the London restaurant guide

Written and edited by
Charles Campion

dditional research by J

So		
Li		
Askews		11-Apr 200
647.954		£8.99

P
PROFILE BOOKS

First published in Great Britain in 2006 by
Profile Books Ltd
3A Exmouth House
Pine Street
Exmouth Market
London EC1R 0JH
www.profilebooks.com

A CIP catalogue record for this book is available from the British Library.

ISBN-10 1 86197 927 4
ISBN-13 978 186197 927 8

Text design by Sue Lamble
Typeset in Humanist 777 by MacGuru Ltd
info@macguru.org.uk

Printed and bound in Italy by Legoprint

The publisher and author have made every effort to ensure that the information in *The London Restaurant Guide* is accurate and up to date, but they can accept no responsibility for any loss, injury or inconvenience sustained as a result of information or advice contained in the guide.

The maps used in this guide are based originally on the 1939 Bartholomew atlas, revised with the assistance of copyright-free material provided by Alan Collinson Design and checked extensively on foot. Subsequent revisions courtesy of Lovell Johns Ltd, Oxford, and David Haslam Publishing. Further revised and extended by ML Design London using Bacon's *Atlas of London* 1948 and out-of-copyright OS 1:25,000 sheets plus checking on foot. Maps © ML Design 2006.

A big thank you

Like the very best Oscar acceptance speeches, this guide must start with a big thank-you for the wholehearted support of everyone at Gonzalez Byass and Profile Books. Tio Pepe occupies a unique position in the affections of many gastronauts as a uniquely versatile stimulator of the appetite – whether you're talking curry or consommé. And without the generous support of Tio Pepe (coupled with a welcome, and almost saintly, lack of interference) this book would never have been written. So saying, the team at Profile must also take credit for putting up with all the tantrums and tribulations that are always part of writing a restaurant guide. I would like to thank Daniel Crewe, Paul Forty and Kate Griffin for Profile, and also Barbara Dixon and Steve Cox for copy-editing and proofreading.

Charles Campion

About the author

Charles Campion is an award-winning food writer and restaurant reviewer. He is a past winner of the Glenfiddich 'Restaurant Writer of the Year' award, and has written about restaurants in the *London Evening Standard* for over a decade. He also contributes to various radio and TV food programmes, as well as to many magazines. He has written a number of cookery books, including *The Real Greek at Home*, which he wrote with chef Theodore Kyriakou, and *Food from Fire*, a book of barbecue recipes published by Mitchell Beazley in 2006. Before becoming a food writer, Charles worked in a succession of London advertising agencies and had a spell as chef-proprietor of a hotel and restaurant in darkest Derbyshire.

Help us update

We've tried to ensure that this book is as up to date and accurate as possible. However, London's restaurant scene is in constant flux: chefs change jobs; restaurants are bought and sold; menus change. There will probably be a few references in this Guide that are out of date even as the book is printed – and standards, of course, go up and down. If you feel there are places we've underrated or over-praised, or others we've unjustly omitted, please let us know: comments or corrections are much appreciated.

Please address letters to:
Charles Campion
Profile Books
3a Exmouth House
Pine Street
London EC1R 0JH

Or send your comments via email to
Charles@CharlesCampion.com

Foreword
by Fay Maschler

How wonderful to have a guide written by an individual whom you can get to know, rather than a collation of varied arbitrary opinions. You know the sort of entries in the sort of booklets I mean – 'Some say the food at the Franco-Iranian La Quelquechose is "right on the button", but others maintain it is "weirdly leaden".' What does that tell you? Charles, my colleague on the *Evening Standard*, an indefatigable, knowledgeable, egalitarian eater, gives you here all the information you will need before making the important investment that is any restaurant meal. He's eaten far and wide, cheaply and indulgently – and also ruthlessly at places that don't deserve inclusion or your contemplation. I have never known his enthusiasm, wry humour or appetite stumble. His guide will unlock the door to familiar pleasures and also fascinating pastures new.

Introduction

Welcome to this new *London Restaurant Guide*, which is the product of over a decade spent eating out and a lifetime obsession with restaurants. In it you'll find over 370 of London's best places to eat.

Anyone who has lived or worked in London knows that while it may seem like one big city to the outsider, it is really a series of villages, each with their own character, their own restaurants and their own secrets. If you're a Londoner you are probably pretty familiar with the restaurants that are close to where you live; but keeping tabs on the whole of the West End or the far-flung suburbs is a full-time job – one made more difficult by the way that restaurants open and close with lightning speed – and that's where this guide comes in.

Given the above, it's therefore strange that almost every other restaurant guide assumes that 'what to eat' is your starting point when you want to go out. It shouldn't be – eating out is much more often about 'where to eat'. If you're meeting friends in Chiswick, your best options might be French or Modern British; in Wembley or Tooting they might be Indian. But you also want to know about that oddball great restaurant, too: whether it's an interesting newcomer like Steins in Richmond, a new gastropub like The Greyhound in Battersea, or a City newcomer like Canteen in Spitalfields. This book divides London into five geographic sections – Central; City and East; North; South; West – and then breaks these down into neighbourhoods. With restaurants arranged alphabetically in each neighbourhood section, it's your key to eating well across the whole city.

This guide reviews restaurants for every possible occasion, from grabbing a bite to pushing the boat out. It also covers many different kinds of food – some sixty cuisines in all. In reality, we cover even more, since for simplicity we have used 'Indian' and 'Chinese' as catch-all terms. The reviews also keep faith with original menu spellings of dishes (for example, you'll find satays, satehs and sates, all of which will probably taste much the same) – so you will certainly find some apparent inconsistencies.

All recommended

Another important thing to note about the restaurants selected and reviewed in this book is that they are all recommended – none has been included simply to make up the numbers.

Prices, websites and credit cards

Every review in this book gives an indication of the prices of starters, mains, sides, desserts, set meals, a figure for the lowest-priced bottle of wine … in fact, everything you need to form a clear picture of how expensive the restaurant will be. At some time in the Guide's life these prices will become out of date, but they were all accurate when the book left for the printer. Even in the uncertain world of restaurants, when prices rise or prices fall, everyone tends to move together. If the prices make it look as if one restaurant is twice as expensive as another, that situation is likely to remain.

Websites are particularly fickle; they were accurate when we went to press, but it only takes a restaurant to change their Internet provider and all bets are off.

Opening hours and days are given in every review, as are details of any service charge and the credit cards accepted. Where reviews specify that restaurants accept 'all major credit cards', that means at least AmEx, MasterCard and Visa. Acceptance of Visa and MasterCard usually means Switch and Delta, too; we've tried to pinpoint any exceptions, but if you're relying on one particular card it's always best to check with the restaurant when you book.

Access

You will also see that the entries for some restaurants display a wheelchair symbol. As provision for the disabled varies wildly, this must be something of a catch-all, so when an entry has the symbol it means that the restaurant has some facilities specifically for disabled diners – that may be a lift, or ramps, or converted loos. It is always best to check exactly what's what before setting out, and all restaurants should be keen to help.

It just remains for me to wish you 'happy eating', and enjoy the Guide.

Charles Campion

Top picks

We've all got favourites. I would happily eat out at any restaurant listed in this book, and there are no makeweights – but only a fool would claim that he had no favourites. Here are some selections, six of the best in each category.

Best newcomers

Bentley's, Piccadilly and St James's, page 110
Canteen, Brick Lane and Spitalfields, page 167
Galvin, Marylebone and Euston, page 64
Imli, Soho, page 135
The Ledbury, Notting Hill and Kensal Green, page 101
Maze, Mayfair and Bond Street, page 84

Best Italian

Assaggi, Notting Hill and Kensal Green, page 94
Enoteca Turi, Putney, page 330
Locanda Locatelli, Marylebone and Euston, page 66
Passione, Bloomsbury and Fitzrovia, page 10
Sardo, Bloomsbury and Fitzrovia, page 15
Zafferano, Knightsbridge, Belgravia and Kensington, page 59

Best for dim sum

Chinese Experience, Chinatown and Covent Garden, page 25
Golden Palace, Harrow and Wembley, page 253
Hakkasan, Bloomsbury and Fitzrovia, page 7
Royal China, Marylebone and Euston, page 72
Yau'atcha, Soho, page 145
Yi-Ban, Docklands, page 206

Best 'élite Indian'

Best 'value Indian'

Best for fish

Best for serious French food

Best for less formal French food

Comptoir Gascon, Clerkenwell and Smithfield, page 189
Gastro, Battersea, Clapham and Wandsworth, page 302
Racine, Earl's Court and South Kensington, page 390
La Trouvaille, Soho, page 143

Best vegetarian dishes

The Gate, Hammersmith and Chiswick, page 396
Kastoori, Tooting, page 338
The Place Below, City, page 181
Ram's, Harrow and Wembley, page 255
Roussillon, Victoria and Westminster, page 156
Morgan M, Islington, page 272

Best gastropub

The Anchor and Hope, Waterloo and South Bank, page 159
The Fox, Hoxton, Shoreditch and Hackney, page 216
The Freemasons, Battersea, Clapham and Wandsworth, page 301
The Gun, Docklands, page 202
The House, Islington, page 270
The White Swan, Clerkenwell and Smithfield, page 198

Best real cheapies

Abu Zaad, Shepherd's Bush and Olympia, page 410
Brula Bistrot, Richmond and Twickenham, page 403
Café España, Soho, page 131
Hung Tao, Queensway and Westbourne Grove, page 121
Masala Zone, Soho, page 138
Zen Satori, Hoxton, Shoreditch and Hackney, page 226

Best for eating alfresco

Le Colombier, Chelsea and Fulham, page 362
Garden Café, Marylebone and Euston, page 65
Metro Garden, Battersea, Clapham and Wandsworth, page 306
El Parador, Camden Town, Primrose Hill and Chalk Farm, page 233
Phoenix Bar and Grill, Putney, page 332
The Real Greek, Hoxton, Shoreditch and Hackney, page 221

Best British

Canteen, Brick Lane and Spitalfields, page 167
Leon, Soho, page 137
Richard Corrigan at the Lindsey House, Soho, page 141
Rivington Grill, Hoxton, Shoreditch and Hackney, page 222
Rules, Chinatown and Covent Garden, page 41
St John, Clerkenwell and Smithfield, page 194

Best for grazing

Amaya, Knightsbridge, Belgravia and Kensington, page 51
Fino, Bloomsbury and Fitzrovia, page 6
Glas, Bermondsey and Borough, page 317
Maze, Mayfair and Bond Street, page 84
Souvlaki & Bar, Clerkenwell and Smithfield, page 196
Al Waha, Queensway and Westbourne Grove, page 125

Best for good, affordable wines

Chez Bruce, Battersea, Clapham and Wandsworth, page 299
Enoteca Turi, Putney, page 330
The Greyhound, Battersea, Clapham and Wandsworth, page 304
Ransome's Dock, Battersea, Clapham and Wandsworth, page 308
RSJ, Waterloo and The South Bank, page 161
Tate Britain, Victoria and Westminster, page 157

Best 'wild cards'

Abu Zaad, Shepherd's Bush and Olympia, page 410
Bodean's, Soho, page 129
Kabul, Southall, page 417
Stein's, Richmond and Twickenham, page 407
La Trouvaille, Soho, page 143
Zen Satori, Hoxton and Shoreditch, page 226

The centre

Bloomsbury and Fitzrovia

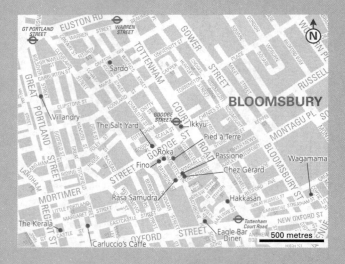

Carluccio's Caffe

8 Market Place, W1 ■ 020 7636 2228

⊖ Oxford Circus

|●| Italian

⊕ Mon to Fri 07.30–23.00; Sat & Sun 10.00–20.00

⌁ www.carluccios.com

⊟ all major credit cards ■ 10% optional service added for parties of 10 or more

££ starters £3.95–£9.95 ■ mains £4.95–£10.95 ■ desserts £3.25–£5.25 ■ sides £3.95–£6.25 ■ lowest bottle price £10.95

✪ Italian shopping, eating and drinking

Branches of Carluccio's Caffe are now springing up almost as fast as Antonio Carluccio's beloved porcini. These are extremely busy restaurants, which means that there is usually a great atmosphere, but the downside is the likelihood of a queue at peak times. The front of the premises is a delicatessen-cum-shop, the mid-section is a bar and the rear is a café-restaurant. Commendable effort has been made to incorporate all that is admirable about Continental coffee shops: Carluccio's is open throughout the day, proper meals are available at all hours, the coffee is notably good and children are welcome. In the morning the temptations are croissants and good coffee ranging from caffè ristretto (the extra strong one) to cappuccino and double espresso. All pukka stuff. This segues into the main menu, on which there are always a couple of good soups, such as zuppa di funghi. The menu starts with sound antipasti and as well as deli-counter items there are specialities like the Sicilian dish arancini di riso, which are crisp, deep-fried rice balls filled with mozzarella or ragù. There's also a range of well-made salads. Main courses range from calzone to a trad parmigiano di melanzane, and from ravioli to osso buco alla Milanese. Puds major in ice cream – gelati artiginali. For a restaurant serving such large numbers of customers, the cooking is pretty decent and the service is efficient enough to cope. Dishes are well seasoned, service is quick and the prices are fair.

→ For branches, see index

Chez Gérard

8 Charlotte Street, W1 ■ 020 7636 4975

___

⊖ Goodge Street

🍽 French

🕐 Mon to Fri 12.00–23.30; Sat 17.00–23.50; Sun 12.30–23.00

🖱 www.sante-gcg.co.uk

🗃 all major credit cards ■ 12.5% optional service added

££ starters £3.95–£9.95 ■ mains £8.95–£24.95 ■ sides £2.25–£4.50
■ desserts £3.65–£7.75 ■ prix fixe menu every evening & weekend
lunch £13.50 & £16.75 ■ lowest bottle price £11.95

___

✪ Steak frîtes, tamed for the English

**There are times when appetite prods the inner man to order a
steak and will not be gainsaid.** When this genuinely carnivorous
impulse strikes, Chez Gérard is a very sound option. Several decades
ago, this kind of simple French cooking (where the steak is good
and the frîtes are better) was a novelty; today Chez Gérard feels
reassuringly old-fashioned. The emphasis on the menu may be
moving gently away from steak, but the approach is resolutely
Francophile, so you'll find escargots; baked Camembert; and crème
brûlée. The bread is crusty, the service Gallic and the red wine decent.
It's not cheap, but the food is generally reliable. The décor is colour-
supplement French, even down to the hat and coat racks, which look
as if they have escaped from a French railway train. Start with fines de
claire oysters, or, for a real belt of nostalgia, a dozen snails in garlic
butter. The steaks come in all shapes and sizes – Châteaubriand is
for two people, while côte de boeuf rib-eye is served on the bone.
There's a 9oz fillet steak and an entrecôte. There is also the wonderful
onglet, a particularly tasty French cut of beef that we know as skirt
steak. Everything from the grill comes with pommes frîtes and sauce
Béarnaise. Other dishes include confit de canard and filet de dorade
royale. But don't kid yourself – you're here for the steak frîtes. Salads,
side orders of vegetables, desserts – including tarte Tatin and a
selection of regional French cheeses – are all in tune with the Gallic
ambience. So too are the good-value cheaper wines.

→ For branches, see index

Eagle Bar Diner

3 Rathbone Place, W1 ■ 020 7637 1418   ♿

⊖ Tottenham Court Road

🍴 North American

🕐 Mon to Wed 12.00–23.00; Thurs & Fri 12.00–01.00; Sat 10.00–01.00; Sun 11.00–18.00

🖥 www.eaglebardiner.co.uk

🖪 all major credit cards except AmEx ■ 12.5% optional service added for parties of 6 or more

££ breakfast £3.95–£6.95 ■ mains £4–£12.95 ■ sides £1.50–£4.75 ■ desserts £3–£4.50 ■ lowest bottle price £12.95

⭐ Anyone for a 4oz emu and mountain black pepper burger?

Unsurprisingly, the Eagle Bar Diner is both a bar and a diner. It's a modern-looking sort of place with the booths for diners on a slightly raised platform. The bar is purposeful and its large size gives a clue as to how busy it gets. Everything seems fairly serendipitous as the crowded times for the bar dovetail with the restaurant's peaks, so sometimes it's a bar and sometimes it's a restaurant. The room is comfortable and service is informal – an agreeably grown-up sort of diner. The menu sticks to tried and trusted diner fare: Caesar salad, to which you can add rosemary chicken or grilled king prawns. An American breakfast – short-stack pancakes, or Belgian waffles with bacon and maple syrup. Pasta dishes and sandwiches – hot salt brisket with spicy onions and rocket, or '24-hour' tomatoes, grilled pepper, feta, avocado and rocket. But the burgers take centre stage here; they are large and sassy and if you plan on taking a bite out of one you'll need jaws that gape like an anaconda. An 8oz ground-rump burger comes with onion marmalade, mustard mayonnaise, lettuce, tomato, gherkin and red onion and is accurately cooked. You'll need spuds, so choose from a variety of styles: hash browns, herb potatoes, fat chips, or skinny chips. The fat chips are good. The speciality burgers range from Greek, made with feta and tzatziki, to South American, with chicken, guacamole and chorizo. Puds are sticky: brownie served warm with ice cream, or cookies-and-cream ice-cream cake.

Fino

33 Charlotte Street, W1 ■ 020 7813 8010

⊖ Goodge Street

🍴 Spanish/tapas

🕐 Mon to Sat 12.00–4.30 & 18.00–22.30

🖰 www.finorestaurant.com

🖫 all major credit cards except AmEx ■ 12.5% optional service added

---

££ tapas £1.80–£6.50 ■ mains £4.50–£15.50 ■ sides £3–£7.40
■ desserts £2–£7.50 ■ menus: Fino Classic Selection (min 2) £17.95pp,
Fino Gourmet Selection (min 2) £28pp ■ lowest bottle price £16

✪ Authentic Spanish food, authentic London setting

**Say tapas, and the mind makes an involuntary leap towards cool,
tiled, old-fashioned places.** Fino approaches the same Spanish
virtues, but from a different angle. There's a stylish bar for drinking
on the mezzanine and a bar for eating tapas while sat along the front
of the open kitchen downstairs. The dining room is large and airy and
very much in the modern restaurant idiom. The food is very sound and
elegantly presented. There's a good range of classic tapas dishes and
some items fresh from the plancha (a no-frills grill). Start with some
pa amb tomaquet, a tomatoey, garlicky toast. Add arroz negro, a
very delicious squid-ink risotto. Also crisp-fried squid, delicious with a
squeeze of lemon. The croquetas are good – filled with ham, or piquillo
peppers. From the meat section there are milk-fed-lamb cutlets, which
are impossibly small, tender and with good gravy, and a good portion
of jamon Iberico bellota gran reserva – top ham, melting in the mouth,
amazing silky texture and gentle richness. From the vegetable section
there is a dish of chickpeas, spinach and bacon to add a welcome
savoury note. From the plancha you could choose queen scallops,
squid, or clams with sherry and ham. In keeping with the smartness of
the surroundings the wine list is priced on the merciless side, although
there are several interesting sherries that are worth investigation.
Ordering from the two set menus will get you five or seven courses,
and relieve you of any responsibility. Fino offers an elegant and
sophisticated Spanish restaurant with slick service and prices to match.

Hakkasan

8 Hanway Place, W1 ■ 020 7927 7000

⊖ Tottenham Court Road

🍴 Chinese/dim sum

🕐 Mon to Fri 12.00–15.00 & 18.00–24.00; Sat 12.00–16.00 & 18.00–24.00; Sun 12.00–16.00 & 18.00–23.00; bar open Mon to Wed to 01.00, Thurs to Sat to 03.00, Sun to 00.30

🖃 all major credit cards ■ 13.5% optional service added

££ dim sum lunch only £3–£8.50 ■ starters £5.50–£18.50 ■ mains £8.50–£68 ■ rice & noodles £1.50–£10.90 ■ desserts £7–£13.50 ■ lowest bottle price £25

✪ Super slick, super cooking, super bills

Twenty-four hours' notice is required if you want to sample 'monk jumps over the wall', a serious soup made with abalone and one that attracts a near-three-figure price tag. This dish rather sets the tone for Hakkasan, which is a very superior kind of Chinese restaurant. The décor is slick (as you would expect when the design budget was a reputed £3,000,000). The double-smart cocktail bar is consistently and fashionably crammed. Top-name designers from the worlds of film and fashion have given their all, and this is a smart and elegant place. The food is novel, well presented, fresh, delicious and, in strangely justifiable fashion, expensive. The starters are called 'small eat' and do not shy away from expensive luxury ingredients. The three-style vegetarian roll teams a mooli spring roll with a bean curd puff and a yam roll. Live native lobster, plus noodles with ginger and spring onion, cannot be many people's idea of a 'small eat'. Or there is grilled Shanghai dumpling. The main dishes are innovative and delicious. Try baked silver cod with Chinese rice wine, or the stir-fry scallop and prawn cake with choi sum. There's also jasmine tea-smoked chicken and sweet-and-sour organic pork with pomegranate. By way of a staple, try the stir-fry glass vermicelli, which enlivens noodles with chicken, crabmeat and fried shallots. The dim sum (served only at lunchtime) are not cheap, but they are very good – prawn puff and sesame prawn toast are exceptional. Whisper it: 'These are better dim sum than you'll find in Chinatown!'

Ikkyu

67a Tottenham Court Road, W1 ■ 020 7636 9280

⊖ Goodge Street

🍴 Japanese/sushi

🕐 Mon to Fri 12.00–14.30 & 18.00–22.30; Sun 18.00–22.30

🗗 Mastercard, Visa, AmEx; no Switch or cheques ■ 10% optional service added at dinner only

---

££ starters £1–£13.50 ■ mains £6.50–£13.50 ■ desserts £2.20–£3.50 ■ lowest bottle price £11; small sake £2.60; shoucho £3.50

✪ Small, shabby and authentic Japanese restaurant

First you will have to find Ikkyu – it is hidden at the bottom of a nondescript stairway with an entrance on the Tottenham Court Road. Ikkyu is busy, basic and full of people eating reliable Japanese food at sensible prices – all of which makes it a good match for any popular neighbourhood restaurant in Tokyo. But it is still an engaging place quite obviously tailored to Japanese customers – although the strangeness of the welcome comes over as politeness, and you won't feel completely stranded. Nigiri sushi is good here and is priced by the piece: tuna, salmon, mackerel, cuttlefish. Or there's sashimi, which runs all the way from mackerel to sea urchin eggs. Alternatively, start with soba – delicious cold, brown noodles. Then allow yourself a selection of yakitori, either a portion of assorted, or mix and match from tongue, heart, liver, gizzard and chicken skin. You will need many skewers of the grilled chicken skin, which is implausibly delicious. Moving on to the main dishes, an order of fried leeks with pork brings a bunch of long, onion-flavoured greens strewn with morsels of grilled pork. Whatever the green element is, it is certainly not leeks. Or there's grilled aubergine, or rolled five vegetables with shrimp, which is like a Swiss roll made with egg and vegetable with a core of prawn. Only the very adventurous will try a shouchu and soda – shouchu is a clear spirit that tastes like … clear spirit!

The Kerala

15 Great Castle Street, W1 ■ 020 7580 2125

⊖ Oxford Circus

🍴 Indian

🕐 daily 12.00–15.00 & 17.30–23.00

💳 all major credit cards ■ 12.5% optional service added

££ starters £3.35–£5.35 ■ mains £4.65–£8.95 ■ sides £1.50–£6.95
■ desserts £3.25–£4.25 ■ lunch buffet £6.95 ■ lowest bottle price £13

✪ Authentic Keralan food, high on hospitality, low on price

This is a straightforward family business and one that takes a genuine pride in home cooking. At the end of the 1980s Shirref's wine bar was taken over by David Tharakan, who sold a good deal of wine and added a short menu of pub food favourites. The big changes came nearly a decade later when David's wife Millie took over the kitchen and changed the menu. Shirref's started to offer Keralan home cooking, with well-judged, well-spiced dishes at bargain-basement prices. Since then The Kerala restaurant – which is what it has become – has gone from strength to strength and achieved a certain notoriety for the great-value lunch deals. Such things are not often found this close to Oxford Street. To start with, you must order a platoon of simple things: cashew nut pakoda; potato bonda; lamb samosa; chicken liver masala; mussels ularthu. These are honest dishes, simply presented and at a price that encourages experimentation. Thereafter, the menu is divided into a number of sections: Syrian Christian specialities from Kerala; coastal seafood dishes; Malabar biryanis; vegetable curries; and special dosas. From the first, try erachi olathiathu, a splendid dry curry of lamb with coconut. From the second, try meen and mango vevichathu, which is kingfish cooked with the sharpness of green mango. From the biryanis, how about chemmin biryani, prawns cooked with basmati rice? Avial is a mixed vegetable curry with yogurt and coconut. The breads are fascinating – try the lacy and delicate appams made from steamed rice-flour. Look out for the 'lunch buffet' – a bargain basement feast.

Passione

10 Charlotte Street, W1 ■ 020 7636 2833

⊖ Goodge Street

⦿| Italian

⏲ Mon to Fri 12.30–14.15 & 19.00–22.15; Sat 19.00–22.15

⌐ www.passione.co.uk

⊟ all major credit cards ■ 12.5% optional service added

££ antipasti £6.50–£15 ■ pasta & risotti £11–£14.50 ■ mains £20.50–£26.50 ■ sides £5.50–£7 ■ desserts £7 ■ lowest bottle price £14

✪ Telly chef Gennaro Contaldo's real passion

Gennaro Contaldo may have been eclipsed in the fame stakes by his protégé Jamie Oliver, but he still cooks delicious and simple food. When Passione opened nobody had heard of Gennaro Contaldo, but gradually Passione has built up a following on its own merits. Simplicity, an unpretentious feel to the place, seasonal ingredients and talent in the kitchen – these are sure bets when it comes to eating. You owe it to yourself to have four courses. The menu changes daily and there is a constant procession of specials. Among the antipasti, there's zuppa di giorno, which sounds so much better than soup of the day, and cinghiale marinato servito freddo con salsa di pesto, marinated wild boar served cold. Then there is pasta and risotti, several of which are available in two portion sizes: tagliatelli con capesante e bottarga teams scallops with dried tuna roe, while risotto all'accetosella has the tasty tang of wild sorrel. Mains are rich and satisfying: orata con endiva belga salsina di miele e aceto bianco, is sea bream with endives and a honey and vinegar sauce; involtini di melanzane alla parmigiano, a rich dish of baked aubergines with mozzarella; coniglio con rosmarino e patate saltate is rabbit with rosemary and sauté potatoes. The service is slick here; this is a place where they understand the art of running a comfortable restaurant. Puddings are serious stuff, though it has to be said that the delicious gelato Passione, a swirl of zesty limoncello ice with a splash of wild strawberry folded into it, is for all the world a grown-up's raspberry ripple. Try Contaldo's fabled focaccia – the one that the pukka chap is always banging on about.

Pied à Terre

34 Charlotte Street, W1 ■ 020 7636 1178

⊖ Goodge Street/Tottenham Court Road

🍴 French

🕐 Mon to Fri 12.00–14.30 & 18.15–23.00; Sat 18.15–23.00

🖰 www.pied-a-terre.co.uk

🖯 all major credit cards ■ 12.5% optional service added

££ du jour lunch (starter & main) £24.50 ■ à la carte (starter & main) £45 ■ dessert £10.50 ■ tasting menu £75 & £122 (with wine) ■ lowest bottle price £17.50

✪ Heavy hitter, reborn and revitalised

Pied à Terre caught fire. Not one of those small flare-ups in the chip pan, but a real raging inferno. Fast forward a year or so and there's a new dining room front and back, a new bar on the first floor and an elegant new private room on the second floor. There is even a completely new kitchen. Things such as fires are wildly inconvenient, but this is a resto that shoots for the Michelin stars and having the ultimate refurb cannot but help. The food is ambitious; dishes are complex both in terms of tastes and textures and in presentation. Service is suave and there is a particularly long and fulsome wine list. The food is very good indeed. Starters may include oxtail and shallot soup with oxtail and horseradish tortellini and celeriac cream – very rich flavours cut by the tang of horseradish, delicious; curry-poached Falmouth oysters with potato blinis and cauliflower purée; or roast breast of teal with choucroute, chanterelles and Scotch quail egg – perfectly cooked duck. Mains range from pan-fried wild sea bass with creamed shallot, roast salsify and cèpes; to best end of salt marsh lamb with roast peppers and a 'braised lamb shank sandwich' – a small crisp parcel with a melting interior. Desserts are elaborate: bittersweet chocolate tart; macadamia nut mousse and stout ice cream; or a prune and walnut frangipane with ginger ice cream, tea-infused prunes and crystallised ginger. If your bank account flinches at the prospect of a visit, try the du jour menu at lunch. This is top-notch cooking.

Rasa Samudra

5 Charlotte Street, W1 ■ 020 7637 0222

⊖ Goodge Street

🍽 Indian/fish

🕘 Mon to Sat 12.00–15.00 & 18.00 to 23.00; Sun 18.00–23.00

🖱 www.rasarestaurants.co.uk

🗗 all major credit cards ■ 12.5% optional service added

££ starters £4.25–£7.50 ■ mains £6.25–£12.95 ■ sides £5.25 ■ desserts £3–£3.50 ■ Kerala feast seafood £30, vegetarian £22.50 ■ lowest bottle price £11.95

✪ Exotic fish dishes, but with a South Indian accent

Das Sreedharan has a triumvirate of high-quality South Indian restaurants. The original Rasa (see p. 294) is a vegetarian gem, Rasa Travancore (see p. 295) offers Southern meat dishes, and Rasa Samudra is unashamedly targeted at fish lovers. The food served here is sophisticated fish cookery, the kind of stuff that would be more at home in Mumbai than in London, consisting as it does of classy Indian fish dishes – a million miles from familiar curry-house staples. At first glance the menu may seem heart-stoppingly expensive, partly due to a strange and exclusively British prejudice that no curry should ever cost more than a fiver, even if made from the kind of top-quality ingredients worth £15 in a French restaurant. All the more expensive choices (often based on fish: always a pricey ingredient) come complete with accompaniments. This makes them substantial enough to allow all but the greediest of diners to dispense with starters, except perhaps for the samudra rasam, a stunning shellfish soup; or the array of pappadoms, papparvardi and achappam. Plus, there are some wicked pickles. For main course, crab varuthathu, a dish of crab stir-fried with ginger, is well offset by pooris and spicy potatoes as side dishes. Other good choices include konju manga curry, prawns cooked dry with turmeric and green mango, and varutharacha meen curry, tilapia cooked with shallots, red chillies and tamarind. The cooking is well judged and the spices well balanced.

Roka

37 Charlotte Street, W1 ■ 020 7580 6464 &

⊖ Goodge Street/Tottenham Court Road

◉ Japanese

⊕ Mon to Sat 12.00–14.30 & 17.30 to 23.00; Sun 17.30–22.30

⌒ www.rokarestaurant.com

⊟ all major credit cards ■ 12.5% optional service added

££ robata £4–£15 ■ sashimi & maki £4–£11 ■ tempura £4.50–£8
■ desserts £6.50–£9 ■ set lunches £8–£9 ■ lowest bottle price £14;
sake from £12

⭐ New wave Japanese, Charlotte Street chic

Roka is little sister to style palace Zuma (see p. 60). It has a striking
dining room with one wall entirely taken up with large jars in which
bits and bobs are marinating. It looks a bit like something you would
find in the Black Museum of police exhibits. The feel of the place is
very modern and very slick, and that is probably how the customers
view themselves. It is hard to sum up the food, except to say that it
is original and elegant – Roka is well adapted to the modern trend of
'grazing' and it is best to order a number of dishes and then share
them. The term 'robata' means cooking on an open flame or, to cut
to the chase, a barbie. The grilled dishes are good – chicken wings
come with sea salt and lime; there are lamb cutlets with Korean
spices; and all sorts of other delights from calf's liver to skewers
of pork and crab. Then there is an array of sashimi and maki rolls,
some of which get quite complex – a cone-shaped roll made with
eel teriyaki, avocado, shiso and sansho pepper, or grilled salmon
belly and skin with cucumber, wasabi and tobiko (flying fish roe).
Or perhaps the rice hot pot with Cornish crab and wasabi, or the
pancake balls filled with prawn and octopus appeal. The set lunch
options help with decision making; all are served with shiro miso
soup and home-made pickles: katsudon is trad pork in breadcrumbs
with egg rice and onion; unadon is teriyaki grilled eel, sansho pepper
and red onion. Sake is a good accompaniment, take advice from the
staff. Roka is suave, slick and somewhat pricey, but the food is good.

The Salt Yard

54 Goodge Street, W1 ■ 020 7637 0657

⊖ Goodge Street

🍽 Spanish (they say Mediterranean)

🕐 Mon to Fri 12.00–15.00 & 18.00–23.00; Sat 17.00–23.00; bar snacks all day

🖱 www.saltyard.co.uk

🗄 all major credit cards ■ 10% optional service added

££ charcuterie £6–£12.95 ■ tapas £2.75–£7 ■ desserts £4.50–£5 ■ cheese selections £6.75–£8.35 ■ pre-theatre menu (18.00–19.30) à la carte less 20% ■ lowest bottle price £14.50

✪ Considered tapas, serious charcuterie

When is a tapas not a tapas? When it's a miniaturised dish picked from a modern grazing menu, that's when. The Salt Yard is a tapas restaurant, but only just. The plain-looking downstairs dining room is very like a good many other modern dining rooms and the concept of ordering 'three or so dishes each and sharing' seems to be all the rage with a host of trendy restos. Rather pleasingly, the food is either very simple – a board with a selection of different Spanish charcuterie: salchichon, cabedaza, lomo and chorizo, or quite sophisticated – a dish of pot-roast rabbit with gnocchi and black olives. The rabbit is good and comes in a middleweight portion, rather more than you would expect as a tapas and only just smaller than you would expect as a pukka main course. Also good from the meat options are the confit of Gloucester Old Spot pork belly with rosemary cannellini beans, and the morcilla croquetas, which are amazing black pudding rissoles with a crunchy outside and creamy, rich interior. From the fish choices, the crispy squid with chickpea purée is a winner: good crisp and dry squidlets on a layer of what is very like a hot and savoury houmous. The piquillo peppers filled with salt cod come with a black olive dressing, and you could order pan-fried bream with chargrilled baby leeks. In the veg section you'll find chargrilled peppers and a panzanella salad with buffalo mozzarella. The wine list is carefully chosen. Service is notably efficient as it needs to be with the dishes coming in waves. Good food in a pleasantly informal atmosphere.

Sardo

45 Grafton Way, W1 ■ 020 7387 2521

⊖ Warren Street

🍽 Italian

🕐 Mon to Fri 12.00–15.00 & 18.00 to 23.00; Sat 18.00–23.00

🖱 www.sardo-restaurant.com

🗗 all major credit cards ■ 12.5% optional service added

££ starters £7.90–£10.90 ■ mains £12–£16.50 ■ sides £3–£7.50 ■ desserts £5–£6 ■ lowest bottle price £14

✪ Sardinia's unofficial gastro-ambassador

Romolo Mudu is from Caligari, and very proud of it. At Sardo his role is one of passionate and ebullient front of house. Coupled with plain but fairly uninspired décor, this may make elderly diners feel that they have wandered into a Soho trattoria circa 1980. Take heart, for the food is more interesting than you would expect and is particularly good when you concentrate on the specials. Start with the bresaola di tonno, cured tuna sliced finely, or the calamari ripieno, baby squid, stuffed and grilled. As a pasta course perhaps the specials will yield culurgiones di formaggio e patate, little pasta parcels filled with potatoes and pecorino cheese. Move on to something simple, but impressive, such as fregola ai gamberi e zucchni – fregola is a Sardinian pasta that comes in small enough pieces to take over the role of rice, and here it is teamed with prawns and courgettes. Or maybe salsiccia Sarda appeals? The proprietor will happily discuss his brother's recipe for these home-made sausages, which have a distinctive aniseed tang. For dessert, go trad Sardinian: sebada is a puff pastry filled with orange peel and cheese and topped with honey. Or there is a splendid array of five or six different Pecorino cheeses. The wine list includes a page of reasonably priced Sardinian specialities, and there are some distinctive, aromatic whites – note the Vermentinas. As well as the listed specials, it is always worth enquiring about even more special specials – occasionally this restaurant has the famous mountain prosciutto made from mutton.

→ For branches, see index

Villandry

170 Great Portland Street, W1 ■ 020 7631 3131 &

⊖ Great Portland Street

🍽 Modern British

🕑 Mon to Sat 09.00–12.00 (breakfast), 12.00–15.00 & 18.00–22.30;
Sun 11.30–16.00 (brunch)

🖰 www.villandry.com

🗗 all major credit cards ■ 12.5% optional service added

££ starters £5.75–£9.75 ■ mains £11.50–£19.75 ■ desserts £4.50–£5.75
■ lowest bottle price £13.50

✪ Slick restaurant grafted onto high ticket food store

This place is both a food store and restaurant and you could end up eating breakfast, elevenses, lunch, tea or dinner. The handsome shop gives onto a modern and rather stark dining room. Passing displays of some of Europe's most extravagant ingredients may jangle the nerves and alarm the wallet, but if you're serious about your food, and you have time to wait for careful preparation, Villandry won't disappoint. The menu changes daily so you won't necessarily find all – or indeed any – of the dishes mentioned here. But as you'd expect at the back of a food store that caters for the well-heeled sector of the foodie faithful, ingredients are scrupulously chosen and prepared with care. At its best, this kind of 'informal' menu is surprisingly demanding on the cook – and exact cooking is crucial to ostensibly simple dishes. To start, you might be offered a leek and potato soup with truffle tapenade; pigeon salad with noodles, chicory, soy and ginger; langoustines and mussels with fish broth; or a plate of charcuterie. Main courses are often hugely impressive: roast rump of lamb with spiced borlotti beans and spinach, or pan-fried lemon sole, wild mushrooms and Jerusalem artichokes. Desserts may include moist chocolate cake with chocolate sauce and, unsurprisingly, given the array in the shop, there's an extensive if expensive cheeseboard, served with terrific walnut and sourdough breads. Wine prices, like the food, are distinctly West End, though there are reasonably priced house selections.

Wagamama

4 Streatham Street, W1 ■ 020 7323 9223

⊖ Tottenham Court Road

🍴 Japanese/Chinese

🕐 Mon to Sat 12.00–23.00; Sun 12.30–22.00

🖰 www.wagamama.com

🖳 all major credit cards ■ no optional service added

££ mains £5.80–£12 ■ sides £1.35–£5 ■ lowest bottle price £10.95

✪ This is the way of the noodle

Wagamama is as good a canteen as you'll find, serving simple and generally rather good food at very reasonable prices, which may explain why it has grown into such a large chain so quickly. What it's not is a place for a relaxed or intimate meal. The basement interior is cavernous and minimalist, and diners are seated side by side on long benches. At regular eating times you'll find yourself in a queue lining the stairway – there are no reservations. When you reach the front, you're seated, your order is punched into a hand-held computer and that spurs the kitchen into action. There's beer and wine available, as well as free green tea. Dishes arrive when they're cooked, so your party will be served at different times. Most people order a main dish – noodles in soup; fried noodles; or sauce-based noodles – or a rice dish. Side dishes can also be pressed into service as a starter: yasai yakitori is chargrilled chicken with the ever-popular yakitori sauce, while gyoza are delicious fried chicken dumplings. The mains include a splendid chilli beef ramen, slivers of sirloin steak in a vat of soup with vegetables. Also good is the yasai katsu curry, which is boiled rice with a light curry sauce and discs of deep-fried vegetables; and yasai chili men, a vegetarian 'everything-in' dish with courgette, ginger, mushroom, carrot, peas, tomato, tofu and so on, plus ramen noodles. If this all sounds confusing, that's because it is. To enjoy Wagamama you'll need to go with the flow. As the cod philosophy would put it, Wagamama is 'Wilfulness or selfishness: selfishness in terms of looking after oneself, looking after oneself in terms of positive eating and positive living'. Now you know.

→ For branches, see index

Chinatown and Covent Garden

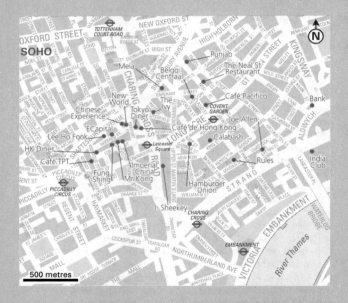

Bank

1 Kingsway (corner of Aldwych), WC2 ▪ 020 7379 9797 ♿

⊖ Holborn

🍴 Modern British

🕐 Mon to Fri 07.00–11.00, 12.00–14.45, 17.30–23.00; Sat 11.30–15.00 & 17.30–23.00; Sun 11.30–16.30

🖰 www.bankrestaurants.com

🖶 all major credit cards ▪ 12.5% optional service added

££ starters £6.45–£13 ▪ mains £12.50–£25 ▪ sides £2.75–£3.50 ▪ desserts £5–£8 ▪ prix fixe lunch & pre- & post-theatre menus £13.50 & £16 (not Sunday) ▪ lowest bottle price £15

✪ A Brasserie to bank on

Remember the all-day buzz and unfussy cuisine of the big Parisian brasseries? Well, that's what you get at Bank, which opens for breakfast, lays on brunch at the weekend, does good-value pre- and post-theatre menus, and has a prix fixe lunch, all underpinned by a popular and busy bar. And then there's the small matter of à la carte lunch and dinner for several hundred. Whatever the time of day, the food is impressive, especially considering the large numbers of people that get fed, and if you like things lively you will have a great time. The menu is constantly changing, so dishes come and go. Start with something simple – simple to get wrong, that is – a Caesar salad, say, or a well-made foie gras parfait with apple and pear chutney. Or go for shellfish. A key role in Bank's history was played by one of London's leading catering fishmongers, so crustacea such as dressed crab with ginger and wasabi dressing should be reliable. The fish dishes range from roast cod with boulangère potatoes and mussels, to a traditional halibut fish and chips, featuring mushy peas and tartare sauce. Meat dishes are well-prepared brasserie fare such as braised beef with parsley mash, or confit of duck with amaretti and butternut squash purée. Puds include an assiette au chocolat, and brioche bread-and-butter pudding. If you want a taxi after 22.00, go for the cabs arranged by the doorman: despite the continual price hikes, black cabs are still a rarity.

→ For branches, see index

Belgo Centraal

50 Earlham Street, WC2 ■ 020 7813 2233

⊖ Covent Garden

🍽 Belgian

🕐 Mon to Wed 12.00–23.00; Thurs to Sun 12.00–23.30

🖥 www.belgo-restaurants.com

💳 all major credit cards ■ 12.5% optional service added

££ starters £5.50–£7.25 ■ mains £8.25–£18.95 ■ sides £1.95–£2.75
   ■ desserts £3.50–£4.50 ■ lowest bottle price £11.95

✪ Moules frîtes stronghold

**'Name five famous Belgians' is a question made a little easier
by the beer at Belgo.** The Belgians invented mussels, frîtes and
mayonnaise, and Belgo has done all it can to help the Belgian
national dish take over London; sensibly they also added beer. The
Belgo group's flagship restaurant is a massive metal-minimalist
cavern accessed by riding down in a scissor-powered lift. Turn left
at the bottom and you enter the restaurant (where you can book
seats); turn right and you get seated in the beer hall, where diners
share tables. With 95 different beers, some at alcoholic strengths
of 8–9 per cent, it's difficult not to be sociable. A kilo of classic
moules marinières served with frîtes has fresh mussels that have
clearly been cooked then and there. Other options include classique,
with cream and garlic; Provençale, with tomato, herbs and garlic; or
even Thai, which comes with a Thai curry sauce. And there's plenty
for the non-mussel eater. Start with a salade Brabançonne, a warm
salad including bacon, black pudding and duck confit, or the cheese
croquettes, made with Orval beer. Move on to carbonnade Flamande,
beef braised in Geuze beer with apples and plums, and served with
frîtes. Desserts include, among many others, traditional Belgian
waffles with dark chocolate. Belgo delights in special offers: there's a
good-value lunch, and a deal called 'beat the clock', where the prices
shift downwards in relation to how early you eat. Beware the '32
stick' – 32 shot glasses of fruit schnapps – 'great to share between
two!' Take a third person to help you home.

→ For branches, see index

Café de Hong Kong

47–49 Charing Cross Road, WC2 ■ 020 7534 9898

✆ Leicester Square

🍽 Chinese

🕐 daily 12.00–23.00

💳 all major credit cards ■ no service added

££ snacks £2.20–£3.20 ■ mains £5–£12.80 ■ sides £1.50–£4.40 ■ rice & noodles £4.80–£5 ■ desserts £1.80–£3.20 ■ lowest bottle price n/a

⭐ Chinese, Jim, but not as we know it

Café de Hong Kong is an engaging place, bustling along, brightly coloured, but spartan, simple with utilitarian booths. There are two dining areas – one on the first floor overlooking the Charing Cross Road and a larger one on the floor above. This place puts a new spin on the term café culture. It's full of young Chinese people lingering over spooky soft drinks and eating hearty stuff from large bowls. There has recently been a great upsurge in the numbers of these basic Chinese cafés (see Café TPT, p. 23) and they look set to displace the trad Italian pasta pitstops as the cheapest way of fuelling up before going out for the night. No bookings are taken. To say that the menu is eclectic would be selling it short. The 'chef 's speciality' is grouper with mango sauce and if that doesn't shock, it's served with 'potatoes and vegetables'. Or how about 'spaghetti Bolognaise'? You get an oval dish full of spaghetti, topped with some tomatoey meat sauce and then cheese, which has been finished in a hot oven. It's O.K. – the kind of cooking you would have expected from an Italian trattoria in about 1980. The menu also offers Russian borscht, pork chop curry and some very good meals-in-a-bowl – such as fried noodles with pork. And to wash it all down? How about sampling one of the tapioca pearl drinks? A tall glass is filled with crushed ice, various flavourings and a secret spoonful of 'pearls' – these are chewy, pea-sized balls of tapioca. You drink your milkshake through a special large-gauge straw and, as you suck up the drink, the pearls shoot into your mouth and rattle around, transforming your head into a giant pinball machine.

Café Pacifico

5 Langley Street, WC2 ▪ 020 7379 7728

⊖ Covent Garden

🍽 Mexican

🕐 Mon to Sat 12.00–24.00; Sun 12.00–23.00

🖰 www.cafepacifico-laperla.com

🖫 all major credit cards ▪ 12.5% optional service added

££ starters £4.95–£10.25 ▪ mains £6.75–£15.95 ▪ sides £1.35–£2.95
▪ desserts £3.95–£4.25 ▪ lowest bottle price £11.45

✪ Beware the worm in the bottle of mescal

The salsa is hot at Café Pacifico – both types. As you are seated,
a complimentary bowl of searing salsa dip with corn chips is put on
your table. As you eat, hot salsa music gets your fingers tapping. The
atmosphere is relaxed and you're soon in the mood for a cold beer;
fortunately, there are several Mexican beers, a good selection of wines
and dozens of cocktails. But Pacifico's tequila list is the highlight,
with more than 60 varieties, including some very old and rare bottles
obscure enough to delight the connoisseur's heart. The menu is a
lively mixture of old-style Californian Mexican and new Mexican, so
while favourites like fajitas, flautas and tacos dominate, there are also
some interesting and unusual dishes. Portions are generous and spicy,
and many main courses come with refried beans and rice. Try nachos
rancheros for starters, and enjoy a huge plate of corn chips with
beans, cheese, guacamole, onions, sour cream and olives. Excellent
for sharing. Taquitos – filled fried baby tacos – are good, as are
smoked chicken quesadillas – flour tortillas with chicken, red peppers
and avocado salsa. Main courses include degustación del Pacifico,
which includes a bit of almost everything. There's the chimichanga
del mar, a seafood-packed, deep-fried, rolled tortilla; burrito especial,
a flour tortilla filled with cheese, refried beans and a choice of roast
beef, chicken or ground beef, covered with ranchero sauce; or Cuervo
swordfish steak asada, grilled fish with a tequila and sun-dried
tomato salsa. Puds are predictable, but pretty soon it will be time to
explore those rare top-shelf tequilas.

Café TPT

21 Wardour Street, W1 ▪ 020 7734 7980

⊖ Piccadilly Circus

🍴 Chinese

🕐 daily 12.00–01.00

🖃 all major credit cards except AmEx (min £10) ▪ 10% optional service added

££ starters £2.50–£6.50 ▪ mains £6–£18 ▪ sides £2–£6 ▪ desserts £3.50 ▪ set menus £9.50–£11 ▪ lowest bottle price £9.50

✪ No frills fast food, the Chinese way

TPT is a busy food factory that is full of happy, predominantly Chinese diners all tucking into large portions of simple food. You'll find Café TPT just across the road from HK diner (see p. 29) and the look of the two places is very similar. The tables in the ground floor dining room have massive angular wooden stools – not very rump-friendly, but you probably won't be lingering over brandy and petits fours as there aren't any! There are two menus at TPT. There's a big one like a book, which is very similar to every other menu in Chinatown – crispy duck with pancakes; hot and sour soup; deep-fried crispy squid – all the old familiar dishes, although at agreeably low prices. The paper 'placemat' menu is a much more rewarding read. It lists the bargain dishes, congee (which is a sort of sloppy, soupy rice porridge allegedly good for hangovers), noodles, rice dishes and barbecued meats. The fried noodle dishes, such as chicken chow mein, are steady; the ho fun dishes (broader noodles), such as fried squid with black bean sauce with ho fun, are much more rewarding. But best of all are the 'pulled noodle' dishes – these are home-made, thick and chewy noodles slightly misshapen like serious pasta, very filling and rich. Try pulled noodles with beef. The barbecued meats are sound here, but the staff insist on warming them through in the microwave, which spoils the texture. The café part of the name is confirmed by the long drinks list. There are all manner of tapioca pearl drinks (as at the Café de Hong Kong), plus fruit juices and floats – 'ice cream with glass jelly and red bean ice'. Good fun with the ho fun?

Calabash

Africa Centre, 38 King Street, WC2 ■ 020 7836 1976

⊖ Covent Garden

🍴 African

🕑 Mon to Fri 12.30–14.30 & 18.00–22.30; Sat 18.00–22.30

🗗 all major credit cards ■ 10% optional service added

££ starters £2.50–£3.25 ■ mains £7.95–£8.10 ■ sides £2.50–£2.75
■ desserts £2.10–£2.75 ■ lowest bottle price £7.50

✪ This place runs on African time – i.e. gently

Deep within the bowels of the Africa Centre, the Calabash is at once worthy, comfortable and cheap. The same complex features a splendidly seedy bar, a live music hall and African arts and crafts for sale. The menu struggles bravely to give snapshots of the extraordinary diversity of African cuisine: they manage dishes from North, East and West Africa, as well as specialities from Nigeria, Ivory Coast, Senegal and Malawi. So if you're looking for a particular dish you may be out of luck. However, if you want a cheerful atmosphere, a small bill and wholesome, often spicy and usually unfamiliar food, the Calabash is worth seeking out. Starters include familiar dishes like avocado salad and houmous, along with interesting offerings such as aloco, which is fried plantain in a hot tomato sauce. Those with an enquiring palate will pick the gizzards, a splendid dish of chicken gizzards served in a rich, spiky pepper sauce. Grilled chicken wings are less exotic, but very good nonetheless. Main courses are identified by origin with the exception of 'Chicken', which is a superb dish of fried chicken served with a ferocious hot sauce. Eat your heart out Colonel. From Nigeria comes egusi, a rich soup/stew with spinach, meat and dried shrimps, thickened with melon seed. Yassa is grilled chicken from Senegal, while doro wot is a pungent chicken stew from Ethiopia, served with injera, the soft and thin sourdough bread. Nyama yo phika is a beef stew from Malawi made with potatoes and sweet peppers. Drink whichever of the African beers is in stock at the time you visit.

Chinese Experience

118 Shaftesbury Avenue, W1 ■ 020 7437 0377

○ Piccadilly Circus

|○| Chinese/dim sum

⏱ Mon to Thurs 12.00–23.00; Fri & Sat 12.00–23.30

⏴ www.chineseexperience.com

⊟ all major credit cards ■ 10% optional service added

££ dim sum £2.50–£5.50 ■ starters £2–£8.50 ■ mains £7–£20 ■ sides £1.80–£9 ■ desserts £2.80–£5 ■ set menus £19–£23 ■ lowest bottle price £12

✪ Bright restaurant, authentic dim sum

A name like Chinese Experience is something of a free shot for any critic who has been to China where the kindest thing to say about the gastronomy in restaurants is that it is remarkably patchy! Thankfully, this light and seriously busy restaurant on Shaftesbury Avenue combines slick service with low prices and has the added bonus of a menu that has not been 'dumbed down'. At lunch there is fierce competition for tables and the dim sum service is fast and furious. Cuttlefish cakes are good – chewy and well flavoured; Shanghai pork buns work well, admirably juicy; the 'BBQ pork pastry' is not as good as the pork puffs at Royal China (see p. 72) or indeed the venison puffs at Yauatcha (see p. 145), but it is pretty good. Prawn dumplings and scallop dumplings are good. There are also all those moody dumplings that sound more adventurous and exciting than they turn out – ducks' tongues, chicken's feet. What's best about this place is that it feels modern – square plates and even square steamers – but prices are still reasonable. The main menu reflects the feel of the dim sum approach; there are some interesting dishes like braised pork belly in five-spice sauce; stir-fried lamb with leek Peking style; deep-fried prawns with salted egg yolk; stir-fried prawns with Chinese tea leaves. And also some intriguing desserts like deep-fried crispy milk, or mango and grapefruit tapioca pearl. An area at the front of the room is set aside for juice-making, and there are a number of healthy fruit and vegetable juices on offer.

ECapital

8 Gerrard Street, W1 ■ 020 7434 3838

⊖ Leicester Square

|●| Chinese

⊕ daily 12.00–24.00

🖨 all major credit cards except AmEx ■ 12.5% optional service added

££ starters £2.50–£11 ■ mains £7.80–£20 ■ sides £1.50–£9.50
■ desserts £1–£4.50 & £18 (for Swallow's Nest in Coconut Milk Soup)
■ daily lunch menu £4.99 & £6.99 ■ set menus £8.50–£24 ■ tasting
menu £19.50 ■ lowest bottle price £12

✪ Let's hear it for the cuisine of Shanghai

**For some while now this restaurant has ploughed a solitary
furrow** while critics have wrangled over just how authentic the
Shanghai dishes are. No matter, some of the dishes here are welcome
and unfamiliar additions to the Chinatown repertoire and valuable
for that if nothing else. The restaurant interior is striking: the ceiling
is painted deep fuchsia, the walls are a nondescript cream, the
lighting is soft – and that's it. For once, less really is more. This is a
comfortable, unpretentious place to eat. For the nervous, the menu
offers a safety blanket of familiar favourites, from crispy seaweed
to sweet-and-sour pork; proceed and you'll find a host of good
things from Shanghai. Starters include drunken chicken; cold chicken
marinated in sweet wine; or the paper-thin seasoned beef, slices of
slow-cooked beef in a chilli-spiked, savoury marinade. Also classic
old-fashioned, pan-fried dumplings, with good crispy bits, and the
wonderful thousand-layer pig's ear. A slight exaggeration, as there
are just 21 layers, but imagine small strips of agreeably chewy,
streaky bacon, cut thin, and tasting gelatinous and savoury. The
grandstand main course is beggar's chicken. The chicken is seasoned
with pickled cabbage and shredded pork, then wrapped in lotus
leaves and given a casing of flour and water paste; the entire parcel
is baked and, when the casing is smashed at table-side, the fragrant
chicken is revealed within. You can also try sea bass West Lake style,
or Shanghai-braised yellow eel. Exploring this lengthy menu and the
surprisingly sophisticated wine list is most rewarding.

Fung Shing

15 Lisle Street, WC2 ■ 020 7437 1539

● Leicester Square

🍴 Chinese

🕐 daily 12.00 to 23.30

🖥 www.fungshing.co.uk

💳 all major credit cards ■ 10% optional service added

££ starters £2–£19 ■ mains £8–£14 ■ sides £1.80–£8.50 ■ lowest bottle price £14.50

✪ Proud Chinatown old-timer

Fung Shing – one of the first restaurants in Chinatown to take cooking seriously. Some decades ago, when the restaurant was still a dowdy little place with a mural on the back wall, Chinatown's number one fish cook, chef Wu, ruled the kitchens. When he died, in 1996, his sous-chef took over. Since those glory days the restaurant has changed beyond recognition and now dining rooms stretch all the way from Lisle Street to Gerrard Street, ever bigger and ever brassier. Critics tend to suggest that there has been a slight decline in overall standards, but that may be rose-tinted hindsight and the menu is still littered with interesting dishes. To start, ignore the crispy duck with pancakes, which is good but too predictable, and the lobster with noodles. Instead try the steamed scallops with garlic and soy sauce – nowhere does them better. Or spareribs, barbecued or with chilli and garlic. The prosaically named 'mixed meat with lettuce' is also good, a savoury dish of mince with lettuce-leaf wraps. You could happily order your mains solely from the chef's specials: stewed belly pork with yam in hot pot; crispy spicy eel; roast crispy pigeon; or oysters with bean thread vermicelli in hot pot. Other dishes are good too: perfect Singapore noodles; crispy stuffed baby squids with chilli and garlic; and steamed aubergine with garlic sauce. The Fung Shing has always been classy, but what is unusual, certainly in Chinatown, is the gracious and helpful service. This a restaurant where you can ask for advice with confidence, although you'll need an unflinching wallet if the recommendation is braised double-boiled shark's fin in hot pot.

Hamburger Union

4–6 Garrick Street, WC2 ■ 020 7379 0412

⊖	Leicester Square
🍴	Burgers
🕐	Sun & Mon 11.30–21.30; Tues to Sat 11.30–22.30
🔗	www.hamburgerunion.com
💳	all major credit cards except AmEx ■ no service added
££	hamburgers £3.95–£9.95 ■ sides 20p–£2.95 ■ desserts £2.95 ■ lowest bottle price £11.95

✪ This resto has a respected butcher as a consultant

Rather than getting fancy, purveyors of hamburgers should get real, because with some dishes simpler is always better, and one of those dishes is the hamburger. Everything starts with decent meat and at Hamburger Union they take their meat very seriously indeed. The meat comes from organic and free-range herds and is properly hung; the burgers are freshly made on the premises. The restaurant occupies two shop fronts: the one on the left is the takeaway part of the operation and also where you order, pay and then go on through to the very modernist dining room. You take a ticket with you and pop it into the metal stand on your table, so that the waitress can find you when your drinks are ready and your meal is cooked. The menu is short. There are burgers, cheeseburgers, bacon cheeseburgers, some veggie options, and a notable fillet steak Adherents to the low-carb cult can have their burger 'protein style', which means that the kitchen replaces the bun with a couple of lettuce leaves. The straightforward burger is very good – juicy, and on an Italian-style bun, it is cooked as requested and comes with some red onion, mayo and lettuce. The chips are described on the menu as 'proper chips, never frozen' and that is what they are. There are reasonably priced drinks and a suitably sticky and unctuous malted milk. 'Cocktail shakes' – Baileys, Tia Maria or crème de menthe – are a bit more puzzling and probably best left to experts.

→ For branches, see index

HK Diner

22 Wardour Street, WC2 ■ 020 7437 1539

⊖ Piccadilly/Leicester Square

|◉| Chinese

⏱ daily 11.00–04.00

🗗 all major credit cards (over £12) ■ 10% optional service added

££ starters £2.50–£9 ■ mains £8.50–£12.50 ■ sides £4.50–£7 ■ lowest bottle price £9.50

✪ Modern vibe, modern interior, trad food

HK Diner really is a diner at heart, and the atmosphere has more in common with American eateries than Chinese restaurants. This a light, bright, busy, modern sort of place, so if you like your Chinese restaurants seedy and 'authentic' you will almost certainly walk past with a shudder. 'It looks more like a burger bar, so how can it possibly …' But pre-judging this place would be a major mistake as the food is very good, and there is no iron rule that slickness means rip-off. Prices are not cheap, but they are not over-the-top either, and the prospect of getting decent food very late at night is a beguiling one. Service is attentive, you don't wait long for food and the tables turn over at a ferocious pace. The menu offers all the Cantonese favourites, from very good salt-and-pepper spareribs, to grilled dumplings and steamed scallops on the half shell. For main course, deep-fried squid with salt, pepper and garlic is as light, crisp and un-rubbery as you could wish, or there's steamed crab with Shao Sing wine. Fried beef with chilli and black bean sauce is rich and delicious, as is honey-barbecued pork. The Singapore noodle is a model of its kind. From the vegetable dishes, choose the fried snow pea shoots with minced garlic – if you love garlic. This is the one dish to guarantee that even good friends will keep their distance for the next couple of days. The simple dishes, such as fried noodles with mixed meat or fried noodle with mixed seafood, always hit the spot.

Imperial China

White Bear Yard, Lisle Street, WC2 ■ 020 7734 3388

⊖ Leicester Square

🍴 Chinese/dim sum

🕑 Mon to Fri 12.00–22.30; Sat & Sun 11.30–22.00

🖥 www.imperial-china.co.uk

🗗 all major credit cards ■ no service added

££ starters £2.80–£9.95 ■ mains £6.95–£23.95 ■ sides £2–£8.95
■ desserts £2.95–£3.95 ■ set menus £30 & £35 ■ lowest bottle price
£12

✪ Large and opulent resto in private backwater

Imperial China should really be called 'Phoenix' something or other since, like so many large Chinatown restaurant sites, this large, smart and aspirational establishment is merely the latest incarnation of an earlier venture. There are various different dining rooms spread over three floors; some are dedicated to karaoke, and the one on the ground floor seems to have been modelled on James Bond's idea of a cocktail bar – it's not often that you see a baby grand piano in a Chinese restaurant, stranger still to have a pianist tinkling the ivories while you're the one playing chopsticks. The dim sum here have a growing reputation – the excellence of the dim sum at Hakkasan (see p. 7) seems to have stung Chinatown into action. Imperial City offers fried pork and spring onion buns; stewed goose web in black bean sauce; preserved egg and sliced fish cheung fun, as well as most of the steadier dim sum favourites. There are also some interesting options on the main menu: starters such as lotus root and straw mushrooms; sliced preserved pork knuckle with jelly fish; and simple soups such as hot and sour, or encouragingly, 'soup of the day – Chinese clear soup'. From the lengthy list of mains, salt-baked chicken appeals; as does shredded pork with ginger and aubergine; stir-fried scallop with lily bud; or deep-fried fillet of eel with chilli. Imperial China tries to be a grown-up sort of restaurant and the pricing reflects this ambition, but there are some interesting dishes, and providing you relish the over-the-top styling it makes a good venue.

India Club

143 Strand, WC2 ■ 020 7836 0650

⊖ Holborn

🍴 Indian

🕐 Mon to Fri & Sun 12.00–15.00 & 18.00–22.30; Sat 18.00–22.30

🖰 cash or cheque only ■ no service added

££ starters £2.50–£3.25 ■ mains £7.95–£8.10 ■ sides £2–£5 ■ desserts (kulfi) £2.50 ■ lowest bottle price £6

✪ A venerable living fossil

Heed the kindly chilli warning of your waiter. The chilli bhajis are extra-hot green chillies deep-fried until crisp – not for novices. When the India Club opened in 1950, the linoleum flooring was probably quite chic. Situated up two flights of stairs, sandwiched between floors of the grandly named Strand Continental Hotel, the Club is an institution, generally full and mostly with regulars, as you can tell by the stares of appraisal given to newcomers. The regulars are in love with the strangely old-fashioned combination of runny curry, low, low prices and time-warp décor. They can be split into two categories: suave Indians from the nearby High Commission, and a miscellany of folk from the BBC World Service down the road in Bush House. The food at the India Club predates any London consciousness of the different spicing of Bengal, Kerala, Rajasthan or Goa. It is Anglo-Indian, essentially, and well cooked of its kind, although to palates accustomed to more modern Indian dishes it is something of a symphony to runny sauce. Mughlay chicken is a wing and a drumstick in a rich, brown, oniony gravy, garnished with the two halves of a hard-boiled egg; while scampi curry is runny and brown, with fearless prawns swimming through it. Masala dosa is a well-made crispy pancake with a pleasantly sharp-tasting potato filling; dhal is yellow and … runny. There are good dishes of bhindi or brinjal. The mango chutney is a revelation: thick parings of mango, which are chewy and delicious. Breads – paratha, puris – are good, while the rice is white and comes in clumps.

The Ivy

1 West Street, WC2 ■ 020 7836 4751

⊖ Leicester Square

|◉| British

🕐 daily 12.00–15.00 (Sun 15.30) & 17.30–24.00

🖰 www.caprice-holdings.co.uk

🖶 all major credit cards ■ no service added

££ starters £7–£11.75 ■ mains £11.50–£26.50 ■ sides £2.75–£5
■ desserts £6.25–£13.50 ■ weekend lunch £21.50 ■ lowest bottle
price £15

✪ Lifestyles of the rich and famous

**The Ivy is a beautiful, Regency-style restaurant, built in 1928
by Mario Gallati.** It has been a Theatreland and society favourite
ever since and never more so than today. The staff, it is said, notice
recessions only because they turn fewer people away. That's no joke:
The Ivy is booked solid, and behaves like a club even if it isn't one. To
get a booking it helps to proffer the name of at least a B-list celebrity.
If your heart is set on a visit, try booking at off-peak times a couple
of months ahead, or at very short notice, or ask for a table in the
bar area. It's also less busy for weekend lunch – three courses for a
bargain price, with valet parking thrown in. And once you're in? Well,
first off, whether you're famous or not, the staff are charming and
un-hurrying. Second, the food is pretty good. The menu is essentially
a brasserie list of comfort food – nice dishes that combine simplicity
with familiarity. You might start with spiced pumpkin and coconut
soup; the risotto of wild mushrooms; or the eggs Benedict. Then
there's deep-fried haddock; grilled pork sausage; and well-made
versions of classic staples such as the Ivy hamburger with dill pickle;
shepherd's pie; and salmon fishcakes. Even the vegetable section is
enlivened with homely delights like bubble and squeak. For dessert
you might turn to chocolate pudding soufflé; rhubarb fool; or go all
Pickwickian and finish with a savoury – herring roes on toast, or a
serious Welsh rarebit.

J. Sheekey

26–32 St Martin's Court, WC2 ■ 020 7240 2565

⊖ Leicester Square

🍽 Fish

🕓 Mon to Sat 12.00–15.00 & 17.30–24.00; Sun 12.00–15.30

🖑 www.caprice-holdings.co.uk

🖫 all major credit cards ■ no service added

££ starters £6.50–£15.25 ■ shellfish/crab/oysters £11.75–£35.50
■ mains £10.25–£31.75 ■ sides £3.25–£4.75 ■ desserts £5.50–£8.50
■ weekend lunch £21.50 ■ lowest bottle price £15

✪ Fresh fish with flair

Sheekey's is one of a handful of restaurants that had shambled along since the war – World War I. Then, towards the end of the last millennium, it was taken over by the team behind The Ivy and Le Caprice (see opposite and p. 111). After a good deal of redesign and refurbishment, it emerged from the builders' clutches as J. Sheekey, with much the same attitudes and style as its senior siblings, but still focused on fish. The restaurant may look new, but it certainly seems old, and its series of interconnecting dining rooms gives it an intimate feel. The cooking is accomplished, the service is first-rate, and the fish is fresh – a good combination. The long menu presents a seductive blend of plain, old-fashioned, classic fish cuisine, such as lemon sole belle meunière, with more modern dishes like whole roast gilthead bream with herbs and olive oil. There are always handwritten dishes on the menu, 'specials' that change on a weekly basis. To start with, there are oysters, crabs and shellfish, plus everything from jellied eels and devilled whitebait, to seared rare tuna. Main courses, like pan-fried wing of skate with capers and brown butter, or Cornish fish stew with celery heart and garlic mayonnaise, are backed up by classics such as fillet of cod and Sheekey's fish pie. Puddings range from spotted dick with butter and golden syrup, to wild strawberry and champagne jelly with Jersey cream. As well as smart wines, there are plenty of options at the cheaper end of the list for sensible drinking. The set lunch at the weekend is a genuine bargain.

Joe Allen

13 Exeter Street, WC2 ■ 020 7836 0651

⊖ Covent Garden

🍽 North American

🕓 Mon to Fri 12.00–24.45; Sat 11.30–24.45; Sun 11.30–23.30

🖰 www.joeallen.co.uk

🖰 all major credit cards ■ 12.5% optional service added for parties over 8

££ starters £5–£7 ■ mains £8–£15.50 ■ sides £3.50 ■ desserts £5.50
   ■ set lunch Mon to Fri £15 & £17 ■ brunch Sat & Sun £15 & £17.50
   ■ lowest bottle price £15 (litre carafe)

✪ American diner for theatrical types

**This is the restaurant with a 'secret' hamburger – not listed on
the menu, but well worth ordering.** By some inexplicable alchemy,
Joe Allen continues to be the Covent Garden eatery of choice for
a wide swathe of the acting profession. It is a dark, resolutely un-
trendy place that dishes up a somewhat refined version of American
comfort food. If your heart is set on a Caesar salad, chilli con carne
or eggs Benedict, this is a great place to come. Joe Allen has a
splendid attitude to mealtimes: the à la carte runs all day, so you
can have lunch when you will. There's also a lunch and a pre-theatre
menu, plus a brunch menu on Saturday and Sunday. The food is
the kind of stuff that we are all comfortable with. Starters include
smoked salmon with new potatoes, chives and sour cream; buffalo
mozzarella, tomato and basil salad; and black bean soup. They
are followed on the menu by a section described as 'salads/eggs/
sandwiches' in which you'll find some of Joe Allen's strengths: the
Caesar salad; the roast chicken salad; and eggs Joe Allen, a satisfying
combination of poached eggs, potato skins, Hollandaise sauce and
spinach. Main courses range from tuna with sesame crust and braised
Chinese cabbage; through barbecue spareribs with rice, wilted
spinach, black-eyed peas and corn muffin; to pan-fried calf's liver
with mashed potato and grilled bacon. As you would suspect, the
dessert offerings provide a serious sugar hit – go for the brownie,
with an extra portion of hot fudge.

Lee Ho Fook

4 Macclesfield Street, W1 ■ 020 7494 1200

⊖ Leicester Square

◉ Chinese

⏱ daily 12.00–12.00

🗄 all major credit cards ■ no service added

££ starters £2.20–£4.50 ■ mains £3.80–£7 ■ desserts £2.80 ■ set meals
£4.50–£17 ■ lowest bottle price £8.80

✪ Barbecued ducks – cheap and cheerful

**There's been a development at this small Chinese barbecue
house and now they appear to be sponsored by the Cherry Valley
Duckling Company.** The resto has also expanded and now has a few
extra tables. Change is always threatening, and where once there
was just a Chinese chef chopping meat and dishing it out, the menu
now lists such extravagances as 'appetisers' and set meals. But the
old-style dishes are still to be had and prices have crept up only a
little. Sit down, enjoy a cup of Chinese tea, splash a dollop of the
chilli sauce onto the pile of rice topped with barbecued meat placed
in front of you, and pick up your chopsticks. This is good, simple,
cheap eating. Choose from lean pork loin; crisp, fatty belly pork;
soya chicken or duck, which all come with a pile of rice and splash
of gravy. You can also mix and match – half pork, half duck, say – or
order a 'combination' of mixed roast pork, soya chicken and duck
with rice. Some choose to order the meats without rice – perhaps a
whole duck, or a portion of soya chicken. Try adding a plate of crisp
vegetables in oyster sauce to your order. And, before the main event,
perhaps a bowl of won ton soup, or the even more substantial won
ton noodle soup. Also attributable to the march of progress is the
series of noodle dishes now listed – soup noodles and ribbon noodles
(ho fan) – the most expensive of which is the 'chicken, and duck leg
with noodle'. This establishment continues to do a simple thing very
well, which is not as easy a trick to pull off as it sounds. There's also a
thriving takeaway trade. Give a duck a home.

→ For branches, see index

Mela

152–158 Shaftesbury Avenue, WC2 ■ 020 7836 8635

◉ Covent Garden

🍽 Indian

🕐 Mon to Sat 12.00–23.30; Sun 12.00–22.30

🖰 www.melarestaurant.co.uk

🖃 all major credit cards ■ 12.5% optional service added

££ starters £3.50–£5.95 ■ mains £6–£15 ■ sides £1.95–£4.50 ■ desserts £3.25–£4.50 ■ set lunch from £1.95 ■ lowest bottle price £10.95

✪ This may be London's best-value set lunch

Mela is a restaurant dedicated to India's regional dishes. Like its newer sibling, Chowki (see p. 132), Mela may even have cracked the great lunch conundrum – Indian restaurateurs find it very difficult to persuade Londoners to eat curry for lunch – and it has done it by offering really good value. At lunchtime there's a 'Paratha Pavilion', which may sound a bit kitsch, but offers a variety of delicious set lunches based around the simple street food of Delhi. Mela has a pleasant modern dining room and service is slick and friendly. At lunch the set meals revolve around bread – which may be made from maize, sorghum, millet, wholewheat flour, or chilli- and coriander-flavoured chickpea flour. The latter is particularly good. It may come with the dhal or curry of the day, or perhaps with a savoury stuffing. There may be other breads, too, such as roomalis (large and thin, wholemeal handkerchief bread); puris (fried chapatis); uttapams (rice-flour pancakes); and naans. Or there is a range of traditional dosas. Fortunately, at Mela's low prices you can experiment. The main menu, which is available at lunch but comes into its own in the evening, makes a real attempt to offer genuine regional dishes. Starters range from gosht utthapams, rice pancakes with lamb, to lehsooni whitebait. Then tandoor dishes like barrah beer kebab lead on to crab moilee; or methi murg, a rich dish teaming chicken with fenugreek. There is also an exemplary gosht rogan josh. Mela is a template for a modern Indian restaurant and it combines good cooking with fair prices.

Mr Kong

21 Lisle Street, WC2 ■ 020 7437 7341

◈ Leicester Square

|◉| Chinese

◷ daily 12.00–03.00

🗗 all major credit cards ■ 10% optional service added

££ starters £1.90–£5.50 ■ mains £5.90–£14.50 ■ sides £1.90–£12
■ desserts £2.90 ■ lowest bottle price £8.90

✪ Late night extra – some moody dishes

Obviously, the modest Mr Kong balked at calling his restaurant King Kong. Despite marathon opening hours, at all regular mealtimes this resto is full of satisfied customers who appreciate King Kong. Go with a party of six or more and that way you can order, taste and argue over a raft of dishes and if any really hit the spot you can always order a second portion to satisfy that craving. Sad to say, but the trend in Chinatown is for restos to abandon some of their more obscure menu items in favour of safety first. Mr Kong is teetering on the brink. The food is good and the menu still sprawls across a vast number of pages, but it is shorter than it once was. Take it as read that the old favourite dishes – baked spareribs with chilli and salt; braised belly pork with preserved vegetables; fried duck with bitter melon – will be consistently good. For a more adventurous time, a good tip is to look out for 'hot pot' dishes – these are casseroles that come to the table in clay pots. Or look on the Chef's special menu – deep-fried oysters in batter; sautéed mixed seafood with fresh mango; crispy beancurd with vegetables; sautéed dragon whiskers (pea shoots) with dried scallops. Portions are generous and prices are reasonable, even when dishes contain exotic ingredients. Just ignore the décor, which despite occasional refurbs remains resolutely ordinary. If you ever get the urge to try the deep-fried pig's intestine with spicy salt, this may be the place to do it.

The Neal Street Restaurant

26 Neal Street, WC2 ■ 020 7836 8368

⊖ Covent Garden

🍴 Italian

🕑 Mon to Sat 12.00–14.30 & 18.00–23.00

🖰 www.carluccios.com

🖻 all major credit cards ■ 12.5% optional service added

££ antipasti & primi £7.50–£18 ■ secondi £15–£23 ■ sides £3.50
■ desserts £5.50–£9 ■ lowest bottle price £18.50

❂ The hall of the mushroom King

This upscale Italian still sticks to a belief in carefully sourced top-quality ingredients and minimal kitchen interference. Antonio Carluccio is the genial mushroom hunter who is behind the chain of Carluccio's Caffes (see p. 3); the Neal Street was his first restaurant and is a much posher affair. When so many dishes reflect the proprietor's love of wild fungi and truffles this can make for pricey dining, but the occasional regional set menus offer some respite. The room is long and the big mirror at the far end makes it seem longer; the walls are (and have been for decades) lined with walking sticks carved by the patron. A homely look in a serious restaurant. The menu changes regularly. There are always specials and they command attention – start with tiny artichokes, deep-fried, or anything mushroomy. The pasta course is a delight: tortelli di granchio, small parcels of crab in a saffron sauce, or tagliolini al tartufo nero, hand-cut pasta with truffle sauce and shavings of black truffle. There is also a tempting array of fish dishes: perhaps the goulash of monkfish and skate with Triestine bread appeals? A dish of boneless oxtail braised in red wine and served with sweet and sour baby onions is top stuff – rich and satisfying. Puds are good – from the bitter chocolate, hazelnut and orange cake, to the Campari and passion fruit sorbet. The wine list offers a guide to Italy, and the coffee is exemplary. But the best advice is to gird your wallet and visit during the autumn mushroom season when you can indulge in Trifolata di funghi del giorno, mixed sautéed mushrooms of the day.

New World

1 Gerrard Place, W1 ■ 020 7734 0396

⊖ Leicester Square

🍽 Chinese/dim sum

🕐 daily 11.00 to 24.00

🖫 all major credit cards ■ no service added

££ dim sum (11.00–18.00) £2.20–£4.10 ■ soups £2–£8 ■ mains £5.50–£15.50 ■ sides £1.30–£8.50 ■ set menus £9.50–£20.50 ■ lowest bottle price £10.50

⭐ A trolley Grand Prix over several floors

This is one of the largest restaurants in Europe, seating as it does between 400 and 600 people depending on how many functions are going on at any one time. However, despite its size, when you arrive you invariably have to wait in a sort of holding pen just inside the door until the intercom screeches with static and you are sent off to your table. The menu, a leather-bound tome and nearly twenty pages long, features everything you have ever heard of and quite a lot you haven't. In any case, you don't need it – go for the dim sum, which are served every day from 11.00 until 18.00. The dim sum come round on trolleys. First, catch the eye of a waiter or waitress with a bow tie, to order drinks, and then you're at the mercy of the trolley pushers. The trolleys are themed: one has a lot of barbecued meat; another is packed with ho fun (broad noodles); another with steamed dumplings; another with soups; another with cheung fun (the long slippery rolls of pastry with different meats inside). A good mix would be to take siu mai and har kau from the 'steamers' trolley, then char sui cheung fun – a long roll with pork. Follow this with some deep-fried won ton, little crispy parcels with sweet sauce. Or perhaps try something exotic like woo kwok, deep-fried taro dumplings stuffed with pork; and something filling such as char sui pow, steamed doughnuts filled with pork. Or perhaps nor mai gai, a lotus-leaf parcel of glutinous rice and meats. If you arrive after 18.00, you're on your own: there are literally hundreds of dishes on the main menus. Dim sum trolleys are a great way to introduce small children to Chinese food.

Punjab

80–82 Neal Street, WC2 ■ 020 7836 9787

⊖ Covent Garden

⦿⦿ Indian

⏱ Mon to Sat 12.00–15.00 & 18.00–23.30; Sun 12.00–22.30

🖰 www.punjab.co.uk

🗗 all major credit cards ■ 10% optional service added

££ starters £2.60–£2.90 ■ mains £8.20–£10.30 ■ sides 95p–£5
■ desserts £2.20–£2.70 ■ lowest bottle price £9.95

✪ One of London's three oldest Indian restaurants

**In 1951 Gurbachan Singh Maan moved his fledgling Indian
restaurant.** He left the City to take over new premises in Neal Street
in Covent Garden, his plan being to take advantage of the trade
from the nearby Indian High Commission. It was a strategy that has
worked handsomely. Today, his grandson Sital Singh Maan runs what
is the oldest North Indian restaurant in the U.K., though one that
has always been at the forefront of new developments – in 1962 the
Maan family brought over one of the first tandoor ovens to be seen
in Britain. Despite these occasional forays into fashion, the cuisine
at the Punjab has always been firmly rooted where it belongs – in
the Punjab. Punjabi cuisine offers some interesting, non-standard
Indian dishes, so start by ordering from among the less familiar items
on the menu – kadu puri, for instance, a sweet and sharp mash of
curried pumpkin served on a puri; or aloo tikka, which are described
as potato cutlets but arrive as small deep-fried moons on a sea of
tangy sauce; or chicken chat, which is diced chicken in rich sauce. To
follow, try the acharri gosht, or the acharri murgha. The first is made
with lamb, and the second with chicken. The meat is 'pickled' in
traditional Punjabi spices and, as a result, both meat and sauce have
an agreeable edge of sharpness. Chicken karahi is good, too – rich
and thick. The anari gosht combines lamb with pomegranate, while
from the vegetable dishes channa aloo offsets the nutty crunch of
chickpeas with the solace of potatoes. Or you could try the benaam
macchi tarkari, billed as a 'nameless fish curry, speciality of chef'.
Nameless, but not tasteless.

Rules

35 Maiden Lane, WC2 ■ 020 7836 5314

⊖ Covent Garden

🍴 Very British

🕐 Mon to Sat 12.00–23.30; Sun 12.00–22.30

🖱 www.rules.co.uk

🖩 all major credit cards ■ 12.5% optional service added

££ starters £6.75–£12.95 ■ mains £15.95–£21.50 ■ sides £3.50
■ desserts £6.95 ■ post-theatre menu £18.95 ■ lowest bottle price
£15.95

✪ London's oldest restaurant

Dickens, Betjeman, H.G. Wells, Thackeray, Graham Greene and King Edward VII are just a few of the celebs who have revelled in Rules. Rules would be a living cliché but for one essential saving grace – all the fixtures, fittings and studied eccentricities that look as if they have been custom-made in some modern factory are real. Rules is the genuine article, a very English restaurant. The proud boast here is, 'We specialise in classic game cookery', and indeed they do, but thankfully the restaurant has become more of a bustling brasserie than the mausoleum it once was. First of all you should note that Rules is open from noon till late, which is very handy when circumstances dictate a four o'clock lunch. Start with scrambled egg and smoked salmon, or a Stilton and watercress soup. Go on to game in season, or the occasional specials: maybe Belted Galloway beef or Tamworth suckling pig, sourced from Rules' own estate in the High Pennines. The steak and kidney pudding with mash is a banker, as is the roast rib of beef for two and the smoked Finnan haddock fishcake with spinach and poached egg. Also noteworthy is the fillet of venison with wild mushrooms and herb mash. Puddings, such as treacle sponge, or sticky toffee, are merciless. Why not go for the traditional blue Stilton cheese with celery and a glass of port? Should you face entertaining out-of-town relatives, or foreign visitors in search of something old and English, Rules is a good place to indulge in nostalgia, but is still forward-thinking enough to have a no smoking rule that applies everywhere but the private rooms.

Tokyo Diner

2 Newport Place, WC2 ■ 020 7287 8777

⊖ Leicester Square

🍴 Japanese

🕐 daily 12.00–24.00

🖰 www.tokyodiner.com

🖻 Mastercard, Visa; no cheques ■ no tips accepted

££ sushi/sashimi sets £3–£9.50 ■ bento boxes £9.20–£13.90 ■ soup noodles £5.90–£6.50 ■ rice meals £4.90–£8.50 ■ sides £1.50–£5.90 ■ lowest bottle price £6.90

✪ Japanese eating house marooned in Chinatown

The place was actually set up by a Nipponophile Englishman, but the kitchen staff are all Japanese and its Far Eastern credentials bear scrutiny. Tokyo Diner offers conclusive proof that you needn't take out a second mortgage to enjoy Japanese food in London. This is fast food, Tokyo-style. The décor is crisp and minimalist, and if you don't know sushi from sumo, you'll be glad of the explanatory notes on the menu. When your food arrives, pick up a set of chopsticks, snap them apart – it's recommended that you rub them together to rid them of splinters – and get stuck in. Top seller is the soba noodle soup – thin brown buckwheat noodles in a soya broth. It's pleasant, filling and very popular with the drop-by lunchtime trade. Don't be afraid of slurping it, slurping is OK. Or try the set lunch in a bento box of rice, noodles, sashimi and your choice of teriyaki. Other bento favourites include the ton katsu bento, which is a kind of superior breadcrumbed pork escalope. If you don't have appetite enough for a full-on bento box, skip the curries – they're a bit like school food – and head straight for the sushi and sashimi. They too come in 'sets': try the nine-piece nigiri set, which is very good value, or the hoso-maki set, which comprises six pieces of salmon, three pieces of cucumber and three pieces of pickled radish. To wash it all down, the Japanese beer Asahi is good, or there's complimentary Japanese tea. For a special treat, try the rich, sweet plum wine, which is surprisingly moreish. Japanese style, the Tokyo Diner does not accept tips.

Edgware Road and Paddington

Abu Ali

136–138 George Street, W1 ■ 020 7724 6338

⊖ Marble Arch

🍽 Lebanese

🕐 daily 09.00–23.00

🗗 cash or cheque only ■ no service added

££ starters £3 ■ mains £7–£8 ■ desserts (Middle Eastern sweets) 25p–50p per piece ■ no alcohol

✪ Clouds of hubble bubble smoke

You can only suppose that in the Lebanon going out to eat is man's work. That certainly seems to be the case around the Oxford Street end of the Edgware Road, where you'll find Abu Ali's bustling café. This is an authentic place, the Lebanese equivalent of a northern working man's club, and men gather to smoke at the pavement tables. It's a bit spartan in appearance, but the food is honest and good value. Although you are unlikely to find many Lebanese women here, female diners get a dignified, if rather formal, welcome as befits their rarity. There's nothing intimidating about the place or its clientele. You will want a selection of starters. Tabbouleh is bright green with lots of fresh parsley, lemon juice, oil and only a little cracked wheat – it even tastes healthy. Houmous is rich and spicy, garnished with a few whole chickpeas and cayenne pepper. Warak inab are thin and pleasantly sour stuffed vine leaves, served hot or cold. Moutabal is also called babaganoush and is a rich dish of aubergine with sesame oil. Kabis is a plate of tangy salt and sour pickles – cucumber, chillies and red cabbage – that comes free with every order. For main dishes there's kafta halabiyeh, minced lamb kebabs with onion and spices. Or there's kafta yogurtliyed, which is the self-same kebab served with good sharp yogurt. The plain grilled meats are also good. Try the boned-out poussin – farrouge moussahab. To drink, there is mint tea – a Lipton's tea bag and a bunch of fresh mint in every pot – or soft drinks. Try a bubble pipe and you will be fussed over by the charcoal man who sets up your pipe and sorts out a new mouthpiece; hardcore hookah puffers replace the water with Appletise and ice, for a really sweet and sickly smoke.

Chai Pani

64 Seymour Street, W1 ■ 020 7258 2000

⊖ Marble Arch

⑩ Indian vegetarian

🕐 Mon to Fri 12.00–14.30 & 18.00–22.30; Sat & Sun 12.00–16.30 & 18.00–22.30

🖰 www.chaipani.co.uk

🗗 all major credit cards ■ no service added

££ starters £3.50–£4.50 ■ thalis £8–£20 ■ mains £5–£7 ■ sides £3.50–£5 ■ desserts £4–£4.50 ■ lunch buffet Mon to Fri £6 ■ lowest bottle price £12.95

✪ Vegging out in Rajasthan

Chai Pani means 'tea' and 'water' – a symbolic offering of Rajasthani hospitality within the home. The name is apt, as not only does this small restaurant, tucked neatly behind Marble Arch, feel welcoming (the décor is almost domestic), but it also serves simple, comforting food that's very fresh and very good. One thing, however, is clear from the menu – modern diet schemes are unlikely to succeed in the Shekhawati region of Rajasthan. Potatoes abound, accompanied by aromatic pulse and vegetable dishes (heaving with mysterious ingredients) and breads – soft, crispy, stuffed, plain … you choose. From the appetizers choose lauki pakoda, bite-sized discs of deep-fried marrow in gram flour, with a mint chutney to die for, or perhaps the wonderful raj kachori, a delicate, puffed, flour shell stuffed with veg and swimming in yogurt and chutney, though it resembles an ice-cream sundae that's fallen from a great height. Delicious. As for mains, either choose one of the speciality thalis on offer – Desert thali; or the Saatvik thali, comprising buckwheat puri, aloo in yogurt gravy, cucumber raita; or a vegan, low-cal or wheat-free thali. Alternatively, take your pick from the selections of rice, curry and dhal dishes. The aloo matar pulao is stir-fried rice and peas in a fragrant heap, laced with deadly dried chillies; panchmela subzi is a rich 'five-vegetable' curry – it's hard to identify all five, but expect pumpkin and … potato. The sweets range from the expected kulfi and gulab jamun, to the unusual badam halwa, a hot ground-almond cousin of treacle pud.

Island

Lancaster Terrace, W2 ■ 020 7551 6070

⊖ Lancaster Gate

|◉| British

⏱ daily 12.00–15.00, 15.00–18.00 (afternoon tea) & 18.00–22.30

🖰 www.islandrestaurant.co.uk

🖫 all major credit cards ■ 12.5% optional service added

££ starters £4.50–£7.50 ■ mains £11.50–£20 ■ sides £3–£3.50
■ desserts £6–£7.50 ■ set menus 12.00–19.00 £12 & £15 ■ lowest
bottle price £15

✪ Think Britain, at this island in the traffic

In a world that sometimes seems full of French food it's a genuine
pleasure to find a restaurant that attempts to fly the flag for the
home team. Although following the current convention of having
its own separate entrance, the Island restaurant still has a faint echo
of 'hotelness' filtering through from the giant Royal Lancaster that
envelops it. The dining room is on a mezzanine level, which lifts it
above the traffic that swirls around a giant not-really-roundabout.
Behind the buses you can see Hyde Park, but this is a rather sterile
dining room despite the best efforts of a modern design firm. So you
are unlikely to pitch up here for the atmosphere, but you may be
tempted by the food. Most dishes are built around strong flavours
and interesting textures, and change with the seasons. Starters may
include simple dishes like cauliflower soup, with thyme foam; or
grilled English goats' cheese, artichoke, Cheltenham beetroot and
green tomato chutney; or Cornish crab, artichoke, mixed cress and
shellfish mayonnaise; or maple-roasted quail, pearl barley and wild
mushroom broth. Mains continue in that vein: confit Clare island
salmon, deep-fried sprats, borlotti beans, and preserved lemon, or
wild rabbit, sweetcorn pancake, peas and girolles. There are some
simple but luxurious dishes from the grill – a T-bone of halibut with
cèpe and horseradish butter, or calf's liver with treacle bacon. Puds
range from poached peaches, with vanilla rice pudding; to a vanilla
panna cotta, with damson sherbet. Service is friendly.

The Mandalay

444 Edgware Road, W1 ■ 020 7258 3696

⊖ Edgware Road

🍽 Burmese

🕒 Mon to Sat 12.00–14.30 & 18.00–22.30

🖱 www.mandalayway.com

🖫 all major credit cards ■ no service added

££ starters £1.90–£3.90 ■ mains £3.90–£7.50 ■ desserts £1.50–£2.50
■ lowest bottle price £7.90

✪ Fancy going out for a Burmese?

Two Scandinavian-educated Burmese brothers, Gary and Dwight Ally, have become famous in the Edgware Road desert – the area north of the Harrow Road but south of anything else. Their restaurant is bizarre, with just 28 seats, an old sandwich counter filled with strange and exotic ingredients, and greetings and decoration in both Burmese and Norwegian. Gary is in the kitchen and smiley; talkative Dwight is out front. The Ally brothers have correctly concluded that their native language is unmasterable by the English, so the menu is written in English with a Burmese translation – an enormous help when ordering. But the food itself is pure unexpurgated Burmese, and all freshly cooked. The cuisine is a mélange of different local influences, with a little bit of Thai and Malaysian, and a lot of Indian. To start there are pappadums or a great bowlful of prawn crackers, which arrive freshly fried and sizzling hot (and served on domestic kitchen paper to soak up the oil). Starters range from spring rolls and samosas, to salads like raw papaya and cucumber, or chicken and cabbage. Main courses are mainly curries, or rice and noodle dishes, spiced with plenty of ginger, garlic, coriander and coconut, and using fish, chicken and vegetables as the main ingredients. The cooking is good, flavours hit the mark, portions are huge, and everything is priced very keenly indeed. Vegetable dishes are somewhat more successful than the prawn ones, but at this price it's only to be expected. The brothers have plans to open a hotel in nearby Paddington, at which point the restaurant may move; you have to hope that it survives.

Ranoush

43 Edgware Road, W2 ■ 020 7723 5929

⊖ Marble Arch

🍴 Lebanese

🕒 daily 09.00–03.00

🖰 www.maroush.com

🖰 cash only ■ no service added

££ starters £1–£5 ■ mains £3–£9 ■ sides £1.50–£2 ■ desserts £3 ■ no alcohol

✪ A cure for the late-night munchies

This branch of Ranoush is part of the Maroush empire, which comprises a dozen Lebanese restaurants all over London, including the Beirut Express, plus (as a wild card) Signor Marco, a slick-looking Italian eatery at the Marble Arch end of the Edgware Road. Ranoush is a fine, unfussy, late-opening, lively sort of pit stop that is justifiably popular with late-night folk. At the back is the juice bar which gives you the healthy bit, at the front is the kebab servery. In between is a counter packed with all the other items from the encyclopedic menu. To eat here you need to know what you want, as you start by paying, then take the relevant piece of the receipt to either the kebab men at the front or the juice men at the rear – it's self-service with attitude. The starters are very sound, lots of meze both cold and hot: houmous, tabbouleh, and warak ineb are good. The pickles are very good. The main course offerings are large plates of grilled meat – lamb shawarma; kafta meshwi (minced lamb); and riash ghanam. Best though to opt for the sandwiches: ordering lamb shawarma brings a fresh round of bread wrapped around slivers of grilled lamb and lubricated with a dollop of yogurt. It arrives wrapped tight in paper and is very difficult to eat without dripping the juices down your clothes. Very good. Variants include chicken shawarma; lahm meshwi, chunks of lamb; and soujok, Lebanese spicy sausages. Have a couple, drink some juice, reflect on the night's adventures. The health-conscious will doubtless opt for the 'low-calorie platter' – six meze plus one skewer of lean meat.

→ For branches, see index

Knightsbridge, Belgravia and Kensington

11 Abingdon Road

Kensington, W8 ■ 020 7937 0120

⊖ High Street Kensington

🍴 Modern British

🕑 daily 08.00–23.00

🔗 www.abingdonroad.co.uk

🏷 all major credit cards ■ 12.5% optional service added

££ starters £5.50–£8.50 ■ mains £10.50–£16.50 ■ sides £2.75
■ desserts £5.50–£6.50 ■ lowest bottle price £12.50

✪ Genuine local: drop in for breakfast, lunch or dinner

Large, cool, comfortable – modern art and modern food – 11
Abingdon Road took over from old-timer Phoenicia and from the
very day the doors opened seemed a part of the scenery. This is
the archetypal local restaurant and comes from the same stable
as Sonny's (see p. 355) and the Phoenix Bar & Grill (see p. 332).
Sensibly enough this place offers breakfast, coffee, lunch, tea,
dinner and supper depending on what time you drop in. The menu
changes continually and every day a couple of dishes are added
and a couple dropped, which allows the kitchen to offer whatever
is in season. The cooking style is Modern British with an elusive
influence from California (think Alice Waters). Starters may include
home-made potato gnocchi with a rich duck ragù, or barrel-aged
feta with marinated chargrilled vegetables and flat-leaf parsley – a
grand combination of textures and flavours. Or how about smoked
haddock, frisée and dandelion, with a soft-boiled egg and mustard
dressing? Mains might include roast Cornish plaice with shiitake
mushrooms, spinach and Parmesan – fresh fish, foreign fungi, Italian
cheese that works surprisingly well. A rib-eye steak comes with garlic-
fried potatoes and red wine and shallot butter, and there's Welsh
chump chop, on celeriac purée with grilled red onion and rosemary
glaze. Puds round up the usual suspects – chocolate brownie; lemon
tart with roast fig; and proper pancakes with lemon. The standard of
cooking is good and presentation just qualifies as unfussy. The service
is helpful and the wine list meets its local restaurant obligations.

Amaya

Halkin Arcade, Motcomb Street, SW1 ■ 020 7823 1166

⊖ Knightsbridge

🍴 Indian

🕐 Mon to Sat 12.30–14.15 & 18.30–23.15; Sun 18.30–22.45

🖰 www.realindianfood.com

🖶 all major credit cards ■ 12.5% optional service added

££ small plates £4–£11 ■ regular plates £4.50–£24 ■ salads & vegetables £3.50–£10 ■ main dishes £12.50–£15.50 ■ set lunch £14 ■ tasting menu £26 (lunch), £35 (dinner), £26 (vegetarian) ■ gourmand menu £55 ■ lowest bottle price £18.55 white, £17 red

---

⭐ Belgravia fashionable meets modern Indian

Over the last few centuries cultured Indians have fine-tuned a very aesthetic way of progressing a meal and over the last few decades Brits have ignored it, until now. Amaya is a very sleek and luxurious place, comfortable, hedonistic and with very good food – striking flavours and textures, very satisfying combinations. But if you expect the familiar curry house way of doing things, think again. At Amaya you start by grazing your way through a succession of 'kebabs': small bites to share that come to table when they're ready rather than in a formal succession of courses. After which the table may share a biryani or a curry by way of a grace note. This unfamiliarity puts a subtle strain on ordering and one good strategy is to leave the choosing to your waiter. Otherwise, the menu is divided up by cooking technique – dishes from the tandoor oven, from the sigiri – a charcoal grill, or the tawa – a flat iron griddle; plus salads and vegetables and, finally, biryanis and curries. All the food is elegantly presented, carefully spiced and very good to eat – from the tandoor the black pepper chicken tikka is notable as are the tiger prawns; from the grill the lamb chops are good, and the fish options are amazing. From the tawa the star dish is the keema kaleeji, which is roughly chopped mince, liver and kidney griddled with rich spices. Very delicious. And if you have room after exploring the small dishes, the curries and biryanis are very good too. Amaya takes Indian dining to another level.

Boxwood Café

The Berkeley, Knightsbridge, SW1 ■ 020 7235 1010

⊖ Hyde Park Corner

🍽 Modern British

🕐 Mon to Fri 12.00–15.00 & 18.00–23.00; Sat & Sun 12.00–16.00 & 18.00–23.00

🖰 www.gordonramsay.com

⊟ all major credit cards ■ 12.5% optional service added

££ starters £7–£13.50 ■ mains £13.50–£25 ■ sides £3.95 ■ desserts £6–7 ■ set lunch £21 (3 courses) ■ Beauty in the Box tasting menu £55 ■ lowest bottle price £18

✪ Society café rather than café society

If the term 'café' conjures up images of fag smoke and fried slice you're better off readjusting briskly and re-pigeon-holing this place simply as Boxwood. When it opened, this part of Gordon Ramsay's stable of hotel eateries was billed as offering simple seasonal dishes in an informal setting. Sure. This is a café in the same way that the Café Royal on Regent Street, or the Union Square Café in New York, is a café. The dining room is stylish and comfortable. The tables are well spaced, the chairs are comfortable, the service swarms over you. The standard of cooking is high. Dishes are well presented, and while the prices may not be café prices they are not wildly 'Knightsbridge'. The menu is seasonal and changes to suit what is on the market. There may be white onion soup with Parma ham, roast potatoes and chives. Or there may be pickled Arctic herrings with new potato salad, or seared beef carpaccio with caviar crème fraîche. Mains are also good. Roast cod fillet with mustard crust and piperade; Black Angus grilled rib-eye with Café de Paris butter; or an accurately cooked piece of roast suckling pig with a grain mustard sauce. And what dish would be more at home in a café than a burger? Here it's a foie gras and veal burger, with port wine onions, cos lettuce, Parmesan and chips. The wine list has some accessibly priced bottles. For dessert, the poppy seed Knickerbocker Glory with roasted apricots and panna cotta is notable, as are the warm sugared doughnuts with espresso sorbet. You do get doughnuts in cafés, but not like these.

The Capital

22–24 Basil Street, SW3 ■ 020 7589 5171

⊖ Knightsbridge

🍴 French

🕐 Mon to Sat 12.00–15.00 & 19.00–23.00; Sun 12.00–14.30 & 19.00–22.30

🖰 www.capitalhotel.co.uk

🖶 all major credit cards ■ 12.5% optional service added

££ lunch £29.50 (3 courses) ■ dinner £29.50 (3 courses) & £68 (5 courses) ■ lowest bottle price £19

✪ Grown-up cooking in a grown-up room

It took the arrival of a voluble and passionate French chef called Eric Crouillère-Chavot to lift things to the current exalted level. Mr Michelin gives The Capital two stars, putting it firmly in the top half-dozen restaurants in London, and for once the tyre folk have got it right. The Capital Hotel has quietly gone about its business since 1971 and the cooking has always been top-flight, but the dining room and bar have had a recent redesign and things have tightened up. The atmosphere has changed – this is still more of a 'temple to gastronomy' than a casual eatery, but it is less old-fashioned. The Capital is not a cheap restaurant. Chavot cooks exciting food and his menus draw on classic French cuisine, which means that dishes are full-flavoured and elegantly plated. Sometimes presentation strays into the fussy zone beloved of Michelin inspectors, but expect classically rich and satisfying flavours. Starters may include crab lasagna with langoustine cappuccino. Or a millefeuille of veal sweetbreads with field mushrooms and potato gnocchi. Or pan-fried duck foie gras 'exotic'. Main courses carry on in the same vein: pot-roast pigeon, potato and bacon galette with mushrooms; fillet of turbot, truffle gnocchi and mushroom ravioli; or saddle of rabbit 'Provençal', white coco beans, deep-fried calamari and a tomato risotto. The wine list here is both expansive and expensive. Puds are elaborate, sculptural and satisfying – Chavot may be offering a praline pear crumble, or an iced-coffee parfait with a chocolate fondant.

Le Cercle

1 Wilbraham Place, SW1 ■ 020 7901 9999 &

⊖ Sloane Square

|○| French

🕔 Tues to Sat 12.00–24.00 (à la carte 12.00–15.00 & 18.00–23.00)

🖯 all major credit cards ■ 12.5% optional service added

££ vegetal £4.50–£6.50 ■ marin £6–£8.50 ■ fermier £6–£8.50
■ terroirs £5.50–£8 ■ plaisirs £9.50–£35 ■ fromagerie £3.50–£4
■ gourmandises £3–£8.50 ■ wine by the glass per course £4–£9.50
■ prix fixe lunch £15 & £19.50 ■ pre-theatre menu £17.50

✪ French grazing – stargazing

The first move outside Smithfield from those wonderful people
who set up Club Gascon (see p. 188), Le Cercle lies deep within the
bowels of a discreet and exclusive 'apartment hotel', which in turn
is tucked away up a side street. You come down a flight of steps
into a modern double-height room; the wine cellar and the cheese
room are on show and there's a long and businesslike bar. It is an
all-day operation running from lunch through afternoon tea to bar
snacks and dinner. The food is modern, resolutely French and is
served in the Club Gascon's trademark style of small portions and
multiple courses. The lengthy menu changes seasonally. Sections are
themed – 'vegetal', 'marin', 'fermier' – and each offers six or seven
options. For two people one dish from each section is probably too
little food and two dishes is too much. The cooking is of a very high
standard. Standouts include crunchy green beans served with pickled
chanterelles; ravioles de romans parfum de cèpes; roast John Dory,
Noilly Prat and citrus; roast veal onglet with shallot sauce; crispy black
pudding pie with apple; tête de veau sauce ravigote; foie gras cercle;
pan-roasted veal sweetbreads, creamy morels – an epic dish, rich and
satisfying. But this selection only scratches the surface of a multi-page
menu. Puds are good, but be careful of the Provençal – three glasses:
green tomato jam, black olive foam, piquillo pepper granita. The wine
list majors in the South West and there are numerous offers by the
glass.

Launceston Place

1a Launceston Place, W8 ■ 020 7937 6912

⊖ High Street Kensington

🍴 Modern British

🕐 Mon to Fri 12.30–14.30 & 18.00–23.00; Sat 18.00–23.00; Sun 12.30–14.30 & 18.00–22.00

🖱 www.egami.co.uk

🖥 all major credit cards ■ 12.5% optional service added

££ starters £7–£11 ■ mains £15–£18 ■ sides £2.75 ■ desserts £6–£6.50 ■ set lunch £15 & £18.50 ■ set supper Mon to Fri £15.50 & £18.50 ■ Sunday roast lunch £22.50 ■ lowest bottle price £16

✪ Top of the list for ladies who lunch

You cannot help feeling a pang of envy for anyone rich enough to live in the slick little houses that line Launceston Place – one of those small, chic streets that looks very pleased with itself. As the road curves you'll find a sprinkling of high-ticket shops and the Launceston Place restaurant. This place sprawls its way through a nest of rooms and is formal but pleasant. Service is efficient without being in your face and there is a traditional feel to everything. This is a neighbourhood restaurant, but one that finds itself in a very swish neighbourhood, which makes some sense of the fact that a couple of years after opening here the team went on to create Kensington Place (see p. 100). The menu changes every six weeks or so and dishes match traditional combinations with fashionable ingredients in an unstuffy way. Starters range from fish soup with rouille; through twice-baked Gruyère cheese soufflé; to marinated duck salad with mango and orange salsa. Mains range from roast cod with mushy peas and fat chips; through John Dory with chardonnay vinegar cream; to meatier offerings such as veal escalope with pancetta and sage, or roast chump of lamb with a saffron pea and chorizo risotto. The dessert menu ticks all the appropriate boxes: there's steamed orange pudding and custard, or a white chocolate tart. The wine list is strong in traditional areas, so think French, and above all do not expect a modest bill in such an affluent location.

Nahm

The Halkin, 5 Halkin Street, SW1 ■ 020 7333 1234

⊖ Hyde Park Corner

🍽 Thai

🕐 Mon to Fri 07.00–10.30, 12.00–14.30 & 19.00–20.30; Sat & Sun
07.00–10.30 & 19.00–20.30 (20.00 Sun)

🖰 www.halkin.como.bz

🖶 all major credit cards ■ 12.5% optional service added

££ traditional Nahm Aharna menu £49.50 (8 dishes over 4 courses)
■ lowest bottle price £25

✪ It's Thai – but not as we know it

David Thompson is a gentle, soft-spoken Australian, which
somehow makes it all the more surprising that he is the world's
leading authority on Thai cooking and consultant to the Thai
government. The dining room at Nahm is chic, stylish and quietly
fashionable – rather like the hotel in which it is hidden away. The food
is amazing. But if you come to it rubbing your hands in anticipation
of familiar dishes brace yourself for disappointment – you are unlikely
to recognise anything on the menu. At Nahm every meal is founded
upon a bowl of jasmine rice and then other dishes are chosen to add
savour to that rice. Nam prik is one such dish – cubes of sweet glazed
pork; a small pancake made with a delicious herb surprisingly called
stinkweed; slivers of raw white turmeric; and a sludge made with
tiny slightly chewy shrimps (much nicer than it sounds) – an amazing
palette of flavours. Or there's yum pak – a 'salad' of different leaves
and vegetables brought together by an amazing citrussy dressing.
Or pla meuk pat sadtor, which is a dish of garlic stir-fried squid with
sadtor beans – wonderfully aromatic and pungent. Even the 'duck
salad' is a complex affair and offers a grand array of textures. There's
an extensive wine list and a helpful sommelier who recommends
drinking Alsace with Thai food. Nahm is a sophisticated place and
not cheap, so it's important to get the most out of the experience
and you should rely on the charming front of house staff to help with
the ordering. Then your meal will be delicious, vibrant and totally
unfamiliar – a strangely alluring and elegant combination.

One-O-One

Sheraton Park Tower, 101 William Street, SW1 ■ 020 7290 7101 &

⊖ Knightsbridge

🍽 French/fish

🕐 daily 07.00–11.00, 12.00–14.30 & 19.00–22.30

🏷 all major credit cards ■ no service added

££ starters £13–£19 ■ mains £21–£28 ■ sides £4.50 ■ desserts £8 ■ set lunch £25 ■ tasting menus £48 & £79 ■ lowest bottle price £26

✪ Upscale temple worships all things fishy

Pascal Proyart is a Breton chef, but more to the point, he is a chef who is obsessive about fish. And for some strange and unaccountable reason that seems somehow inevitable. This restaurant is one of those svelte organisms that lives within a pricey hotel rather like a hermit crab in an old whelk. That means a spacious dining room, a slick bar and a three-day march to the toilets. The front of house staff are really on the ball here and they'll take you off in search of a urinal without batting an eyelid; maybe they have to escort punters to avoid them getting lost. The standard of cooking is very high, as is the quality of the fish, and consequentially the prices. Starters range from a page of witty ways to serve Royal King Crab legs (flown in from the Barents Sea) and you could choose to have them grilled with spring onions and sweet chilli ginger sauce, to another page of different ways with smart French oysters. Every dish is precise: a starter of sautéed tiger prawn comes with a coconut and tamarind sauce – sophisticated stuff. Or red mullet soup Provençal; saffron shellfish chowder; lobster salad with green mango remoulade. Mains are grandstand numbers – a whole sea bass comes to table baked under a mound of salt. A pavé of Dover sole is roast and served with pan-fried langoustines. There's a whole roast baby monkfish. Everything glides to table in an elegant fashion. The wine list prices scamper out of reach pretty quickly. Puds are exceedingly ornate. But if you want top fish this is the place to get it.

Wódka

12 St Alban's Grove, W8 ■ 020 7937 6513

⊖ High Street Kensington

🍴 Polish

🕐 Mon to Fri 12.00–15.00 & 18.30–23.15; Sat & Sun 18.30–23.15

🖰 www.wodka.co.uk

🖰 all major credit cards ■ 12.5% optional service added

££ starters £5.90–£7.90 ■ mains £12.90–£15 ■ sides £3 ■ desserts £4.50–£5.50 ■ special lunch £11.50 & £14.50 ■ lowest bottle price £13

✪ Vodka, soup and good cheer

What has become, you wonder, of the streak of madness that inspired the Polish cavalry to take on German tank regiments with sabres drawn? It's on the shelves behind the bar, in the extensive collection of moody and esoteric vodkas, which are for sale both by the shot and by the carafe. Like the spirits, Wódka is a restaurant that lies in wait for you. It's calm and bare, and the food is better than you might expect – well cooked and thoughtfully seasoned. There's a daily lunch menu that represents extremely good value, a large proportion of the dishes being refugees from the evening à la carte. Otherwise, the soup makes a good starter: barszcz is a rich, beetrooty affair and comes with little sauerkraut and mushroom parcels called pasztecik. Blinis are also the business: they come with smoked salmon, aubergine mousse, or 40g of Oscietra caviar. Choosing a selection will get you all except the caviar. Also good is the kaszanka – grilled black pudding with pickled red cabbage and pear purée. For a main course, the fishcakes with creamed leeks is a firm favourite with the regulars. In line with the Polish love of wild game, when partridge is available it is roasted and served with a splendid mash of root vegetables; wild boar is served with roast baby beetroot and red wine shallots; or there may be braised rabbit with mustard sauce, spatzle dumplings and black cabbage. Puddings tend to be of the oversweet, under-imaginative gateau variety. Opt for the chocolate truffle cake, and your twelfth glass of vodka.

→ For branches, see index

Zafferano

15 Lowndes Street, SW1 ■ 020 7235 5800

⊖ Knightsbridge

🍽 Italian

🕐 Mon to Sat 12.00–14.30 & 19.00–23.00; Sun 12.00–15.00 & 19.00–23.00

🖰 www.zafferanorestaurant.com

🖻 all major credit cards ■ 12.5% optional service added

££ lunch £25.50 (2 courses), £29.50 (3 courses) & £32.50 (4 courses)
■ dinner £29.50 (2 courses), £37.50 (3 courses) & £45 (4 courses)
■ lowest bottle price £14.50

✪ Italy in Belgravia

When Zafferano opened, the combination of modern Italian food and decent value fixed-price menus was a rare and dazzling new development that attracted a host of diners and a number of awards. People felt that although it wasn't cheap per se you did get a good deal. Now Zafferano has matured and expanded – more tables, a luxurious bar and a private room. But the deal is still a simple one, you are faced with a series of multiple-course options and you merely have to decide how greedy you want to be. This is one place where you should go through the card: antipasti, pasta, main and pud. The cooking is good here, the menu is seasonal, and the ingredients carefully chosen. Fortunately, the service is slick and the wine list long, so the 'essence of Italy' mood remains unbroken. Starters may include sliced duck speck and pig's cheek with mustard fruits; warm octopus salad; tuna carpaccio with fennel, orange and mint. Go on to the stunning pheasant ravioli with rosemary, or the fish. Then there may be something simple like pan-fried veal cutlet with mushrooms and rosti; or roast partridge with cabbage, chicken livers and capers; or truffles dishes in season – they attract a hefty supplement, but it is worth it for the baked onion filled with cheese fondue and topped with truffle. Puddings are serious – the tortino al cioccolato, chocolate fondant pudding, is worth the 12-minute wait. The tiramisù is formidable.

Zuma

5 Raphael Street, SW7 ■ 020 7584 1010

■ valet parking from 19.00

♿

⊖ Knightsbridge

🍴 Japanese

🕐 Mon to Fri 12.00–14.30 & 17.30–23.30; Sat & Sun 12.30–15.30 & 18.00–22.30

🖥 www.zumarestaurant.com

💳 all major credit cards ■ 13.5% optional service added

££ small dishes/salads/maki rolls £3.80–£22.30 ■ sushi/sashimi/tempura £3.30–£30.30 ■ mains £10.30–£60 ■ sides £1.80–£7.70 ■ desserts £5.80–£12.80 ■ tasting menu £96 ■ lowest bottle price £19

✪ Uber-cool celeb haven, elegant Japanese food

Chef-proprietor Rainer Becker chose the unspeakably chic Japanese design team Super Potato and they created a huge restaurant, now filled with crowds of both celebs and celeb spotters. This place is all stone, rough-hewn granite and unfinished wood. The approach to eating is modernist – the menu claims that it is a 'contemporary Japanese Izakaya' – so now you know. In practice this means a long menu with dishes prepared either at the sushi bar, on the robata grill, or in the kitchen. Everything is designed for sharing and the dishes will pitch up in a gentle procession rather than the more formal starters, mains and puds. By way of a prelude, order some edame, these are soya beans that have been steamed in the pod – strip the beans out with your teeth and leave the pods. Or there is tosa dofu, which is deep-fried tofu with daikon and bonito flakes, or age watarigani, a dish of fried soft-shell crab with wasabi mayonnaise. The sashimi and sushi are exquisite and pricey. The skewers from the robata grill are fresh and appealing. Try satsumaimo no goma shoyo gake, sweet potato glazed with sesame; or Suzuki no shioyaki, salt-grilled sea bass with burnt tomato; or tori no tebasaki, chicken wings with sea salt and lime. Then there are tempura, seafood dishes, meat dishes – every dish is presented stylishly. The sake list features over twenty different kinds – thankfully there's a 'sake sommelier' to help.

Marylebone and Euston

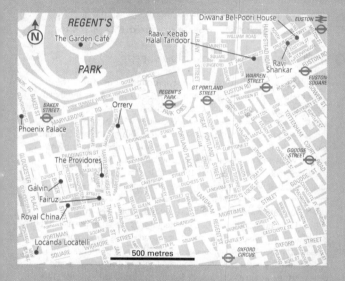

Diwana Bel-Poori House

121 Drummond Street, NW1 ■ 020 7387 5556

⊖ Euston

▣ Indian/vegetarian

🕐 Mon to Sat 12.00–23.30; Sun 12.00–22.30

🖱 www.diwanarestaurant.com

🗗 all major credit cards ■ 10% optional service added

££ starters £3–£4 ■ mains £4–£7.75 ■ sides £3.80–£4.20 ■ desserts £1.80–£3.20 ■ buffet lunch £6.50 ■ unlicensed, BYO (no corkage)

✪ Veggie heaven, and implausibly cheap

This place is enough to make the style police cringe with its heady combination of varnished pine and shag-pile carpets. Only the Indian woodcarvings dotted around the walls give the game away – that and the heady scent of freshly blended spices. It's a busy place, with tables filling up and emptying at a fair crack, though the atmosphere is convivial and casual rather than rushed. You can bring your own beer or wine and a full water jug is supplied on each table. This, the awesomely low prices, a chatty menu listing 'tasty snacks', and fast, friendly service combine to create a deceptively simple stage for some fine Indian vegetarian cooking. There's even a lunch buffet where you can overeat to your heart's content. Starters are copious, ladled out in no-nonsense, stainless steel bowls. The dahi bhalle chat is a cool, yogurty blend of chickpeas, crushed pooris and bulghur wheat, sprinkled with 'very special spices'. The dahi poori is a fragrant concoction of pooris, potatoes, onions, sweet and sour sauces and chilli chutney, again smothered in yogurt and laced with spices. Stars of the main menu are the dosas, particularly the flamboyant deluxe dosa, a giant fan of a pancake with coconut chutney, potatoes and dhal nestling beneath its folds. Also superb is the house speciality, thali Annapurna – a feast of dhal, rice, vegetables, pickles, side dishes, mini bhajees and your choice of pooris or chapattis, which overcomes any ordering reticence by bringing what seems like everything. There are extras like Bombay aloo, but the main course portions are large enough to make them seem pretty ambitious.

Fairuz

3 Blandford Street, W1 ■ 020 7486 8182

⊖ Bond Street

🍽 Lebanese

🕐 daily 12.00–23.30

🖱 www.Fairuz.uk.com

🖽 all major credit cards ■ no service added

££ mezze £4.50 cold, £4.95 hot ■ mains £9.95–£18.95 ■ sides £2.95–£3.95 ■ desserts £4.95 ■ set mezza (min 2) £18.95 & £26.95 ■ lowest bottle price £13.95

✪ Authentic food, but un-intimidating atmosphere

Fairuz may look as if it has been squeezed in between two self-consciously modernist Blandford Street eateries, but it happily carries on doing its own thing, which is Lebanese cooking. As you open the front door, jolly souk music, the smell of spices and the light of the warm, mud-coloured room provide a warm welcome. This is one of London's most accessible Middle Eastern restaurants, even though the menu is set out in traditional style. To start there's an epic list of mezze, both hot and cold, followed by a selection of charcoal grills. You can leave the selection up to the restaurant and order a set mezza, or a set menu, which combines a mezza with a mixed grill. The set mezza delivers eight or ten little dishes – plenty for lunch or a light supper. But if you prefer to make your own selection, the à la carte lists 47 different mezze for you to choose from: cold and hot dishes. Particularly recommended are the wonderfully fresh and herby tabbouleh; the warak inab (stuffed vine leaves); the houmous; and makanek (spicy lamb sausages). Even that most dangerously indigestible of delicacies, the falafel, is fine here. Main course grills are generous. Kafta khashkhash, lamb minced with parsley and grilled on skewers, is unexpectedly delicate and fragrant, while the shish taouk, chicken marinated in garlic and lemon, really is finger-licking good. Round off your meal with excellent pastries and real Lebanese coffee. Gentle service helps make this a good place for a first foray into Lebanese cuisine. If you can, get there early to secure one of the nook-and-crannyish, tent-like tables.

Galvin

66 Baker Street, W1 ■ 020 7935 4007

⊖ Baker Street

🍴 French

🕐 Mon to Sat 12.00–14.30 & 18.30–23.00; Sun 12.00–15.00 & 18.30–22.30

🖰 www.galvinbistrotdeluxe.co.uk

🖫 all major credit cards ■ 12.5% optional service added

££ starters £4.95–£10.50 ■ mains £12.50–£15.25 ■ desserts £5.50–£6.50 ■ prix fixe menus: lunch £15.50, early dinner (18.00–19.00) £17.50 ■ lowest bottle price £13.75

✪ Les frères Galvin cooking up a storm

Chris Galvin and his brother Jeff get on well together and after parallel careers in some of London's top kitchens, at last they get their own place. This is a French restaurant, as French as only two Englishmen who genuinely love classic French food can make it. It's comfortable. It represents excellent value for money. The wine list doesn't pillage your plastic. The menu is short and seasonal. A great deal of time and effort goes into sourcing fine ingredients. Galvin burst onto the scene and has been busy from the moment the doors opened. Keep in mind 'seasonal' and 'classic French' – starters may range from a splendid, almost juicy terrine pressé of pork and foie gras; to a salad of Roquefort, pear and walnut; a beautifully made little Pithiviers of pigeon with a glazed chestnut – very delicious; to an omelette aux cèpes – it's hard to find a good omelette, and harder still to find one as good as this, plenty of mushrooms, well seasoned. Main courses range from a risotto of courgette and saffron; to wing of skate Grenobloise; and parmentier of oxtail and black pudding – stunning mashed potato with a dark frazzled and sizzled disc of oxtail and b.p. sitting on top. Gutsy cooking. The braised pig's trotter is served with the same spud, but is a light and ethereal dish – stuffed with a chicken mousseline and surrounded by small morels. Puds are hardcore: St Emilion au chocolat comes in a small glass and is impressively rich. As you would expect, there's a decent cheeseboard. For people who like food, Galvin 'Bistrot de Luxe' really hits the spot.

The Garden Café

Inner Circle, Regent's Park, NW1 ■ 020 7935 5729 &

● Regent's Park

|●| Modern British

🕒 daily 10.00–dusk (no bookings taken)

🖰 www.thegardencafe.co.uk

🖺 all major credit cards ■ no service added

££ starters £4.50–£7.50 ■ mains £7.50–£12.95 ■ desserts £3.25–£4.25
   ■ prix fixe menu £13.50 & £15.50 ■ lowest bottle price £13.50

✪ A hidden gem by the rose garden

Merely the words 'park café' are enough to make a gastronaut cower, but with the arrival of the Garden Café that view may have to change. In 1964 the new café (built under a roof made up of 31 copper hexagons) was the height of modernity and lovers of gastro trivia will enjoy the fact that this was the first 'Little Chef' in Britain. Now the building is a cherished part of our architectural heritage, but thankfully something has been done about the food, which is now also worth cherishing. Service is friendly in an egalitarian sort of way – no bookings are taken – and there is plenty of room both inside and al fresco. The menu changes with the seasons, so winter starters range from honey-roast parsnip and Cox apple soup, to Parma ham served with shaved Parmesan and rather good sour dough toast. Home-made potted shrimps are very good. The menu writing sets the tone for the main courses: 'proper roast duck, sloe gin and damson braised red cabbage, mashed potato' – with the one caveat that the duck skin could be crisper, this is a very good dish. Or there is leek and Roquefort tart, with a green salad; a macaroni cheese made with Montgomery's Cheddar; or a rib-eye steak. There is always a decent salad served in a large, no-nonsense bowl and, to finish up, workmanlike puds. The Garden Café is a pretty restaurant with good food, a friendly atmosphere and reasonable prices.

Locanda Locatelli

8 Seymour Street, W1 ■ 020 7935 9088

⊖ Marble Arch

🍴 Italian

🕐 Mon to Thurs 12.00–15.00 & 19.00–23.00; Fri & Sat 12.00–15.00 & 19.00–23.30; Sun 12.00–15.00 & 19.00–23.00

🖥 www.locandalocatelli.com

💳 all major credit cards ■ no service added

££ antipasti £7–£12 ■ pasta £8–£14 ■ mains £19.50–£29.50 ■ sides £3.50 ■ desserts £6–£12 ■ lowest bottle price £12

⭐ Stars in the dining room, stars in the kitchen

Giorgio and Plaxy Locatelli run a chic modern Italian restaurant and despite being blisteringly fashionable, the food is very good indeed. When Giorgio Locatelli moved here it took until the end of the second week for everybody from the Prime Minister to Madonna to visit and sample the startlingly good North Italian food. The room is elegant and has a real buzz to it. Which may be part of the reason there's phone frenzy at the beginning of each month when everyone struggles to book a table – spontaneous here means five to eight weeks ahead. The restaurant now opens on Sunday, but that has done little to cut the waiting list. To start, there's a splendid basket of mixed breads to keep you busy. There is a large turnover of dishes, but the cooking is always spurred on by the seasons. There may be antipasti such as wild chicory and caper salad with Parmesan foam; cured venison with celeriac and black truffle; or layered potatoes with pancetta and Taleggio cheese. Pasta dishes delight: spaghetti comes with octopus; gnocchi with morel mushrooms; or how about a risotto with sausage and peas? Every dish looks elegant on the plate, and combines tastes and textures to their best effect. Main courses may include steamed hake in garlic and vinegar; bollito misto with salsa verde; or roast duck with broccoli and spelt. The service is slick and the restaurant has an established and comfortable air. Dolci range from tiramisù, to a serious chocolate soufflé. Service runs smoothly and the wine list pays homage to the Italian greats.

Orrery

55 Marylebone High Street, W1 ■ 020 7616 8000

⊖ Baker Street/Regent's Park

🍴 French

🕐 Mon to Sat 12.00–15.00 & 19.00–22.30; Sun 12.00–14.30 & 19.00–22.30

🖰 www.orrery.co.uk

🖃 all major credit cards ■ 12.5% optional service added

££ starters £8.50–£16.50 ■ mains £12–£28.50 ■ desserts £6.50–£10 ■ set lunch £25 ■ tasting menu £55 & £90 (with wine) ■ potager vegetarian tasting menu £40 & £75 (with wine) ■ lowest bottle price £15

✪ Classy French food in a classy restaurant

This is one of Sir Terence Conran's restos and you have to admire the way that he has moved heaven and earth to ensure that there is no 'formula' in the restaurants within his elastic portfolio. Orrery certainly stands out – this is a very good restaurant indeed, driven by a passion for food. At Orrery they cherish their own network of small suppliers, going for large, line-caught sea bass above their smaller, farmed cousins, and selecting the best Landes pigeon and Scottish beef. The service is slick and friendly, the dining room is beautiful, the cheeseboard has won prizes and the wine list is exhaustive. All of the above is reflected in the bill. Your meal will start well – white onion and thyme soup, truffle emulsion with coco beans and chanterelles; or langoustine and frog's legs, wild mushrooms, grilled baby leeks and jus; or partridge mousseline. These are sophisticated dishes featuring well-judged combinations of flavours. Mains may include roast fillet of halibut, pommes purée, salted grapes and verjus; roast Landes pigeon, polenta galette, foie gras and preserved vegetables; filet of Scottish beef, creamed spinach, bone marrow beignet. Presentation is ultra-chic, flavours are intense – this is serious stuff. Puddings span the range from classics such as fondant of Amedei chocolate and milk ice cream, to a raspberry soufflé. One way to eat well here is to rely heavily on the set menus: the three-course menu du jour is one way to control the cost.

Phoenix Palace

3–5 Glentworth Street, NW1 ■ 020 7486 3515 &

⊖ Baker Street/Marylebone

⦿ Chinese

⦿ Mon to Sat 12.00–23.00; Sun 11.00–22.30

⦿ all major credit cards ■ no service added

££ dim sum £2–£4 ■ starters £4–£8.80 ■ mains £5.80–£25 ■ sides
£1.50–£7.80 ■ desserts £3.80 ■ set dinner £13.80–£23.80 ■ lowest
bottle price £9.80

✪ Chinese outpost in the far North

**It comes as a bit of a shock to find a rather good, large, bright,
busy Chinese restaurant** marooned this far north by the stream of
traffic intent on dodging the Congestion Charge as they crawl past
Tussaud's. Over the years the menu has become more and more
interesting here. Thankfully the chefs seem to know what they are
doing, so this has become a place to try out something new. Starters
include all the old favourites, such as chicken wrapped in lettuce
leaf, but try the jellyfish with sesame seed; the soft-shell crab with
chilli and garlic; the pork trotters with vinaigrette; or chilli potsticker
dumplings. The menu is a long one and it is worth a careful read as
there are some interesting discoveries to be made, and a good many
dishes that push the envelope. Whenever you visit an ambitious
Chinese restaurant it is always worth trying one dish that you have
never had before. Salt-baked chicken is a wonderful savoury roast
chicken with juicy meat and crisp skin. There's steamed turbot with
Tientsin cabbage and garlic. The fried minced pork patties with salted
fish are very classy, the salt fish seasoning the pork mix successfully.
There's baked crab and salty yolk served with steamed buns; eel
with pickled mustard green; pork and stuffed beancurd cooked in a
clay pot; venison with yellow chives and celery. To find any Chinese
restaurant in this out-of-the-way location is a puzzle – to find such a
good one is positively inscrutable.

The Providores

109 Marylebone High Street, W1 ■ 020 7935 6175 &

⊖ Baker Street/Bond Street

🍽 Fusion

🕐 Mon to Fri 12.00–15.00 & 18.00–23.30; Sat & Sun 10.00–15.00
(brunch) & 18.00–23.30

🌐 www.theprovidores.co.uk

💳 all major credit cards ■ 12.5% optional service added

££ starters £5.60–£12.80 ■ mains £17.30–£23.80 ■ sides £3–£4
■ desserts £8.40 ■ lowest bottle price £15

✪ Fusion without confusion

When you nervously mention the word 'fusion' there is only
one chef in London with a 24-carat bankable reputation and
that is Peter Gordon, the amiable New Zealander. His showcase
is this restaurant, which he opened with a consortium of friends.
The resto part occupies an elegant room on the first floor. Chairs
are comfortable, tablecloths are white and simplicity rules – which
is just as well, as the dishes are among the most complicated in
town. But these dishes all taste fresh, every flavour distinct, and
each combination cunningly balanced. The menu descriptions
read like lists: smoky coconut and tamarind laksa with grilled tiger
prawn, green tea noodles, crispy shallots, chicken-hijiki dumpling
and coriander. Puzzled? The rich, creamy, sweet coconut broth is
covered with a scattering of crisp bits of shallot and laced with the
contrasting textures of ribbon noodles and tiger prawns. Or how
about grilled kangaroo loin on a cassava fritter with spiced quandong
relish and Greek yogurt? Mains may include roast sea bass on white
bean and rosemary purée, lemon-braised fennel, lemongrass dressing
and wasabi tobiko; roast lamb chump on bonita potatoes with roast
beetroot and apple relish; or roast Barbary duck breast on sesame
miso aubergines and bok choy with shiitake. Desserts are equally
elaborate: chocolate liquorice 'delice' with soured pink grapefruit,
runny cream and chocolate almond wafers. Downstairs there's a
walk-in, informal, gentler-paced sort of eatery.

Raavi Kebab Halal Tandoor

125 Drummond Street, NW1 ▪ 020 7388 1780

⊖ Euston/Euston Square

🍽 Indian

🕐 daily 12.30–22.30

🖪 all major credit cards ▪ 10% optional service added

££ starters £2.50–£5.95 ▪ mains £1.75–£5.50 ▪ sides £3.25 ▪ desserts £1.75–£3 ▪ lunch buffet £7.65–£9.85 ▪ no alcohol

---

✪ Cheap grills, hot food

Over the last 30 years Drummond Street has become one of the main curry centres in London and for all that while this small restaurant has gone about its business. Competition here is more than just fierce – it is ludicrous, as well-established vegetarian restaurants compete to offer the cheapest 'eat-as-much-as-you-can' lunch buffet. It is lucky that vegetables are so cheap. But the Raavi is not just about bargain prices – or vegetables, come to that. It is an unpretentious Pakistani grill house that specialises in halal meat dishes, and could be said to have a special way with the chilli. The grills here are good but hot: seekh kebab straight from the charcoal grill in the doorway is juicy, well flavoured and hot; chicken tikka is hot; mutton tikka is hot. The mixed grill brings a bit of everything – everything hot. Lamb quorma is rich with fresh ginger and garlic and topped with a sprinkle of shaved almonds. Chicken daal brings chunks of chicken on the bone, bobbing on a sea of savoury yellow split pea dhal, and is thoroughly delicious. Naan breads are light and crispy. Nihari, the traditional Muslim breakfast dish of slow-cooked curried mutton, vies with haleem for the title of bestseller here. Haleem is made by taking some meat and cooking it, adding four kinds of dhal, a good deal of cracked wheat, and two kinds of rice, plus spices. Cook for up to seven hours, then add some garam masala. The result is a gluey slick of smooth and spicy glop from which any traces of the meat have all but disappeared. And how does it taste? You'd be hard pushed to be more enthusiastic than 'not bad'. Enjoy the Raavi for what it is, but do not expect sharp décor or super service.

Ravi Shankar

131 Drummond Street, NW1 ■ 020 7388 6458

⊖ Euston/Euston Square

|◉| Indian vegetarian

🕐 daily 12.00–22.00

🖥 Mastercard, Visa ■ 10% optional service added

££ starters £2.60–£3.15 ■ mains £4.10–£7.85 ■ sides £1.25–£2.25
■ desserts £1.25–£1.65 ■ daily specials £4.50–£4.75 ■ lowest bottle
price £7.95

✪ Trad veggie bottom-dollar belly buster

It's likely that in the 1980s when this place opened, a good many
more of the customers would have heard of Ravi Shankar, but fast
forward to the present day and the restaurant is still going strong,
even if the décor is firmly wedged in an era when plain enough was
good enough. The Ravi Shankar may look plain, and the seating
may not be ultra-comfortable, but the vegetarian food is honest and
cheap – something that weighs heavily with the loyal clientele. The
daily specials are impressive – maybe a cashew nut pilau rice and
cauliflower curry, served with salad and mint yogurt chutney and
all costing less that a smart sandwich – there are not many cheaper
meals left anywhere in London, let alone a meal at such a price
that is well cooked and satisfying. The cashew nut pilau is rich and
nutty, and the cauliflower curry has been made substantial by the
addition of chunks of potato. Or there's vegetable biryani with curry,
or, on another day, maybe aloo palak with chapati. And the specials
wind onwards to the extravagance of chana bhatura – a delicious
fried bread with a chickpea curry. The main menu starters fall into
two categories. There are hot snacks from Western India, including
samosas, bhajis and potato bonda – a solid, tasty, deep-fried sphere
made from potato and lentils. Then there are cold 'snacks and chat',
billed as coming from Mumbai's famed snack city, Chowpatty Beach.
Breads are good – treat yourself to an ace stuffed paratha. But above
all you will leave Ravi Shankar full, and with that smug feeling that
comes from having nailed a genuine bargain.

Royal China

24–26 Baker Street, W1 ■ 020 7487 4688

⊖ Baker Street

🍴 Chinese/dim sum

🕓 Mon to Sat 12.00–23.00; Sun 11.00–22.00; dim sum until 16.45

🖰 www.royalchinagroup.co.uk

🖬 Mastercard, Visa ■ 13% optional service added

££ dim sum £2.20–£3.50 ■ mains £7–£18 ■ sides £2.50–£8.50
■ desserts £4 ■ set lunch £13 ■ set dinner £28 ■ lowest bottle price £14

✪ Dim sum star

You'll find the Royal China Group's number one restaurant on Queensway and this, their West End outpost, used to be at no. 40 Baker Street. However, the recent move a few doors down to this new establishment has proved a big success. All the Royal China restos are kitted out in shiny black and gold, very 1980s and very glitzy, which makes the more modern, less glossy, rather calmer look of the new dining room all the more welcome. There is a large wall mural in the black and gold idiom, but it is no longer oppressive. The dim sum are terrific. There is a long menu featuring much the same array of dishes as you find in every other Chinese establishment, but go before 16.45 and stick with the dim sum. Until Hakkasan (see p. 7) introduced the venison puff, the roast pork puff from Royal China was thought by many to be the best dim sum in town. It is still very good, light, flaky and rich. The regulars such as steamed prawn dumplings and minced pork dumplings are fresh and well seasoned, and the prawn cheung fun are well made and commendably thin. Even dishes that sound prosaic, like 'crispy spring roll', are very good, fresh and crisp with good complementary textures. Also noteworthy are the prawn and chive dumplings, and the steamed curry squid. Bulk out your order with the glutinous rice in lotus leaves – a dish that is done very well here. Service is slick and quick and after you've made the choice between Chinese tea and Tsing Tao beer try as many different dumplings as you dare. Look at the specials list where you might find unusual delicacies like 'pig's skin and turnip in broth'. A treat for Baldric.

→ For branches, see index

Mayfair and Bond Street

NORTH ROW
REEN STREET
LEES PL
Truc Vert
ER BROOK STREET
Le Gavroche
ROSS STREET
PPER GROSVENOR ST
Angela Hartnett
at the Connaught
WEIGHHOUSE ST
NORTH AUDLEY ST
DERTON ST
DAVIES STREET
BROOK STREET
GROSVENOR STREET
GROSVENOR
SQUARE
MOUNT ROW
ADAM'S ROW
SOUTH AUDLEY STREET
MOUNT STREET
Maze
GROSVENOR
Gordon Ramsay
at Claridge's
NEW BOND STREET
ST GEORGE ST
MADDOX
Sketch – the Glade
CONDUIT STREET
KINGL
RE
Patterson's
SAVILE ROW
CLIFFORD ST
OLD BURLINGTON ST
Momo
MODD

GROSVENOR HILL
BOURDON STREET
BRUTON PL
Umu
BRUTON ST
The Square
BERKELEY
CORK ST
The Berkeley Square
FARM ST
Benares
SQUARE
Chor Bizarre
GRAFTON
ALBEMARLE ST
DOVER STREET
OLD BOND ST
BURLINGTON AR

MAYFAIR

Kai
AUDLEY STREET
CHESTERFIELD STREET
HAY'S MEWS
WAVERTON ST
HAY'S HILL
The Greenhouse
CHARLES STREET
CLARGES MS
HAY'S MEWS
MAY HILL
BERKELEY STREET
Automat

MOUNT STREET
STRATTON STREET

The Mirabelle
CLARGES ST
BOLTON ST
PICCADILLY
ARLINGTON ST
PARK PL
ST JAMES

PARK LANE
PARK LANE
DEANERY STREET
HILL
DERBY STREET
CURZON STREET
MARKET M
CURZON PLACE
SHEPHERD STREET
HALF MOON ST
WHITE
QUEEN STREET
Kiku
GREEN
PARK
ST JAMES

HYDE PARK

HERTFORD ST
DOWN STREET
Nobu
BRICK STREET
OLD PARK LANE
HAMILTON PL

GREEN PARK

250 metres

N

Angela Hartnett at the Connaught

16 Carlos Place, W1 ■ 020 7592 1222

Green Park

Modern European

Mon to Fri 12.00–14.45 & 17.45–23.00; Sat 12.00–15.15 & 17.45–23.00; Sun 12.00–15.15 & 19.00–22.30

www.gordonramsay.com

all major credit cards ■ 12.5% optional service added

££ à la carte £55 (3 courses) ■ set lunch £30 (3 courses) ■ menu prestige £70 (8 courses) ■ lowest bottle price £26

Old warhorse, rejuvenated by charismatic lady chef

Gordon Ramsay's empire is a good deal more subtly organised than at first appears. Some of the restos are held fairly close to the master and are branded accordingly, while some get more leeway and become sub-brands in their own right. Angela Hartnett has made her mark at the Connaught, where for many years a hushed atmosphere, high prices, top ingredients and menus written in 19th-century menu French were the inviolable rule. Hartnett is a very good cook and, possibly through her Italian ancestry, has a respect for ingredients that shines through. Dishes are elegant to look at and team strong flavours; they are also, whisper it, modern. The wine list surges off into famous names at famous prices, the service is very slick and the dining room walks a knife-edge between comfortable (for the new clients) and formal (for the older, long-term clientele). Starters range from hand-made tagliatelle with baby courgettes, goats' cheese and broad beans; to sautéed langoustine with a salad of fresh almonds and baby artichokes; or confit foie gras, roasted Braeburn apples, with star anise and ginger and lime glaze. Mains are in a similar vein: canon of monkfish wrapped in Parma ham with vegetable tempura and pepperonata; Moulard duck breast, sautéed foie gras, braised orange slices and new season English turnip; or rabbit from Anjou – roast rack, confit shoulder and loin, girolles and summer truffle vinaigrette. Puds are sophisticated: roast quince with Pedro Ximinez jelly, Catalan cream and almond biscotti, or milk chocolate with caramelised banana ice cream and ginger foam.

Automat

33 Dover Street, W1 ■ 020 7499 3033

● Green Park

|●| North American

🕐 Mon to Fri 12.00–01.00; Sat & Sun 11.00–24.00

🖰 www.automat-london.com

🗃 all major credit cards ■ 12.5% optional service added

££ starters £5–£10 ■ mains £6–£24 ■ sides £3 ■ desserts £6 ■ lowest bottle price £14.50

✪ Mayfair plush meets Americana

It's always worth travelling for a good hamburger, and the one at Automat is on the cusp of greatness. Setting aside delightful images of rich, little old Mayfair ladies pitching up with their laundry for a service wash, Automat doesn't seem like a good name for this combination of chic, slick and Yank that opened in 2005. The dining area is divided into three parts – to the rear is a bar and seating with a greenhousey feel, in the middle are solid and trad booths, and to the front, smaller, less comfortable tables and chairs crowd a sort of 'shop-window' area. The menu also splits into appetisers, sandwiches, entrées and sides. The starters are American dishes seen through European eyes, so a clam chowder is marginally less chunky (although it does come with Saltine crackers). There's chicken liver and foie gras mousse; an iceberg wedge with 'house ranch dressing'. A grilled portabello mushroom salad is very delicious – sliced marinated mushroom, small endive leaves, beetroot and mozzarella, a winning combo. Sandwiches include the Automat burger – good meat, check; cooked as requested, check; good bun, check; good size, check. Also on offer the soft shell 'po boy'. The entrées include macaroni and cheese; sea bass baked in parchment with clams; a crispy fried duck leg; and hanger steak. The hanger steak (a.k.a. onglet or skirt steak) comes to table accurately cooked and is very tender and full of flavour – the French fries are very sound. Puds range from apple pie, to a New York cheesecake and Mississippi mud pie with soured cream. The prices on the wine list reflect the Mayfair location, but thankfully the service is informal and cheerful.

Benares

12 Berkeley House, Berkeley Square, W1 ■ 020 7629 8886   &

⊖ Green Park

🍴 Indian

🕐 Mon to Fri 12.00–14.30 & 17.30–23.00; Sat 17.30–23.00; Sun 12.00–14.30 & 18.00–22.30

🖥 www.benaresrestaurant.com

🖳 all major credit cards ■ 12.5% optional service added

££ starters £6.95–£11.95 ■ mains £15.50–£24 ■ sides £2.95–£6.95 ■ desserts £6.50 ■ set lunch £14.95 ■ tasting menu £59 ■ lowest bottle price £19.50

✪ Top-drawer Indian in plush surroundings

Atul Kochar is the man who secured one of the first Michelin stars ever awarded to an Indian restaurant in Britain, and you can be sure that at Benares he is striving to repeat the trick. It is certainly a deluxe affair: acres of polished stone floors, pools strewn with blossoms and little candles bobbing about. The dining room is modern and stylish. Some of the pricing, and most of the wine list, 'goes Mayfair' pretty briskly, but considering the elegance of the setting, the friendliness of the service and the undoubted quality of the cooking, this is a good option as a special occasion Indian restaurant. When each dish arrives it is beautiful on the plate – lots of influences from smart French chefs, but still matching textures with good assertive tastes. Kekdae ki chaat aur tille ka jhinga is a crab salad teamed with a tangy kumquat chutney and topped with prawns deep-fried in a crisp coat – very fresh, very delicious. The tandoor work is exemplary – lamb chops are exceedingly plump and tender. A classic dish such as rogan josh is as good as you can get – unless you can find it served on the bone. Or there's hare masala ki machchi, which is pan-fried John Dory served with a broth of curried mussels. The vegetable side dishes are most interesting. Pani singara aur faliyon ki subji is superb and an exercise in crunchy textures – water chestnuts and French beans with onion seeds and dried mango.

The Berkeley Square

7 Davies Street, W1 ■ 020 7629 6993

⊖ Green Park

🍽 French

🕐 Mon to Fri 12.00–14.30 & 18.00–22.00

🖱 www.theberkeleysquare.com

🗗 all major credit cards ■ 12.5% optional service added

££ lunch menu £21.50 (3 courses) ■ dinner menu £49.50 (3 courses)
■ surprise menu £55 (7 courses) ■ lowest bottle price £21.50

✪ A calm place with good cooking

When it opened, this place was called the Berkeley Square Café, but it quickly became apparent that it was really a restauranty sort of restaurant and the word café was quietly dispensed with. It is now established as an elegant and comfortable restaurant where chef-patron Stephen Black serves remarkably good food with unpretentious style. Dishes are ambitious, and pretty on the plate, but thankfully the menus are market driven and there's a welcome emphasis on British produce. Service is slick and there is a handful of roadside tables for lunching outdoors on bright days. The lunch menu offers a choice of three starters, three mains and three puds and is something of a bargain: smoked trout and crushed potato terrine with dill crème fraîche; slow-roast belly pork glazed in honey and lavender; poached rhubarb with clotted-cream ice cream – good dishes, with nicely judged combinations of flavour. The à la carte is a three-course offer and there's a seven-course 'surprise menu' that must be ordered for the whole table. Dishes are appealing – Sennen Cove crab salad with avocado purée, pink grapefruit and peas; shavings of confit foie gras, white asparagus and wild salad leaves; morel mushroom risotto with asparagus and Parmesan; fillet of halibut with brandade fritters, cauliflower and truffle purée; Welsh Black Mountain organic chicken – you get the supreme roast, plus an open herb ravioli of the confit thigh, with a carrot and tarragon salad. The wine list is extensive and can get expensive. Puds are elaborate, but the ice creams are very good – particularly the black cardamom.

Chor Bizarre

16 Albemarle Street, W1 ■ 020 7629 9802

🚇 Green Park

🍽 Indian

🕐 Mon to Sat 12.00–15.00 & 18.00–23.30; Sun 18.00–22.30

🔗 www.chorbizarrelondon.com

💳 all major credit cards ■ 12.5% optional service added

££ starters £7–£18 ■ mains £7–£15 ■ desserts £4–£5 ■ tasting menu (Wazwan) £25 ■ lowest bottle price £16

✪ Good Indian food, genuine Indo-kitsch dining room

This is one of a handful of London's Indian restaurants with a 'head office' in India. Our Chor Bizarre is a straight copy of the one in the Broadway Hotel, Delhi. Its name is an elaborate pun (*Chor Bazaar* translates as 'thieves' market') and, like the Delhi branch, the London restaurant is furnished with Indian antiques and bric-a-brac. Every table, and each set of chairs, is different, and you may find yourself dining within the frame of an antique four-poster bed. The food is very well prepared and encouragingly authentic. Care is taken over the detail; Chor Bizarre does, however, carry the kind of price tag you'd expect in Mayfair. Start with simple things such as pakoras, which are tasty vegetable fritters, or coconut mussels, which come in a coconut fish broth. Kebabs are taken seriously here, too: try gazab ka tikka, a bestseller in Delhi, which is a kind of chicken tikka deluxe. Then, for your main course, choose dishes such as baghare baingan, a Hyderabadi dish combining aubergine, peanuts and tamarind. Or Malabar prawn curry, which is marinated king prawns with a kick of chilli, or goshtaba, the famous Kashmiri lamb curry – very velvety. Breads are also impressive, including an excellent naan; pudina paratha, a mint paratha; and stuffed kulcha. The many imposing set meals are a good way to tour the menu without watching your wallet implode. Try the Maharaja thali – a complete meal on a tray. TV dinners will never be the same again. Bravehearts will tackle the Wazwan, which is a multi-course banquet, rich food from the North of India.

Le Gavroche

43 Upper Brook Street, W1 ∎ 020 7408 0881

⊖ Marble Arch

🍴 French

🕐 Mon to Fri 12.00–14.00 & 18.30–23.00; Sat 18.30–23.00

🖱 www.le-gavroche.co.uk

🏷 all major credit cards ∎ 12.5% optional service added

££ starters £19.90–£43.80 ∎ mains £26.90–£42.80 ∎ desserts £15.80–£30.60 ∎ set menus: £46 (set lunch) up to £130 (tasting menu with wines) ∎ lowest bottle price £16.50

✪ Temple to gastronomy

The Roux family business is cheffing and at Le Gavroche Michel (Jnr) plys his trade to some purpose. This is an awesome French restaurant. Service is super slick. The dress code is super formal (jacket and tie). The wine list is littered with superstar bottles. And the cooking? The cooking is as good as it gets. The only teeny drawback is the bill – have your heart pills handy at the end of the meal. The best way of dodging this minor fiscal problem is to opt for the set lunch, which is one of the bargains of the age. For a relatively minor sum you can choose from three starters, three mains, three puds and enjoy half a bottle of wine, water, coffee and petits fours. If you enjoy 'proper' French cooking almost anything on the menu will ring a bell, but the soufflé Suissesse – a cheese soufflé with extra cream – is very charming; or scallops pan-fried with five-spice mixture; or an artichoke heart filled with foie gras and truffles. Mains are equally self-indulgent: a tournedos comes with pan-fried foie gras and truffled macaroni cheese. Or there's roast Anjou pigeon; wild salmon; turbot. Serious stuff. Then it's time to hit the trolleys – the cheese trolley is a monster, laden with cheeses all in perfect condition. Or there's one groaning with different ice creams and sorbets. The rest of the puds are stellar. Meanwhile, the service glides around you, not too pushy, but you never seem to wait – it's uncanny. The wine list has sound bottles at the bottom end for people whose priority is the food, and then it soars off to the top for people whose priority is spending.

The Greenhouse

27a Hay's Mews, W1 ■ 020 7499 3331

⊖ Green Park

🍴 French

🕐 Mon to Fri 12.00–14.30 & 18.45–23.00; Sat 18.45–23.00

🖱 www.greenhouserestaurant.co.uk

🖴 all major credit cards ■ 12.5% optional service added

££ lunch £28 (2 courses) & £30 (3 courses) ■ dinner £60 (3 courses)
■ tasting menu £75 (7 courses) ■ lowest bottle price £30

✪ High ambitions and high prices

The Greenhouse is a very Mayfair concept. The coda of this place
is excellence – the ingredients, cooking, service and wines all aim for
excellence. And the price? If you are genuinely at home in the Mayfair
village that should be of no concern. If you can muster the ante, a
visit to the Greenhouse is most enjoyable; the room is comfortable
and elegant, service attentive, the wine list an absolute monster
with a great many fine wines and the cooking is very accomplished.
The kitchen works with seasonal ingredients and what seems like
an absolute disregard for ingredient costs. Starters may range from
a 'Shed bush farm bio-dynamic duck egg', which is cooked in a
different fashion each day and has 'limited availability'; to sheep's
milk ricotta gnocchi, cèpes, Parmesan and parsley pistou – a complex
combination of tastes and textures; or pan-seared foie gras, espresso
syrup and amaretto foam. And how does organic cauliflower velouté,
with diver scallop and pistachio-truffle vinaigrette sound? Main
courses continue the theme; considered dishes predominate, like
Lincolnshire rabbit served with a bean ragout, the rabbit leg braised,
and snails; or there may be a dish of halibut poached in truffle milk
and served with a lemon sabayon, spiced dates and a red wine sauce.
Desserts are elaborate – mascarpone parfait, roasted figs, Sauternes
jelly and walnut ice cream. Meanwhile, the giant wine list tries to
tempt you with ever more fabulous first growths and moody pudding
wines. You will like this place, but your bank manager may have
another view.

Gordon Ramsay at Claridge's

Brook Street, W1 ■ 020 7499 0099 &

⊖ Green Park

🍴 French

🕐 Mon to Fri 12.00–14.45 & 17.45–23.00; Sat 12.00–15.30 & 17.45–23.00; Sun 12.00–15.00 & 18.00–22.30

🖰 www.gordonramsay.com

🗗 all major credit cards ■ 12.5% optional service added

££ à la carte £60 (3 courses) ■ set lunch £30 (3 courses) ■ tasting menu £70 (6 courses) ■ lowest bottle price £18

✪ Classic French food within a classic luxury hotel

When Gordon Ramsay took over the restaurant at Claridge's, various regular customers both old and young held their collective breath. But within a couple of years everything was set fair. The dining room is still large, the service is still slick, but the food is much better than it used to be and, it could be argued, better value, too. There's a good-value set lunch, which some reckon to be an even better bargain than the set lunch at Ramsay's Chelsea flagship (see p. 366). Unfortunately, like its sibling, Claridge's is booked up far in advance. While Gordon Ramsay has his name over the door, the head chef here is Mark Sargeant. The menu changes with the seasons and among the starters you may find a velouté of cauliflower with a fricassée of wild mushrooms, artichokes and rocket; crisp ventrêche and poached quails' eggs; and a tian of Cornish crab with fennel, rocket and herb salad. Presentation on the plate is elegant and seasoning spot-on. Main courses might include roast canon of Cornish lamb served with confit shoulder, white bean purée, baby leeks and rosemary jus; pan-fried fillet of dorade with grilled asparagus, globe artichokes and vanilla sauce; or fillet of monkfish wrapped in Parma ham on a bed of cèpes risotto, white asparagus and five-spice sauce. The desserts are equally considered: Valrhona chocolate fondant with feuillatine and malt ice cream. Those with stalwart wallet and an inquisitive nature should consider booking the chef's table, which seats six in an alcove overlooking the kitchen.

Kai

65 South Audley Street, W1 ■ 020 7493 8988

⊖ Bond Street/Marble Arch

🍴 Chinese

🕐 Mon to Fri 12.00–13.45 & 18.30–22.45; Sat 12.30–14.15 & 18.30–22.45; Sun 12.30–14.15 & 18.30–23.15

🖰 www.kaimayfair.com

🖰 all major credit cards ■ 3.5% optional service added

££ starters £7.50–£36 ■ mains £13–£52 ■ set lunch £23 ■ tasting menu £75 ■ lowest bottle price £23

✪ Exquisite cooking, merciless Mayfair pricing

Outside, in the huge and glossy cars, the chauffeurs sit waiting. Inside, the diners take their time over elegant and often elaborate dishes. Make no mistake, at Kai you can spend as much on your meal as you want to. If you have the foresight to pre-order, there's even a bowl of soup costing over £100! And you'll find a full complement of all those fabled Chinese dishes, with all those fabulously expensive ingredients – abalone, shark's fin, deer's pizzle… hereabouts truffles and lobster are run of the mill. So, having established the ground rules (i.e. this place is not for those of feeble wallet), what's it like? The standard of both the cooking and invention is very high, flavours are well matched, textures are inspired – eating here is an aesthetic experience. You'll find all your favourite Chinese dishes – prawns Kung Po, spareribs, crispy duck – but you're better off trying some of chef Alex Chow's more elaborate flights of fancy. There's a dish called 'Oriental lamb shank', which comes to table in a Martini glass, the bottom layer is brown soup-sludge-slow-braised-lamb and it is topped with a garlic cream – delicious. Or there are tempura prawns with a wasabi mayonnaise – crisp, crunchy, well balanced. The braised abalone (cooked for three days) has 'best-ever' status and comes with a white truffle jus. The deep-fried, soft-shell crabs with fried garlic and chilli are very good. The sirloin with black pepper and garlic flakes is a rich and sticky beef dish. The service at Kai is exemplary, careful and friendly, and the wine list matches the ambitions of the menu. Save up and visit.

Kiku

17 Half Moon Street, W1 ■ 020 7499 4208 &

🚇 Green Park

🍴 Japanese

🕐 Mon to Sat 12.00–14.30 & 18.00–22.15; Sun 17.30–21.45

🖰 www.kikurestaurant.co.uk

🖃 all major credit cards ■ 12.5% optional service added

££ sushi £1.50–£5 ■ mains £7.50–£19.50 ■ sushi combinations £22 & £30 ■ desserts £4–£8 ■ lowest bottle price £14.50, sake £12

✪ Good sushi, blissfully un-intimidating atmosphere

Brace yourself, because this is all going to sound like a bit of a porky. Kiku is a Japanese restaurant (translates as pricey), deep in the heart of Mayfair (translates as very pricey) and one that serves top-class sushi with a classical ambience – but without charging the earth. Your bill will prove it. In helpful Oriental fashion, it lists the huge number of sushi portions you are alleged to have consumed and an average price. What is odd, however, is how reasonable it all ends up. Kiku is laid out around a traditional sushi bar, so you can sit and wonder at the dexterity of the knife man. Wander along smack on opening time, snatch a seat at the counter and go for it. Knowledgeable Japanese folk always start a meal of sushi with tamago – the sweetish, omelettey one that allows the diner to properly assess the quality of the rice. Who knows? The toro, or tuna belly, is good; the suzuki, or sea bass, is good; the amaebi, or sweet prawn, is … sweet. Hiramei, or turbot, is very delicate. You must have hotate, which is slices of raw scallop, translucent and subtle – very good indeed. From the rolled sushi section, pick the umeshiso maki, made from rice with pickled plums and fresh green shiso leaves. Tobiko is slightly advanced and surprisingly good. A successful strategy might be to try a few sushi and then turn to the main menu: perhaps tempura moriawase, which is mixed tempura, or sake teriyaki, which is grilled teriyaki salmon. If you suffer from 'long foreign menu fatigue system', there are good sushi combinations such as tokujyo nigiri or jyongiri. Drink the very refreshing Asahi beer and only venture into the realms of sake if you understand it.

Maze

10–13 Grosvenor Square, W1 ■ 020 7107 0000 &

⊖ Bond Street

|○| French

⏱ Mon to Sat 12.00–15.00 & 18.00–23.00; Sun 12.00–15.00 & 18.00–22.30

⌂ www.gordonramsay.com

⊟ all major credit cards ■ 12.5% optional service added

££ small dishes £3.50–£8 ■ dishes à la carte £7–£16 ■ desserts £2.50–£8 ■ tasting menu dishes £3.0–£8.50 ■ lowest bottle price £18

❂ Every day is a grazing day

Part of the Gordon Ramsay empire, with inspired cooking made complicated by the mechanics of the menu. First things first, the menu here is a seasonal one, which is a wholly commendable approach. It quickly gets more complicated; to start with, about twenty small dishes are listed and you are invited to choose between six and eight per person. But if the grazing approach doesn't ring your bell, the next spread is more conventional and offers six starters and six mains – but all dishes drawn from the first selection. The room is pleasant and modern, the service is sound enough, although all the explaining necessary tends to drag on. 'Grazing' – and all the other derivatives of the tasting menu – is a mixed blessing. When a dish arrives that you like, you feel disappointed that there is not more of it on the plate; when a dish arrives that you don't like, you're just disappointed. If you were to visit in the spring you might be offered pressed foie gras and smoked eel with pickled ginger and rhubarb, ginger brioche – good complementary textures, or Orkney scallops roasted with spices, golden raisin purée and cauliflower – sweet and subtle. Other highlights might be a risotto made with peas, broad beans, wood sorrel and grated truffle; or roast turbot with five-spice oxtail, confit baby leeks and crushed peas; or pork cheeks with honey and cloves, roast chorizo, coco beans. Desserts appeal – Valrhona chocolate fondant with green cardamom caramel, sea salt and almond ice cream. Even as you find yourself wondering whether this is all triumph or gimmick, you realise that Maze is saved by the quality of the cooking.

The Mirabelle

56 Curzon Street, W1 ■ 020 7499 4636

⊖ Green Park

🍴 French

🕐 Mon to Fri 12.00–14.30 & 18.00–23.30; Sat 12.00–14.30 & 18.30–23.30; Sun 12.00–15.00 & 18.00–22.00

🖰 www.whitestarline.org.uk

🖃 all major credit cards ■ 12.5% optional service added

££ starters £9.50–£16.95 ■ soup £9.50 ■ mains £15–£25 ■ desserts £8.50 ■ set lunch £17.50 & £21.50 ■ lowest bottle price £18

✪ Mayfair stalwart grows middle-aged gracefully

While Marco Pierre White's restaurant empire is changing focus and élite dining places become less formal, The Mirabelle is still the jewel in the crown. A gratifyingly pukka restaurant. This site has been home to a fashionable restaurant since the 1950s and it is hard to grasp that it is over a decade since MPW took it over, gutted and restored it. The Mirabelle has graduated from new kid on the block to neighbourhood stalwart gradually, but it now has real gravitas. Overlook the pretensions of an extensive and expensive wine list (the 1847 d'Yquem priced at £30,000 has been on offer since opening day) and concentrate on the food, which is quite reasonably priced for this kind of cooking. The surroundings are elegant, the service attentive and the bar is inviting. Start with a classic: omelette 'Arnold Bennett' with sauce Mornay. It's no wonder that Arnold liked this so much – rich, buttery and light, made with good smoked haddock. Or there's ballottine of salmon Maison Prunier. Step up a level for some triumphant foie gras 'en terrine' dishes: with green peppercorns, gelée de Sauternes and toasted brioche, or 'parfait en gelée'. Very delicious. For a fishy main course, how about an escalope of tuna with aubergine caviar? Or the classical grilled lemon sole served on the bone with sauce tartare. In the meat section, choose from roast venison au poivre, sauce grand veneur, or braised pig's trotter with morels, pommes purées, sauce Périgueux. Puddings are deftly handled. The star is tarte sablée of bitter chocolate.

Momo

25 Heddon Street, W1 ■ 020 7434 4040

⊖ Oxford Circus

🍴 North African

🕒 Mon to Sat 12.00–14.30 & 19.00–23.00; Sun 19.00–23.00

🖱 www.momorestaurant.com

🖻 all major credit cards ■ 12.5% optional service added

££ starters £6.50–£12.50 ■ mains £9.75–£19.50 ■ desserts £5.50–£7
■ set lunch £11 & £14 ■ lowest bottle price £18

✪ The men's urinal is an installation of some beauty

Blisteringly trendy, Momo is not only the eponymous owner, but an attractive Moroccan restaurant tucked away in a backwater off Regent Street. For dinner, you usually have to book at least a week in advance and to opt for an early or late sitting. If you apply for the late shift, be prepared for a noisy, nightclub ambience. The design of the place is clever, with bold, geometric, kasbah-style architecture, plush cushions and lots of candles. Downstairs there's an even more splendid Moorish bar, annoyingly reserved for members only – a shame, as Momo is the kind of place where you could happily carry on the evening, especially if you're booked in for the earlier (19.00–21.00) dining slot. The starters include 'Momo kemia', which combines méchouia – red pepper purée, chicken bourek and briouat au cabillaud (mouthwatering little parcels of paper-thin pastry filled with cod, potatoes and chermoula). Or there is 'millefeuille' made with aubergine and asparagus. For main course, choose from four tagines, which are North African-style stews served in a large clay pot. Try the tagine of chicken with preserved lemons, or the tagine of lamb with prunes, quinces and almonds. Alternatively, opt for couscous méchouia, based around roasted, spiced lamb. Or treat yourself to the Fès speciality of pastilla, the super-sweet pigeon pie in millefeuille pastry – a main course that has been relegated to the starters list. Desserts include pastries, deep-fried filo parcels of fruit, pancakes and meringues. There is a 'tearoom' next door, which makes a pleasant spot to pause during any afternoon rampage through the West End.

Nobu

19 Old Park Lane, W1 ■ 020 7447 4747

⊖ Hyde Park Corner

🍽 Japanese

🕐 Mon to Thurs 12.00–14.15 & 18.00–22.30; Fri & Sat 12.00–14.15 & 18.00–23.00; Sun 18.00–21.30

⌁ www.noburestaurants.com

🖪 all major credit cards ■ 15% optional service added

££ special dishes & appetisers £5–£29.50 ■ tempura £1.25–£6 ■ kushiyaki £4.50–£9.50 ■ mains £14–£23.50 ■ desserts £6–£9 ■ bento box set lunch £24.50 ■ sushi lunch £20–£21 ■ 'Omakase' chef's choice: lunch £50 & £60, dinner £70 & £90 ■ lowest bottle price £26

✪ Good food in celeb-spotter's heaven

Nobu is home to the actual broom cupboard where Boris Becker qualified for his paternity suit. It's hard to know just what to make of Nobu. On the face of it, a restaurant owned by Robert de Niro, Drew Nieporent and Matsuhisa Nobuyuki sounds like the invention of a deranged Hollywood producer. And then there is the cocoon of hype: the restaurant is amazingly expensive, but don't worry, the food is innovative and superb. Ingredients are fresh, flavour combinations are novel and inspired, and presentation is elegant and stylish. See for yourself – start with the lunchtime bento box, which is something of a bargain and includes sashimi salad, rock shrimp tempura, black cod and all the trimmings. Matsuhisa worked in Peru, and South American flavours and techniques segue into classical Japanese dishes – some of the dishes here defy classification. The sashimi is terrific: salmon is sliced and just warmed through to 'set' it, before being served with sesame seeds – the minimal cooking makes for a superb texture. The black cod with miso is a grandstand dish – a piece of perfectly cooked fish with an elaborate banana-leaf canopy. Other inspired dishes are the rock shrimp tempura and the chocolate and almond parfait. The 'Omakase' is a menu based around the chef's selection – serious stuff at a serious price.

→ For branches, see index

Patterson's

4 Mill Street, W1 ◼ 020 7499 1308

⊖ Oxford Circus

|◉| French

⏲ Mon to Fri 12.30–15.00 & 18.00–23.00; Sat 18.00–23.00

⌂ www.pattersonsrestaurant.com

🖶 all major credit cards ◼ 12.5% optional service added

££ starters £5 (lunch), £12 (dinner) ◼ mains £10 (lunch), £17 (dinner)
◼ desserts £5 (lunch), £11 (dinner) ◼ lowest bottle price £15.50

✪ Ask the family for good French food

While family-run restaurants serving top-quality, classical, French food are occasionally sighted in France they are as rare as hen's teeth in Mayfair. Patterson's is the exception. Raymond Patterson won his spurs during a fourteen-year stint in the kitchens at the Garrick Club, and somehow he has persuaded most of his family to join him in his restaurant. The menu here is littered with those satisfying, classical dishes that are so very difficult to do well. A smoked haddock soufflé served with a chive caviar sauce comes to table towering and quivering, the beurre blanc concoction in a jug to pour into its depths – a stunning dish. Or there may be a ham hock and duck egg ravioli with roast chanterelles. Other starters may include roast foie gras with peach caviar, or a venison and wild boar terrine with a white pear cake. These are dishes that put the kitchen through its paces. The mains continue the theme – steamed halibut with crab mousse and fondant leeks; saddle and civet of rabbit with a Swiss chard gateau; or tournedos of beef with foie gras and wild mushroom cannelloni. The puds are good – a textbook tarte Tatin, an epic white chocolate soufflé with cherry sauce. The wine list at Patterson's seems un-aggressively priced – and there are a good many classic bottles at just about accessible prices. The service is charming, and there is plenty of both ambition and technical ability in the kitchen. At lunch prices shrink a good deal – and there is sometimes a very reasonable and quintessentially civilised 'oyster lunch' on offer here: a dozen oysters, cheeseboard and coffee.

Sketch – the Glade

9 Conduit Street, W1 ■ 0870 777 4488

⊖ Oxford Circus

🍴 French

🕐 Mon to Sat 12.00–15.00

🖰 www.sketch.co.uk

🖬 all major credit cards ■ 12.5% optional service added

££ starters £5–£14 ■ dishes £8–£24 ■ desserts £3.50–£5 ■ Market Menu
£18 & £21 ■ lowest bottle price £12

❂ Complex French food at simple prices

When Sketch opened, a succession of critics arrived, ate and went
home to write pretty similar reviews. The food at 'Sketch, the Library'
– Pierre Gagnaire's London fine-dining outpost – was certainly cutting
edge, but it was also so blisteringly expensive that even the stoutest
expense accounts quickly hit meltdown. Time passed and the other
half of the Sketch equation, restaurateur Mourad Mazouz, opened
Glade, a lunch-only restaurant offering Gagnaire's food at less
extravagant prices. Like the rest of the Sketch, Glade drips with high
style. Lofty ceiling, odd décor, spooky chandelier made from gnarled
tree branches. The food does likewise, the menu listing a variety of
dishes some marked as starter-sized, some not; many of these are
very good indeed. Gagnaire's strengths are presentation, combining
textures, balancing flavours and an impish sense of humour.
'Hommage à M. L'Ambassadeur…' works incredibly well: an assembly
of rice, fresh green peas, pomegranate seeds, cubes of almost raw
salmon, hazelnuts, grapes and a fried duck egg. Also delicious: the
bitter sake sorbet and the rye bread pudding that accompany oysters;
the Yorkshire partridge terrine; the 'salad' of white beans, rocket,
confit tomato and globe artichoke. Braised oxtail is teamed with
tagliatelle and creamy Gorgonzola. A rib-eye steak comes with a
sauce made from walnut, beer and maple syrup. This is cooking at its
most masterful, and for once these flights of fancy come at accessible
prices.

The Square

6–10 Bruton Street, W1 ■ 020 7495 7100

⊖ Green Park

|◉| French

🕐 Mon to Fri 12.00–15.00 & 18.30–22.45; Sat 18.30–22.45

🌐 www.squarerestaurant.com

🖅 all major credit cards ■ 12.5% optional service added

££ set lunch £25 (2 courses) & £30 (3 courses) ■ dinner £60 (3 courses) ■ tasting menu £75 (8 courses) ■ lowest bottle price £18

✪ Splendid food, splendid wines, splendid service

Eating here is a palate-expanding experience. The Square is very French, and food is terribly important here. And in the gastro premier league – an arena where almost every commentator bows to the supremacy of French chefs and French cuisine – you cannot help a slight smirk that head chef Philip Howard, a softly spoken Englishman, has got it all so very, very right. At The Square, the finest ingredients are sought out, and then what is largely a classical technique ensures that each retains its essential character and flavour. This is a very gracious restaurant. Service is suave, silent and effortless. Seasoning is on the button. Presentation is elegant. The wine list seems boundless in scope and soars to the very topmost heights (where mortals dare not even ask the price). The menu changes on a broadly seasonal basis. Starters are dishes such as lasagne of crab with a cappuccino of langoustines and basil; assiette of foie gras: roast with fig and apple, mousse with redcurrant jelly, smoked ballotine with celeriac, cappuccino with beignet and truffle. Mains may include baked turbot with a warm potato pancake, a fondue of leeks and velouté of truffle; loin of lamb with goats' cheese tortellinis, aubergine and apricot; twice-cooked pigeon from Bresse with a tarte fine of caramelised endive, five-spice and cherries. Puddings – such as a fondant of chocolate with malted-milk ice cream – are classics. Howard is an able man and Michelin's two-star measure of his worth is an underestimate. There's also an eight-course 'tasting' menu (only for the entire table). This is one treat you will never regret.

Truc Vert

42 North Audley Street, W1 ■ 020 7491 9988

⊖ Bond Street

◉ Modern British

🕒 Mon to Fri 07.30–21.30; Sat 12.00–16.00; Sun 09.30–18.00

🖰 www.trucvert.co.uk

🖻 all major credit cards ■ 10% optional service added

££ starters £4.95–£9.95 ■ mains £12.50–£16.50 ■ sides £2.50
■ desserts £4.75–£4.95 ■ pre-theatre menu £15 & £18.50 ■ lowest
bottle price £13

✪ Delicious in-deli eating

Truc Vert is one of those hybrid restaurants. You want it to be
a deli, with fine cheeses, artisan chocolate and obscure wild boar
salami? Then it's a deli. You want it to be a restaurant, with proper
starters, mains and puds? Then it's a restaurant. The Truc is open
all day during the week, and it makes a very decent fist of being
all things to all customers. The menu comes in two halves. 'From
the shop' means quiche, salads, chicken from the rotisserie, pâtés,
cakes, pastries and cookies. There is also a novel approach to the
magnificent cheese counter: you nominate a few different cheeses,
they make up an elegant plateful and then weigh it, and you are
charged by weight. The same deal works for charcuterie. But despite
competition from these instant assortments, the main dishes are well
done and the seasoning spot on. The menu is rewritten daily, but
by way of starter you could be offered a sweet potato and ginger
soup; saffron crab cakes; or baked goats' cheese with artichoke and
grilled mixed peppers. Mains run the gamut from grilled halibut fillet;
through penne pasta with roast broccoli, cherry tomatoes and spicy
ricotta sauce; to grilled lamb cutlets with roast butternut squash and
French bean salad. Puds are accomplished – try baked plums with
coconut and rum sorbet – but they pale beside the prospect of the
epic array of fine cheeses. At lunch the quiches, rotisserie chickens
and the selection of pâté with cornichons make the 'From the shop'
option most appealing. And thankfully there's a very un-Mayfair wine
policy – you pay the shop price and they add nominal corkage.

Umu

14–16 Bruton Place, W1 ■ 020 7499 8881   ♿

⊖ Green Park/Bond Street

🍴 Japanese

🕐 Mon to Sat 12.00–14.30 & 18.00–23.00 (tasting menus to be
ordered before 14.00 & 22.30)

🖥 www.umurestaurant.com

🖶 all major credit cards ■ 12.5% optional service added

££ starters £5–£16 ■ sushi £2–£8 per piece ■ mains £10–£45 ■ sides
£2–£14 ■ desserts £6–£8 ■ set lunch from £22 ■ Kaseki tasting
menus £60, £90 & £130 ■ wines by the glass £7–£16 ■ lowest bottle
price £23

⭐ Rarefied Japanese food, rarefied prices

**The publicity blurb for this resto mentions that the chef imports all
the water he uses for cooking from Japan,** an obsessive attention to
detail that seems a little more credible when you have eaten the food at
Umu. This place makes no bones about targeting the A-list: the décor is
slick; the service is very slick under the aegis of a talented French maitre
d'; the sake list is refined and extensive; the food is very sophisticated
indeed; and when it comes, the bill is large enough to make a
lottery winner wince. The menu offers appetisers; sashimi; classic
sushi; modern sushi; main courses; soups; rices and desserts. A few
generalities: the combinations of taste and of texture are magnificent;
every dish looks beautiful on the plate, and the attention to detail is
amazing. Simple starters like mackerel tartare or sesame tofu with fresh
wasabi and nori seaweed work well. Sweet shrimp comes with sake
jelly and caviar; or there's makizukuri of salmon and chives; or deep-
fried oyster with lemon vinaigrette. These are all delicate and delicious.
The sushi verge on 'best ever'. Modern sushi contenders are blue crab,
courgette, pine nuts, red ichimi; foie gras with lily roots; and scallop,
lemon confit, langoustine bisque. Main courses range from a deep-
fried lobster yuba roll with yuzu salt; to grilled venison with spring
onions, sesame sauce; or tempura of prawn, rabbit and ginger bud.
Although pricey, the 'Kaseki' tasting menus offer a balanced choice of
dishes and also suggest matched sake and wine.

Notting Hill and Kensal Green

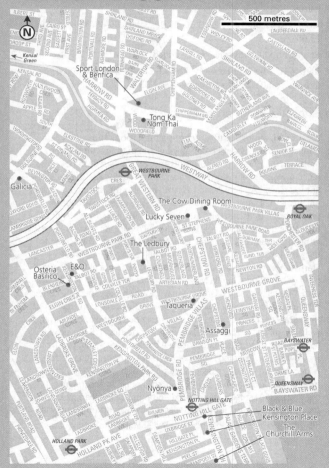

500 metres

N

← Kensal Green

Sport London & Benfica

Tong Ka Nom Thai

WESTBOURNE PARK

Galicia

The Cow Dining Room

Lucky Seven

ROYAL OAK

The Ledbury

Osteria Basilico

E&O

WESTBOURNE GROVE

Taqueria

Assaggi

BAYSWATER

QUEENSWAY
BAYSWATER RD

Nyonya

NOTTING HILL GATE

Black & Blue
Kensington Place
The
Churchill Arms

HOLLAND PARK

Assaggi

39 Chepstow Place, W2 ■ 020 7792 5501

⊖ Notting Hill Gate

🍽 Italian

🕐 Mon to Fri 12.30–14.30 & 19.30–23.00; Sat 13.00–14.30 & 19.30–23.00

🖫 all major credit cards ■ no service added

££ starters £8.90–£15.90 ■ mains £16.90–£19.90 ■ sides £2.90 ■ desserts £6.50 ■ lowest bottle price £17.95

✪ Elite Italian with prices to match

For a small, almost scruffy, ochre-painted room above the Chepstow pub, Assaggi is enviably full and getting a table can be a problem. The prices are unforgiving and, on the face of it, paying so much for such straightforward Italian dishes could raise the hackles. But the reason Assaggi is such a gem, and also the reason it is always full, is that selfsame straightforwardness. The menu may appear simple, but it is littered with authentic and luxury ingredients, and the cooking is very accomplished indeed. Prepare yourself for a meal to be remembered. You'll find a dozen starters – with the option to have the pastas as main courses – and half a dozen main courses. Start with pasta, maybe rotolo con asparagi e ricotta al forno, or a plate of sensational bufala Mozzarella. Or choose grilled vegetables with olive oil and herbs. Or there may be a dish like capesante con salsa alla zafferano, a simple plate of perfectly cooked, splendidly fresh scallops. Main courses are even more pared down: calf's liver; a plainly grilled veal chop with rosemary; fritto misto. But even a humble side salad of tomato, rucola e basilico is everything you would wish for. Puddings change daily. Look out for panna cotta – a perfect texture – and the beautifully simple dish made from ultra-fresh buffalo ricotta served with 'cooked' honey. To accompany, the short wine list features splendid and unfamiliar Italian regional specialities. Be careful if offered 'specials' made with truffle or wild mushrooms – they are delicious but wallet bruising.

Black & Blue

215–217 Kensington Church Street, W8 ■ 020 7727 0004 ♿

⊖ Notting Hill Gate

🍽 Steak

🕐 Mon to Thurs & Sun 12.00–23.00; Fri & Sat 12.00–23.30

🖰 www.blackandblue.biz

🖫 all major credit cards ■ 12.5% optional service added

££ starters £5 ■ steaks £12–£20 (hamburger £9) ■ desserts £5 ■ lowest bottle price £15

✪ Black for the Angus cattle, blue for Scotland

Say the words 'steak house' to a Londoner and they conjure up a very 1970s' image – lots of tartan and red plush, with hapless tourists reaffirming their worst misgivings about British food. It's about time we had a decent chain of steak houses, and Black & Blue may just be a contender. For a start, this establishment, which is part of a lengthening chain, has the very best provenance for its meat. All the steak here comes from Donald Russell of Inverurie – a company that is king of the Aberdeen Angus beef trade. For a steak house, Black & Blue looks smart and modern. There are banquettes, wood panelling, a stylish bar and some rather nice vintage Bovril posters. Starters are predictable. There's a prawn cocktail – half a dozen large prawns in pink stuff. Or that American abomination, a whole deep-fried onion sometimes called a 'Texas Rose'. Thereafter there's an 'all day breakfast', salads, baguettes, two chicken dishes, salmon, prawns and tuna – ignore them all in favour of the steaks. Aberdeen Angus is well-flavoured meat and, commendably enough, when you say rare you get rare. Each steak comes with a very decent mixed salad – steer clear of the proffered dressings – and tolerable fries. There are five steaks: sirloin, rib-eye, fillet, T-bone and a côte de boeuf for sharing, and there is a wide choice of sizes. It's also worth checking out the very decent hamburger, which proves the point that most dishes are only as good as their ingredients. There's a small choice of simple desserts: chocolate mousse and lemon tart are served with clotted cream. The wine list is not long, but is agreeably un-grasping.

→ For branches, see index

The Churchill Arms

119 Kensington Church Street, W8 ■ 020 7792 1246

⊖ Notting Hill Gate	

🍴 Thai

🕐 daily 12.00–21.30

🖻 all major credit cards ■ no service added

££ mains £5.85 ■ desserts £2.50 ■ lowest bottle price £10.95 white, £11.50 red

✪ Great pub out front, great Thai out back

Over the years the Churchill has nurtured its clientele (who are largely students and bargain hunters) by the simple expedient of serving some of the tastiest and most reasonably priced Thai food in London. The main dining area is in a back room featuring acres of green foliage, but don't despair if you find it full (it fills up very quickly) – meals are served throughout the pub. Service is friendly, but as the food is cooked to order, be prepared to wait – it's worth it. If you really can't wait, pre-cooked dishes such as chicken with chillies (along with that other well-known Thai delicacy, Stilton ploughman's) are also available. Dishes are unpronounceable, and have thoughtfully been numbered to assist everybody. The pad gai med ma muang hin-maparn is a deliciously spicy dish of chicken, cashew nuts and chilli served with a generous helping of fluffy, boiled rice. The khao rad na ga prao is described as very hot. For once this is not an understatement; how wonderful to find a menu where hot means hot. This prawn dish with fresh chillies and Thai basil is guaranteed to bring sweat to the brow of even the most ardent chilliholic. For something milder, try the pad neau nahm man hoi, which is beef with oyster sauce and mushrooms, or the khao rad na, a rice dish topped with prawns, vegetables and gravy. Both are good. Puddings are limited in choice and ambition, but for something sweet to temper the heat, try apple pie – a strange accompaniment to Thai food, but surprisingly welcome. Still a real pub with real beer; seek out a pint of well-kept Fuller's London Pride.

The Cow Dining Room

89 Westbourne Park Road, W2 ■ 020 7221 5400

⊖ Westbourne Park

◉ Modern British/gastropub

🕐 Mon to Sat 12.00–23.00; Sun 12.00–22.30

🔲 all major credit cards ■ 12.5% optional service added

££ starters £4–£7 ■ mains £7–£15 ■ sides £2.50 ■ desserts £4.50
   ■ lowest bottle price £13

⭐ Haven for Notting Hillbillies

The Cow is something of a conundrum. On the one hand it is a
genuine pub – a proper pub, with beer and locals – and on the other,
owner Tom Conran has managed to make it something of a meeting
place for Notting Hill's smart set. Downstairs all is fierce drinking and
loud debate, while upstairs you'll find an oasis of calm and, at its
centre, a small dining room. It is a good place to eat. The atmosphere
is informal, but the food is accomplished. The menu changes daily
and delivers fresh, unfussy, seasonal food. Starters deliver tried and
tested combinations of prime ingredients – rabbit, white bean and
chorizo soup; tuna sashimi, spinach oshitashi, soy and wasabi; skate
wing, capers and beurre noisette; or lamb's kidney, black pudding
and mustard sauce. Main courses cover most of the bases, from
goats' cheese and herb ravioli; through roast monkfish, ratatouille
and pesto; to braised milk-fed kid; or line-caught Cornish cod, spiced
chickpeas and gremolata. The menu finishes triumphantly with slow-
roast belly of Old Spot pork with wild mushrooms. Puddings are a
suitable mix of the comfortable and the desirable: crème brûlée; tarte
Tatin with vanilla ice cream. Or you could go for cheese, which comes
with the imprimatur that signifies well-chosen and well-kept cheeses
– 'Neal's Yard' cheeses with oatcakes. The wine list is sound, and if
asked nicely your waiter will fetch a pint of De Koninck beer from the
bar. The true Notting Hill resident will probably pop in for the 'Cow
special' – six Irish oysters and a pint of Guinness, in the bar.

E&O

14 Blenheim Crescent, W11 ■ 020 7229 5454

⊖ Ladbroke Grove

⦿ Asian eclectic

🕐 Mon to Fri 12.15–15.00 & 18.15–23.00; Sat 12.15–16.00 & 18.15–23.00; Sun 13.00–16.00 & 18.15–20.30

🖰 www.eando.nu

🖶 all major credit cards ■ 12.5% optional service added

££ starters £4.50–£6.50 (dim sum) ■ mains £9.50–£27 ■ sides £3–£4.50 ■ desserts £5–£6.50 ■ lowest bottle price £13.50

✪ E&O stands for Eastern & Oriental

It must be hard for a resto like E&O to make the transition from hot new destination to well-established local hero. Even the kind of non-traditional eating that started out here is now commonplace as grazing sweeps London's restos. Cooking is based on Japanese with added influences. The venue itself is modern Japanese in feel, and forks, knives, spoons and chopsticks sit in stone pots on the table. Staff are knowledgeable and take trouble to explain if you're unfamiliar with dishes or the spirit of the place. But even more than the taste, it is the presentation of the food that makes it exceptional. The menu divides into soups, dim sum, salads, tempura, curries, futo maki rolls/sashimi, barbecue/roasts, specials, sides and desserts. Edamame, soy and mirin is a dish of soybeans in the pod to pop and suck out. Fun and delicious. Among the dumplings, chicken and snow pea gyosa, and mushroom and chestnut, green tea dumplings stand out. Chilli-salt squid is well-seasoned, crispy squid served in a Japanese newspaper cone, while baby pork spareribs come with a sauce good enough to eat with a spoon. In the barbecue/roasts section, black cod with sweet miso is as good as this fish gets. Under curries you'll find sour orange monkfish. When you get to the puds you must choose from ices; chocolate pudding (which comes with a 20-minute wait); and a shockingly trans-cultural ginger tiramisù. Wines are well chosen and reasonably priced, and there's a selection of six teas served in large Chinese pots. Can't get a table? Opt for the dim sum served in the bar.

→ For branches, see index

Galicia

323 Portobello Road, W10 ▪ 020 8969 3539

⊖ Ladbroke Grove

🍴 Spanish/tapas

🕐 Tues to Sat 12.00–15.00 & 19.00–23.30; Sun 12.00–15.30 & 19.30–22.30

🖫 all major credit cards ▪ no service added

££ tapas £2.95–£6 ▪ mains £8–£12 ▪ sides £2.75 ▪ desserts £2.75 ▪ lowest bottle price £9.50

⭐ Experience the Spanish side of W10

Ambling up the Portobello Road, it would be only too easy to walk straight past Galicia – this restaurant has that strange Continental quality of looking shut even when it's open. Make it through the forbidding entrance, however, and Galicia opens out into a bar (which is in all probability crowded), which in turn opens into a small, 40-seat restaurant (which is in all probability full). The tapas at the bar are straightforward and good, so it is no surprise that quite a lot of customers get no further than here. First secure your table, then cut a swathe through the starters. Jamón is a large plate of sweet, air-dried ham; gambas a la plancha are giant prawns plainly grilled; pulpo a la Gallega is a revelation – slices of octopus grilled until bafflingly tender and powdered with smoky pimentón. Galicia does straightforward grilled fish and meat very well indeed. Look for the chuleto de cordera a la plancha, which are perfect lamb chops; or lomo de cerdo, which are very thin slices of pork fillet in a sauce with pimentón. Or there's the suitably stolid Spanish omelette, tortilla. And you should have some chips, which are very good here. Galicia is a pleasant place without pretension. The wine list may have the occasional lurking bargain – older, and overlooked, Spanish vintages at prices that have stayed reasonable. The waiters are all old-school – quiet and efficient to the point of near-grumpiness – and the overall feel is of a certain stilted formality. The clientele is an agreeable mix of Notting Hillites and homesick Iberians, both of which groups stand between you and that table reservation, so book early.

Kensington Place

201–207 Kensington Church Street, W8 ■ 020 7727 3184 ♿

⊖ Notting Hill Gate

🍴 Modern British

🕐 Mon to Sat 12.00–15.30 & 18.30–23.45; Sun 12.00–15.30 & 18.30–22.15

🔗 www.egami.com

🗄 all major credit cards ■ 12.5% optional service added

££ starters £6–£12.50 ■ mains £12.50–£28.50 ■ sides £3 ■ desserts £7.50 ■ set lunch Mon to Fri £18.50 & Sunday £21.50 ■ set dinner £24.50 & £39.50 (with matched wines) ■ lowest bottle price £14

✪ Mighty fine neighbourhood stalwart

The first thing to know about Kensington Place is that it is noisy – the dining room is large, echoing, glass-fronted and noisy with the racket of hordes of people having a good time. The service is crisp, the food is good and the prices are fair. The menu changes from session to session to reflect whatever the market has to offer, and there is a set lunch that offers a limited choice of three good courses throughout the week, and a set dinner with the option of matched wines. Rowley Leigh's food is eclectic in the best possible way. The kitchen starts with the laudable premise that there is nothing better than what is in season, and goes on to combine Mediterranean inspirations with classic French and English dishes. Thus you may find, in due season, starters such as carrot soup with risotto and dill; endive, beetroot and orange salad; or omelette fines herbes. These are sophisticated dishes, and well-chosen combinations of flavours. Main courses (depending on the season) might be mackerel roast to a crisp and served on a bed of potatoes and apples; a perfectly roast partridge; roast white asparagus with pimentón and pepper cream; or roast baby lamb with persillade. The dessert section of the menu offers what some hold to be London's finest lemon tart and a selection of well-made ice creams. There are also traditional favourites with a twist: Beaujolais pears with Financiers, or a hot bitter chocolate mousse. Service is attentive and your meal will swing along in a jolly and businesslike fashion.

The Ledbury

127 Ledbury Road, W11 ■ 020 7792 9090

⊖ Westbourne Park

|●| French

⏱ Mon to Fri 12.00–14.30 & 18.30–22.45; Sat 18.30–22.45

🖰 www.theledbury.com

🖶 all major credit cards ■ 12.5% optional service added

££ lunch £19.50 (2 courses) & £24.50 (3 courses) ■ dinner £44 (3 courses) ■ tasting menu £55 (8 courses) ■ lowest bottle price £17.50

✪ Into the front rank ... from a standing start

The last time the Ledbury had plenty of spare seats available was during the week it opened in 2005. Restaurateur Nigel Platts Martin is unusual in that he never opens a new resto until he is absolutely ready. The chef here is Brett Graham, who served time at head office (The Square, page 90), and his food is sophisticated, elegant to look at and well balanced, all of which translates as extremely good. What is most impressive is the instant maturity achieved here; already the Ledbury seems like a tried and tested, highly polished old-timer. Starters include a lasagne of rabbit and girolles with a velouté of thyme – a dish that quickly became the critics' favourite; a parsley soup with mousserons, wild wood sorrel and frog leg beignets; or roast scallops with pumpkin purée. Main courses are equally complex – a roast Dover sole comes with a gratin of macaroni, cockscombs, chicken wings and pine nuts; a fillet of beef is teamed with a red wine sauce and a croustillant of snails, oxtail and celeriac; or perhaps an assiette of lamb with borlotti beans, artichokes and herb oil appeals? The cooking is accomplished, flavours are upfront and textures varied. The wine list is comprehensive, but the wine service manages the trick of being both informal and knowledgeable. Puds are seriously ambitious – jasmine tea and milk chocolate Chantilly with hazelnut dacquoise and milk ice cream; a tarte fine of figs with truffle honey ice cream; or raspberry soufflé with mascarpone and lemon verbena. The Ledbury delivers very good French food in an elegant dining room and at a price that represents good value – even if the bill seems more West End than W11.

Lucky Seven

127 Westbourne Park Road, W2 ■ 020 7727 6771

⊖ Westbourne Park

|◉| North American

⏱ Mon to Thurs 11.00–23.00; Fri & Sat 09.00–23.00; Sun 09.00–22.30

🃏 all major credit cards except AmEx ■ 12.5% optional service added

££ breakfast £4.95–£7.95 ■ mains £5–£9 ■ sides £3.50–£5 ■ desserts £4–£5 ■ blue plate specials £8–£12 ■ lowest bottle price £15

✪ American diner given Notting Hill gloss

Following the success of The Cow (see p. 97), Tom Conran shifted his attention a few hundred yards up the road to a site that was previously a shabby café-restaurant-drinking den and set up Lucky Seven. The kitchen runs across the back behind a high counter and the tiny dining area accommodates 36 people in two sets of booths. There are engraved mirrors. A Pepsi clock. Sally didn't meet Harry here, but doubtless she will soon. The menu is on a pegboard over the kitchen and it opens with breakfast dishes: two eggs any style; with sausage; with bacon; with Portobello mushrooms – wending its way through omelettes and eggs Benedict to buttermilk pancakes. Then there's a section of 'soups, stews, salads, sides' before it moves towards 'sandwiches and fries'. In the evening there's a blue plate special dish, which ranges from club sandwich to gammon and eggs. For chips choose between 'fat' and 'French fries'. The burgers are well made, although on the small side for serious trenchers – but, as they start at a reasonable price with the 'Classic hamburger', perhaps that is best resolved by ordering two separate Classics or a special with an extra patty of meat. In the stews section you will come across such delights as New England clam chowder, and a Cuban black bean chilli (both of which are sold in two sizes, by the cup or by the bowl). And then there are salads – Cobb, Caesar and 'Garden of Eden', plus the ominously but accurately named 'Exterminator chilli'. Sounds like fair warning.

Nyonya

2a Kensington Park Road, W11 ▪ 020 7243 1800

⊖ Notting Hill Gate

🍽 Malaysian/Chinese

🕐 Mon to Fri 11.30–15.00 & 18.30–22.30; Sat & Sun 11.30–22.30

🖰 www.nyonya.co.uk

🖶 all major credit cards ▪ no service added

££ starters £4.50–£8 ▪ mains £6.50–£8.50 ▪ desserts £3.50 ▪ set lunch £8 ▪ lowest bottle price £13.50

✪ Fast food meets Malay home cooking

Nyonya is ultra modern, sensibly cheap and seriously informal and all of the above gains added piquancy as the cuisine is downright moody. The French may crow about traditional 'cuisine grandmère' but the Straits Malays are just as proud of their 'nyonyas' who have much the same credentials. In Nyonya dishes you'll find plenty of coconut cream, some chilli heat, souring from tamarind, and that musty-savoury tang you get from fish sauce or blachan – the seriously stinky shrimp paste. The room is light and bright, and considering how modern everything looks, the stools are surprisingly comfortable. There are four, long, curved tables, so sharing is the order of the day. Service is friendly and the food arrives briskly. Starters include the ubiquitous chicken satay and it is well done here. The dumplings are good, especially if you splash out on a small saucer of 'sambal blachan' – a red sludge made from prawns and chillies, not over-the-top hot, but it does add a welcome belt of heat. Main courses come in decent portions. Beef rendang arrives in a clump, and so it should – this dish should be served almost dry with the coconut sauce reduced to a paste. Upfront flavours. A dish of cashew nut prawns is agreeably mild. It's worth ordering the nyonya fried rice, which is very rich and sticky and contains a variety of odds and ends – shrimp, chicken, peas, egg. There is also a long list of 'hawker favourites' that includes several 'meals-in-a-bowl' – a Penang Assam laksa, or hokkien prawn mee soup. It is hard to oppose a cold Tiger beer with this kind of spicy food.

Osteria Basilico

29 Kensington Park Road, W11 ■ 020 7727 9372

⊖ Ladbroke Grove

¶O¶ Italian

🕔 Mon to Fri 12.00–15.00 & 18.30–23.30; Sat 12.00–16.00 & 18.30–23.30; Sun 12.30–15.30 & 18.30–22.30

🖰 www.osteriabasilico.co.uk

🖶 all major credit cards ■ 12.5% optional service added

££ starters £7.50–£8.50 ■ pasta £7.50–£13.50 ■ mains £12.80–£16.50 ■ sides £3–£4.50 ■ desserts £4–£5.50 ■ lowest bottle price £10.50

✪ Laid-back, neighbourhood Italian

Osteria opened in 1992 and has flourished ever since. Daytime star-gazing is enlivened by arguments between parking wardens, clampers and their victims, while the traffic comes to a standstill for the unloading of lorries and for a constant stream of minicabs dropping off at the street's numerous restaurants. At dusk you get more of the same, with the streetlights struggling to make the heart of Portobello look like the Via Veneto. Inside, pizza and pasta are speedily delivered with typical chirpy Italian panache to cramped, scrubbed tables. Go easy on the baskets of warm pizza bread, since the antipasti – various grilled and preserved titbits arranged on the antique dresser – are a tempting self-service affair. Of the other starters, the carpaccio di manzo con pesto, rucola e Parmigiano (cured beef with pesto, rocket and Parmesan) is delicious. Specials change daily and have no particular regional influence – perhaps there is a classic such as fettuccine con tartufo bianco, Parmigiano e salsa al rosmarino, fettuccine with white truffle, Parmesan and rosemary. Among the permanent fixtures, spigola alla griglia con olio aromatizzato is a simply grilled sea bass; and carre d'agnello al forno con patate arrosto is roast rack of lamb cutlets with roast potatoes. Pizzas vary in size depending on who is in the kitchen – perhaps staff with shorter arms throw the dough higher, resulting in a wider, thinner base – but all are on the formidable side of large. The wine list has a good many sound Italian wines and at pretty decent prices.

Sport London & Benfica

988 Harrow Road, NW10 ■ 020 8964 5142

⊖ Westbourne Park

🍴 Portuguese

🕐 daily 11.00–23.00

🗗 all major credit cards ■ no optional service added

££ starters £1–£6.50 ■ mains £8.50–£17 ■ desserts £2–£2.50 ■ lowest bottle price £9

✪ Football on the telly, football in the soul

A quarter of a century ago 'Sport London & Benfica' was a successful football team based in W11 – then they moved their base up to 988 Harrow Road and set up a large restaurant, a no-frills bar and club room. In the resto all the customers watch football on large-screen tellies. The food is very good, honest, straightforward, giant portions, uncompromising. The starters range from the familiar – deep-fried squid; ham; melon with ham, to the odd – ordering chourico assado brings a ribbed earthenware dish with two substantial chorizo sausages on it. As it is placed on the table, the waiter casually flicks his cigarette lighter and a deep pool of eau de vie is set alight under the sausages. The star starter is the ameijoa à marinheira, a plate of stunning fresh clams swimming bravely through a butter sauce. For mains, fish gets priority – fourteen fish dishes, including the classic dish for two arroz de marisco, shellfish rice. The portions are daunting; bacalhau na brasa is salt cod soaked in water and milk to de-salt it and then grilled before being served with boiled potatoes. On the meat side of things posta à Mirandesa is subtitled 'big beef cube'. You get about 500g of perfectly cooked rump steak cut about 3cm thick and dressed with oil, herbs, green onion and garlic. This may be London's best-value steak. The wines come from Portugal and are gently priced. Puddings are very serious, try the Molotov – a sort of baked-egg yolk mousse with a caramel dressing. Even if you are not Portuguese, everyone here will make you very welcome … but if you are not a football fanatic it is probably best not to mention the fact. They would find that very puzzling.

Taqueria

139–143 Westbourne Grove, W11 ■ 020 7229 4734

⊖ Notting Hill Gate

🍴 Mexican

🕐 Mon to Sun 12.00–15.30 & 17.30–23.00

🖰 www.coolchiletaqueria.com

🖫 all major credit cards except AmEx ■ no service added

££ small dishes £1–£5 ■ large dishes £10–£11 ■ sides £1–£3 ■ desserts £3.50 ■ lowest bottle price £14.50

✪ Any time is taco time

Dodie Miller (chilli fanatic and proprietor of importers the Cool Chile Company) opened her first restaurant in 2005 and this is it. The Taqueria took over from an old-established but chaotic Sudanese establishment and is certainly a more stylish affair. Granted it is still a tad utilitarian on the design front, but the Taqueria offers workmanlike food at accessible prices and seems to strike a chord with the locals since it is a busy place. The menu suggests that you graze your way through between two and four small dishes per person and given that there are plenty of unfamiliar things on offer it seems sensible. Under 'antojitos' (snacks) you'll find jicama sticks – these are large, cold chips cut from a tuber that has a bland taste but the crisp crunch of a giant water chestnut, dusted with hot chilli powder. Or there's ceviche, sea bass 'cooked' by marinating it in lime juice. Or there are stuffed chillies – helpfully subtitled chilli roulette – these little chillies vary in hotness, some are mild but every now and then you get a real whizzer that's Hades hot. The ready-made tacos range from al pastor, slow roast pork, to achiote sea bass; chargrilled skirt steak; and chargrilled flat cap mushroom. You can order the sea bass or the steak as large 'self-assembly' platters and build your own tacos. Tostadas range from chicken and crumbly cheese, to beef salpicon, a well-made salad of shredded beef plus avocado on a tortilla. The side dishes are worth investigation: garlicky greens is a good dish. The refried beans are dark and sludgy – those learned writings about cooking beans with the herb epazote and so avoiding the flatulent results are all hot air!

Tong Ka Nom Thai

833 Harrow Road, NW10 ■ 020 8964 5373

⊖ Kensal Green

🍽 Thai

🕐 Mon to Fri 12.00–15.00 & 18.00–22.00; Sat 18.00–22.00

🗗 cash or cheque only ■ no service added

££ starters £4–£4.50 ■ mains £4–£4.50 ■ sides £1.30–£3.50 ■ desserts £2.50 ■ Unlicensed, BYO (but buy soft drinks)

✪ Cheerful Thai cafe

At its best, Thai cuisine means intense and distinct flavours, a concept that so many establishments selling Thai grub seem to have mislaid. However, the good news is that fresh, cheap and authentic Thai food is alive and well and living on the Harrow Road. Tong Ka Nom Thai is a small and garish Thai restaurant with a wonderful view of the railway tracks. It is implausibly cheap, the food is very good, and the service friendly. For an astonishingly modest outlay you get six well-spiced tod mun (delightfully chewy Thai fishcakes); or eight popia tod (well-made mini vegetarian spring rolls); or six goong hompha, which are prawns in filo. But the star turn is gai bai toey – six morsels of chicken that are marinated, wrapped in pandan leaf and then fried; they are seriously good. The curries are splendid. And splendidly cheap. Gaeng kheaw wan is a well-made green curry that comes with a choice of main ingredients. Other options are a red curry, a yellow curry and a 'jungle curry'. The house speciality is called 'boneless fish fillet'. This is a large hunk of tilapia that comes in a mesmerizing light and elegant sauce with plenty of holy basil. The sauces here are good – not thickened to a sludge with cornflour, but rich on their own account. You'll need some rice and you should have a noodle dish – perhaps the pad phrik, which is well balanced. At Tong Ka Nom Thai they serve delicious and authentic Thai food. It is truly remarkable that they can do so at what are almost Thai prices.

Piccadilly and St James's

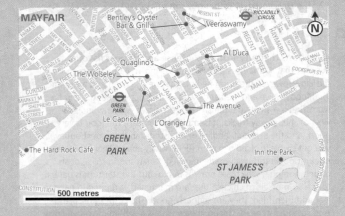

The Avenue

7–9 St James's Street, SW1 ■ 020 7321 2111   ♿

⊖ Green Park

🍴 Modern British

🕐 Mon to Fri 12.00–15.00 & 17.45–24.00; Sat 17.45–24.45; Sun 12.00–15.30 & 17.45–22.00

🖰 www.theavenue.co.uk

🖩 all major credit cards ■ 12.5% service added

££ starters £6–£10 ■ mains £13–£20 ■ sides £4 ■ desserts £6.50 ■ prix fixe menu £17.95 & £19.95 ■ lowest bottle price £16

⭐ Stark yet stylish, a busy barn of a place

The Avenue was one of the first banker-led restaurants in London – a bunch of City folk set up the kind of restaurant where they would choose to eat – which may be the first recorded instance of investors putting their mouths where their money was. This strategy was a great success and now the Avenue is part of a sprawling empire, which includes Kensington Place (see p. 100) and Circus (see p. 133), to name just two. The entrance is through a large glass door (part of a great glass plate fronting the restaurant), and your greeting will be from designer-clad hosts. Inside it's a very buzzy place with an upbeat atmosphere, dominated by a bar that is much more cocktail than aperitif. The cooking is well executed and the menu is a fashionable mix of English and the Med, leavened with a few comforting dishes to appeal to the inner banker. First courses are generally light and bright: chicken consommé and mushroom ravioli; escarole, Roquefort and pear salad; pickled herring with warm potato pancake and scallion sour cream; or Vietnamese prawn and papaya salad. Main courses may include salmon fishcakes with dill butter sauce; roast bream with artichokes, red pepper confit and thyme; salt beef with bubble and squeak and charcuterie sauce; grilled lamb steaks with soft polenta and slow-roast onions; or calf's liver with champ and devils on horseback. Puddings range from jam roly-poly with custard; through lemon tart; and flourless chocolate fudge pudding with clotted cream; to chocolate and honeycomb semifreddo.

Bentley's Oyster Bar & Grill

11 Swallow Street, W1 ■ 020 7734 4756

⊖ Piccadilly Circus

🍽 British/fish

🕐 (Oyster Bar) Mon to Sat 12.00–24.00; Sun 12.00–14.30; (Restaurant) Mon to Sat 12.00–14.30 & 17.30–23.00; Sun 17.30–22.30

🗗 all major credit cards ■ 12.5% optional service added

££ starters £5.75–£26 ■ mains £12–£23 ■ desserts £6.50–£9.50 ■ lowest bottle price £14

✪ Classic restaurant re-born

Strangely enough, the new Bentley's is a restaurant that pays homage to the old Bentley's. Richard Corrigan is the ebullient chef/proprietor of the Lindsay House (see p. 141) and he has refurbed Bentley's in a way that is both sensitive and very effective. Downstairs there is both a charming bar and the famous oyster bar; upstairs there is the more formal dining room. The oyster bar has the best feel to it, the craic is good here! So are the oysters. Downstairs the menu is a tad shorter and all fish, upstairs half a dozen meat dishes are added. Everything is underpinned by Corrigan's obsession with carefully sourced, top-quality ingredients. The smoked salmon comes from Frank Hederman in Ireland, the fillet of beef comes from West Cork. From the starters the smoked sturgeon with crème fraîche is teamed with delicate miniature blinis; there's a Mediterranean fish soup; and home-cured herrings with warm potato and grape mustard. From the fish dishes the Bentley's fish pie is worth noting; also the breaded fillet of plaice with tartare sauce – what a delicious and meaty fish plaice can be. Or you could opt for a classic Dover sole; or zander with smoked eel and pickled cabbage. And hurrah! There are savouries on the menu: a Guinness rarebit, or perhaps a Crozier Blue cheese that has been soaked in Banyuls. Puds range from delightful steamed stodge to vanilla ice cream with rosehip sauce. The wine list is accommodating, if pitched at Piccadilly prices. A very good place to eat.

Le Caprice

Arlington House, Arlington Street, SW1 ■ 020 7629 2239 ♿

⊖ Green Park

🍴 Modern European

🕐 Mon to Sat 12.00–15.00 & 17.30–24.00; Sun 12.00–15.30 & 18.00–24.00

🔗 www.capriceholdings.co.uk

💳 all major credit cards ■ no service added

££ starters £5.75–£15.75 ■ mains £14.25–£26.50 ■ sides £3.25–£5.75 ■ desserts £6.25–£7.50 ■ lowest bottle price £15

✪ Establishment comfort zone

Every London socialite worthy of the label is a regular at this deeply chic little restaurant and everyone from royalty downwards uses it for the occasional quiet lunch or dinner. That's not because they'll be hounded by well-wishers or because photographers will be waiting outside. They won't. This restaurant is discreet enough to make an oyster seem a blabbermouth. It's not even particularly plush or comfortable, with a black-and-white-tiled floor, a big black bar and cane seats. What keeps Le Caprice full day in, day out is an amazing level of personal service, properly prepared food and a bill that holds no surprises. The much-imitated menu is enticing from the first glance. Plum tomato and basil galette is simplicity itself. Crispy duck comes with watercress salad, while dressed Dorset crab with celeriac remoulade is very fresh and clean. In season there are splendid specials – River Spey sea trout with steamed clams and parsley. Or perhaps Tamworth pork chop with white asparagus and rosemary butter. Or there may be loin of yellow fin tuna with spiced lentils. This kitchen expends time and effort on finding small producers and securing the best of everything. If you are still up for pudding, try banana sticky toffee pudding, or the baked Alaska with cherries and Kirsch to see just what classic English puds are about. In the winter there is an array of more solid rib-stickers. Expense aside, the only trouble with Le Caprice is the struggle to get a table. Try booking well in advance, or go for a last-minute place at the bar.

Al Duca

4–5 Duke of York Street, SW1 ■ 020 7839 3090

⊖ Piccadilly

¶●¶ Italian

⊕ Mon to Fri 12.00–14.30 & 18.00–23.00; Sat 12.30–15.00 & 18.00–23.00; Sun 18.00–22.30

⌁ www.alduca-restaurant.co.uk

⊟ all major credit cards ■ 12.5% service added

££ lunch £18.50 (2 courses), £21.50 (3 courses) & £24.50 (4 courses)
■ dinner £21.50 (2 courses), £24.50 (3 courses) & £29 (4 courses)
■ lowest bottle price £16

✪ Low prices, high standards

With this kind of deal it's best not to think London – think Italy. You get high-quality, sophisticated food, an agreeable setting, slick service, and all at modest prices – what you get here seems to be far more than you pay for. Such regularly changing menus are commonplace in Italy and you can only speculate as to why they are not more widely available in London. The entire menu changes regularly and has a seasonal bias to it. There are six or more starters at Al Duca: dishes such as chargrilled marinated mixed vegetables with balsamic vinegar, or pan-fried wild mushrooms with chicken livers, bacon and crisp polenta. Then there is a raft of dishes under the heading pasta: home-made fettuccine with rabbit ragù and black olives; linguine with clams and garlic; or reginette with peas and bacon. This is followed by an array of main courses: pan-fried salmon with poached potatoes in butter and spinach with balsamic; sea bass; chicken. Finally, six desserts, ranging from a stracchino cheesecake with acacia honey to a classic almond and pear tart. Or you could try the dessert called seadas, 'puff pastry ravioli with ricotta and honey'. The standard of cooking is high, with dishes bringing off that difficult trick of being both deceptively simple and satisfyingly rich. Overall there is much to praise here, and the slick service and stylish ambience live up to the efforts in the kitchen; best of all, you get an opportunity to have a multi-course meal. This is the place to try four courses Italian-style.

The Hard Rock Café

150 Old Park Lane, W1 ■ 020 7629 0382 ♿

⊖ Hyde Park Corner

🍴 North American/burgers

🕐 Mon to Thurs & Sun 11.30–24.00; Fri & Sat 11.30–01.00

🖥 www.hardrock.com

🗄 all major credit cards ■ 12.5% optional service added to bills over £30

££ starters £3.95–£7.50 ■ mains £8–£9 ■ sides £1.95–£3.25 ■ desserts £4–£6 ■ lowest bottle price £12

✪ Burger palace – the original and genuine

The 'Museum and memorabilia' outlet is over the road in what was once Coutts bank, which just about says it all. The Hard Rock Café was one of the first restos to understand both merchandising and the tourist market. This place is the original theme restaurant, and as such a hard act to follow. The queue out front is legendary. There's no booking and you'll find a queue almost all day long, every day of the year. Once in, there is a great atmosphere, created by full-on rock music, dim lighting and walls dripping with rock memorabilia. The Hard Rock food is not bad, either, predominantly Tex-Mex and burgers. Scanning the menu is a serious business here – dishes get short but complex essays attached to them – so Tupelo chicken tenders are explained as 'boneless chicken tenders, lightly breaded and coated in our Classic Rock (medium), Heavy Metal (hot) sauce or tangy Bar-B-Que sauce. Served with celery and Bleu cheese dressing'. The job of copywriter is an important one here. The burgers cover the spectrum from HRC burger to the hickory Bar-B-Que bacon cheeseburger. Veggies are catered for by the HRC veggie sandwich. Further along, among the Smokehouse Specialities, there's the pig sandwich and Bruce's famous Bar-B-Que ribs. Puddings are self-indulgent, and the hot fudge brownie elevates goo to an art form. If sweet is truly your thing there's a shooter called 'bubblegum' – Bailey's, blue curaçao, banana liqueur!

Inn the Park

St James's Park, SW1 ■ 020 7451 9999

⊖ St James's Park

|◉| British

◷ daily 08.00–23.00

🖰 www.innthepark.co.uk

🖶 all major credit cards ■ 12.5% service added

££ breakfast £2.50–£12.50 ■ starters £5–£12.50 ■ mains £12.50–£18.50 ■ desserts £5.50–£6 ■ afternoon tea, bookings taken for parties of 10 or more ■ lowest bottle price £15

✪ Kicks park catering into the next century

This building is stunning – like the dwelling of an A-list hobbit. There are lots of gentle curves, plenty of wood, and everything is built into a grassy mound. The food is good, too – British produce, commendably fresh, unfussy presentation and simply cooked. This place opens for breakfast, then serves snacks, then lunch, then afternoon tea, then dinner. The waiting staff seem friendly and service is slick – which will all come as something of a shock to anyone accustomed to the hot-dog-from-a-barrow that used to be the only kind of sustenance available within the park. Breakfast ranges from a boiled egg and soldier, to a duck egg on sourdough, the Great British breakfast and 'poor knights of Windsor' – which rather disappointingly is French toast, or eggy bread to you and me. The tea comes in pots, pots with real leaves in. At lunch and dinner the 'proper' cooking is well done: wild garlic and potato soup; jellied ham hock and parsley terrine; oxtail with purple sprouting broccoli; seared salmon with a warm salad of potatoes and Denhay bacon. There are also home-made ice creams and farmhouse cheeses from Neal's Yard. The afternoon tea of sandwiches, cakes and scones is a serious contender, and even the snacks appeal – 'plate of British cured and cooked meats with chutneys and pickles'. What good, honest food and what a splendid place to eat it, and due to a change in policy you can make bookings for any time.

Quaglino's

16 Bury Street, SW1 ▪ 020 7930 6767   &

⊖ Green Park

|◉| Modern British

🕐 Mon to Thurs 12.00–15.00 & 17.30–23.30; Fri & Sat 12.00–15.00 & 17.30–01.30; Sun 12.00–15.00 & 17.30–23.00

⌁ www.conran.com

🗗 all major credit cards ▪ 12.5% service added

££ starters £6–£16.50 ▪ crustacean £6.50–£31 ▪ mains £10–£29.50 ▪ sides £3–£4.50 ▪ desserts £4–£7 ▪ prix fixe lunch & pre-/post-theatre £17.50 & £19 ▪ lowest bottle price £14.75

✪ Spiritual home of the Essex crowd

In 1929 Giovanni Quaglino opened a restaurant in Bury Street that became an instant success and the one thing it had, above all else, was glamour. His other claim to fame was that he was the first restaurateur to offer a hot dish as hors d'oeuvre. When Sir Terence Conran redesigned and reopened Quaglino's, more than 60 years later, his vision was essentially the same. The ambience is still impressive – an elegant reception, the sweeping staircase into the bar that overlooks the main restaurant, and the second stairway down to restaurant level. If this kind of thing rings your bell you will be happy here. The menu is simple, classy and brasserie-style, with very little to scare off the less experienced diner. The plateau de fruits de mer (extravagantly priced and for a minimum of two people) is as good as you would hope, as is the whole lobster mayonnaise. Fish and chips is served with home-made chips and tartare sauce and is excellent, while a 42-day-aged Glen Fyne sirloin steak is a treat when served properly cooked, as it is here. Puddings are straightforward and agreeably predictable – blackcurrant parfait; apple Charlotte, clotted cream. Quaglino's staff can be brusque, but then marshalling large numbers of glamour-seekers is a testing job. You can avoid this altogether by staying in the bar, which offers highlights from the menu – including all the seafood. Furthermore, Quag's is open late, which makes it perfect for a genuine after-theatre dinner.

Veeraswamy

Victory House, 99 Regent Street, W1 ■ 020 7734 1401

⊖ Piccadilly Circus

|●| Indian

🕘 Mon to Thurs 12.00–14.30 & 17.30–23.00; Fri 12.00–14.30 & 17.30–23.30; Sat 12.30–15.00 & 17.30–23.30; Sun 12.30–15.00 & 18.00–22.30

🖰 www.realindianfood.com

🗗 all major credit cards ■ 12.5% service

££ starters £5.50–£10.50 ■ mains £11.50–£26 ■ sides £3.50–£6.50 ■ desserts £5.50 ■ set lunch & pre-/post-theatre £13.50 & £15.50 ■ Indian Sunday lunch £16 ■ lowest bottle price £16.50

⭐ London's oldest Indian restaurant

Ever since it opened in the 1920s, Veeraswamy has been a magnet to lovers of Indian food. It was opened by Edward Palmer (a bright young man keen to capitalise on his success providing Indian food for the Empire Exhibition), and under various owners managed to cling to its reputation as a society restaurant until the 1960s. Today it is part of the Masalaworld Group and it recently emerged from a thorough redesign to successfully recapture some of the glitz and glamour of the early days. The room is elegant, the chairs are comfortable, the lighting is subtle and dramatic. The food is very good indeed, the dishes are drawn from several regions and the cuisine of Maharajahs jostles with street food. Start with the green leaf bhajias – an amazing mini-haystack of herbs given a tempura-like treatment in the lightest possible batter. Sholay chicken tikka is smoky and very subtle. The duck seekh kebab is well spiced. The giant 'green prawns' are huge and juicy. From the mains choose the chicken chatpatta – rich with tomato and spices; or the sea bream paturi, fillets of fish in a mustard marinade steamed in banana leaf; or the stunning Hyderabadi lamb biryani. Breads are exemplary. Puds are interesting if you dodge the over-sweet trad Indian confections. Service is friendly; advice is freely given and worth taking.

The Wolseley

160 Piccadilly, W1 ■ 020 7499 6996

⊖ Green Park

🍴 European

🕐 daily 07.00–11.30 (breakfast) (09.00–11.30 Sat & Sun); 15.00–17.30 (tea) (15.30–18.00 Sat & Sun); (restaurant) 12.00–14.30 & 17.00–24.00

🔗 www.thewolseley.com

🗄 all major credit cards ■ no service added

££ breakfast £1.75–£26.50 ■ starters £5.25–£17.25 ■ mains £6.50–£28.50 ■ desserts £4–£6.75 ■ afternoon tea £7.25 & £17.50 ■ lowest bottle price £15.50

⭐ A European Grand Café docks in Piccadilly

Christopher Corbin and Jeremy King are the best known double act in London restaurants. They are the people who developed the Caprice (see p. 111), nursed the Ivy (see p. 32) back to health, and revived J. Sheekey (see p. 33) before retiring. Then they un-retired and opened the Wolseley, turning what was once a car showroom into a buzzing restaurant. The room is tall and theatrical, gloriously dramatic. The atmosphere is 'celebrity chic' and the feel of the place owes plenty to middle European grand cafés, as does the menu. One enterprising critic started with breakfast, and then stayed for elevenses, lunch, afternoon tea and dinner – it's probably the one sure way to secure a table for dinner! This place is so busy that it is very hard to get into, but worth it. Try early or late. The food is good here – unfussy, old-fashioned, and well presented. There are good reports about the breakfast, the cakes and pastries. Starters include some nostalgic numbers such as chopped liver; steak tartare; and half a dozen escargots. There are salads, such as frisée aux lardons; shellfish, including dressed Cornish crab; soufflé Suisse. Onwards! Nürnberger bratwurst and potato salad; grilled Dover sole; a hamburger; spit-roast suckling pig. There is even a classically presented Wiener Holstein complete with crossed anchovies and fried egg. Among the puds are a Vacherin Mont Blanc, a 'fruit bowl' and serious ice-cream coupes. The wine list is comprehensive. The service is slick and the celebrity count is very high.

Queensway and Westbourne Grove

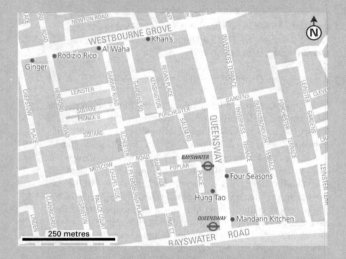

Four Seasons

84 Queensway, W2 ■ 020 7229 4320

🚇 Queensway/Bayswater

🍴 Chinese

🕐 Mon to Sat 12.00–23.15; Sun 12.00–22.45

🗂 all major credit cards ■ 12.5% service added

££ starters £1.80–£16.50 ■ mains £4.50–£13.50 ■ sides £2.80–£16.50
■ desserts £1.20–£2.80 ■ set menus £13.50–£18 ■ lowest bottle
price £9

⭐ Genuine Chinese food, good value

The Four Seasons is an old-established restaurant that has always had a special reputation for roast duck. Something reinforced by the mound of roasted ducks in the window. As with so many good Chinese restaurants, there is a stream of rumours concerning the Four Seasons – maybe that the chef has moved to a neighbouring eatery, that the duck oven has been changed, and anything else diners care to invent. But standards seem high, and they seem to stay high. That doesn't mean that service won't be brusque and that the front of house won't look at you blankly when you claim to have made a reservation. Be prepared to sit, order, eat and have a bill slapped on the table in short order. The food is good; starters tick all the boxes from crispy seaweed to steamed scallops. The barbecued meats are splendid – the roast duck is meaty with a crisp skin; the crispy pork has a salty savoury bark that shatters in the mouth. The menu wanders on through familiar and unfamiliar dishes; turn to the chef's specials: 'stuffed bitter melon with salted fish and minced pork' is a triumph – very bitter and very rich. Or there's that hot pot classic 'double-cooked belly pork with yam' – everything melted down to a glorious mix of flavours. There are plenty of adventures to be had without going as far as 'duck's feet with sea cucumber and fish lips in hot pot'. A fine and workmanlike Chinese restaurant where the menu has not been dumbed-down.

Ginger

115 Westbourne Grove, W2 ■ 020 7908 1990

⊖ Bayswater/Notting Hill Gate

|●| Indian

⏰ Mon to Fri 17.00–23.00; Sat 12.00–24.00

🖰 www.gingerrestaurant.co.uk

🖫 all major credit cards ■ 12.5% service added

££ starters £3.25–£7.95 ■ mains £7.50–£12.95 ■ sides £3.95–£4.50 ■ desserts £3.95–£4.50 ■ set meals £10–£25 ■ lowest bottle price £11.95

✪ Real Bangladeshi food goes upscale

Given that nearly every curry house on nearly every high street in the land is owned and manned by Bangladeshi businessmen you might think that Ginger, which serves traditional Bangladeshi food, would be pretty run-of-the-mill. Until you eat there, that is. This is a restaurant that offers genuine Bangladeshi home cooking. Not the sweet and tomatoey dishes worked up to suit the British palate, but the real deal. Expect lots of fish dishes, and delicious light stews (known as jhols). Plus attentive service, a thoughtful wine list and some slick cocktails. But, most important of all, the men in the kitchen really know their stuff. There are some stunning dishes. Start with the shingara – imagine a solid vegetable samosa that has been made with shortcrust pastry, like a deep-fried pasty. The katti kebab is also good (roast lamb in a kind of wrap). The difficult choices continue among the main courses. Surma macher biryani is epic – a fish biryani. Bangladeshis are besotted with fish – try the macher kobiraji, which is an aromatic fish curry from West Bengal. Carry on to the raj ash kalia, which is a Bengali stir-fry of duck, or the moni puri prawns, a dish named after one of the tribespeople of Bangladesh. There are a good many prawn dishes on the menu – try the ajwani chingr jhol, which presents king prawns in a thin sauce that is both hot and sour. Lau dal is a revelation: moong lentils cooked with white pumpkin and garlic. The parathas are very good – flaky and suitably self-indulgent. Mishti doi is a lurid, sweeter than sweet set yogurt. Toothkind it is not.

Hung Tao

51 Queensway, W2 ▪ 020 7727 5753

● Bayswater/Queensway

◉ Chinese

⏱ daily 11.00–23.00

◢ cash only ▪ 10% service added

££ starters £2 ▪ noodle soups £4.20–£5.70 ▪ mains £5.30–£7.50 ▪ no alcohol

⧭ Fast food, cheap food, good food

It is easy to find the Hung Tao: just look out for the much larger and glossier New Kam Tong restaurant and two doors away you'll see this small and spartan establishment. They're actually part of the same group, as is another restaurant over the road. The reason to choose the Hung Tao above its neighbours is if you fancy a one-plate (or more accurately, one-bowl) meal. One of the first items on the menu is the 'hot and sour' soup. Uncannily enough, this is hot – with fresh red chillies in profusion, sour, and delicious. There are also a dozen different 'noodle' soups, at bargain prices: these are the perfect all-in-one student meal – carbs and protein swimming in a tasty broth. Then there are twenty dishes that go from duck rice to fried fish with ginger. Plus about thirty noodle, fried noodle and ho fun dishes, all at blow low prices. The fried ho fun with beef is a superb rich dish – well-flavoured brisket cooked until melting, on top of a mountain of ho fun. And the barbecued meats displayed in the window are very tasty, too: rich, red-painted char sui; soya chicken; duckling; and crispy pork. Towards the front of the menu you'll find a succession of congee dishes. Congee is one of those foods people label 'interesting' without meaning it. It is a thick, whitish, runny porridge made with rice, stunningly bland and under-seasoned, but tasting faintly of ginger. Plunge in at the deep end and try preserved egg with sliced pork congee. As well as containing pork, there's the 'thousand-year' egg itself, the white of which is a translucent chestnut brown and the yolk a fetching green. Inscrutably, it tastes rather like a cheesy hard-boiled egg.

Khan's

13–15 Westbourne Grove, W2 ■ 020 7727 5420

⊖ Bayswater/Queensway

⦿ Indian

🕓 Mon to Thurs 12.00–14.45 & 18.00–23.45; Fri–Sun 12.00–23.45

🖰 www.khansrestaurant.com

🖭 all major credit cards ■ 10% service added

££ starters £1.70–£3.25 ■ thalis £7.75 & £8.25 ■ mains £3.25–£8.50
■ sides £1.85–£3.15 ■ desserts £2.60–£3.60 ■ no alcohol

✪ Cavernous and echoing Indian food factory

Khan's is the business if you're after a solid, inexpensive and familiar
Indian meal. Gastronomy it ain't. This restaurant, in busy Westbourne
Grove, is a long-standing favourite with students and budget-wary
locals who know that the curries here may be the staples of a
thousand menus across Britain, but that they're fresh, well cooked
and generously portioned. Just don't expect a restful evening. Tables
are turned in a trice, service is perfunctory (this isn't a place to dally
over the menu), and it's really noisy. Try to get a table in the vast,
booming ground floor, where blue murals stretch up to the high
ceilings – it feels a bit like dining in an enormous municipal swimming
pool. There are some tasty breads on offer. Try the nan-e-mughziat, a
coconut-flavoured affair with nuts and sultanas, or the paneer kulcha,
bulging with cottage cheese and mashed potatoes. You might also
kick off with half a tandoori chicken, which is moist and well cooked,
or a creditable chicken tikka. For main dishes, all those curry house
favourites are listed here – meat Madras or vindalu; prawn biryani;
chicken chilli masala; king prawn curry – and they all taste unusually
fresh. Especially good is the butter chicken, while for lovers of tikka
masala dishes, the chicken tikka masala will appeal. There's a typical
array of vegetable dishes, too: bhindi, sag aloo, vegetable curry.
Desserts include kulfi and various ice creams from Häagen Dazs.
Then, just when you think that Khan's is an unreconstructed curry
house, you spot the heart symbols on the menu – they are positioned
beside 'low fat' dishes.

Mandarin Kitchen

14–16 Queensway, W2 ■ 020 7727 9012

⊖ Queensway/Bayswater

🍴 Chinese/fish

🕒 daily 12.00–23.00

🍽 all major credit cards ■ no service added

££ starters £2.80–£11.80 ■ mains £5.90–£22 ■ lobster 'seasonal price' (about £28.50) ■ lowest bottle price £13.50

✪ Lobster HQ

London has its fair share of French fish restaurants and there are famous English fish restaurants, so why does it seem odd to come across a Chinese fish restaurant? This is a large place, busy with waiters deftly wheeling four-foot diameter tabletops around like giant hoops as they set up communal tables for parties of Chinese, who all seem to be eating … lobster. Whatever you fancy for the main course, start with as many of the steamed scallops on the shell with garlic soya sauce as you can afford. They're magnificent. Then decide between lobster, crab or fish. If you go for the lobster, you can have it as sashimi; steamed; with ginger and spring onions; or with black bean and green pepper chilli sauce (whichever way it will be 'seasonally priced'). Be sure that you order the optional extra soft noodle to make a meal of it. The crab is tempting, too. Live crabs are shipped up from the south coast, and you can opt for a handsome portion of shells, lots of legs and four claws baked with ginger and spring onion. Fish dishes require more thought – and an eye to the seasonally changing per-pound prices, which do reflect the gluts and shortages of the fish market. The menu lists sea bass, turbot, Dover sole, red snapper and pomfret. The steamed eel with black-bean sauce is notably rich. The squid in chilli and black-bean sauce is good. The Mandarin Kitchen serves good fresh fish, but the downside is that reservations are a waste of time – you'll be greeted by blank stares.

Rodizio Rico

111 Westbourne Grove, W11 ■ 020 7792 4035

⊖ Notting Hill Gate

🍽 Brazilian

🕐 Mon to Fri 18.30–24.00; Sat 12.30–16.30

🖰 all major credit cards ■ 10% service added

££ set meal £18 ■ desserts £3.90 ■ lowest bottle price £11.90

⭐ Meat, then meat and some more meat!

In southern Brazil this restaurant would be seen as pretty run-of-the-mill, but in W11 churrascarias are the exception rather than the rule. If you're a lover of smoky grilled meat, Rodizio Rico will come as a godsend, but it can be a rather puzzling experience for first-timers. There's no menu and no prices – but no problem. 'Rodizio' means 'rotating', and refers to the carvers who wander about the room with huge skewers of freshly grilled meat from which they lop off chunks on demand. You start by ordering and then help yourself from the salad bar and hot buffet. As the carvers circulate they cut you chunks, slivers and slices from whichever skewer they are holding. You eat as much as you like of whatever you like, and then pay the absurdly reasonable price. When you're up helping yourself to the basics, look out for the tiny rolls, no bigger than a button mushroom, called pão de queijo – a rich cheese bread from the south of Brazil. Return to your seat and await the carvers – they come in random order, but they keep on coming. There's lamb, and ham, and pork, and spareribs, and chicken, and silverside beef (called lagarto after a similarly shaped iguana). Then for offal aficionados there are grilled chicken hearts. But the star of the show is picanha – the heart of the rump, skewered and grilled in huge chunks. Taste it and the arguments over the relative merits of rump and fillet are over forever. Brazilians seem to revere the crispy bits, but if you want your meat rare you only have to ask.

→ For branches, see index

Al Waha

75 Westbourne Grove, W2 ▪ 020 7229 0806

⊖ Bayswater/Queensway

🍴 Lebanese

🕙 daily 12.00–24.00

🖱 www.waha-uk.com

🖃 all major credit cards except AmEx ▪ no service added

££ meze £3.50–£7 ▪ main dishes £9.50–£18.50 ▪ sides £3–£3.75 ▪ desserts £3.50 ▪ 'Days of the Week speciality' £10 ▪ lowest bottle price £12.50

✪ Top-notch Lebanese cooking

Anissa Helou, writer of the definitive book on Lebanese cuisine, nominates Al Waha as London's best Lebanese restaurant. And after cantering through a few courses here you will probably agree with her. Lebanese restaurants are all meze obsessed, and Al Waha is no exception. What is different, however, is the way in which the chef at Al Waha is obsessive about the main course dishes as well. When you sit down, a dish of fresh, crisp crudités will be brought to the table. It includes everything from some quartered cos lettuce to a whole green pepper – get the healthy eating part over early. Choosing is then the problem, as there are 21 cold starters and 23 hot ones. Go for balance and include one dish that you have never had before. Houmous is good here; tabbouleh is heavy on the parsley; and the foul moukala is good, despite its name – broad beans with garlic, coriander and olive oil. From the hot section, try manakeish bizaatar, which is a mini-bread topped with thyme, like a sophisticated pizza. Or there's batata harra, potatoes with garlic and peppers. The makanek ghanam are tiny Lebanese lamb sausages, like very refined cocktail sausages. For main courses, grills predominate, and they are all spanking-fresh and accurately cooked. Good choices include shish taouk, made with chicken, and samakeh harrah, a whole sea bass. Star turn is kafta khashkhash – a superb cylinder of minced lamb with parsley, garlic and tomato. Drink the good Lebanese beer or the very good Lebanese wines.

Soho

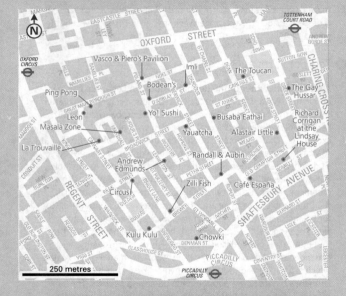

Alastair Little

49 Frith Street, W1 ■ 020 7734 5183

⊖ Leicester Square

🍴 Mediterranean

🕐 Mon to Fri 12.00–15.00 & 18.00–23.30 Sat 18.00–23.30

🗗 all major credit cards ■ no service added

££ lunch £33 (3 courses) ■ dinner £38 (3 courses) ■ lowest bottle price £17.50

⭐ Reassuringly traditional modern Italian cooking

The eponymous Alastair Little may have moved on to run a traiteur called Tavola on Westbourne Grove (just down from the Taqueria, page 106), but his legacy remains. Alastair Little was the chap who led us out of a world where an Italian restaurant was judged by the size of its pepper mills. He championed simple, strong flavours, fresh produce, joyful meals, and although it is a very long while since he was a full-time presence in the kitchen, the flame still burns brightly. Although the chef has changed, the restaurant retains the name Alastair Little, which in some ways is appropriate because it still serves his kind of food. Unlike the décor, which has stayed much the same, the menu changes twice a day. Pricing is simple and forgiving, three-course meals have an accessible price tag, and the wine list is equally moderate save for a sprinkling of more ambitiously priced famous names. The menu runs the gamut, but everything is seasonal. So starters may include spinach soup, dhal and rava dosa; sizzling prawns with chilli, garlic and parsley; a salad of seared tuna, artichokes, French beans and quails' eggs; and, at something of a tangent, six native oysters with shallot vinegar and spicy sausages. The main courses follow on in similar vein: skate with black butter and capers; pork fillet, chorizo, bacon, white beans and cabbage sprouts; Gressingham duck breast, egg-and-bacon salad, chips and Béarnaise. To end your meal there are splendid puds, such as a café Liégeoise, or panna cotta with blood orange jelly – and the satisfying alternative of a plate of British cheeses with oatcakes.

Andrew Edmunds

46 Lexington Street, W1 ▪ 020 7437 5708

⊖ Oxford Circus

🍴 Modern British

🕐 Mon to Fri 12.00–15.00 & 18.00–22.45; Sat 13.00–15.00 & 18.00–22.45; Sun 13.00–15.30 & 18.00–22.30

🏛 all major credit cards except AmEx ▪ 12.5% service added

££ starters £2.95–£8.95 ▪ mains £8.25–£17 ▪ sides £2.50 ▪ desserts £3.75–£5.75 ▪ lowest bottle price £11.50

✪ Local hero from the days of old Soho

Soho locals determined to rub in their savoir faire refer to this restaurant by its original name – Andrew Edmunds' Wine Bar. This place has been an institution in the area for nearly two decades – a long time when you consider how speedily so many restaurants come and go. It all started when the lease on the wine bar next door to his print gallery became vacant and Andrew decided that, as he wanted to go on eating there himself, he should take it on. The restaurant now has a loyal band of regulars who like the imaginative bistro-style dishes, strong flavours and bold combinations. It's cosy, dark and very crowded. The menu changes weekly and combines solid favourites with bright new ideas. Start with parsnip and apple soup; or dressed crab; or black pudding, caramelised apples and horseradish crème fraîche. Main courses may include stalwart and straightforward dishes such as best end of lamb, with haricot beans and thyme purée and roast aubergines; confit duck leg with red cabbage and potato wedges; roast monkfish with mash and purple-sprouting broccoli; or an impressive vegetarian option like vegetable tagine with couscous, toasted almonds and coriander. This is very like stumbling on a neighbourhood restaurant in some affluent suburb, only you are in the very heart of Soho. Puddings include chocolate mousse cake; the ubiquitous tiramisù; nutmeg ice cream. Wines are a passion with Andrew Edmunds. The constantly changing, broker-bought list is long and special and, because of his low mark-up policy, there are some genuine bargains. Booking is essential as the dining room has a limited number of covers.

Bodean's

10 Poland Street, W1 ■ 020 7287 7575

⊖ Oxford Circus

🍴 Modern British

🕐 Mon to Fri 12.00–15.00 & 18.00–23.00; Sat & Sun 12.00–23.30

🖥 www.bodeansbbq.com

🖬 all major credit cards ■ 12.5% service added

££ starters £3.95–£5.25 ■ mains £6.95–£12.35 ■ sides £1.95–£2.50
■ desserts £2.75–£3.50 ■ lowest bottle price £11.95

✪ Yankophile rib palace

It's a fair old leap from Belgian mussels to American barbecue,
but Bodean's seems to have struck a chord and is a friendly, busy
place. This unashamedly American eatery is the brainchild of one of
the men who set up Belgo (see p. 20). Upstairs is a kind of diner/
deli/sandwich shop. Downstairs is a restaurant. Only somewhere
paying serious homage to Americana would have a strident tartan
carpet, wall lights made to look like antelope horns and a red-painted
ceiling. Even the service is American gushy and there is an authentic
'commercial' ring to the place, something that you will either love
or hate. The starters are not very impressive – smoke-fired chicken
wings come either hot or mild and they are the best of the bunch,
or perhaps the clam chowder. Cut to the chase and get amongst the
real smoky barbecued stuff. Baby back ribs (served by the whole or
half 'slab') are considered by ribologists to be too tender and a bit of
a cop-out. The pork spareribs (again sold by the whole slab, eleven or
twelve ribs; or the half, five or six ribs) are terrific. Mains come with
average coleslaw and pretty good beans. Fries are good and crisp.
The star dish is the beef back ribs – a Fred Flintstone dish with large
flat bones, this is dry and chewy. Very good. There are other delicacies
such as Boston butt, a pulled pork sandwich. But only the ribs will
stick to your ribs. Puds tread the ice-cream and pie route, while
to drink there is a flotilla of different Bloody Marys, wine or beer.
Happily, this place is very child-friendly and there is usually some sort
of enticing deal on offer.

→ For branches, see index or website

Busaba Eathai

106–110 Wardour Street, W1 ■ 020 7255 8686

⊖ Piccadilly Circus

🍽 Thai

🕐 Mon to Sat 12.00–23.00; Sun 12.00–22.00

🖰 www.busaba.com

🗗 all major credit cards ■ no service added

££ mains £5.80–£9 ■ sides £1.50–£5.50 ■ set Thai £13.70 & £14.90 ■ lowest bottle price £12

✪ Easy Thai, by the bowlful

Busaba occupies a West End site that was once a bank – you remember the days when banks were conveniently positioned all over the place? Former customers stumbling into 106 Wardour Street would be more than a little surprised by the dark, designery and implacably trendy Thai eatery that is now well bedded in. This place serves decent Thai food at low prices, and with consummate lack of pretension. For all the cod philosophy, this is a jolly and energetic restaurant and you will probably have a very good time. There's no booking so there may be queuing, and the tables are large so there may be sharing. Food, grouped into categories, veers towards one-pot dishes, and vegetarians are particularly well served. If you want starters you need to peruse the side dishes. Choose from such things as po-pea jay, which are vegetable spring rolls; or fishcakes; or Thai calamari, which are not unlike everyone else's calamari. There are curries: Mussaman duck curry; green chicken curry; green vegetable curry; and aromatic butternut pumpkin curry. You'll find genuine Thai veg, such as pea aubergines, sweet basil and lime leaves, although dishes do tend to be on the sweet side. Or there's phad Thai, and thom yam chicken. Stir-fries include chargrilled duck in tamarind sauce with Chinese broccoli; ginger beef; and chargrilled cod with lemongrass and tamarind sauce. The power juice phenomenon has reached Busaba. Nam polamai is organic, and combines carrot, apple and celery with dandelion and nettle extract. Mekhong Thai whiskey with ice is listed for the more adventurous.

→ For branches, see index

Café España

63 Old Compton Street, W1 ■ 020 7494 1271

⊖ Piccadilly Circus/Leicester Square

🍽 Spanish

🕐 Mon to Sat 12.00–24.00; Sun 12.00–23.00

🗐 Mastercard, Visa ■ no service added

££ starters £2.50–£5.95 ■ mains £6.25–£11.95 ■ desserts £2–£2.50
■ lowest bottle price £9.95

✪ No frills and small bills at this trad Spanish

Nestled among the hardcore shops and video stores in the heart of
Soho's pink strip at the Wardour Street end of Old Compton Street,
Café España is a remarkably balanced restaurant. From the outside it
looks rather small and shabby – not very prepossessing at all, in fact,
and much like the more tourist-focused trattorias. But once through
the door, tripping over the dessert trolley, you'll be greeted by a
friendly maître d' and led up the stairs to join a hubbub of hungry
Soho folk with a nose for a bargain. The menu does give a nod to
the trattoria, with a short list of pastas, but it is the Spanish cooking
that you should be here for. From the tapas, mejillones a la plancha
delivers a hefty portion of mussels; a tortilla Española is the size of
a saucer; and ordering the jamón serrano brings a decent portion
at a price you'd be hard to match wholesale. Chipirones, a plate of
baby squid, and boquerones, the classic white anchovies, are good.
For something more substantial, there's plenty of choice, mostly in
the form of simple grills. Ordering chuletas de cordero a la brasa
will bring lamb chops; higado de ternera, calf's liver and bacon; and
rodaballo a la plancha, grilled turbot. Or there are the traditional
Valenciana and marinera paellas (for two), though these are slightly
less exciting. Service is swift, if a little harassed. To enjoy Café España
to the maximum, go mob-handed and allow yourself the luxury of
running amok with the tapas selections before pouncing on the
paella. Be warned – the sangria is a dark and dangerous West End
concoction, with only a nodding acquaintance to the Iberian drink of
the same name.

Chowki

2–3 Denman Street, W1 ■ 020 7439 1330

⊖ Piccadilly Circus

🍴 Indian

🕐 Mon to Sat 12.00–23.30; Sun 12.00–22.30

🖰 www.chowki.com

🗗 all major credit cards ■ no service added

££ starters £1.95–£4.25 ■ mains & thalis £5.95–£9.50 ■ sides £2.95
■ desserts £2.75 ■ lowest bottle price £10.95

✪ Regional Indian dishes, un-Piccadilly prices

Kuldeep Singh is the head chef behind Chowki and he is also the
mainspring of Mela (see p. 36). Chowki is a large, cheap restaurant
serving authentic home-style food in stylish surroundings. The menu
changes every month in order to feature three different regions of
India. Thus April might feature the North-West Frontier, Lucknow,
and Goa, then by June it could be Kashmir or Maharashtra. During
a whole year Chowki showcases 36 different regional styles of food.
All the dishes are authentic and all come with accompaniments.
Chowki has 120 seats spread across three dining areas, but you'll
still probably have to wait for a table at peak times. There are three
or four starters and three or four mains from each region. When the
menu showcases the cuisine of Rajasthan, Hyderabad and Mangalore,
starters might include an epic dish of Rajasthani quail; dumplings
stuffed with banana from Hyderabad; and a dish of prawns
marinated in tamarind. Mains follow the lead and come with an
appropriate vegetable and the correct rice or bread. From Hyderabad
comes a sour mutton stew. From Mangalore there might be a dish
of chicken cooked with coconut, or a mackerel poached in spice
paste. All the dishes have the unmistakable stamp of homely cooking
– rich, simple, appetising flavours. Service is friendly, and this is a
comfortable, modern place. Finding anywhere this good – and this
cheap – within earshot of Piccadilly Circus is little short of miraculous.
The regional feast – three courses – enables a strategy whereby
sharing three different feasts allows you to sample most of the menu.

Circus

1 Upper James Street, W1 ■ 020 7534 4000

⊖ Oxford Circus

🍴 Modern British

🕐 Mon to Fri 12.00–15.00 & 17.45–24.00; Sat 17.45–24.00

🖰 www.egami.com

🏪 all major credit cards ■ 12.5% service added

££ starters £6–£12.50 ■ mains £13.50–£18.50 ■ sides £3.50 ■ desserts £6.50 ■ prix fixe lunch & pre-/post-theatre £14.50 & £16.50 ■ lowest bottle price £13.50

⭐ Fashionable dining place, chattering crowd

When it opened towards the end of the 1990s, Circus was everything a fashionable fin-de-siècle restaurant should be. The décor was cool shades of black and white, there was a de rigueur members' bar downstairs, open till late, and there were spiky 'statement' flower arrangements. The service was efficient and good-looking, and the food was very much of the moment. It took little time for Circus to become a destination restaurant for media and design professionals. A few years and several trends later, Circus has proved that it can stand the test of time. The menu works hard to offer something for everyone. Tucked in alongside the pan-fried risotto with smoked haddock and soft poached egg, and globe artichoke, ratte potato and Parmesan salad, you'll find starters as diverse as spring onion and potato soup, or 30g of Sevruga caviar with trimmings. Main courses offer the traditional – roast rump of lamb with Provençal vegetables; honey-roast Gressingham duck breast – as well as more modern dishes such as roast ostrich with black bean rice and kasundi. Everything about this place suggests that whatever you choose will be well executed and pleasing to the eye. The kitchen is obviously at ease, cooking good-quality ingredients properly and with predictable results. This being an expense-account eatery ideal for business lunches and dinners, desserts are often skipped. Which is a shame, as the pastry chefs obviously delight in flights of fancy – amaretto cheesecake with coffee sauce. Note the decently priced set lunch and pre- and post-theatre offers.

The Gay Hussar

2 Greek Street, W1 ▪ 020 7437 0973

⊖ Tottenham Court Road

🍽 Hungarian

🕐 Mon to Sat 12.15–14.30 & 17.30–22.45

🖱 www.simplyrestaurants.com

🗗 all major credit cards ▪ 12.5% optional service added

££ starters £3.80–£6.75 ▪ mains £10.75–£16.50 ▪ sides £2.50–£4
▪ desserts £4–£4.50 ▪ prix fixe lunch £16.50 & £18.50 ▪ lowest
bottle price £13.95

✪ Unashamedly old-fashioned power lunchery

**The ground-floor dining room of The Gay Hussar stretches before
you like an old-style railway carriage** – there are banquettes,
there are waiters in dinner jackets, there is panelling and the walls
are covered with political caricatures. 'Aha!' the knowledgeable
restaurant-goer murmurs. 'How very retro – some chic designer has
replicated an entire 1950s' restaurant dining room.' Not so. Granted,
it has been spruced up, and the room is clean and comfortable, but
The Gay Hussar is the real thing, right down to the faded photo of
a naked Christine Keeler. Perhaps the politicos like the food, which is
solid, dependable, comfortable and tasty. It can also be good value,
especially if you stick to the decent value set lunch. In the evening
dishes get a trifle more complicated, but the Hungarian specialities
are still to the fore. Starters include a fish terrine with beetroot sauce
and cucumber salad, and hási pástétom – a fine goose and pork pâté.
But the most famous (a house speciality that has featured in various
novels) is chilled wild cherry soup, which is like a thin, bitterish,
sourish yogurt and is rather good. Main courses are blockbusters.
Try the hortobágyi palacsinta, a pancake filled with a finely chopped
veal goulash and then sealed, deep-fried and served with creamed
spinach. Or there are fish dumplings, which are served with rice and
a creamy dill sauce. Or cigány gyors tal, a 'gypsy fry-up' of pork and
peppers. Puds are also fierce – poppy-seed strudel comes with vanilla
ice cream; options like chestnut purée have real substance.

Imli

167–169 Wardour Street, W1 ■ 020 7287 4243   &

⊖ Oxford Circus

🍽 Indian

🕐 daily 12.00–23.00

🌐 www.imli.co.uk

💳 all major credit cards except AmEx ■ 12.5% optional service added

££ dishes £2.95–£6.95 ■ mains £7–£12 ■ sides 50p–£1.50 ■ desserts
£2.96 ■ set meal £10.95 ■ lowest bottle price £12

⭐ Graze away at this slick Indian

Imli is one of the more recent recruits to the grazing revolution,
which is odd, because when it is done well (and it is done well here)
the grazing menu and Indian food make perfect partners. Sharing
a number of different curries has long been the modus operandi of
the curry house and formalising matters and booting the concept
upmarket is a grand idea. Mercifully, prices at Imli are wholly
reasonable and allowing three or four dishes per person will leave
you happy if not belly-busted. The menu headers are rather coy,
but persevere – from 'light and refreshing' the spiced potato cakes
are very simple and good; the over-stuffed samosas are delightful;
and the 'banana dosa' – which seems to be the potato cake dish
but made with bananas – is delicious. Under 'New Traditions'
you'll find fenugreek wraps – breads flecked with green herb and
stuffed with chicken, or a seafood platter – good crisp squid rings,
a commendable fishcake and some very large prawns. Undermining
the grazing idyll some of the 'Signature Dishes' come with a choice of
paratha or rice. These are well-balanced curries --a dish of Saunfiya
lamb comes in a rich and finely textured sauce thickened with ground
cashew, while Goan pork is rich and red with enough chilli heat
to give the nod towards the fabled vindalho. Puds feature some
moody ices – raspberry and black salt sorbet. This is a large, elegant
restaurant with plenty of attentive staff and high standards in the
kitchen… only by being a busy place will the management be able to
keep the prices so reasonable.

Kulu Kulu

76 Brewer Street, W1 ■ 020 7734 7316

⊖ Oxford Circus/Piccadilly Circus

🍴 Japanese

🕐 Mon to Fri 12.00–14.30 & 17.00–22.00; Sat 12.00–15.30 & 17.00–22.00

🗐 Mastercard, Visa ■ no service added

££ sushi £1.20–£3.60 ■ sishu combinations £4.80–£9.60 ■ mains £12.80–£30 ■ desserts £1.80 ■ lowest bottle price £12

✪ Well-made sushi at conveyor belt prices

Serving good sushi without being impersonal or intimidating
is a difficult trick for any conveyor-belt sushi restaurant, but Kulu
Kulu pulls it off. This place is light and airy and there are enough
coat hooks for a small army of diners. The only thing you might
quibble over is the rather low stools – anyone over six feet tall will
find themselves dining in the tuck position favoured by divers and
trampolinists. The atmosphere is Japanese utilitarian. In front of you
is a plastic tub of gari (the rather delicious pickled ginger), a bottle
of soy and a small box containing disposable wooden chopsticks.
The plates come round on the kaiten, or conveyor, and are coded by
design rather than colour, which could prove deceptive. Do not worry
too much as prices are reasonable and having a couple of plates from
the top price band rather than the lowest won't break the bank.
All the usual nigiri sushi are here, and the fish is particularly fresh
and well presented. Choose from maguri, or tuna; amaebi, or sweet
shrimp; salmon roe; hotategai, or scallops – very tender, very sweet.
Futomaki is a Californian cone-shaped roll with tuna. The top plates
tend to be ritzier fishes such as belly tuna. As well as the sushi, the
conveyor parades some little bowls of hot dishes. One worth looking
out for combines strips of fried fish skin with a savoury vegetable
purée. It counts as a basic sushi, as does the bowl of miso soup.
For the indecisive, mixed tempura is good and crisp and there's also
mixed sashimi. To drink there is everything from oolong tea to Kirin
beer, by way of a special sake made in Rocky Mountains of the good
ol' U.S.A.

Leon

35 Great Marlborough Street, W1 ■ 020 7437 5280

⊖ Oxford Circus

🍽 Modern British (they say Mediterranean)

🕐 Mon to Fri 07.00–20.00; Sat 08.30–20.00; Sun 10.30–18.30

🖱 www.leonrestaurants.co.uk

🖫 all major credit cards ■ no service added

££ salads £3.95–£5.90 ■ wraps £2.95–£4.55 ■ big dishes £4.30–£5.60 ■ sides £2.80–£3.75 ■ desserts £1.80–£4.80 ■ lowest bottle price £6.50

✪ Fast food, but wholesome

Imagine a typical Carnaby Street fast food joint: the bright lights, garish uniforms and ghastly food – then forget all that. Leon is from another planet and deserves your support. As soon as this place opened it collected a hatful of awards from judges grateful that at last someone was prepared to serve good food fast. Starting with a really decent breakfast – dry-cured English bacon, two free-range soft-boiled eggs, roast tomatoes, grilled mushrooms, hand-made wholemeal toast and home-made tomato ketchup or brown sauce – the attention to detail, and the care taken sourcing the ingredients, is impressive. Like the ethos of the place, the décor is a blend of the stylish and the utilitarian. The lunch and dinner menu is written seasonally and offers dishes in a variety of sizes and styles. The food is an amalgam of modern British and Mediterranean influences, so Moroccan meatballs nudge a charcuterie plate and chicken nuggets (but home-made, from real chicken – there's a shock). There are also 'Superfood Salads', like the warm mushroom and tarragon fish superfood salad: subtitled 'white fish from sustainable shoals, baked with sautéed mushrooms and freshly chopped tarragon, broccoli, baby spinach, toms, alfalfa, seeds, rocket and aioli'. These are good dishes, appetising and thoughtfully put together. For a tad more indulgence look no further than the puds section and the Leon hot Valrhona chocolate brownie with organic Herefordshire ice cream. You can eat well, and fairly cheaply, at Leon – while basking in the knowledge that the food is PC.

→ For branches, see index

Masala Zone

9 Marshall Street, W1 ■ 020 7287 9966

◉ Oxford Circus/Piccadilly Circus

🍴 Indian

🕐 Mon to Fri 12.00–15.00 & 17.30–23.00; Sat 12.00–23.00; Sun 12.00–23.30

🖰 www.realindianfood.com

🖰 all major credit cards ■ 10% service added

££ starters £3.50–£5.50 ■ thalis £5.50–£11.55 ■ mains £5.50–£11.55 ■ sides 85p–£1.75 ■ desserts £2.60–£3.50 ■ lowest bottle price £10.10

✪ Good-value Indian fast food, quite at home in Soho

Masala Zone is impossible to pigeonhole. The food is Indian, but modern Indian, with a commendable emphasis on healthy eating – as would be the norm in India – and also, because it's an authentically Indian menu, there's a long list of attractive vegetarian options. The dining room is smart and large with a handsome mural (look out for the stretch limo in the mural – it impressed the visiting tribal artists greatly), but the prices are low. The fast-food dishes on the menu tend to be the roadside snacks of Mumbai. In all, this is an informal, stylish and friendly place, serving food that is simple and delicious. The gentle informality extends to the menu, which begins with small plates of street food. There are sev puris, dahi puris, samosas and a particularly fine aloo tikki chaat. Pick several dishes and graze your way along – at these prices it doesn't matter if there's the occasional miss among the hits. At lunch there are splendid Indian sandwiches, including a large masala chicken burger and a Bombay layered-vegetable grilled sandwich. There are also half a dozen curries that are well balanced and richly flavoured – served simply, with rice. But you should move straight on to the thalis, which are the authentic option. At Masala Zone these are steel trays with eight little bowls containing a vegetarian snack (to whet the appetite), a curry, lentils, a root vegetable, a green vegetable, yogurt, bread, rice and pickles. You just choose the base curry and a complete, balanced meal arrives at your table.

→ For branches, see index or website

Ping Pong

45 Great Marlborough Street, W1 ■ 020 7851 6969 &

⊖ Oxford Circus

🍽 Chinese/dim sum

🕐 Mon to Sun 12.00–24.00; Sun 12.00–22.30

🔗 www.pingpongdimsum.com

🖥 all major credit cards ■ 10% optional service added

££ set meals £9.90–£11.90 ■ dim sum £2.30 (most)–£3.10 ■ desserts £3.50 ■ lowest bottle price £14

✪ Plenty of seats at this modern dumpling factory

'Little steamed parcels of deliciousness' is what it says on the signage, cards and every printed surface and this is probably fair enough. Ping Pong is a cavernous dim sum palace. There are two floors and the chef twirling the noodles, or his colleagues steaming the baskets, provide a floorshow for diners. There are seats at tables and stools at sinuous counters; all is black and stylish. This place is like a cocktail bar with a strange emphasis on food, and soon after it opened in 2005 it started to attract the see-and-be-seen crowd. The food is simply pigeonholed on the one hand (good) and most of the dumplings are priced very reasonably; on the other hand (less good) dim sum purists will find some of the wrappers a bit thick, some dumplings a bit lacklustre, and some a tad dried out. But Ping Pong is a jolly place, service is brisk and efficient, and those prices go a long way to calming the inner gastronome. Roast pork puffs are good (maybe not quite as good as the venison puffs at Yauatcha, p. 145). Old favourites like pork siu mai, char sui pau, and vegetable spring roll are sound enough. Prawn toast is reinterpreted and seems less greasy than the trad version. Crispy prawn balls are surrounded by a sphere of deep-fried noodles. There is Chinese beer on draught, but the most elegant refreshment is the Jasmine Flower Tea – you get a glass containing a ball of leaves and when they pour on the boiling water it 'flowers' and unravels. The owners of Ping Pong are convinced that they have found the modern-day philosopher's stone – a new and popular fast food restaurant.

Randall & Aubin

16 Brewer Street, W1 ■ 020 7287 4447

⊖ Piccadilly Circus

🍽 Modern British

🕐 Mon to Sat 12.00–23.00; Sun 16.00–22.30

🗐 all major credit cards ■ 12.5% optional service added

££ starters £2.90–£9.75 ■ mains £7.25–£28 ■ sides £2.65–£5.10
■ desserts £4–£4.50 ■ lowest bottle price £12.50

✪ Ex-butcher shop becomes stylish bar restaurant

Fruits de mer and champagne – if Randall & Aubin had a signature dish this combo would be it. The team behind this eatery took over a trad butcher shop and remoulded it as a sharp restaurant – as the studied informality and huge flower displays would suggest – but it's also a rotisserie, sandwich shop and charcuterie to boot. Randall's serves good food speedily, to folk without a lot of time. In summer the huge sash windows are opened up, making this a wonderfully airy place to eat, especially if you grab a seat by the window. There's an extensive menu. An eclectic choice of starters roams the globe, with soupe de poisson, Japanese fishcakes, and salt-and-pepper squid with fresh coriander and teriyaki dressing. Main courses range from 'original' Caesar salad; through spit-roast herb chicken; and sausage with butter-bean mash and onion gravy; to organic sirloin steak with pommes frîtes and sauce Béarnaise. There are also some interesting sides, such as gratin Dauphinoise, or zucchini frîtes with basil mayonnaise. If you don't mind crowds, drop in at lunchtime for a hot filled baguette. How about a lamb souvlaki, tzatziki and salad baguette? Also available in the evening, the baguettes provide an inexpensive yet satisfying meal, something to fuel the bar hopper for the night ahead. The list of fruits de mer offers well-priced seafood, ranging from a whole dressed crab; through grilled lobster, garlic butter and pommes frîtes; to 'the works' (for a minimum two people). Puddings range from tart and brûlées to the more adventurous pear and caramel galette, or chocolate truffle cake.

Richard Corrigan at the Lindsay House

21 Romilly Street, W1 ■ 020 7439 0450

⊖ Leicester Square

🍽 British

🕓 Mon to Fri 12.00–14.30 & 18.00–23.00; Sat 18.00–23.00

🌐 www.lindsayhouse.co.uk

🖥 all major credit cards ■ 12.5% optional service added

££ lunch £27 (3 courses) ■ dinner £54 (3 courses) ■ tasting menu £64 (6 courses) ■ 'Garden' menu £64 (6 courses) ■ lowest bottle price £21

✪ The best of British, and Irish, cooking

Chefs are not usually held to be overly calm and levelheaded and it is a testament to his impressive powers of stamina that even in such company Richard Corrigan is regarded with awe. At Lindsay House his cuisine has gone from strength to strength and has won the approval of Mr Michelin. The restaurant is split into a series of small rooms, the service is attentive, and the food is very good indeed. The menus are uncomplicated and change regularly to keep in step with what is available at the market. As well as three-course lunch and dinner menus there is an epic six-course tasting menu. Starters surprise with warm potato and goats' cheese terrine, or are lusciously opulent – roast foie gras, potato blini and caramelised apples. Or there are intriguing combinations such as tea-roasted sweetbread with aubergine. Main courses follow the same ground rules (or lack of them): squab pigeon with chorizo and black pudding; scallops with pork belly and spiced carrots; or halibut with turnip gratin, steamed cockles and clams. The puddings may include Seville orange tart with chocolate soufflé and buttermilk sorbet. The wine list is extensive and expensive. One thing distinguishes the cuisine at the Lindsay House – Corrigan's love affair with offal. Sweetbreads, kidneys and hearts all end up on the menu – dishes that perfectly illustrate his deft touch with hearty ingredients. The wine list is particularly well matched to the cooking style, with plenty of serious reds to complement the rich dishes.

The Toucan

19 Carlisle Street, W1 ■ 020 7437 4123

⊖ Leicester Square/Tottenham Court Road

🍴 Irish

🕒 Mon to Sat 11.00–23.00

🖰 www.thetoucan.co.uk

🖼 all major credit cards except AmEx ■ no service added

££ starters £2.50–£6.95 ■ oysters £6 for 6 ■ mains £5.95 & £6.95
■ specials £5.95 ■ lowest bottle price £10

✪ There's eating and drinking in a pint of Guinness

When The Toucan opened, over a decade ago, the proprietors'
first priority was to approach Guinness and ask if they could retail
the black stuff. They explained that they wanted to open a small bar
aimed single-mindedly at the drinking public, just like the ones they
had enjoyed so much in Dublin. Guinness replied that, providing they
could shift two barrels a week, they'd be happy to put them on the
list. Neither party imagined that the regular order would end up at
more like 30 barrels a week! It's an impressive intake, but then The
Toucan is an impressive place, serving home-made, very cheap, very
wholesome and very filling food, along with all that Guinness. Start
with six Rossmore Irish oysters, or the vegetable soup with bread.
Go on to the steak and ale pie and champ, or sausage and champ
with onion gravy – champ is a kind of supercharged Irish mashed
potato, with best butter playing a leading role alongside the spring
onions. It features in a couple of novelty items such as chilli and
champ, or garlic mushrooms and champ. And just when you think
you have the measure of the place, there's Thai chicken curry and
rice. The JPs (jacket potatoes) come with various fillings, and there's
an array of sandwiches. One thing to bear in mind if you've come
here hungry is that there are times when The Toucan becomes so
packed with people that you can scarcely lift a pint. At those times,
all attempts at serving food are abandoned. Those with deep pockets
may be tempted by the long list of Irish whiskies including the
stratospherically expensive Middleton Rare – don't ask.

→ For branches, see index

La Trouvaille

12a Newburgh Street, W1 ■ 020 7287 8488

⊖ Oxford Circus

⦿ Very French

🕐 Mon to Sat 12.00–15.00 & 18.00–22.00

🖰 www.latrouvaille.co.uk

🖶 all major credit cards ■ 12.5% optional service added

££ lunch £17.95 (2 courses) & £20.50 (3 courses) ■ dinner £25 (2 courses) & £30 (3 courses) ■ lowest bottle price £13.50

✪ The Frenchness may be over the top, but the prices aren't

French haute cuisine has topped the European Champions League for about a century and although the English may resent such total dominance, there is a particular kind of French eatery they still adore. At La Trouvaille the proprietors understand the English longing for really French Frenchness; they even know that they should provide one or two dishes that are a step too authentic for most Brits. They know that waiters who would be considered too over-the-top for *Allo, Allo* are admired here. They know that their clientele want good food at a price that doesn't break the bank. There are good-value set lunches offering two or three courses plus cheese. Dinner ups the price a little, but the cooking here is very sound. The kitchen take carefully sourced produce – not slavishly French or dogmatically British, but rather whatever is best – and then add some Gallic flair. Starters may include watercress soup with goats' cheese, or artichoke vinaigrette, which comes with an improbably large artichoke simply presented. Main courses stay in character: onglet de 'Galloway'; glazed roast duck leg; canon de mouton 'Herdwick' Someone in the kitchen has a truly French respect for the integrity of ingredients. So pick bavette frîtes, sauce Béarnaise and then revel in excellent Scottish beef. When considering the puds – choccy mousse; crème brûlée; roast pears – divert to the weekly cheese plate, which is outstandingly good: three cheeses – a chunk of melting Livarot, a wedge of waxy Brebis, richly blued Fourme d'Ambert and a little pot of truffled honey.

→ For branches, see index or website

Vasco & Piero's Pavilion

15 Poland Street, W1 ■ 020 7437 8774

⊖ Oxford Circus

|O| Italian

⏱ Mon to Fri 12.00–15.00 & 18.00–23.00; Sat 19.00–23.00

⌂ www.vascosfood.com

🗗 all major credit cards ■ 12.5% optional service added

££ à la carte lunch only starters £6–£8.50 ■ mains £9.50–£18.50 ■ sides £2.50–£3.50 ■ desserts £6.50 ■ set menu (dinner only) £22 (2 courses) & £26 (3 courses) ■ lowest bottle price £13

✪ Family-run Italian stalwart

The Pavilion has been a Soho fixture for a couple of decades, but there's nothing old or institutional about the cooking or décor. Vasco himself cooks for his regulars, and the establishment has long been a favourite with diners who appreciate his food, which is fairly simple but made with top-class ingredients. Dishes are biased towards Umbrian cuisine. Customers include the great and the good, and the Pavilion's comfortable atmosphere guarantees them anonymity. There's an à la carte menu at lunch, but in the evening the basic deal is that you choose either two courses or three. Given the quality, freshness of ingredients and attention to detail, this restaurant delivers exceptional value, albeit with a slightly old-fashioned vibe. Starters may include roast beetroot, tomato, eggs and anchovies. Or there may be duck salad, mixed leaves and mostarda di cremona. Pastas, all home-made, are excellent, too, particularly the tagliolini with king prawns and zucchini – perfectly cooked and with a sauce that is prepared from fresh ingredients and tastes like it. For carnivores, however, there is nothing to beat the calf's liver with fresh sage – paper-thin liver that literally melts in the mouth. Piscivores should turn to the scallopine of swordfish with garlic, parsley and cannellini beans, or to the sautéed monkfish with saffron and lentils. Puddings continue the theme – they're simple and top-quality. A panna cotta is gelatinously creamy; a praline semi freddo is rich and soft as well as being crunchy. Service is in the old-style, attentive and well organised, as you'd expect in such a well-established resto.

Yauatcha

15 Broadwick Street, W1 ■ 020 7494 8888

⊖ Piccadilly Circus

🍽 Dim sum/teahouse

🕐 (Teahouse) Mon to Sat 08.00–23.30; Sun 09.00–22.30; (Dim sum) Mon to Sat 10.00–23.30; Sun 10.00–22.30

🗗 all major credit cards ■ 13% optional service added

££ teas £3–£12.50 ■ dim sum £3.50–£26 ■ desserts £6–£13.50 ■ lowest bottle price £20

✪ Long on dim sum, long on style

For a relative newcomer, Yauatcha has attracted a gratifying amount of controversy. On the one hand, the critics raved (one gave it five stars), and on the other hand, the snipers sniped about the concept of a booking only securing your table for 90 minutes. This place is a new, bright, designer take on dim sum from Alan Yau, the man behind Hakkasan (see p. 7) and the food is amazingly, blisteringly good. The little dishes here sweep effortlessly to a 'best ever' rating, and if you cannot stuff yourself greedily in 90 minutes you should be ashamed. It is hard to oppose tea by way of accompaniment – there's a lady who is a kind of tea sommelier and there are half a dozen regional and specialised Chinese teas. There are dumplings – all are good, some are amazing, most come three to a portion. Chinese chive dumpling is a delicate green pastry basket with a savoury middle; prawn and enoki mushroom dumpling has a thin, translucent casing; box dumpling is round and solid, with pastry outer and savoury middle; five-spice roll is like an über sausage roll, meaty with crisp exterior; pork and spring-onion cake – ring-shaped, with light pastry crust and rich filling; venison puffs – the best puff pastry with a meaty filling. Don't worry, choose what you like and you will not be disappointed. At ground level there is a tearoom, which offers an appealing combo of fine Chinese teas and super slick French pâtisserie – really good, really elegant little cakes. Well worth a mid-afternoon pause to enjoy some refreshment.

Yo! Sushi

52 Poland Street, W1 ■ 020 7287 0443

⊖ Piccadilly Circus/Oxford Circus

|◉| Japanese

⏲ daily 12.00–24.00

⌐ www.yosushi.co.uk

⊟ all major credit cards ■ no service added

££ sushi/sashimi/maki £1.50–£5 ■ desserts £5 ■ lowest bottle price
£12.50

✪ Let the sushi come to you

This was the first Yo! Sushi to open and jolly shocking the whole
conveyor belt concept all was, too. So it is no surprise that this is
generally the first branch to adopt any new developments, whether
that means a new décor or changes to the menu. This is a place
of dark wood and comfortable booths, and the somewhat harsh
techie feel that was part of the original design is no more. In among
all this, the food has been refined and, while purists may shudder,
it continues to be more consistent than the hype would have you
suspect. Plates are colour-coded according to their price, and when
satiated you simply call for a plate count, and your bill is prepared.
You sit at the counter with a little waiters' station in front of you
– there's gari (pickled ginger), soy and wasabi, plus some little
dishes and a forest of wooden chopsticks. By way of refreshment
Kirin beer, a small warm sake and unlimited Japanese tea vie for
your attention. You're ready to begin. Yo! Sushi claim to serve more
than one hundred sushi, so be leisurely and watch the belt – and,
if in doubt, ask. The sushi range from roasted pepper and avocado;
through salmon, crabstick and avocado; and tuna, grey mullet and
salmon skin; and so on up to yellowtail and fatty tuna – which carry a
warning that they are on offer 'as available'. There are about twenty
different maki rolls (with vegetarians well catered for), at all prices.
The ten different sashimi and five different gunkan all command the
higher orange and pink prices. Occasional 'Specials' broaden the
appeal still further.

→ For branches, see website and index

Zilli Fish

36–40 Brewer Street, W1 ■ 020 7734 8649

⊖ Piccadilly Circus

🍴 Italian/fish

🕒 Mon to Sat 12.00–23.30

🖥 www.zillialdo.com

🗄 all major credit cards ■ 12.5% optional service added

££ starters £7–£10.50 ■ mains £8–£28 ■ sides £3–£4 ■ desserts £7
■ express menu £16.90 & £19.90 ■ lowest bottle price £14.90

✪ Telly chef cooks fish for glitterati

Bright, brittle and brash, Zilli Fish is a part of Aldo Zilli's empire, which extends to books, telly stardom and anything else that buoys the profile up. You can see into the surprisingly calm kitchen through a large window as you walk along Brewer Street. Inside, in a hectic atmosphere, the restaurant serves a modern Italianate fish menu to London's media workers and the rest of the young Soho crowd. Tables are close and everything is conducted at a racy pace. Not ideal for a secret conversation or for plighting your troth, unless you want the whole place to cheer you on. The starters here are an attractive bunch: pan-fried squid with Thai sauce; mussels arrabiatta with bruschetta; tuna carpaccio with rocket and Parmesan. Then there are the pasta dishes, such as penne arrabiatta and spaghetti vongole (clams with Italian cherry tomatoes and basil). The menu goes on to feature a modestly entitled section, 'What we are famous for'. These are dishes like traditional deep-fried cod, chips and tartare sauce; spaghettini with whole fresh lobster. Or baked sea bass fillet, wrapped in banana leaf and cooked with cherry tomatoes, ginger, garlic, basil, olive oil and lemon dressing. From the side orders the rocket, Parmesan and roast tomato salad is a winning combination of flavours. Puddings include a ricotta and amarena cherry tart with cherry coulis; a home-made tiramisù with Pavesini; and pecorino and Gorgonzola with honey. But for something genuinely excessive, who could oppose 'fried banana spring rolls with white chocolate ice cream'?

→ For branches, see index

Victoria and Westminster

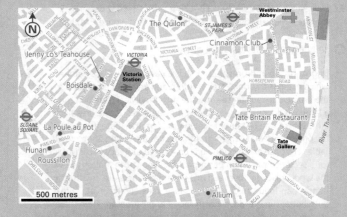

Westminster Abbey

The Quilon

Cinnamon Club

Jenny Lo's Teahouse

Boisdale

La Poule au Pot

Hunan

Roussillon

Tate Britain Restaurant

Tate Gallery

Allium

500 metres

Allium

Dolphin Square, Chichester Street, SW1 ■ 020 7798 6888

⊖ Pimlico

🍽 Modern British

🕒 Tues to Fri 12.00–15.00 & 18.00–22.30; Sat 18.00–22.30; Sun 18.00–22.30

🔗 www.allium.co.uk

🗄 all major credit cards ■ 12.5% service added

££ starters £7.50–£14.50 ■ mains £17–£24.50 ■ desserts £7.20 ■ set lunch £18.50 & £23.50 ■ set dinner £29.50 ■ lowest bottle price £16.50

⭐ Passport to Pimlico's finer dining

Anton Edelmann spent several decades heading the Savoy kitchens during that establishment's glory years and as chef-proprietor of Allium he follows the same star – carefully sourced, top-quality ingredients cooked carefully: Buccleuch beef, foie gras, frogs' legs, everything fresh and every dish designed to bring out the intrinsic flavours. Allium is a very sophisticated restaurant; it has a somewhat mannered style, but the cooking is first rate. Sitting in the dining room is rather like being in the first class lounge on a transatlantic liner – there's a plush feel with plenty of dark colours and chrome. The service has a similar polish and panache. The menu comes in three sections. There's a prix fixe two or three courses: poached skate; loin of pork with sautéed potatoes and wild mushrooms; hazelnut parfait – these are carefully chosen combinations and good value. The à la carte is full-on. Starters may include seared scallops on caramelised sweetbreads, lemon and thyme reduction, or a tortellini of cèpes. The menu changes gradually and continually, but mains may include herb-crusted loin of lamb on rosemary, Provençal vegetables, or roast suckling pig with black pudding spatzle – the spatzle are absolutely marvellous, as you expect from an Austrian chef. Puds are delicious: whole baked peach with ginger, or blueberry financier with lemon curd ice cream. The wine list offers good scope and you do not have to spend too wildly to get the best from it.

Boisdale

15 Ecclestone Street, SW1 ■ 020 7730 6922

⊖ Victoria

|O| Scottish

🕐 Mon to Fri 12.00–01.00; Sat 19.00–01.00

🖰 www.boisdale.co.uk

🖃 all major credit cards ■ 12.5% service added

££ starters £7.50–£17.50 ■ mains £15–£28.50 ■ sides £3.50–£3.95
■ desserts £6.50 ■ Flying Scotsman lunch £14 ■ '1780' menu £17.80
■ lowest bottle price £13.95

✪ Braveheart – the restaurant

Ranald Macdonald, who is next in line to be the Chief of Clanranald, owns Boisdale, and if that information gives you a premonition of what the restaurant is like you are probably thinking along the right lines. This is a very Scottish place, strong on hospitality, and with a befuddlingly large range of rare malt whiskies. Fresh produce – correction, fresh Scottish produce – rules wherever possible, and it is no wonder that the clubby atmosphere makes this a haven of choice for local businessmen. There are various Boisdale menus: one is a two-course menu with choice of five starters and five mains. Or there's the 'Flying Scotsman', a limited choice lunch presumably for people in a rush. Starters range from marinated Orkney herring and mini roast Macsween haggis, to dill-marinated Scottish salmon. Main courses veer from crofter's pie, to smoked haddock fishcakes, to – you've guessed it – roast Macsween haggis. The à la carte includes a good many luxury ingredients. As well as Lochcarnan smoked salmon from South Uist, and Rannoch Moor smoked venison with black truffle dressing, there's a rabbit, pigeon and foie gras terrine with pear chutney. Commendably, the mains feature fresh fish of the day, and fresh offal of the day. There are various Aberdeen Angus beef steaks: fillet with Béarnaise sauce and chips, or rib-eye with black truffle, pommes Dauphinoise, spinach and wild mushrooms. Puds also favour north of the border – look out for raspberry cranachan made with oatmeal and cream.

→ For branches, see index or website

Cinnamon Club

Old Westminster Library, Great Smith Street, SW1

■ 020 7222 2555

⊖ St James's Park

⦿ Indian

🕐 Mon to Fri 07.30–10.00, 12.00–14.45 & 18.00 to 22.45; Sat 18.00–22.45

🔗 www.cinnamonclub.com

🖥 all major credit cards ■ 12.5% optional service added

££ breakfast £10–£16 ■ starters £8–£12 ■ mains £11–£29 ■ sides £2.50–£6 ■ desserts £6–£8 ■ prix fixe weekday lunch & pre-/post-theatre £19 & £22 ■ lowest bottle price £16

✪ Sleek and accomplished modern Indian restaurant

Libraries and restaurants can have a good deal in common – lofty ceilings, large doors, old wood floors, plenty of panelling – just the features you need for a cracking formal restaurant. So it shouldn't surprise that what was once Westminster Library is now the Cinnamon Club. The whole operation is elegant, substantial and very pukka. Service is polished and attentive, the linen is snowy-white, the cutlery is heavy, the toilets opulent, and there are huge flower arrangements. The cooking is very good, and each dish offers a finely judged combination of flavours, every one distinct. There's an informed wine list. You can even pitch up for a power breakfast if you're seeking to influence the nearby parliamentary movers and shakers. And yes, unlikely as it may sound, this is an Indian restaurant. From the 'Appetisers' section of the menu there's tandoori halibut in Rajasthani spices; or sandalwood-flavoured chicken breast; or Bengali-style grilled half lobster. Such dishes set the tone. Mains are also well conceived: spice-crusted tandoori monkfish with tomato and lemon sauce; or Goan-style wild boar chop with vindaloo sauce – not something you'd find on the High Street. Go for the basket of breads as a side dish, a selection of unusual parathas, naans and rotis. Desserts are elegant: try the warm apple lassi with champagne granita, or the spiced banana tarte Tatin, with a deep-purple berry sorbet.

Hunan

51 Pimlico Road, SW1 ■ 020 7730 5712

⊖ Sloane Square/Victoria

⦿ Chinese

⏱ Mon to Sat 12.30–14.00 & 18.30–23.00

🗗 all major credit cards ■ 12.5% service added

££ à la carte (lunch only) starters £8 ■ mains £8.50–£9.50 ■ sides £7 ■ desserts £4 ■ tasting menus £31.80–£50 (multi-course) ■ lowest bottle price £12

✪ Interesting Chinese food, providing you do as you're told

The Hunan is now the domain of Mr Peng, Junior. As you venture into his restaurant you put yourself into his hands, to do with you what he will. It is rather like being trapped in a 1930s' B-movie. You order the boiled dumplings … and the griddle-fried, lettuce-wrapped dumplings turn up, 'because you will like them more'. Peng Junior is following principles established by his father, Peng Senior, who invented the 'feast' or tasting menu arrangements. But for most of the Hunan's regulars it was ever thus. The 'feast' is a multi-course extravaganza, varied according to the maestro's whims and the vagaries of the market, and it might include pigeon soup. Or goose. Or a dish of cold, marinated octopus. This fine food and attentive service is matched by the Hunan's elegant surroundings, but be warned – the prices are Pimlico rather than Chinatown, and they continue to escalate. If you want to defy two generations of Pengs and act knowledgeable, there is an à la carte at lunchtime. Standouts include hot and spicy beef; sizzling prawns; braised scallops in Hunan sauce; and spicy braised eggplant. However, for all but the strongest wills, resistance is useless and you'll probably end up with what is described on the menu as 'Hunan's special leave-it-to-us-feast – minimum two persons. We recommend those not familiar with Hunan cuisine and those who are looking for a wide selection of our favourite and unusual dishes to leave it to us to prepare a special banquet. Many of the dishes are not on the menu.' Even Alexis Gauthier, Roussillon's Michelin-starred head chef (see p. 156), leaves it to the Pengs.

Jenny Lo's Teahouse

14 Eccleston Street, SW1 ■ 020 7259 0399

⊖ Victoria

🍜 Chinese noodles

🕙 Mon to Fri 12.0–15.00 & 18.00–22.00; Sat 18.00–22.00

🗐 cash or cheque only ■ no service added

££ mains £5.75–£7.95 ■ sides £3.50–£5.95 ■ lowest bottle price £12.50

⭐ Homely Chinese noodle shop and teahouse

Jenny Lo's Teahouse is bright, bare and stylishly utilitarian – the complete opposite of trad, over-designed, Chinese restaurants. From the blocks of bright colours and refectory tables, you gather instantly that this is a somewhat smart, but still comfortable, place to eat. And that just about sums up the food, too. Service makes you think that you're in the politest cafeteria in the world and the prices don't spoil the illusion. Although portion sizes and seasoning can vary, the food is freshly cooked and generally delicious, which meets with unqualified approval from a loyal band of sophisticated regulars. The menu is divided into three main sections: soup noodles, wok noodles and rice dishes. Take your pick and then add some side dishes. The chilli beef soup is a good choice: a large bowl full of delicate, clear, chilli-spiked broth is bulked out with yards of slippery ho fun (ribbon noodles like thin tagliatelle), plus slivers of beef and fresh coriander. The black bean seafood noodles are an altogether richer and more solid affair, made from egg noodles with prawn, mussels, squid and peppers. Rice dishes range from long-cooked pork and chestnuts, to gong bao chicken with pine nuts. The side dishes are great fun, with good spareribs and guo tie, which are pan-cooked dumplings filled with either vegetables or pork. Spring onion pancakes are a Beijing street food made from flat, griddled breads laced with spring onions and served with a dipping sauce. Also on offer is a range of moody and therapeutic teas; perhaps you would benefit from Dr Xu's cleansing tea: 'A light tea for strengthening the liver and kidneys'.

La Poule au Pot

221 Ebury Street, SW1 ■ 020 7730 7763

⊖ Sloane Square

|⚈| French

🕑 Mon to Sat 12.30–14.30 (Sat 15.00) & 18.45–23.00; Sun 12.30–15.30 & 18.45–22.00

🖃 all major credit cards ■ 12.5% service added

££ starters £6.25–£16 ■ mains £14.25–£22 ■ sides £2.50–£3.75 ■ desserts £4.50–£6 ■ prix fixe lunch £15.75 & £17.75 ■ lowest bottle price £26 (magnum) or £3.40 (glass)

✪ La belle France – as found in Chelsea

La Poule au Pot is unreservedly a bastion of France in England, and has been for more than three decades. What's more, several of the staff have worked here for most of that time, and the restaurant itself has hardly changed at all, with its huge dried-flower baskets and a comfortable rustic atmosphere. The wide windows brighten lunch and there are tables outside under parasols, but by night, candlelight ensures that La Poule is a favourite for romantic assignations. Many a Chelsea affair has started (and finished) here, fuelled by the decidedly basic house wine. You are in trouble at La Poule au Pot if you don't understand at least some French, as the waiters have a Gallic insouciance and delight in incomprehension. A small dish of crudités in herb vinaigrette is set down as a bonne bouche. Different fresh breads come in huge chunks. The menu is deceptive, as there are usually several additional fresh daily specials. As a starter, the nine escargots deliver classic French authenticity with plenty of garlic and herbs. The soupe de poisson is not the commonly served thick soup, but a refined clear broth with chunks of sole and scallop, plus prawns and mussels. A main course of bifteck frîtes brings a perfectly cooked, French-cut steak with red-hot chips. The gigot aux flageolets is pink and tender, with beans that are well flavoured and not overcooked. There's calf 's liver, and carré d'agneau à l'ail, rack of lamb with garlic. The pudding menu features standards such as crème brûlée – huge, served in a rustic dish, and classically good. The wine list is unadventurous.

The Quilon

41 Buckingham Gate, SW1 ■ 020 7821 1899

⊖ Victoria

🍴 Indian

🕐 Mon to Fri 12.00–14.30 & 18.00–23.00; Sat 18.00–23.00

🖱 www.quilon.co.uk

🖥 all major credit cards ■ 12.5% service added

££ starters £5.50–£8.25 ■ mains £8.50–£23 ■ sides £2–£8.50 ■ desserts £5–£5.25 ■ prix fixe lunch £12.95 & £15.95 ■ lowest bottle price £19.50

✪ Classy South Indian cooking

The Quilon is a sophisticated restaurant – as it is part of the Taj hotels group this should come as no surprise, but words like sophisticated and élite are the exception rather than the rule when the subject is Indian restos. Given that this restaurant is tacked onto the end of a hotel, that the dining room is large, and that the plush décor is rather anodyne, it has a very good feel to it. The staff are helpful and there is an appreciative buzz. The stellar bargain is the set lunch, which is priced very keenly indeed. Starters include some interesting South Indian delicacies: banana flower vada – the flower is chopped and fried with lentils; karvari fried fish – very crisp and very dry outside, firm within; pepper shrimps – agreeably spicy; crab cakes – rich with curry leaves and ginger. As befits any Keralan restaurant, when you come to choose main courses fish is a good option – there is 'black cod Vattichathu', truly splendid, the black cod (not an Indian species by several thousand miles) is marinated in a tamarind mixture that accentuates its butteriness. Very good. The West Coast lamb curry is good and rich. The chicken masala admirably intense and dry. Veg dishes are very good – a raw jackfruit thoran is perfectly balanced with coconut and curry leaves. The breads are good as well, particularly the flaky, buttery Malabar paratha. The cooking here is very accomplished and dishes have finesse without losing the rich spicing of Southern India.

Roussillon

16 St Barnabas Street, SW1 ■ 020 7730 5550

⊖ Sloane Square/Victoria

🍽 French

🕘 Mon & Tues 18.30–22.45; Wed to Fri 12.00–14.30 & 18.30–22.45;
Sat 18.30–22.45

🖰 www.roussillon.co.uk

🖥 all major credit cards ■ 12.5% service added

££ set lunch £30 (3 courses) ■ dinner £45 (3 courses) ■ tasting menu
£65 (7 courses) ■ vegetarian tasting menu £55 (7 courses) ■ lowest
bottle price £17

⭐ Top-notch French cooking, in the modern style

The mainspring here is a young French chef called Alexis Gauthier
and he is obsessed with the quality and freshness of his ingredients.
Despite a dining room that has always looked rather stuffy, Roussillon
has gathered a shelf full of awards – even impressing the inspectors
from Michelin. To see the advantages of being seasonal, and market-
driven, try the excellent set lunch. The main menu offers three courses
and if you feel the urge to splash out there are multi-course showing-
off menus – the vegetarian 'Garden Menu' and the 'Seasonal Menu'.
Service is formal and slick. The menu is broken down into various sub-
sections: the classics, the garden, the land, the sea and river – and
changes with the seasons. You might open with a terrine of duck foie
gras with conference pear. Into 'the garden' for thin cream of broad
beans and radish leaves; royale of chicken liver; or autumn vegetables
and fruits cooked together in a pot with aged balsamic. Fish dishes
may include roast Dublin Bay prawns, salad of purple artichoke
and lemon pepper. 'The land' brings pan-fried, lightly battered
sweetbreads, sautéed cèpes and creamed flat parsley, or Gloucester
Old Spot pork prepared in two ways – tenderly braised and pink-
roasted, with pommes boulangère. Gastronomic stuff. You have to
warm to anyone so keen on chocolate puddings. There's white and
black chocolate pyramide; chocolate praline finger; and a chocolate
soufflé. Vegetarians (and anyone treating a vegetarian guest) can dine
particularly well here.

Tate Britain Restaurant

Millbank, SW1 ■ 020 7887 8825   ♿

⊖ Pimlico

🍽 Modern British

🕐 Mon to Sat 11.30–15.00 (lunch) & 15.00–17.30 (tea); Sun 10.00–
11.30 (breakfast), 11.30–15.00 (brunch) & 15.00–17.50 (tea)

🌐 www.tate.org

🗄 all major credit cards ■ 12.5% optional service added

££ breakfast £4.75–£6.95 ■ starters £6.75 ■ mains £14.50–£17.50
■ sides £2.25 ■ desserts £5.50–£7.50 ■ set menus (only during
exhibitions) £17.50 & £19.95 ■ afternoon tea £3.75–£9.95 ■ lowest
bottle price £15

⭐ Still a place of pilgrimage for wine lovers

In these days of a 'sandwich at the desk' office culture you have to
think before recommending a restaurant that doesn't open for dinner.
For the foodie, the Tate Britain Restaurant is worth a visit; for the
winey, a visit is essential. This restaurant's love affair with wine began
in the 1970s, when the food was dodgy and it seemed as if the only
customers were wine merchants smug at the impossibly low prices.
Today there may be fewer florid gents enjoying a three-bottle lunch,
but the atmosphere is soothing and the wine list not only fascinates,
but offers outstanding value as well. The menu changes on a regular
basis and offers admirably seasonal dishes. Although there is no
indication on the menu, there are dishes to suit the oenophiles, and
dishes for civilian diners. Thus wine folk might choose simple starters
such as dressed Cornish crab mayonnaise, while the others can opt
for eggs Benedict with smoked haddock. Mains touch most of the
bases: seared skate wings with capers, parsley and crisp potatoes;
roast squab pigeon with butternut squash and cranberry jus. There
are tempting puddings to team with dessert wines. The wine list is
wonderful, and changes constantly. Don't be intimidated by the vast
book – take your time, the wine waiters are knowledgeable. Bottles
are served at the right temperature and decanted without fuss when
necessary. Two tips – look at the half bottles, and ask advice.

Waterloo and South Bank

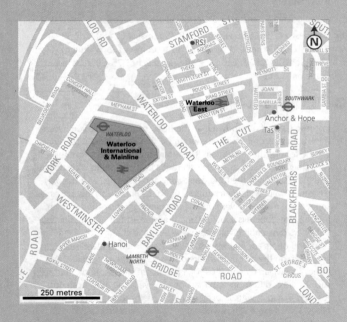

Anchor & Hope

36 The Cut, SE1 ■ 020 7928 9898

⊖ Southwark/Waterloo

🍽 British/gastropub

🕐 Mon 18.00–22.30; Tues to Sat 12.00–14.30 & 18.00–22.30

🖻 all major credit cards except AmEx ■ no service added

££ starters £4–£7 ■ mains £10–£22 ■ shared dishes (for 4) £40–£60 ■ sides £2.80–£3.20 ■ desserts £4.50–£6.80 ■ lowest bottle price £10

⭐ Champion gastropub

There's one marker that infallibly signals really excellent food.
You might spot it in the way the menu is written, in the presentation of the dishes, or in the way things taste, but the key quality is confidence. And at the Anchor & Hope there's confidence aplenty. This gastropub has deservedly won a shed load of awards – despite various minor eccentricities. It's a rough-looking dining area and there is no booking (which may mean queuing unless you are ready and waiting when the doors open), but the pricing is fair and the cooking is very confident indeed. The menu changes twice a day, but starters may include smoked sprats with horseradish, or crab on toast – how understated is that? Leeks gribiche; a warm snail and pig's head salad, or Spanish ham and green tomatoes on toast. Among the mains are the economically named tripe and chips; roast pigeon and semolina gnocchi; scallops escarole and morels; and slow-cooked Middle White pork with choucroute. Then there are a few dishes that are for sharing, such as a slow-cooked stuffed duck. Or how about ordering up a Lancashire hotpot to feed six? The cooking is inspired and owes a good deal to the time one of the chef-proprietors spent at St John (see p. 194). The wine list is un-graspingly priced and service, which can get ruffled, is in tune with the surroundings. Puds are pukka – chocolate pot; pear and almond tart; or a lemon and almond cake with blood oranges. The Anchor & Hope is strongly recommended.

Hanoi

139 Westminster Bridge Road, SE1 ■ 020 7207 9747

⊖ Waterloo /Lambeth North

⑩ Vietnamese

🕐 Mon to Fri 12.00–15.00 & 17.30–23.30; Sat & Sun 17.30–23.30

🗗 all major credit cards ■ no service added

££ starters £2–£3.50 ■ mains £5.50–£7 ■ sides £2–£3.50 ■ desserts £2–£3 ■ menus: set lunch £12; dinner £15 & £17 ■ lowest bottle price £9

✪ Family-run, homely Vietnamese

This is still the Long family's restaurant. Formerly known as the Little Saigon, the Hanoi still sells good, homely Vietnamese food from a comprehensive menu. You will eat best by sticking to the trad dishes, and should take this opportunity to get to grips with Vietnamese spring rolls – both the crispy deep-fried kind and the 'crystal' variety. The latter are round discs of rice pastry like giant, translucent Communion wafers, which you soak in a bowl of hot water until pliable, and then roll around a filling of fresh salady things, interesting sauces, and slivers of meat grilled on a portable barbecue. Run amok with the starters. Vietnamese imperial spring rolls are of the crispy fried variety, but they are served cut into chunks and with lettuce leaves to roll them up in. Topping the bill are crystal spring rolls – delicate pancakes (in this case 'pre-rolled'), which are quite delicious. Also good is the strangely resilient Vietnamese fish cake. Each of the starters seems to come with its own special dipping sauce, and the table is soon littered with an array of little saucers – look out for the extra-sweet white plum sauce and the extra-hot brown chilli oil. For mains, Hanoi grilled chicken with honey; stir-fried monkfish with lemon grass and chillies; special Saigon prawn curry; and the house special, fried crispy noodles, which comes with chicken and shrimps, can all be recommended. But the best recommendation is to ask the helpful staff to compose you the perfect meal, it may not all be familiar but it will certainly be delicious.

RSJ

13a Coin Street, SE1 ■ 020 7928 4554

⊖ Waterloo

🍴 Modern European

🕐 Mon to Fri 12.00–14.00 & 17.30–23.00; Sat 17.30–23.00

🖰 rsj.uk.com

🖰 all major credit cards ■ 12.5% service added

££ starters £5.75–£8.75 ■ mains £10.95–£17.95 ■ sides £2.50–£2.95
■ desserts £5.25–£5.95 ■ lowest bottle price £14.95

❂ The definitive Loire wine list

Rolled Steel Joist may seem a curious name for a restaurant, but it is appropriate – they can point out the RSJ holding up the first floor if you wish! What's more interesting about RSJ is that it's owned by a man with a passion for the wines of the Loire. Nigel Wilkinson has compiled his list mainly from wines produced in this region, and it features dozens of lesser-known Loire reds and whites – wines that clearly deserve a wider following. Notes about recent vintages both interest and educate, and each wine is well described. The menu is based on classical dishes, but with a light touch and some innovative combinations as well. The starters might include purple sprouting broccoli and garlic leaf risotto; smoked haddock soup with baby spinach and crème fraîche; or terrine of free-range chicken and foie gras. Moving on to the main courses, typical choices might include roast cod fillet with a casserole of spicy butter beans; fillet of beef, black pepper and chive butter, braised potatoes; and breast of guinea fowl, Jersey royal potatoes, spring greens, shallot and carrots. The menu also features an above-average number of vegetarian options, such as fresh sage gnocchi with a blue cheese sauce, new season peas and broad beans. The puddings can be serious stuff: white chocolate and passion fruit mousse, or pear and pistachio tart with camomile ice cream. Wine lovers captivated by the Loire should check out the RSJ Wine Company, or visit the website if they have a penchant to do their shopping online.

Tas

33 The Cut, SE1 ■ 020 7928 1444   ♿

⊖ Waterloo

🍽 Turkish

🕐 Mon to Sat 12.00–23.30; Sun 12.00–22.30

🖥 tasrestaurant.com

🖫 all major credit cards ■ 12.5% service added

££ starters £3.55–£4.45 ■ mains £5.25–£14.45 ■ sides £2.15–£4.15
■ desserts £3.35–£3.85 ■ set menus £8.25–£18.50 ■ lowest bottle
price £11.95

✪ Lively, cheap and Turkish

This place is heaving with office parties and stag or hen nights,
so not only can you expect colourful crockery, but also an overdose
of noise and liveliness. Tas is a bright and bustling Turkish restaurant
where eating is cheap. The various menus and set menus offer a
baffling choice and there is often live music. Consider the set menus
as a simple way through the maze. Sahan menu includes starter and
main; renk menu is a mixed mezze. There's even a set menu called
the 'Aslan', which is presumably aimed at lion-sized appetites. The
main menu rushes off in a great many directions at once. There are
four soups, a dozen cold starters, a dozen hot starters, eight salads,
a dozen vegetarian dishes, plus casseroles, fish and grilled meats
aplenty. Take a breath and then treat Tas like a simple Turkish eatery.
Start with some mezze. There's tarama salata; calamari; houmous;
cacik, a simple cucumber and yogurt dip; hellim, which is grilled
cheese – in fact all the usual suspects. Then go on to some grilled
meats: tavuk shish is chicken kebab; kofte is a minced lamb kebab.
Or there are the casseroles. Hunkar begendi is aubergine topped with
lamb; and incik is lamb cooked on the bone. One element of the menu
that makes Tas stand out from most Turkish eateries is the long list of
fish and shellfish dishes. As well as kalamari, there is balik bugiulama,
which is steamed cod, and pirasali mercan, pan-fried dorade. Baklava
is all very well, but it is probably outsold by chocolate cake.

→ For branches, see index or website

The City and east

Brick Lane and Spitalfields

Arkansas Café

Unit 12, Old Spitalfields Market, E1 ■ 020 7377 6999   ♿

⊖ Liverpool Street

🍴 North American/steak

🕐 Mon to Fri 12.00–14.30; Sun 12.00–16.00

💳 Mastercard, Visa ■ no service added

££ starters £3.50–£6.30 ■ mains £6–£16 ■ sandwiches £4–£10.95
■ sides 60p–£1 ■ desserts £2.50 ■ lowest bottle price £9.25

✪ Worship at the smoky altar of genuine Arkansas BBQ

American Bubba Helberg and his wife Sarah claim that they serve the best barbecue this side of the pond and they may just be right. As you approach the Arkansas Café the glow from its steel-pit barbecue invites you in. Their food is fresh and simple, and Bubba chooses his own steaks from Smithfield Market to ensure that the meat is marbled through for tenderness. He marinates and smokes his own beef brisket and ribs, and his recipe for the latter won him a soul-food award back home. His secret home-made barbecue sauce is on every table. Décor is spartan – clean-scrubbed tables, canvas chairs and paper plates. It's folksy but fun. There are no starters and 'No fries'. Any of the steaks – like the Irish steak platter – are good bets, chargrilled with Bubba's special sauce and served with seasonal vegetables. Note that the price is genuinely market-sensitive and can rise and fall. Corn-fed French chicken is tender and full of flavour, and a side order of chilli provides a spicy sauce-like accompaniment. Most of the other dishes on the menu are platters or sandwiches, the latter including choices like chargrilled Barbary duck breast sandwich; free-range pork sandwich; beef brisket Texas-style sandwich, which comes meltingly tender and smoky; and, of course, hot dog. Puddings include New York-style lemon cheesecake and New Orleans pecan pie. They are as sweet and as solid as they should be. The wine list is short and to the point, but the beer list is long. Bubba will be happy to bring his magnificent travelling barbecue and pig roaster to your party, unless it happens to be scheduled for the fourth of July – he's usually booked by the American Embassy.

Bengal Village

75 Brick Lane, E1 ■ 020 7366 4868

⊖ Aldgate East/Liverpool Street

|⚫| Indian

🕐 Mon to Fri 12.00–14.30 & 18.00–23.30; Sat & Sun 12.00–24.00

🖰 www.bengalvillage.com

🖨 all major credit cards ■ no service added

££ starters 60p–£3.95 ■ mains £4.50–£8.50 ■ sides £1.25–£3.50
■ desserts £1.95–£3.50 ■ lunch menu £5.95 ■ lowest bottle price
£5.95

✪ Bangladeshi cooking – the genuine article

Ignore the rabidly commercial curry houses and seek out
something more satisfying. Brick Lane is becoming ever more
sophisticated. Where once all was BYO restaurants serving rough-
and-ready curries at bargain-basement prices to impoverished punters
seeking chilli, there's now a growing crop of slick new establishments
serving authentic Bangladeshi cooking. The Bengal Village is one
such place. There's a blond wood floor and modernist chairs, but it's
about more than just design. The menu touches all the bases: trad
curryholics can still plough their way through more than a hundred
old-style curries, but now they can also try some more interesting
Bangladeshi dishes. Bucking what seems to be becoming the trend,
starters are not the best dishes at the Bengal Village. Bowal mas biran
is boal fish that has been deep-fried and is served with a rich sauce.
There are four shatkora curries, the shatkora being a small green fruit
that has a delightful bitter-citrus tang and goes very well with rich
meats – lamb shatkora, for example. Then there are ureebisi dishes,
traditionally made with the seeds of a large runner-bean-like plant
– try chicken ureebisi. There are also some interesting vegetarian
options: chalkumra – subtitled 'ash-ground', made with a pumpkin-
like gourd. The marrow kofta is a curry with large and satisfactorily
dense vegetable dumplings floating, or rather sinking, in it. If charm
is to be the decider, you must try bhug mas bhuna – 'A large fish
spotty like a leopard found in Bangladesh'.

Canteen

2 Crispin Place, EC1 ■ 0845 686 1133

⊖ Liverpool Street

🍴 British

🕐 Mon to Fri 11.00–23.00; Sat & Sun 09.00–23.00

🖱 www.canteen.co.uk

🗄 all major credit cards ■ 12.5% optional service added

££ starters £4.50–£8 ■ mains £7–£12 ■ sides £3 ■ desserts £5 ■ lowest bottle price £12

✪ The modern face of traditional cooking

The re-birth of the Liverpool Street end of Spitalfields Market has not been without trauma, but it's a pleasure to announce that the outcome is rather slick, with office blocks jostling with boutiquey food shops and various restaurants. Canteen's manifesto bangs on about 'honest food, nationally sourced, skilfully prepared and reasonably priced' and in the main this is a resto that lives up to its billing. The dining room is modern and you get to choose between booths and long tables. The menu changes with the seasons and starts with various breakfast favourites – bacon sandwich; black pudding with bubble and squeak; and eggs Benedict – served throughout the day. Then there are starters like hot buttered Arbroath Smokey; devilled kidneys on toast; and the rather good potted duck, which comes with piccalilli. Mains range from macaroni cheese, to fishcake with mushy peas, and a 'pie of the day' – which might be as simple, and as good, as chicken, ham and mushroom: a tall-sided pie like a pork pie, but with good pastry and a well-seasoned filling, served with decent mash and buttered cabbage. This is a very successful dish and something of a bargain. Order 48 hours in advance (and take four or in some cases six people) and you can have a roast – leg of lamb; chicken; loin of pork. Canteen is a 'helpful', unfussy sort of place – there is a section of the menu listing dishes that are for 'fast service', but everything else is cooked to order. Puds are trad, with a 'cake counter' offering a sugar rush for those mid-afternoon moments.

Herb & Spice

11a White's Row, E1 ■ 020 7247 4050

⊖ Aldgate East/Liverpool Street

🍴 Indian

🕐 Mon to Fri 11.30–14.30 & 17.30–23.30

🗗 all major credit cards ■ no service added

££ starters £2.25–£4.75 ■ mains £3.95–£9.95 ■ sides £2.25–£2.75 ■ desserts £2.25–£2.95 ■ lowest bottle price £7.95

✪ A charming and unreconstructed curry house

Do not let the tiny, rather cramped and garish dining room put you off this treasure of a curry house on White's Row, a small road just off Commercial Street and tucked in behind Spitalfields. A loyal clientele from the City means that to secure one of the 22 seats you'll probably have to book. What sets Herb & Spice apart from the pack is that the dishes are freshly cooked and well prepared, and yet the prices are still reasonable. When the food arrives it will surprise you: it's on the hot side, with plenty of chilli and bold, fresh flavours. It's not often that the pappadoms grab your attention. They do here. Fresh, light and crisp, they are accompanied by equally good home-made chutneys – perky chopped cucumber with coriander leaf, and a hot, yellowy-orange, tamarind-soured yogurt. The kebabs make excellent starters: murgi tikka – chicken, very well cooked; shami kebab – minced meat with fresh herbs; gosht tikka – tender lamb cubes. For a main course you might try the excellent murgi biryani, chicken cooked with saffron rice and served with a good, if rather hot, vegetable curry. Or there's bhuna gosht, a model of its type – a rich, well-seasoned lamb curry with whole black peppercorns and shards of cassia bark. Murgi rezalla is chicken tikka in sauce; it's much hotter and comes with more vegetables than its cousin, the chicken tikka masala. The breads are good, too: from the decent naan to the shabzi paratha, a thin, crisp wholemeal paratha stuffed with vegetables. If you are inclined towards masochism, try a real tongue-trampler – the dhal shamber, very hot, and very, very sweet indeed.

The Lahore Kebab House

2–10 Umberston Street, E1 ■ 020 7481 9737

⊖ Whitechapel/Aldgate East

🍽 Indian

🕐 daily 12.00–24.00

🖶 all major credit cards ■ no service added

££ starters 75p–£6.50 ■ mains £5 & £6 ■ sides £2.50–£6.50 ■ desserts £2 ■ unlicensed, BYO (no corkage)

⭐ A chillied success story

This is a nondescript, indeed dowdy-looking, kebab house serving excellent and very cheap fare. Recent years, however, have seen a few changes, and now the 'Original' Lahore Kebab House is bent on world domination. The resto here has spread up the street and now seats 500 or so. What was once a cherished secret among a handful of curry lovers is now big business. Thankfully, the food in Umberston Street is still good and spicy, prices are still reasonable, and the service brusque enough to disabuse you of any thoughts that the smart, round, marquetry tables and posh shop front are signs of impending mediocrity. What they do here, they do very well indeed. Rotis tend to arrive unordered – the waiter watches how you eat and brings fresh bread as and when he sees fit. For starters, the kebabs are standouts. Seekh kebab, mutton tikka and chicken tikka are all very fresh, very hot and very good, and served with a yogurt and mint dipping sauce. The meat or chicken biryanis are also splendid, well spiced and with the rice taking on all the rich flavours. The karahi gosht and karahi chicken are uncomplicated dishes of tender meat in a rich gravy. And on Friday there is a special dish – lamb chop curry. Also noteworthy is the masala fish. The dal tarka is made from whole yellow split peas, while sag aloo brings potatoes in a rich and oily spinach purée. For dessert try the delightful home-made kheer, which is a special kind of trad rice pudding with cardamom. BYO by all means – but remember, when it comes to chilli burn, lassi is more cooling.

New Tayyab

83–89 Fieldgate Street, E1 ■ 020 7247 6400

⊖ Whitechapel/Aldgate East

🍴 Indian

🕐 daily 12.00–24.00

🖰 www.tayyabs.co.uk

🗗 all major credit cards ■ no service added

££ starters 70p–£10 ■ mains £3.50–£10 ■ sides £3.50 ■ desserts £2
■ unlicensed, BYO (no corkage)

✪ Join the queue, relish the prices

The Tayyab group has come a long way since those first days in 1974. After the initial café came the sweet shop, and then the New Tayyab took over what was once the corner pub. So no. 83 was transformed from a scruffy converted pub into a smart new designer restaurant. Now it's a slick 180-seater, there's art on the walls, smart lighting and the chairs are leather and chrome. Miraculously, the food remains straightforward Pakistani fare: good, freshly cooked and served without pretension. And more miraculous still, the prices have stayed lower than you would believe possible. Booking is essential if you don't want to spend your evening in a queue and service is speedy and slick. This is not a place to um and er over the menu. The simpler dishes are terrific, particularly the five pieces of chicken tikka, served on an iron sizzle dish alongside a small plate of salady things and a medium-fierce, sharp, chilli dipping sauce. They do the same thing with mutton, or there's a plate of four large and splendid lamb chops. Sheekh kebabs and shami kebabs are bought by the skewer. There are round fluffy naan breads, but try the wholemeal roti, which is deliciously nutty and crisp. The karahi dishes are simple and tasty: 'karahi chicken' is chicken in a rich sauce, and karahi aloo gosht is lamb with potatoes in another rich sauce, heavily flavoured with bay leaves. Or there's karahi mixed vegetables. A list of interesting daily specials includes dishes such as the trad mutton curry nihari, which is served every Monday.

St John Bread & Wine

94–96 Commercial Street, E1 ■ 020 7247 8724

⊖ Liverpool Street

🍽 British

🕐 Mon to Fri 09.00–23.00; Sat 10.00–23.00; Sun 10.00–18.00

🖰 www.stjohnbreadandwine.com

🖫 all major credit cards ■ 12.5% service for parties of 6 or more

££ breakfast £2.50–£6.80 ■ starters £2–£10 ■ mains £11.80–£14
   ■ desserts £6–£7.40 ■ lowest bottle price £14.50

⭐ Best British Restaurant – award winner

**This place is younger brother to St John in nearby Clerkenwell
(see p. 194)**, and is home to what may be London's most civilised
elevenses – 'Seed cake and a glass of Madeira'. It's a stylish but
utilitarian room with small, tightly packed tables and chairs, and
the whole place is dominated by an open-plan bakery and kitchen:
wafts from the racks of cooling bread will boot your tastebuds into
life. The food is honest here. Simple. Delicious. Very good value, as
you would expect with a menu written by Fergus Henderson. Said
menu has a time line running down the side of it: 08.00 could mean
an Old Spot bacon sandwich or porridge and prunes. The seed cake
combo features at 11.00. By lunchtime at noon you'll find oysters;
game broth; pickled herrings; roast shallots; and goats' curd; or you
could splash out on langoustines and mayonnaise. The menu changes
with the seasons and what is available at market, so perhaps there'll
be braised cuttlefish or red mullet served with chicory and anchovy.
Maybe pigeon with mushy peas appeals? Beside the timeline for
19.00 there's roast Large Black pork with fennel. All these dishes are
supported by fabulous bread, and a fairly forgiving selection of wines.
You shouldn't expect anything elaborate or fancypants, but you can
be sure of big flavours and intriguing combinations of taste and
texture. Puds are good – meringue, pomegranate and cream; baked
cheesecake with Marc. Should you be feeling Proustian, take half a
dozen madeleines home with you.

Wild Cherry

241 Globe Road, E2 ■ 020 8980 6678

⊖ Bethnal Green

🍴 Vegetarian

🕐 Mon 11.00–15.00; Tues to Fri 11.00–19.00; Sat 10.00–16.00

🖅 Mastercard, Visa ■ no service added

££ Sat £3.90–£5.95 (all-day breakfast) ■ starters £2.50–£5.25 ■ mains
£1.75–£4.75 ■ desserts £1.80–£3.25 ■ unlicensed, BYO (£1 corkage)

✪ Vegetarian, and proud of it

Wild Cherry is an offshoot of the London Buddhist Centre and was
once a soup kitchen for workers and devotees. A genuine vegetarian
restaurant that, as the mission statement by the door proclaims,
'exists firstly to provide fresh home-cooked vegetarian meals for
the local community'. This is a bright, clean, self-service venue with
modern wooden tables and Arne Jacobsen chairs. A blackboard lists
the daily menu and you choose from selections like miso and aramé
soup; cream cheese and spinach and polenta with roast vegetables;
or chickpea and spinach curry with coriander and coconut served
with basmati rice; and there's a hot quiche of the day (such as Stilton
and celery) with two salads. On to a choice of three different salads
every day – maybe beetroot, carrot and ruby chard with orange
hazelnut dressing, and there's always a quiche and two further hot
dishes. Baked potatoes include a choice of comforting fillings like
houmous, grated Cheddar and tzatziki. Salads (which vary in size
from a single scoop to regular or large) include choices like aramé
rice; ruby chard, cherry tomato and fresh chive; mixed leaf; Moroccan
chickpea with rocket; and coleslaw with vegan mayonnaise. Puddings
include chocolate and beetroot cake or prune and honey cake.
Choose from fourteen different teas, ten of them herbal, plus Free
Trade coffee (by the mug, or by the cafetière), and a choice of soya or
cow's milk. There are usually wheat-free, gluten-free and sugar-free
options available and all the portions here are huge; everything tastes
wholesome and it's amazing value.

The City

1 Lombard Street – the Brasserie

1 Lombard Street, EC3 ■ 020 7929 6611 ♿

⊖	Bank
🍴	French
🕐	Mon to Fri 07.30–11.00 (breakfast) & 11.30–22.00
🖰	www.1lombardstreet.com
🗗	all major credit cards ■ 12.5% optional service added
££	breakfast £9.50–£16.50 ■ starters £6.50–£9.75 ■ mains £9.95–£27.50 ■ sides £3.50–£4.75 ■ desserts £6.50–£7.50 ■ lowest bottle price £16.50

✪ City stuff for City people

The Brasserie at 1 Lombard Street was formerly a banking hall, so many of the suited and booted clientele will feel at home here. It's an imposing room (doubtless it was designed to be so) and the circular bar sits under a suitably impressive glass dome. The brasserie menu is a model of its kind, long but straightforward with a range of dishes that is up to any meal occasion. It delivers on pretty much every front, serving satisfying dishes made with good fresh ingredients, both stylish and unfussy at the same time. The bar, meanwhile, is like any chic City watering hole – loud, brisk and crowded, with simultaneous conversations in every European language. There is a smaller, 40-seater room at the rear, set aside for fine dining at fancy prices. The brasserie menu changes every couple of months to satisfy the band of regulars, and there are daily specials in addition. The starters can be ambitious, such as seasonal game terrine, or simple, like Scotch broth, while further down the menu there will be some even more comfortable options such as soft-boiled, free-range egg served with smoked haddock and spinach gratin. There's enough listed under shellfish and crustacea to fuel even the wildest celebrations, including griddled scallops with black pudding leeks and brown butter, and casserole of mussels and clams. The Classics section has coq au vin à la Bourguignon; the Meat section lists steak, sausages, and liver. Puds triumph – there's an indulgent warm chocolate fondant – and there's something on the wine list to suit most tastes.

Aurora

Great Eastern Hotel, 40 Liverpool Street, EC2

■ 020 7618 7000   ♿

⊖ Liverpool Street

🍽 Modern British

🕐 Mon to Fri 12.00–14.30 & 18.45–22.00 8

🖰 www.aurora.restaurant.co.uk

🗗 all major credit cards ■ 12.5% optional service added

££ starters £9–£16.50 ■ mains £17.50–£23 ■ desserts £7.50–£8 ■ set lunch £28 ■ tasting menu £50 ■ lowest bottle price £22

✪ A genuine City slicker

The lofty dining room, with soaring pillars and a stained glass dome, is a period piece. The cooking is more modern in style, but equally polished and elegant. Aurora is in the City and pretty much of the City and for the City. So expect diners in waistcoats, plenty of linen, cigars, and a knowledgeable sommelier with a giant book. Aurora is not over-formal, however, and there are some interesting and good-value bottles scattered throughout the wine list. The food is very good, and there is an admirable reliance on seasonal dishes and carefully sourced ingredients. Starters range from pan-fried quail, marinated white radish, sunflower seeds and prunes; to slow confit pork belly, served with a sauté of Bourguignonne snails – a brilliant dish, richly melting pork complemented by the earthiness of the snails. Another stunner is the salad of melon and Cornish crab, with nostraline olives, and shellfish dressing – the balance between the sweet crab and the slight crunch of the thin disc of watermelon just about perfect. These are considered dishes and very pretty on the plate. The main courses range from pan-fried brill, baby leeks, with roast cèpes and claret butter sauce; to pot-roast wild duck, fig and port sauce (very tender and suitably rich); by way of roast and confit partridge, with chestnut gnocchi and smoked bacon jus – a splendid dish with well-balanced flavours. Puds are good and the cheese trolley is an epic vehicle laden with goodies. Service is whisper slick and the whole experience is a very comfortable one. Just the place to take your broker to lunch.

Barcelona Tapas Bar

1a Bell Lane, E1 ■ 020 7247 7014

⊖ Aldgate

🍽 Spanish/tapas

🕔 Mon to Fri 11.00–23.00

🖰 www.barcelona/tapas.com

🖰 all major credit cards ■ 12.5% optional service added

££ tapas £2.95–£13.95 ■ mains £5.95–£11.95 ■ sides £2.95–£3.50
■ desserts £2.95–£3.95 ■ menus (min 2 people) £9.99–£19.99
■ lowest bottle price £10.95

⊗ Barca fans will feel at home

The original link in a growing chain, there are now five Barcelona tapas bars. You'll find this branch at the start of the East End, not a hundred yards from the towering buildings of the City, and close to the market stalls of Petticoat Lane and Middlesex Street. On one of the less salubrious corners you'll see a banner bearing the legend 'tapas'. Descend the stairs into a cramped basement that seats about twenty and you're in the Barcelona – one of London's best tapas bars. The range of snacks wouldn't be sniffed at in Barcelona or Madrid, and it includes a fair few Catalan specialities, including the classic tomato- and garlic-rubbed bread – a good accompaniment to any tapas session. There are a number of tapas lined up in typical Spanish style along the back half of the bar, but these are just a few of the selection on offer. The Barcelona has a vast (in more ways than one) menu, written in Spanish and Catalan with English translations. Many are simple, such as Serrano ham, or queso manchego, or aceitunas (olives), and rely on the excellent quality of the raw ingredients. More skill is involved in creating the paellas; the paella Valenciana is particularly good. Unusually for such a small place with such a huge choice, there's no need to worry about freshness. One of the other bigger, smarter, newer and less charming branches of Barcelona is nearby, and the apparent lull between ordering and receiving your order may be because the girl is running around the corner to another kitchen to fetch some.

→ For branches, see index or website

Café Spice Namaste

16 Prescot Street, E1 ■ 020 7488 9242 &

⊖ Aldgate/Tower Hill

🍴 Indian

🕑 Mon to Fri 12.00–15.00 & 18.30–22.30; Sat 18.30–22.30

🖑 www.cafespice.co.uk

🗗 all major credit cards ■ 12.5% optional service added

££ starters £4.25–£7.25 ■ mains £9.75–£15.95 ■ sides £4.50–£5.50
■ desserts £3.75–£4.75 ■ lowest bottle price £14.50

⭐ Gifted chef lifts Indian cooking

During the week this restaurant is packed with movers and shakers, all busily moving and shaking. They come in for lunch at 11.59 am and they go out again at 12.59 pm. Lunchtimes and even weekday evenings the pace is fast and furious, but come Saturday nights you can settle back and really enjoy Cyrus Todiwala's exceptional cooking. The menu, which changes throughout the year, sees Parsee delicacies rubbing shoulders with dishes from Goa, North India, Hyderabad and Kashmir, all of them precisely spiced and well presented. The tandoori specialities, in particular, are awesome, fully flavoured by cunning marinades. Start with a voyage around the tandoor. The murg kay tikkay tastes as every chicken tikka should, with yogurt, ginger, cumin and chillies all playing their part. Or there's venison tikka aflatoon, which originates in Gwalior and is flavoured with star anise and cinnamon. Also notable is the papeta nay eeda na pattice – a potato cake perked up with egg, coconut, green peas and Parsee-style hot tomato gravy. For a main course, fish lovers should consider the patra ni machchi, pomfret stuffed with green coconut chutney. Choose meat and you should try the dhansaak, which is a truly authentic version of the much-misrepresented Parsee speciality; it is served with a small kebab and brown-onion rice. Breads are also excellent, and some of the accompaniments and vegetable dishes belie their lowly status at the back of the book-sized menu. Try baingan bharta – an aubergine classic. It's also worth checking out the weekly changing 'specials menu'.

→ For branches, see index

Christopher's in the City

18 Creechurch Lane, EC3 ■ 020 7623 3999

⊖ Aldgate/Bank

🍴 North American

🕐 Mon to Fri 12.00–15.00 & 18.00–21.00

🔗 www.christophersgrill.com

🗄 all major credit cards ■ 12.5% optional service added

££ starters £4.50–£7 ■ mains £11.50–£19.50 ■ sides £2.50–£3.50
■ desserts £5.50 ■ lowest bottle price £14

✪ Modern and comfortable City resto

If green is your favourite colour, Christopher's in the City will not be
for you. The dining room seems shockingly modern with lime green
chairs, green strip lights and … much else that is green besides. Do
not be put off, as you sit in the comfortable chairs and tuck into the
very accessible food, you will warm to this place. It doesn't seem so
very outlandish when you spot the many favourites on the menu.
The food seems somehow familiar as it is broadly North American in
style, but with the rough edges smoothed away. Starters may include
a very creamy sweetcorn and scallop chowder – good thick soup,
sweet shellfish; carpaccio of beef 'Harry's Bar' dressing; Maryland
crab cakes with red pepper mayo and rocket salad – well seasoned
and nicely crisped outside. Other options might be linguine with fried
prawn and chilli, or a goats' cheese mousse, with confit tomatoes
and pecan dressing. Main courses go from the straightforward: a
New York striploin steak, with fries and Béarnaise sauce – cooked as
asked for, sound chips; to more complex – a hunk of grilled swordfish
comes with a 'clams *'Casino'* sauce'. Double-cooked shoulder of lamb
comes with minted pea purée and spiced broth; in season there may
be a roast red leg partridge, with Napa cabbage, California raisins
and a reduction of white port. Puds are steady – chocolate tart with
raspberries; baked New York cheesecake; or crème brulée. Service is
friendly and the wine list has something to please the parsimonious
as well as those with a record bonus to squander.

The Don

20 St Swithins Lane, EC4 ■ 020 7626 2606

○ Bank

🍽 Modern European

🕐 (Restaurant) Mon to Fri 12.00–14.30 & 18.30–22.30; (Bistro) Mon to Fri 12.00–15.00 & 18.00–22.00

🖱 www.thedonrestaurant.com

💳 all major credit cards ■ 12.5% optional service added

££ starters £5.90–£9.95 ■ mains £8.95–£23.95 ■ desserts £5.95–£7.50 ■ lowest bottle price £16.95

⭐ Rich food in a rich setting

George Sandeman first took over the cellars at 20 St Swithin's Lane in 1798. And very fine cellars they are too, complete with an ornate black iron 'Capital Patent Crane' for lowering barrels into the depths. Now it is home to The Don restaurant and bistro, which takes its name from the trademark portrait of Sandeman port's 'Don', which has been re-hung, with due ceremony, at the gateway to this hidden courtyard. The lofty room on the ground floor makes a striking restaurant, while the vaulted brick cellars make a grand backdrop for the Bistro. The feel of the smart ground floor restaurant is sophisticated – this place is aiming directly for the fine-dining market, and the strategy seems to be working. The food is accomplished: starters range from a terrine of foie gras, with a prune and Cognac dressing and toasted brioche; to scallops baked 'en croûte' with lime and vanilla. Mains may include Shetland salmon in leaf spinach, preserved lemon and sauce Jacqueline; rack of young New Zealand venison on pancetta with a Reblochon and potato gateau; and a well-judged dish of calf's liver with braised chicory and champ potatoes. The kitchen knows its stuff: strong flavours and good combinations. Puds are comforting – dark chocolate tart with eau de vie Mandarine sorbet; hazelnut pistachio parfait. And hurrah, there are savouries, including a delicious French rarebit of grilled Reblochon on toasted potato and garlic bread. Party throwers note: there is a grand private room in the cellar adjoining the Bistro.

Paternoster Chop House

Warwick Court, Paternoster Square, EC4 ■ 020 7029 9400 &

⊖ St Paul's

🍽 Very British

🕐 Mon to Fri 10.30–15.00 & 17.30–23.00; Sun 12.00–16.00

🖰 www.conran.com

🖅 all major credit cards ■ 12.5% optional service charge added

££ starters £5–£6.50 ■ mains £10.50–£18.50 ■ sides £3.50 ■ desserts £5.50–£6 ■ lowest bottle price £15

✪ British food – carefully chosen, carefully cooked

In its present guise Paternoster Square may be a relatively new creation, but admirably the food and hospitality on display in this corner of the Conran empire is top stuff. The restaurant makes no bones about targeting City folk: there's real ale on offer, simple fish dishes, roast meats, plenty of shellfish and seafood, while the prices are pretty much what you would expect. So saying, everything is done well. Ingredients are carefully sourced from the length and breadth of Britain, the menu changes seasonally and the cooking style is sympathetic. Start with bradan orach smoked salmon; Dublin bay prawns; or watercress soup. Comfort food fans may be tempted by the corned beef hash with a fried egg. They are proud of the meat cookery here and pure-bred Angus beef is hung for five weeks before ending up as twelve-hour roasted brisket, or a flank steak. In season, there's plenty of game. You could opt for a cottage pie (made from the same well-matured beef), or a pork and veal faggot with mustard mash. As befits anywhere showcasing British food, fine cheese plays a leading role – the Cheddar comes from Keen's; the Stilton from Cropwell Bishop; while the Welsh rarebit is made with Lancashire cheese and comes topped with a poached egg. The wine list runs from reasonable to rarefied and the service is slick; but best of all this place flies the flag for British cuisine.

The Place Below

St Mary-le-Bow Church, Cheapside, EC2 ■ 020 7329 0789

Bank/St Paul's

Vegetarian

Mon to Fri 07.30–15.30 (lunch 11.30–14.30)

www.theplacebelow.co.uk

all major credit cards ■ no service charge

££ breakfast £1.15–£2.30 ■ soup £2.70–£3.10 ■ mains £4.30–£7.50 ■ sandwiches £2.95–£4.50 ■ desserts £1.30–£3 ■ unlicensed, BYO (no corkage)

✪ Wholesome veggie food that tastes good as well

The Place Below is a vegetarian restaurant, and yes it is in the crypt of the St Mary-le-Bow Church. But persevere: it has a splendidly low worthiness rating. Wander into the wonderfully elegant Wren church and look for the staircase down to the crypt – you'll see that the resto is split into two halves. The first has an open kitchen at one end and acts as coffee shop and servery – good pastries and breakfast buns. The other side is the restaurant proper, which is open at lunch (with prices a pound or two cheaper between 11.30 and noon). Choose from the daily changing menu, push a tray along the canteen-style rails, and the chefs will fill a plate for you. The ever-changing menu is reassuringly short and the dining room is lofty, with the large, central, communal dining table being the only one with a tablecloth. There are a couple of soups, a hot dish, a quiche option, a salad of the day, good trad puds and that's about it. The soups are hearty, such as leek and potato with Thai flavours, or spicy lentil and chickpea with harissa. The salad of the day can be triumphant: crisp green beans, a rich savoury dollop of wild rice, shredded carrot with sesame seeds and plenty of fresh leaves. Or how about a hot dish like Emmental and white wine hotpot with root vegetable mash? The field mushroom, fennel and Gruyère 'quiche of the day' is also well made. There are always puddingy puddings like a marzipan and cranberry cake or passion fruit syllabub with lavender shortbread. Good cooking, great value.

Prism

147 Leadenhall Street, EC3 ■ 020 7256 3888   ♿

⊖ Bank/Monument

🍽 Modern British

🕐 Mon to Fri 11.30–15.00 & 18.00–22.00

🖰 www.harveynichols.co.uk

🗗 all major credit cards ■ 12.5% optional service added

££ starters £9–£12.50 ■ mains £15–£24 ■ sides £3.50–£4.50 ■ desserts £7.50 ■ lowest bottle price £21

✪ Lofty dining room, lofty food, lofty prices

Part of the Harvey Nichols plan for world domination, Prism is an expensive City restaurant, although recent years have seen prices easing back somewhat and the menu getting shorter – both of which are most encouraging trends. Eating here is rather like being inside a towering, white-painted cube; it's very slick, and very much a towering ex-banking hall. The food is a well-judged blend of English favourites and modernist influences. There is the obligatory (for the City) long bar and the obligatory suave service. Starters are well executed: Cornish crab and mango salad, with coriander and mild curry dressing; Sudtirol speck with a salad of roast artichokes; terrine of ham hock, foie gras and Puy lentils sauce gribiche; or a risotto made with peas and crisp Carpegna ham. When it comes to main courses, the menu splits into three fish, three meat and a veggie. So there are dishes such as Glenarm organic salmon, served with a fresh herb risotto, as well as more adventurous offerings such as seared Canadian halibut, celeriac and Bramley apple purée and curly kale. The meat side offers roast cutlet of Dutch veal, braised onion and chargrilled polenta, and roast rump of English lamb with a cassoulet of cannellini beans. Veggies can look forward to a cannelloni of ricotta and spinach, red pepper coulis and shaved truffle – which is certainly a step up from the 'stuffed vegetables' so many chefs keep in reserve for anyone awkward enough to be vegetarian. Puddings include chestnut and chocolate mousse with Swiss meringue, and the wine list has some high-ticket numbers.

Refettorio

Crowne Plaza Hotel, 19 New Bridge Street, EC4

■ 020 7438 8052

⊖ Blackfriars

🍴 Italian

🕐 Mon to Fri 12.00–14.30 & 18.30–22.30; Sat 18.30–22.30

🖰 www.tableinthecity.com

🗗 all major credit cards ■ 12.5% optional service added

££ pre-selected combinations £8.50–£20 ■ antipasti £6–£8.50 ■ pasta/
risotti £6–£12.50 ■ mains £16–£21.50 ■ desserts £6–£7 ■ lowest
bottle price £15

✪ Honest Italian – specialist charcuterie

**When Refettorio opened it looked as if it was going to be the
start of a major trend,** but somehow it never caught on, which is
something of a pity. What we have here is a brave idea. This resto
is to be found within the Crowne Plaza Hotel just to the north of
Blackfriars Bridge. The menu stems from his love of top-quality,
artisan-produced Italian foods, and the first thing to note is that the
same menu, and the same prices, apply whether you eat in the less
formal Convivium or end up at the tables with tablecloths. As you
walk into the room there is a counter with a slicing machine and a
glass-fronted refrigerator – the contents of which would put any
London deli to shame. The menu starts with an epic list of about
thirty Italian cheeses and a similar number of regional salamis and
cured meats. The idea is that you graze your way to a full tummy. If
the choice intimidates, opt for the pre-selected combos – cheeses,
salami. Otherwise, standouts are the lardo di collonata, the salami
di cinghale – made from wild boar, and an implausibly creamy
Gorgonzola. Then there's a section of fritti: arancini are good, deep-
fried spheres of saffron rice stuffed with cheese. The pasta dishes
are very good – tagliolini gratinata is green pasta, baked under
unbelievably good cheese and ham sauce. Main courses are trad
– veal chop, or sea bass in white wine. Puds range from well-made
tarts to Italian delicacies such as pastiera. The wine list is long and
Italian. The service is slick and Italian.

Rosemary Lane

61 Royal Mint Street, E1 ■ 020 7481 2602

⊖ Tower Hill/DLR Tower Gateway

🍴 French/Californian

🕐 Mon to Fri 12.00–14.30 & 17.30–22.00; Sat 17.30–22.00

💻 www.rosemarylane.btinternet.co.uk

💳 all major credit cards ■ 12.5% optional service added

££ starters £8–£12 ■ mains £13–£22 ■ desserts £6 ■ prix fixe lunch £14 & £17 ■ tasting menu Sat £30 ■ lowest bottle price £12

✪ Californian charisma, fresh seasonal food

The prime mover here is a Californian chef called Christina Anghelescu and her menus show an agreeable reliance on seasonal produce while displaying the same dogged determination to use only the best-quality ingredients that we associate with Alice Waters and the other West Coast stars. This even extends to running a 'pot luck' tasting menu on Saturdays that is based around whatever was good at Borough Market that morning. The main menu changes every six weeks or so. The dining room looks like a lick-of-paint-makeover of a dodgy saloon bar – which is just what it is. Service is slick, in a Gallic sort of way. The food is good. Dishes are pleasantly light, and presentation just about manages to stay elegant without tipping over the edge into elaborate. In the winter starters may include oxtail ragout ravioli served with celeriac cream and sage-flavoured port reduction – good clear-cut flavours; or Devon crab served in the shell with creamy spinach, orange caviars and cresses; or a forest mushroom savoury pudding, watercress soup and salad of watercress and Parmigiano. Mains are considered combinations – sea bass en papillote, truffled fennel beurre blanc, caramelised chicory; a French rabbit daube, toasted brioche, roast winter vegetables and sherry glaze; or slow-roast poussin, warm salad of Puy lentils, lardons and figs and a creamy tarragon white wine sauce. Puds are good – there's a bitter chocolate shortbread truffle tart, and the 'satsuma curd sandwich' – a somewhat tongue-in-cheek description, but a pleasant surprise. As befits the City location, there's a grown-up wine list with some good stickies.

Thai Square City

136–138 The Minories, EC3 ■ 020 7680 1111

⊖ Aldgate/Tower Hill

🍴 Thai

🕐 Mon to Thurs 12.00–20.00; Fri 12.00–23.30

🖥 www. thaisq.com

🗔 all major credit cards ■ 12.5% optional service added

££ starters £4.50–£6 ■ mains £6.95 ■ sides £4.75 ■ desserts £3.50–£3.95 ■ Lunch Express (in Bar) £6.95–£8 ■ set menus £18 & £27 ■ lowest bottle price £9.95

✪ Loud City Thai for loud City types

It is claimed (admittedly mainly by PRs) that this is Europe's largest Thai restaurant, but it may well be true. In a vast room decorated with temple bells, Buddhas, pots, carved panels, teak, wooden flowers and gold-mosaic rooftop dragons, friendly staff greet customers with a genuine smile. Downstairs there's a 100-seater cocktail bar with a 16.00–19.00 happy hour. On Thursday and Friday the basement turns into a club with a 02.00 drink and dancing licence. The lengthy menu lists both familiar favourites and more novel ideas. Toong thong is a dish of minced prawn and chicken in purse-like little sacks, and very moreish. Tod man poo, or Thai crab cakes, will satisfy connoisseurs seeking this favourite, and tom yam kung will delight lovers of the classic lemongrass soup. Moo ping, or barbecued pork served with a sweet and incredibly hot sauce, is tender and good. The menu suggests that it's especially good with sticky rice, and it is. Six Thai curries offer a choice of red or green and different main ingredients. There are the classic noodle dishes like pad Thai. Other treats include Chu-chee lobster, which is deep-fried lobster with special curry paste, coconut milk and lime leaves. Puddings include banana with coconut syrup and sesame seeds; Thai egg custard; and ice creams and sorbets. The wine list starts gently, threads its way through some decent choices at the accessible verging on expensive mark, and then rockets to cosset City boys with show-off bottles like a Château Cheval Blanc St Emilion.

Clerkenwell and Smithfield

Bleeding Heart

Bleeding Heart Yard, off Greville St, EC1 ■ 020 7242 2056

Farringdon/Chancery Lane

Modern British

Mon to Fri 12.00–14.30 & 18.00–22.30

www.bleedingheart.co.uk

all major credit cards ■ 12.5% optional service added

£975 starters £5.95–£9.75 ■ mains £11.95–£21.50 ■ desserts £5.95
■ dinner £24.95 (3 courses) ■ lowest bottle price £16.95

⭐ Traditional dining rooms, trad food, trad pricing

According to the *New Yorker,* **Bleeding Heart Yard is** 'bleeding
hard to find', and for once they have got it about right. Just
supposing you make it, your first glance around the panelled
basement rooms at Bleeding Heart Yard will tell you instantly what
kind of a place this is. The clientele is from the City, the menu is
written with Square Mile superiority, and the wine list is priced for
bonus-laden wallets. Just right for the pukka, suit-wearing, claret-
loving kind of City folk. Even during a glorious summer these plush
dining rooms will still be packed, and booking is doubly necessary
should the forecast veer towards the windy and rain-swept. There's
also an accessible dinner offer. The menu changes seasonally and
dishes form a bridge between classical French cooking and its
Modern British descendants. Starters may include lightly smoked foie
gras pressé with roasted apple and a pourpier salad; warm asparagus
with creamy goats' cheese quenelle; or a millefeuille of fresh crab and
confit tomato. The mains range from dishes like fillet of halibut in red
wine with a polenta galette and prune and red wine sauce, to rack of
Welsh lamb with sweet potato purée and rosemary jus. The owners
of the Bleeding Heart empire – restaurant, bistro, tavern, crypt, plus
The Don restaurant (see p. 179) – also have interests in the antipodes,
so New Zealand venison is often featured. There's always Stilton
cheese on offer and sound, trad puds. The wine list is formidable. The
Wine Spectator says that this place has 'one of the most outstanding
restaurant wine lists in the world'.

Club Gascon

57 West Smithfield, EC1 ■ 020 7796 0600

⊖ Farringdon

🍴 Very French

🕐 Mon to Thurs 12.00–14.00 & 19.00–22.30; Fri 12.00–14.00 & 19.00–23.00; Sat 19.00–23.00

🗗 all major credit cards ■ 12.5% optional service added

££ starters £4.50–£42.00 ■ mains £1–£19 ■ desserts £7–£9 ■ tasting menu £38 & £60 (inc. matched wines) ■ déjeuner club menu £35 ■ lowest bottle price £12

✪ Notably authentic food, from south-western France

It's hard to believe it, but Club Gascon is nudging its way towards the end of a first decade. It's amazing that the place still seems new and still seems fresh, although a cabinet full of awards testifies to how very successful it has become. If you want a booking, they advise calling two or three weeks ahead, though you may strike lucky with a cancellation. Pascal Aussignac is chef here, and his cooking is an authentic taste of south-western France. The menu is set out in sections and the portions are larger than some starters, but smaller than most mains, the idea being that you indulge in your very own *dégustation* – which isn't the cheapest way of eating. The sections are 'La route du sel' – cured meats and charcuterie; 'Le potager' – vegetables and cheese; 'Les foies gras'; 'L'océane' – fish and shellfish; 'Les pâturages' – mainly duck, game and cassoulet. There are 40 different dishes so it's important to spread your ordering. Here are some promising combinations: three 'pousse en claire' oysters with seaweed tartare; warm Gascon pie of duck and chanterelles; roast foie gras 'lemon lemon'; royal of hare with smooth and crispy parsnips; old-fashioned cassoulet Toulousain. Or does the home-made 'confit' French fries with fleur de sel appeal? The problem with eating like this is that you can hit on a dish that is amazing and therefore too small. You must have the confidence to order a second or even third serving. The wines – mainly from the South West – are splendid.

→ For branches, see index

Comptoir Gascon

61–63 Charterhouse Street, EC1 ■ 020 7608 0851

⊖ Farringdon

🍴 Very French

🕐 Tues to Thurs 12.00–14.00 & 19.00–22.00; Fri & Sat 12.00–14.00 & 19.00–23.00

🗄 all major credit cards ■ 12.5% optional service added

££ starters £4–£6.50 ■ mains £6–£12 ■ sides £3–£5 ■ desserts £2.50–£3.50 ■ lowest bottle price £14

✪ A shop and a bistro, both Gascon through and through

The Club Gascon gang seem to be taking over this section of the book. No matter. Don't you sometimes wish that a really ace restaurant (like Club Gascon, see opposite) had a slightly simpler sidekick? The same glorious food naturally, but a bit less elaborate and a bit less expensive. In Paris some of Monsieur Michelin's favourite chefs have spotted this 'gap' in the market and plugged it with a 'bistro en face' – quite literally a bistro opposite. Hurrah! That's the role played by the Comptoir Gascon. On one side of Smithfield Market there's the Club and on the other there's the Comptoir. At the Comptoir you can drop in to buy fine bread, pâtisserie, cheeses and the wines of the South West. You can also sit down to a bowl of cassoulet. The food is good, well cooked, simply presented and comes in satisfyingly large portions. Prices are reasonable and you can even drink very well without breaking the bank. Starters may include the cheekily named 'piggy treats' – a serious pork-fest; duck rillettes; steamed oyster with crépinette; epic black pudding with caramelised apple; and a great deal of well-made rustic bread. Mains range from a perfect steak tartare; to grilled squid with barley and tomato confit; to confit of duck; steamed haddock and greens; mini cheese ravioli with trompettes; and a poulet grand-mère des Landes. The cassoulet is stellar, but everything is good. For pud run amok at the cake counter. This bistro provides a friendly and inexpensive way to eat some very good dishes indeed.

The Eagle

159 Farringdon Road, EC1 ■ 020 7837 1353

● Farringdon

◉ Mediterranean/gastropub

🕐 Mon to Fri 12.30–15.00 & 18.30–22.30; Sat 12.30–15.30 & 18.30–22.30; Sun 12.30–15.30

🖥 Mastercard, Visa, Switch ■ no service added

££ tapas £3 ■ mains £6.50–£13.50 ■ desserts £1.20 ■ lowest bottle price £10.50

✪ Gastropub, the original and genuine

For most of its lifetime The Eagle was merely a run-down pub in an unpromising part of London. Then, way back in 1991, it was taken over by food-minded entrepreneurs who transformed it into a restaurant-pub turning out top-quality dishes. They were pioneers: there should be a blue plaque over the door marking the site as the starting place of the great gastropub revolution. The Eagle has remained a crowded, rather shabby sort of place, and the staff still displays a refreshing full-on attitude. The kitchen is truly open: the chefs work behind the bar, and the menu is chalked up over their heads. It changes daily, or even hourly, as things run out or deliveries come in. The food is broadly Mediterranean in outlook with a Portuguese bias, and you still have to fight your way to the bar to order and pay. The menu changes like quicksilver, but you may find the likes of the famous caldo verde – the Portuguese chorizo and potato soup that takes its name from the addition of spring greens. There may be a grilled swordfish with peppers, mint, new potatoes and balsamico; a delicious and simple dish like roast spring chicken with preserved lemons, potatoes, mustard leaves and aioli; cuttlefish stew with chilli, garlic, parsley, onions and broad beans; or a rib-eye 'tagliata' with green beans and mixed leaves, radishes and horseradish. To finish, choose between a fine cheese – perhaps Wigmore served with rhubarb jam and toast – or the siren charms of those splendid, small, Portuguese, cinnamony custard tarts – pasteis de nata. Enjoy the lack of frills and the service that comes with a helping of attitude.

Medcalf

40 Exmouth Market, EC1 ▪ 020 7833 3533 ♿

⊖ Farringdon/Angel

🍴 Modern British

🕐 Mon to Thurs 12.00–23.30; Fri 12.00–15.30; Sun 12.00–16.00

🖰 www.medcalfbar.co.uk

🗄 all major credit cards ▪ 12.5% service added for parties of 5 or more

££ starters £4.50–£5.50 ▪ mains £12.50–£17.50 ▪ sides £2.50
▪ desserts £5.50 ▪ lowest bottle price £12.50

❂ A resto that thinks it's a gastropub

The frontage may look like Albert Sydney Medcalf's 1912 butcher shop, but the long bar looks very like a pub bar, the tables look like pub tables and the menu is a pubby sort of menu. All of which doesn't matter a damn because, whichever pigeonhole you choose to file it in, Medcalf makes a very decent job of being an informal eatery. The menu is seasonally driven and changes every session, so starters may range from Welsh rarebit to sweet potato soup; a duck confit salad with poached egg; squid with chilli and ginger – a good, well-balanced dish with assertive flavours and accurately cooked squid; and a well-made rabbit terrine with home-made piccalilli. The main courses listed may include one that is for sharing – Shorthorn rib of beef for two, served with chips and horseradish (the chips are good here). Or how about a serious and suitably trad fish pie, fluffy mash on top and creamy gunk within? There's braised beef with Guinness and neeps; and a roasted fig and goats' cheese tart. A fillet of sea bass comes with a herb risotto – good texture and flavours. The pud list is headed by 'selection of British cheeses with oatcakes and chutney', but for the sweeter tooth there is chocolate and almond cake; rice pudding with blackberry compôte; or plum syllabub. The wine list is priced sensibly, there is real beer on offer and service is confident and attentive without getting too pushy.

Moro

34–36 Exmouth Market, EC1 ■ 020 7833 8336

⊖ Farringdon/Angel

🍴 Spanish/tapas

🕐 Mon to Fri 12.30–14.30 & 19.00–22.30; Sat 12.30–15.00 & 19.00–22.30

🖰 www.moro.co.uk

🖯 all major credit cards ■ 12.5% service added for parties of 6 or more

££ starters £5–£7.50 ■ mains £13.50–£18 ■ desserts £5–£6.50 ■ sherry tasting Saturday only £40 (4 courses) ■ lowest bottle price £12.50

✪ Good food – both Moorish and more-ish

Moro has a secure place on the list of London's 'must visit' eateries. In feel it's not so very far away from the better pub-restaurants, although the proprietors have given themselves the luxury of a slightly larger kitchen. This has also become a place of pilgrimage for disciples of the wood-fired oven, and the food here hails mainly from Spain, Portugal and North Africa. You'll probably have to book. The à la carte changes every fortnight. There's usually a soup, and it's usually among the best starters. How does cauliflower, yogurt and coriander soup sound? Or you may be offered starters such as pan-fried calf's sweetbreads and artichoke hearts with cardamom, or blood orange, crisp bread and feta salad. Main courses are simple and often traditional combinations of taste and textures. As with the starters, it's the accompaniments that tend to change rather than the core ingredients. Look out for wood-roasted brill, braised sweet and sour leeks with red pepper and walnut sauce; charcoal-grilled lamb with roast squash, cumin chickpea purée; or perhaps charcoal-grilled sea bass with wilted escarole and lentils. Do not miss the splendid Spanish cheeses served with membrillo – traditional quince paste. And there's no excuse for avoiding the Malaga raisin ice cream, or the serious bitter chocolate, coffee and cardamom truffle. This is a place that effortlessly combines top-quality ingredients with very good cooking and comfortable service, and there is a grand list of moody sherries into the bargain.

Portal

88 St John Street, EC1 ■ 020 7253 6950

⊖ Barbican

🍽 Portuguese

🕐 Mon to Sat 12.00–15.00 & 18.00–22.15; bar food 12.00–22.15

🖥 www.portalrestaurant.com

🗄 all major credit cards ■ 12.5% optional service added

££ starters £4.50–£9.50 ■ mains £10.50–£17.50 ■ desserts £6.50–£9.50
■ lowest bottle price £11

✪ Sophisticated Portuguese wine-lover opens posh resto

Portal is neither one thing nor the other, but it still offers a
good time to the discerning diner. This restaurant may claim to
serve Modern European food, but what you get is slightly bland
Portuguese-meets-International grub. The strengths of the place lie
in a grand modern dining room – the glassed-in section at the rear
is particularly elegant, with a good view of the original City Walls
(an appreciation of medieval brickwork will help). The wine list is
fascinating and there are some real bargains here, particularly the
gently priced 'Quinta de Portal' house wines. The food is not as wizzy
as everything else. Starters include tuna with foie gras and an onion
confit; veal carpaccio with wild mushrooms, Parmesan and lime
ice cream and a raspberry vinaigrette; and the famous Portuguese
cabbage soup called calde verde. The soup tastes terrific, but is more
calde beige than verde. Mains are also from all over: roast lamb with
thyme crust, ratte potatoes and serra cheese gratin is a dish that
could be from several European countries (save only for the cheese),
but it is well done – pink rack of lamb, waxy spuds. Guinea fowl
comes with black olive crust and a pea and corn risotto. A more
Portuguese dish is the bacalhau confit with a corn bread and herb
crust – good meaty cod, not too salty, but not gutsy Portuguese-
rustic either. Puds include creamed rice with coconut ice cream, and
chocolate parfait with a nougat and lemon butter snap. There is a
tantalising list of Quinta de Portal ports including magnums of 2000.
Wine buffs will be happy here.

St John

26 St John Street, EC1 ■ 020 7251 0848

◉ Farringdon

🍽 British

🕐 Mon to Fri 12.00–15.00 & 18.00–23.00

🖰 www.stjohnrestaurant.com

🖬 all major credit cards ■ no service added

££ starters £4–£12.80 ■ mains £12.80–£22.50 ■ sides £3.20–£7.20
   ■ desserts £3.40–£7.40 ■ lowest bottle price £14.50

✪ A national treasure, the best British cooking

**American chef, food writer, wild man and all-round good egg
Antony Bourdain** names the St John bone marrow and parsley
salad as his 'desert island dish'. Good call. One of the most frequent
requests, especially from foreign visitors, is, 'Where can we get some
really English cooking?' Little wonder that the promise of 'olde
English fare' is the bait in so many tourist traps. The cooking at St
John, however, is genuine. It is sometimes old-fashioned and makes
inspired use of strange and unfashionable cuts of meat. Technically
the cooking is of a very high standard, while the restaurant itself is
completely without frills or design pretensions. You'll either love it
or hate it. The menu changes every session, but the tone does not,
and there's always a dish or two to support the slogan 'nose to tail
eating'. Charcuterie, as you'd imagine, is good: a simple terrine will
be dense but not dry – well judged. Or, for the committed, what
about a starter of crispy pig's skin and dandelion? Or celery soup?
Main courses may include calf's liver and swede, or oxtail and mash.
Maybe there will be a dish described simply as 'fennel and Berkswell
cheese'; perversely, in this den of offal, the veg dishes are a delight.
Puddings are traditional and well executed: custard tart and rhubarb,
or a slice of strong Lancashire cheese with an Eccles cake. Joy of joys,
sometimes there is even a seriously good Welsh rarebit. St John has
won shedloads of awards, and booking is a must. St John serves
good food at its most genuine.

→ For branches, see index

Smiths, the Dining Room

67–77 Charterhouse Street, EC1 ■ 020 7251 7950

⊖ Farringdon

⦿ Modern British

⏲ (Café) Mon to Fri 07.00–23.00; Sat & Sun 12.30–17.00; (Restaurants) Mon to Fri 12.00–15.00 & 18.00–23.00; Sat 18.00–3.00 (top floor); Sun 12.30–15.30 & 18.30–22.30

🗗 all major credit cards ■ 12.5 % service added

££ larder/starters/soups £5.50, £5.75 & £3.75 ■ mains/grills £11.75 & £11.50 ■ daily lunch Market Special £10.50 ■ sides £2.50 ■ Sweet Tooth £4.50 ■ lowest bottle price £12.75

✪ The Café is allegedly Jamie Oliver's favourite breakfasting place

You have only to rebuild a Grade II listed warehouse in ultra-modern-meets-*Blade Runner* style and, hey presto, you could have two restaurants, two bars, private rooms, kitchens and whatever, spread over four floors. On the ground floor there's a bar and café serving drink and practical, sensible food. The 'top floor' is a 70-seater where they pay particular attention to quality meat with good provenance. On the second floor is the 130-seater 'Dining Room'. The culinary mainspring here is an enlightened buying policy – quality, quality, quality. The Dining Room is a large space around a central hole that looks down onto the smart bar area. Eating here is rather like sitting at the centre of a deactivated factory. The menu is divided into Larder, Starters, Soups, Mains, Grills, Daily Lunch Market Specials, Sides, and Sweet Tooth. The starters are simple and good: grilled mushrooms and Taleggio on toasted sourdough; Portuguese-style salt cod fritters; foie gras and chicken liver parfait. Main courses may include crisp belly of pork with mashed potato and green sauce; roast cod with roast salsify and Hollandaise. The lunch specials are from the comfort-eating school, and feature such delights as cottage pie. Puds are good. Try chocolate and pear pithivier. The 'Top Floor' is an élite affair specialising in well-matured steaks from rare-breed steers – expensive, but very good indeed; rather naturally it has become something of a favourite with bonus boys from the City.

Souvlaki & Bar

140–142 St John Street, EC1 ■ 020 7253 7234 &

⊖ Farringdon

|O| Greek

🕘 Mon to Sat 12.00–23.00

🖳 www.therealgreek.co.uk

🖬 all major credit cards ■ 12.5% service added

££ mezedes £3.20–£5.95 ■ souvlaki £4.85–£5.85 ■ sides £2.75–£3.75
■ desserts £3.50 ■ menus: meze, souvlaki & drink (to 19.30) £8.75;
children's menu £4.95 ■ lowest bottle price £11.75

✪ London's best, and most authentic, kebab

**This was the first of a gradually lengthening chain at the head
of which** you'll find The Real Greek (see p. 221). These 'Souvlaki &
Bar' restaurants tend to be busy from day one, partly because the
food is cheap and top-quality, and partly because the tone of the
place is perfectly in tune with the mood of the times. The bar with
its open kitchen dominates the room and there is a series of high,
narrow island tables with stools. As it says on the menu, 'Souvlaki &
Bar offers Real Greek street food. Regional wines, beers and ouzos
complement the flavours' and the good-value Greek wines will
convince you. The menu is very short. There are ten mezedes, among
them dolmades, taramosalata, gigandes plaki – a trad bean stew,
and htipiti, which is a delicious mishmash of cheese, red peppers and
roast red onions. The bread is terrific: round, Greek flatbreads, lightly
oiled and then crisped on the grill. Then there is the souvlaki. In
Greece souvlaki changes with the seasons, so that during the months
that pork is at its best the kebabs are pork and when lamb comes to
the fore then they are lamb. Here, ordering kebab gets you a delicious
hot flatbread with a splosh of yogurty tzatziki and some tomato
and pepper purée and then a skewer of meat. It is rolled tightly and
wrapped in greaseproof paper. Or you can order a 'double' (two
kebabs, unsurprisingly). Options include the same kind of thing, but
made with chicken. Non-souvlakists will find crevettes with a warm
potato salad, and grilled pork cutlets to stop them going hungry.

→ For branches, see index

The Well

180 St John Street, EC1 ■ 020 7251 9363

⊖ Farringdon/Angel

🍴 Modern British/gastropub

🕑 Mon to Fri 12.00–15.00 & 18.30–22.30; Sat & Sun 10.30–22.30

🖰 www.downthewell.com

🖅 all major credit cards ■ 12.5% service added

££ starters £5.50–£8.50 ■ mains £9.95–£15.95 ■ sides £2.50–£3.50 ■ desserts £5–£7.50 ■ daily specials on blackboard £13–£15 ■ lowest bottle price £12.50

✪ Sound gastropub with good atmosphere

Takes its name from the well that served the clerken hereabouts, so leading to the name of the area. The Well is a buzzy bar-cum-gastropub where the diners and staff all appear to be friends having a good time. Scrubbed tables and old church chairs give a fresh, accessible feel to this corner venue, which is open as a bar throughout the day and as a restaurant during kitchen hours. A couple of daily specials on a blackboard complement the modern mixed menu. The menu changes regularly, but starters may include bread, garlic and sage soup; 'pint o' prawns' with mayonnaise; or seared chicken livers with a balsamic reduction and mixed leaves. Main courses are equally eclectic. Sausages come with herb mash and gravy; or there may be saddle of rabbit cooked in grain mustard with borlotti beans and Savoy cabbage; or chargrilled rib-eye steak, which comes with grilled tomatoes, flat mushrooms and French fries. Fish dishes get good representation: pan-fried skate wing with potato and leek compôte and brown butter, or fillet of salmon with risotto cake and seafood saffron sauce. The desserts range from the classic – chocolate brownies with vanilla cream, or whisky bread-and-butter pudding with custard, to the more adventurous – cranberry and cinnamon crème brûlée. British cheeses are from the admirable Neal's Yard Dairy. The wine list scoots from a respectable house red or white to Dom Pérignon – for the Clerkenwell-heeled.

The White Swan

108 Fetter Lane, EC1 ■ 020 7243 9696

⊖ Chancery Lane

¶◎¶ Modern British/gastropub

🕓 Mon to Fri 12.00–15.00 & 18.00–22.00

⌐🖰 www.thewhiteswanlondon.com

🗗 all major credit cards ■ 12.5% optional service added

££ starters £4.50–£9 ■ mains £12–£19 ■ sides £3–£3.50 ■ desserts £4.50 & £9.50 for cheese ■ prix fixe lunch £20 & £25 ■ lowest bottle price £12.50

✪ A good restaurant posing as gastropub

'It's certainly a pub, but not as we know it'. The White Swan is sister to The Well (see p. 197), but is one of a completely different breed of gastropub. These places are not content to knock out homely food in homely surroundings; their aspirations are tuned to a world of fine dining where there is little room for junkshop tables and mismatched cutlery. Downstairs the pub ethic dominates with real ale and decent bar food; upstairs there's the dining room. The seating is luxurious beige leather, the ceiling is mirrored, there's a cheese trolley. The food is blisteringly good. The presentation is simple but elegant. Flavours are well matched. For cooking of this quality prices are very fair. Start with courgette and mint soup, or a leek and Lancashire risotto. Or something seasonal, like purple sprouting broccoli, focaccia and Hollandaise sauce. On to the mains: grilled calf's kidney with bacon and mustard; rib-eye with Roquefort butter; or a dish described as 'roast cod with boulangère potatoes, pancetta and rosemary lemon sauce' – a very decent chunk of cod wrapped in boulangère potatoes and then the whole thing swaddled in pancetta. Very satisfying. Puds are good, the 'blood orange marmalade sponge pudding with custard' has a real tang. Having a go at the extensive cheeseboard ups the ante, but it is worth it to see so many fine British cheeses. Service is slick and the wine list has some decent bottles at the cheap end. This is a really good place to eat.

The Zetter

86–88 Clerkenwell Road, EC1 ■ 020 7324 4455

⊖ Farringdon

🍴 Modern Italian

🕐 Mon to Fri 07.30–10.30, 12.00–14.30 & 18.00–23.00; Sat 07.30–11.00, 11.00–15.00 (brunch) & 18.00–23.00; Sun 07.30–11.00, 11.00–15.00 (brunch) & 18.00–22.30

🖰 www.thezetter.com

🖃 all major credit cards ■ 12.5% optional service added

££ breakfast £4–£15 ■ starters £4–£6.50 ■ mains £11–£15.50 ■ sides £3.50 ■ desserts £2–£6.50 ■ menus: lunch & dinner £30 & £40 ■ lowest bottle price £12

⭐ Boutique hotel, boutique restaurant

Formerly HQ to Zetter's Football Pools, this place has become the spiritual home of the style police – at the Zetter they have enough front to describe themselves as a 'restaurant with rooms'. But one where you'll find 59 bedrooms and 7 rooftop suites, so maybe this particular cart has nudged in front of the horse. This resto is a hotel restaurant; granted it's a very good one, and granted it would survive as a stand alone. The plus side of this arrangement is that the Zetter is open all day. The dining room curves around a large bar, the tables and chairs are utilitarian and the high ceiling can make for a noisy, echoey experience. The food is Italian, but seen through Modern British eyes; it changes monthly and strives to keep in step with the changing seasons. Winter will see hearty soups – pumpkin and chestnut soup with salame N'Duia, very rich with a welcome belt of chilli; other starters include a decent chicken liver risotto dressed with fried sage leaves, or buffalo mozzarella with puntarelle and anchovies. Pasta dishes are well done – bucatini comes with a sauce made from octopus, tomatoes and red onion. Mains range from grilled scallops with chard and chickpeas, to roast mallard with savoy cabbage and polenta. Puds are considered – pear and Strega sorbet, or perhaps a chestnut ice cream with bitter chocolate sauce. The wine list is eclectic – but whether it lives up to its self-billing as 'illustrious' may be a moot point.

Docklands

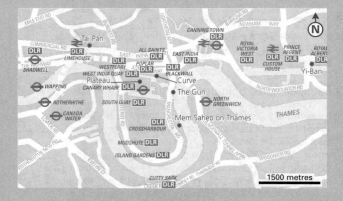

Curve

Marriott Hotel, 22 Hertsmere Road, EC4

■ 020 7093 1000, ext 2622 &

⊖ DLR West India Quay

🍴 North American/steak

🕐 Mon to Fri 06.30–11.00, 12.00–14.30 & 17.00–22.30; Sat & Sun 07.00–11.00, 12.00–14.30 & 17.00–22.30

🖥 www.marriott.com

🗄 all major credit cards ■ 12.5% optional service added

££ breakfast £13–£20 ■ starters £6–£14 ■ mains £13–£20 ■ sides £3–£4 ■ desserts £5–£6 ■ prix fixe menus £20, £25 or £30 ■ lowest bottle price £16

✪ Simple dishes done with a certain panache

For a resto in a large, faceless, international chain hotel, Curve does a pretty good job. The dining room is large and there are tables outside that on a sunny day could justifiably claim a pleasant view across the water. The chairs are comfortable, the service is crisp. Granted, some of the touches are a bit overblown, but the quality of cooking is generally high. Remember this is a place peopled by singletons reading a book throughout their meal, having been entombed in a Docklands hotel before, after or during some meeting or other. Starters range from a decent chowder to an acceptable prawn cocktail (large prawns, palatable pink gloop) and a Caesar salad that dodges most of the prevalent mistakes (plenty of Parmesan, mercifully no anchovies). There are oysters – cheap oysters. And oysters Rockefeller, too. The mains are encouraging – wild mushroom risotto offers Mrs Tee (of New Forest mushroom hunting fame) as provenance. The steaks are from Cornish beef 'hung for five weeks'. Forgive them the Americanism of offering 'fillet Mignon', turn to the hanger steak – good meat, accurately cooked. Or there's surf'n'turf; there are even some dishes marked with a symbol to show they are 'fit for you', i.e. low-carb. Puzzlingly, the mint julep cocktail is so described. Puds include an English apple dessert plate comprising apple crumble, apple shot and a calvados chocolate mousse. For what it is, and where it is, Curve is a grand option.

The Gun

27 Coldharbour, E14 ■ 020 7515 5222 &

⊖ DLR South Quay/Canary Wharf

◉ Modern British/gastropub

⏰ Mon to Fri 12.00–15.00 & 18.30–22.00; Sat & Sun 10.30–16.30 (brunch) & 18.30–22.00

🖱 www.thegundocklands.com

💳 all major credit cards ■ 12.5% optional service added

££ starters £6–£10.50 ■ mains £14.50–£25 ■ sides £4–£5 ■ desserts £5–£5.50 ■ bar menu £4.50–£12.95 ■ lowest bottle price £12.50

✪ A slick restaurant – disguised as an award-winning gastropub

It is said that Horatio Nelson liked The Gun. But that may be on account of the charms of Emma Hamilton, whom he is supposed to have met regularly in an upstairs room. This sprawling riverside pub has a warren of rooms and a splendid terrace. First things first, the pub side of The Gun works very well; there's real beer and a roast suckling pig sandwich with apple sauce. The restaurant side of things also delights: well-cooked food, river terrace, suave service, private dining room, rampaging wine list. But if your idea of a gastropub is somewhere scruffy with good food at rock-bottom prices, The Gun doesn't qualify. This place is a ten-minute walk from Canary Wharf (don't even think of trying to park here) and it's full. Full to bursting with happy customers who can afford these prices. The menu changes regularly, dishes are seasonal, and ingredients are carefully chosen – venison from the Denham estate, lamb from Hampshire. The cooking is very sound, even a testing dish like a black truffle and pecorino omelette is very delicious. Or there's an inspired combination of grilled morteux sausage with sauerkraut and a poached egg. Or potted duck with pear chutney. Mains include a series of daily specials from the blackboard, like a roast grouse, or a whole sea bass, well cooked and well presented. A dish of braised pig's cheeks with mash is very sticky and unctuous. Puds range from chocolate fondant to Sharrow Bay sticky toffee pudding.

Mem Saheb on Thames

65–67 Amsterdam Road, E14 ■ 020 7538 3008 ♿

⊖ DLR Crossharbour

🍽 Indian

🕐 Mon to Fri 12.00–14.30 & 18.00–23.30; Sat & Sun 18.00–23.30

🖰 www.memsahibuk.com

🗗 all major credit cards ■ 10% optional service added

££ starters £2.95–£6.95 ■ mains £6.50–£12.95 ■ sides £2.75 ■ desserts £2.95–£4.50 ■ menus 'Kitchen Curry' (from 19.00) still £7.95 ■ lowest bottle price £9.95

✪ An honest and appealing curry house

'Amsterdam Road' conjures up pictures of old-fashioned docks and wharves, rolling fog banks and cheery East Enders. In practice, this bit of Docklands is a lot like Milton Keynes. The redeeming factor is the river. As the Thames sweeps round in a majestic arc, the restaurant has a superb view across the water to the Millennium folly. As a result there's a good deal of squabbling for the middle table in the non-smoking section (pole position as far as the view is concerned). Ultimately, however, the lucky winner must balance the grandstand view of the Millennium folly with the piped-music speaker directly above the table. Start by sharing a tandoori khazana, which is a platter of mixed kebabs from the tandoor, including good chicken tikka. Or some salmon samosas? Or the kabuli salad, a winning combination of chickpeas and hard-boiled egg in a sharp tamarind dressing? Of the main courses, macher jhul is tilapia cooked Bengali-style with aubergine and potato. Rajasthani khargosh is an unusual dish pairing rabbit with a mild sauce and served with garlicky spinach. Konju papas is a prawn curry in the South Indian style – tamarind, mustard seeds and coconut. The breads and vegetable dishes are good, particularly the aloo chana – a simple dish of potatoes and chickpeas. The kitchen is to be commended for avoiding artificial additives and colourings. And for the 'Kitchen Curry' – 'Each day our chefs cook a different staff curry for themselves. Usually fairly hot, sometimes very hot. Only available from 7pm.'

Plateau

Canada Place, Canary Wharf, E14 ■ 020 7715 7100

⊖ Canary Wharf

|●| Modern British

⏱ (Restaurant) Mon to Fri 12.00 –15.00 & 18.00 –22.30; Sat 18.00–
22.30; (Bar & Grill) Mon to Sat 12.00–15.00 & 18.00–22.30; Sun
12.00–16.00

⤴ www.conran.co.uk

🖰 all major credit cards ■ 12.5% optional service added

££ starters £8–£14.75 ■ mains £14.50–£27 ■ sides £4.50 ■ desserts
£6.50 ■ prix fixe dinner Mon to Sat £24.75 & £29.75 ■ lowest bottle
price £18

✪ High-level room, high level of ambition

Plateau juts out from the fourth floor of a giant glass office block
and looks out over a square that is surrounded by even larger towers.
Visit at night, the view is amazing – spooky in a slightly *Blade Runner*
sort of way, but incredible. Because the other offices tower above
you there is no feeling of vertigo until you catch sight of a tiny bus
moving round the square below. The menu at Plateau is of stalwart
construction. You can have seared foie gras with fig, date and lime
chutney; or butternut squash and mascarpone ravioli; or seared
scallops, celery, cranberry sauce. Main courses tick a few comfortable
boxes: Dover sole with herb crust, or braised beef cheeks, purple
mash potato; wild sea bass comes with crushed potato and pistachio;
aligot translates as pretty desirable mashed potato. The service is
sound and unruffled. The wine list is refreshingly egalitarian – in such
a lofty and aspirational establishment it is hard not to feel nervous,
but before winging off into the stratosphere, there is plenty of good
drinking at more earthbound prices. Puds are sound: chocolate
fondant, or tarte Tatin. At lunch Plateau is odds on to do good
business in a directors' dining room sort of way, but in the evening
it is worth a visit purely to gaze out of the window. It is also worth
noting that the adjacent Plateau bar and grill shares the view and
offers a slightly less formal menu.

Tai Pan

665 Commercial Road, E14 ■ 020 7791 0118

⊖ DLR Limehouse

|●| Chinese

🕐 Mon to Fri 12.00–23.30; Sat 18.00–24.00; Sun 12.00–24.00

🗗 all major credit cards ■ no service added

££ starters £2.90–£8.30 ■ mains £5.60–£8.70 ■ sides £2–£5.50 ■ set meals £14.50–£22.50 ■ lowest bottle price £10.50

⭐ Neighbourhood Chinese restaurant

As fans of Sherlock Holmes will know, Limehouse was London's first Chinatown, complete with murky opium dens, laundries and inscrutable coolies in cone-shaped hats. Nowadays all it has to boast about is the Tai Pan. This restaurant is very much a family affair – out front there's a light, bright dining room, to the rear a bustling kitchen. The kitchen fires out a constant stream of well-cooked, mainly Cantonese dishes, many of them dressed with intricately carved vegetables, which lift the presentation. After the complimentary prawn cracker and seriously delicious hot-pickled shredded cabbage, start with deep-fried crispy squid with Szechuan peppercorn salt, or fried Peking dumplings with a vinegar dipping sauce – both are excellent. Or try one of the sparerib dishes, or the soft-shell crabs. Alternatively, go for the nicely done, crispy, fragrant aromatic duck with pancakes and the accoutrements. Otherwise, relax and order the Imperial mixed hors d'oeuvres, which removes any burdensome choosing and offers a sampler of ribs, spring rolls, seaweed, and prawn and sesame toast, with a carrot sculpture as centrepiece. When ordering main dishes, old favourites like deep-fried shredded beef with chilli, and fried chicken in lemon sauce, are just as you'd expect. Fried seasonal greens in oyster sauce is made with choi sum, and is delicious, while the fried vermicelli Singapore-style will suit anyone who prefers their Singapore noodle pepped up with curry powder rather than fresh chillies. There are often good deals to be had here offering various permutations on an 'eat as much as you like' theme.

Yi-Ban

London Regatta Centre, Royal Albert Dock, E16

■ 020 7473 6699

⊖ DLR Royal Albert Dock

▶◎❘ Chinese/dim sum

🕒 Mon to Sat 12.00–23.30; Sun 11.00–22.30

⌐ www.yi-ban.co.uk

🗗 all major credit cards ■ 10% optional service added

££ dim sum £2–£3.50 ■ mains £7–£25 ■ sides £7–£8 ■ desserts £3.50
■ set menus £18–£35 ■ lowest bottle price £13

⚙ Sophisticated Chinese, good dim sum

If your mission was to find a rather good Chinese restaurant, it's
unlikely that your first thought would be to go to a barren corner of
Docklands and then make your way upstairs to a rowing club bar.
Persevere – at one end of the room you'll find Yi-Ban, complete with
lots of tables, a licence to conduct weddings and friendly staff. But
beware, this is not an easy place to find: best to navigate yourself to
the north-west corner of the Albert Dock and start from there. If you
turn up at lunch you'll find the room full of happy Chinese customers,
which is somehow very reassuring. The room is comfortable in a
modernist sort of way, so settle yourself at a large round table. The
dim sum are good and cheap: snow pea dumplings are prawny,
green herby numbers; mini glutinous rice rolls are mini and suitably
glutinous; the crystal prawn dumplings are good, as are the prawn
fun guo. The fried options are dry and crisp: sweet and sour wan
tun; deep-fried seafood dumplings; Vietnamese sugar cane prawns.
Strangely there are no steamed cheung fun on the menu here, but
you can indulge any whims for exotica by ordering chicken claws
Thai-style. The lengthy main menu is 'standard Chinese sophisticated':
steamed scallops; baked lobster (beware, it attracts the dreaded
'seasonal price'); honey spare ribs; lemon chicken. This is a very
pleasant restaurant with a terrific view, smiling helpful staff, and
bargain dim sum for lunch – not bad for a converted rowing club bar.

→ For branches, see index

Hoxton, Shoreditch and Hackney

Istambul İskembecisi • • Mangal II

CANONBURY

DALSTON LANE

HACKNEY DOWNS

ST PAUL'S ROAD

BALLS POND ROAD

DALSTON KINGSLAND

DALSTON LANE

GRAHAM ROAD

ESSEX

NEW

AGATH

KINGSLAND ROAD

Huong Viet •

Green Papaya

LONDON FIELDS

Faulkner's •

Santa Maria del Buen Ayre

Armadillo •

MARE STREET

KINGSLAND ROAD

Sòng Quê •

HACKNEY ROAD

CAMBRIDGE HEATH

CITY ROAD

Fifteen •

Viet Hoa Café •
Zen Satori •

Cày Tre

Fish Central •

EAST ROAD

BATH STREET

LEVER STREET

The Real Greek •

OLD STREET

CURTAIN ROAD

Rivington Grill, Bar, Deli

GREAT EASTERN STREET

GREEN

ROAD

OLD STREET

OLD STREET

Anakana
Chaibar •

Eyre Brothers •

BETHNAL

Carnevale •

• The Fox

SHOREDITCH HIGH STREET

SHOREDITCH

500 metres

Anakana Chaibar

1 Oliver's Yard, City Road, EC1 ■ 0845 262 5262

⊖ Old Street

🍴 Indian

🕐 Mon to Sat 11.30–23.00; Sun 11.30–22.30

🖻 all major credit cards ■ 10% service added for parties of 5 or more

££ salads £7–£7.50 ■ dosas £6.50–£7.50 ■ thalis £9.50–£10.50 ■ mains £7–£12 ■ sides £1.50–£4.50 ■ lowest bottle price £11.50

✪ Modern bar, modern Indian food

Anakana describes itself as a 'Chaibar', which doesn't stop the waiter opening with the line, 'Would you like a Martini while you are waiting?' And, in truth, tea bars were never like this. The bar area has seating at the front and the dining room lies behind the bar. All is screamingly modern. The tables are large (if a touch low) and the stools are broad (if a touch hard-cornered); this place is edgy rather than comfortable. It's a non-smoking environment and they don't take bookings. But after getting that lot off one's chest, the food is good. Old favourites like the masala dosa are well presented, crisp, thick and chewy all at the same time; the giant pancake is sound and the filling is … filling! From the rice dishes the kale pilau is very good – grilled cuttlefish with a black ink-stained pillau. The chennai jungli soer is a rich dish of pork belly with apples that has a good depth of flavour. You'll also find familiar dishes like korma and rogan josh. The tandoor and grilled dishes includes sikandari ran, which is a slow-cooked lamb shank – billed as having been marinated with vinegar; somewhat surprisingly, this pitches up on a bed of pickled red cabbage – for all the world like Lancashire hotpot. From the bread selection pick the supremely self-indulgent bhatura – you can't beat the appeal of fried bread. Once you have got over the incredible modernity of the place, Anakana is fun, the food prices are fair and the standard of cooking is above average.

Armadillo

41 Broadway Market, E8 ■ 020 7249 3633

⊖ Bethnal Green

🍽 Latin American

🕐 Tues to Fri 18.30–22.30; Sat 12.00–16.00 (tapas) & 18.30–22.30; Sun 12.00–16.00 (tapas)

🖱 www.armadillorestaurant.co.uk

🖰 all major credit cards ■ 12.5% service added for parties of 6 or more

££ tapas £3.50–£5 ■ mains £9.50–£16.50 ■ sides £2.50 ■ desserts £3.50–£5 ■ lowest bottle price £11

✪ South American embassy to the republic of Hackney

Armadillo is that rare thing, a small neighbourhood restaurant with an unusual menu and staff who care. The staff care because this resto has an owner-driver, the menu is unusual because it is based on South American home cooking, and the standard of that cooking is good enough to have won several awards. The dining room is bright and colourful, and although the menu uses some unfamiliar South American terms, after a couple of the excellent caipirinhas (a mixture of fierce white spirit called cachaçà, sugar, crushed limes and ice) the friendly explanations from the staff will start to make sense. To start there may be a Bolivian cheese, onion and chilli pasty served with a green tapenade; fried squid and cassava with sauce criolla; tilapia in a ceviche made with peppers, red onions and blood oranges; or chicken anticucho, potato and black mint crema. Mains range from the slightly bizarre – ostrich meatballs, corn cake and watercress, to more straightforward dishes like roast suckling pig with Columbian beans and chorizo, or sea bream baked in a banana leaf with coconut and ginger sauce and fried plantain. Puddings are equally novel. Spicy chocolate ice cream and amaretti is home-made and delivers what it promises, while pionon with manjar is a kind of Peruvian Swiss roll. Wines are mainly from South America and Spain and are reasonably priced. Or perhaps 'Quentão' appeals – a Brazilian spirit, mulled and served with ginger and orange? For the summer there are four or five tables in the courtyard – booking is essential.

Carnevale

135 Whitecross Street, EC1 ■ 020 7250 3452

⊖ Old Street

|⊙| Vegetarian/fusion

🕔 Mon to Fri 10.00–22.30; Sat 17.30–22.30

🖱 www.carnevalerestaurant.co.uk

🖶 all major credit cards except AmEx ■ 12.5% service added for parties of 6 or more

££ starters £3.95–£5.25 ■ mains £11.50 ■ sides £2.50–£4.50 ■ desserts £4.95 ■ lunch deli plates £5.95 & £9.50 ■ lowest bottle price £12

✪ Friendly, if eccentric, vegetarian stalwart

This scruffy street is all sprawling market by day and dingy grubbiness by night, and you'll find a rather strange little restaurant called Carnevale tucked into an ordinary shop-like space halfway along. Step inside to a clean, light but cramped space, full of blond wood tables and chairs, with carefully selected (if not particularly original) prints on the walls and a faux garden to the rear. The interior has been put together in workable form to meet the needs of the customers. Mercifully, the enduring tendency of vegetarian restaurants to litter the premises with hippy references has been brought under control. Instead, close attention seems to have been paid to the food, which is cooked with care. The menu changes every couple of months, and is not overlong. Starters may range from flageolet bean fritters with marinated red peppers; through soup of the day; to purple sprouting broccoli with goats' cheese and kalamata olives. They are good enough to be served in many grander establishments. Main courses are equally grounded: potato gratin with fried free-range egg, buffalo mozzarella and wild mushrooms, or radicchio and red wine risotto with Parmesan and herbs. There is a plentiful list of side orders, though given the size of the portions it is unlikely that you'll need any. If your stamina is up to them, puddings are good, too: try the chocolate and chestnut roulade with passion fruit, or the caramelised blood orange tart. Service is relaxed, coffee is good and there are a number of alternative drinks on offer.

Cây Tre

301 Old Street, EC1 ■ 020 7729 8662

⊖ Old Street

❙❍❙ Vietnamese

🕒 Mon to Thurs 12.00–15.00 & 17.30–23.00; Fri & Sat 12.00–15.30 & 17.30–23.30; Sun 12.00–22.30

🖰 www.vietnamesekitchen.co.uk

🖺 all major credit cards ■ 10% optional service added

££ starters £1.50–£9 ■ mains £3.50–£7 ■ sides £3.50–£6 ■ desserts £3–£3.50 ■ special menus £15 (meat) & £19 (seafood) ■ lowest bottle price £10.95

✪ Jolly, bustling Vietnamese – strong on fish

There used to be something of a demarcation line between the trendy clubs and restaurants on Old Street and the more functional throng of Vietnamese restaurants just up the Kingsland Road. But then Cây Tre opened on Old Street. What is most surprising is that the food is so good, the prices are so reasonable and that the resto has retained that engaging family-run feel that is now getting harder to find. The menu is fascinating and includes many authentic and complicated Vietnamese dishes. Start with the bò cuôn bánh tráng (for two). A griddle is set up on your table for you to grill thinly cut steak; while you're waiting, soak rice papers until soft, then add sauce and parcel up the beef with pickles. Also prepared at table is cha cá La Vong, a dish that hails from a notable restaurant on Cha Cá Street in Hanoi. Sliced marinated monkfish is cooked in a frying pan at table on fresh fennel with a shrimp sauce. Another superb starter is the bò lá lôt, parcels of minced savoury beef wrapped in aromatic sapu leaves. From the mains, bò lúc lâc, shaking beef, is made with tender rib-eye steak. There is a wide selection of noodle soups including the classic pho, and you can get that most delicious of Vietnamese vegetable dishes, rau muông xào to'i, stir-fried water spinach with garlic dressing. There are two ways to make the most of Cây Tre's charming service and very good food: either opt for one of the 'meals-in-a-bowl' and dine quickly, or order up an array of starters and feast.

Eyre Brothers

70 Leonard Street, EC2 ■ 020 7613 5346 &

⊖ Old Street

🍴 Mediterranean

🕐 Mon to Fri 12.00–15.00 & 18.30–22.45; Sat 18.30–22.45

🖱 www.eyrebrothers.co.uk

🗗 all major credit cards ■ 12.5% optional service added

££ starters £6–£16 ■ mains £14–£21 ■ sides £3 ■ desserts £6 ■ menus
£17 & £33 ■ lowest bottle price £13.50

✪ Good food, sleek and slick room

The eponymous David Eyre will forever be pigeonholed as one of
the creators of The Eagle (see p. 190) and, as such, a founding father
of the gastropub revolution. Which makes it all the more surprising to
find Eyre and his brother at the helm of a very large, very swish, very
elegant 80-seat restaurant. Eyre Brothers is on Leonard Street, deep
in the trendy part of EC2. There is a long bar and a good deal of dark
wood and leather – the overall feel is one of comfortable clubbiness.
The food is ballsy, with upfront flavours and textures, and scarcely
a day goes by without some dishes falling off the menu and being
replaced by new ones. David's cuisine is hard to categorise – there are
a few Spanish and Italian dishes, a lot of Portuguese specialities and
some favourites from Mozambique. Starters range widely and include
octopus salad with mussel and chilli vinaigrette; warm pimentos
de picquillo stuffed with duck confit; fried king scallops with Leon
chorizo. You may also be offered jamón Ibérico 'Joselito' gran
reserva – quality is the watchword here. Main courses include grilled
Mozambique tiger prawns piri-piri – these are large and meaty with a
belt of heat from the Portuguese chilli. Or there may be grilled black
leg chicken with garlic. Puds are classics with a twist, such as basil
and mascarpone ice cream, or chocolate fondant with almond milk
sorbet. This is one place where you can indulge in really good sherry.
A rare Manzanilla Passada, a Palo Cortada or an old Oloroso by the
glass, or the half bottle.

Faulkner's

424 Kingsland Road, N8 ■ 020 7254 6152   ♿

⊖ BR Dalston Kingsland

🍽 Fish & chips

🕐 Mon to Thurs 12.00–14.30 & 17.00–22.00; Fri 12.00–14.30 & 16.30–22.00; Sat 11.30–22.00; Sun 12.00–21.00

🏧 all major credit cards except AmEx ■ no service added

££ starters £2.90–£4.95 ■ mains £8.90–£18.90 ■ sides 60p–£2
■ desserts £3 ■ menus: children's £4.90, set £13.90 & £16.90
■ lowest bottle price £9.50

✪ Old-time fish and chips

Among the kebab shops that line the rather scruffy Kingsland Road, Faulkner's – a spotless fish-and-chip restaurant combined with a takeaway – is a clear highlight. It is also reassuringly old-fashioned with its lace curtains, fish tank and uniformed waitresses, and it holds few surprises – which is probably what makes it such a hit. Usually Faulkner's is full of local families and large parties, all ploughing through colossal fish dinners while chatting across tables. It also goes out of its way to be child-friendly, with highchairs leaned against the wall and a children's menu. House speciality among the starters is the fishcake, a plump ball made with fluffy, herby potato; genuine French fish soup imported from Perard in Le Touquet, peppery and dark; or there's prawn cocktail. For main courses, the regular menu features all the British fish favourites, served fried or poached and with chips, while daily specials are chalked up on the blackboard. Cod and haddock retain their fresh, firm flesh beneath the dark, crunchy batter, while the subtler, classier Dover sole is best served delicately poached. The mushy peas are just right – lurid and lumpy like God intended – but the test of any good chippy is always its chips, and here they are humdingers: fat, firm and golden, with a wicked layer of crispy little salty bits at the bottom. Stuffed in a soft doughy roll they make the perfect chip butty. Most people wet their whistles with a mug of strong tea, but there is a wine list for those dining in style.

Fifteen

Upstairs Trattoria, 15 Westland Place, N1 ■ 0871 330 1515

⊖	Old Street
ᅵ◉ᅵ	Italian
⏱	Mon to Sat 12.00–14.30 & 18.00–23.30; Sun 17.30–21.30
⌂	www.fifteenrestaurant.com
⊟	all major credit cards ■ 12.5% optional service added
££	antipasti £3 ■ secondi £9–£18 ■ desserts £6 ■ menus: lunch Mon to Fri £22.50 & £25; dinner tasting menu £60 ■ lowest bottle price £20

✪ Your way to support the Fifteen Foundation Charity

When Jamie Oliver's restaurant Fifteen first burst onto our television screens it quickly became apparent that the stated objective, 'To give opportunities to unemployed youngsters and help them change their lives by becoming the next generation of star chefs', would not be an easy task. Some years further on and dogged determination seems to be paying off. The more pukka establishment downstairs is very busy and somewhat pricey, while the Trattoria on the ground floor offers customers sound Italian food, chirpy service and glimpses of the telly stars, and then makes them pay enough to support the endeavour. For a cold-hearted, careful-with-money diner, the prices here will be high enough to elevate the wince factor, certainly higher than you would pay for this level of cooking elsewhere. But come on … this is for charity, so evaluate the rosy glow instead. The menu copy is very gushy: 'Fifteen's amazing antipasti – beautifully dressed seasonal vegetables, the biggest olives, superb cured meats' … you get the idea; this plateful is good, but not amazing. In a similar vein, 'the lightest potato gnocchi' are very good; tagliatelle with horse mushrooms, mascarpone, thyme and Parmigiano is sound enough. 'Secondi' offers roast monkfish wrapped in prosciutto; roast spatchcocked poussin; chargrilled swordfish; and pan-fried calves' liver with Italian sausage, oozy polenta, red onions and Belazu balsamic. The cooking is sound and the service is slick, so be charitable when you catch sight of the bill.

Fish Central

151 King's Square, Central Street, EC1 ■ 020 7253 4970

⊖ Barbican

🍴 Fish & chips

🕐 Mon to Sat 11.00–14.30 & 16.45–22.20

🏧 all major credit cards ■ no service added

££ starters £3.25–£7.95 ■ mains £6.95–£13 ■ sides £1.50–£2 ■ desserts £3.50 ■ lowest bottle price £8.95

✪ Top-notch fish and chip restaurant

The Barbican may appear to be the back of beyond – a black hole in the heart of the City – but perfectly ordinary people do live and work around here. Apart from the theatres and concert hall and the proximity to the financial district, one of the main attractions of the place is Fish Central, which holds its own with the finest fish-and-chip shops in town, and indeed a good many snootier restaurants. People tend to be very snobbish about fish-and-chip shops, but Fish Central is just the place to dispel such delusions. Though at first sight it appears just like any other superior chippy – a takeaway service one side and an eat-in restaurant next door – a glance at its menu lets you know that this is something out of the ordinary. All the finny favourites are here, from cod and haddock to rock salmon and plaice, but there's a wholesome choice of alternatives, including grilled Dover sole and roast cod with sautéed potatoes. These dishes are cooked to order, and a menu note prepares you for a 25-minute wait. You can eat decently even if you are not in the mood for fish. Try the Cumberland sausages, with onions and gravy. If you think your appetite is up to starters, try the prawn cocktail – the normal naked pink prawns in pink sauce, but genuinely fresh. Chips come as a side order, so those who prefer can order a jacket potato or creamed potatoes. There are mushy peas, which are, well, mushy, and pickled onions and gherkins. In keeping with its role as fish restaurant rather than fish shop there is even a wine list. Champagne anyone?

The Fox

28 Paul Street, EC2 ■ 020 7729 5708

⊖ Old Street

🍽 Modern British/gastropub

🕐 Mon to Fri 12.30–15.00 & 18.30–22.00

🗗 all major credit cards except AmEx ■ 12.5% service added for parties of 6 or more

££ menus £15 (2 courses) & £19.75 (3 courses) ■ lowest bottle price £11

✪ Great food in a genuine gastropub

It may raise a few eyebrows amongst biologists, but this fox is the direct descent of an eagle – The Fox is sibling to the original gastropub, The Eagle (see p. 190). Downstairs it is a grand, pubby sort of pub, with decent real ale and the kind of serious pub food that really appeals. Upstairs is the dining room, which has much in common with the style of the original Eagle: the tables and chairs are an eclectic mix, the cutlery and china are gleefully mismatched, and the whole has a passing resemblance to Steptoe's lair. The cooking at The Fox is 'school of' The Eagle. Dishes are robust, well seasoned, honest and driven by the seasons. The menu changes every day, and while there isn't a huge amount of choice there should be something to please everyone. Pricing is straightforward: either a two-course or a three-course set menu. For starters, a typical choice is between a potato and sorrel soup; smoked trout, dandelion and soft-boiled egg; beetroot, feta and rocket. Note the homeliness of these dishes, their balance and the comfortable combinations of flavour and texture. Main course options may include crab Newburg; cod, peas and escarole; pigeon, bubble and squeak; or gammon and parsley sauce. This food is as sophisticated as it is simple. Finish off with a delicious pud, such as buttermilk pudding with blood orange salad, or chocolate tart, as well as a well-chosen cheese. With food like this, and a sensibly priced wine list, The Fox makes for a pleasant, good-value and unpretentious place to eat. And there is even an agreeable little suntrap terrace, with a few tables for hardened lovers of the alfresco.

Green Papaya

191 Mare Street, E8 ■ 020 8985 5486

⊖ BR Hackney Central

🍽 Vietnamese

🕐 Tues to Sun 17.00–23.00

🕸 www.greenpapaya.co.uk

🖃 all major credit cards except AmEx ■ no service added

££ starters £3.25–£5.95 ■ mains £5–£8.50 ■ desserts £2.80–£3 ■ lowest bottle price £10.50

✪ Value from Vietnam

There are a great many Vietnamese restaurants in East London, but Green Papaya stands out by virtue of sound cooking, excellent value and a casual café-bar atmosphere. The menu claims, 'for a true experience of Vietnamese cuisine', and for once this may be true, as there are some remarkably economical dishes that are also full of authentic flavours – like a large bowl of vermicelli, shiitake mushrooms, black fungi and kohlrabi soup. There is also a wine list with a good selection of workmanlike New World wines at accessible prices. The cooking is accomplished and makes use of the fresh ingredients and herbs to be found from the many Vietnamese suppliers nearby. You know that on Mare Street they are unlikely to run out of purple basil. Starters include the usual suspects such as Vietnamese herb rolls with prawns; banana flower salad; and the eponymous green papaya salad. They are fresh, crisp and delicious. Try the banh tom for a change and experience lightly battered strips of sweet potato and king prawn deep-fried and presented as a nest. Very moreish. There are enough variations of braised, stir-fried and steamed meats, seafood and poultry to satisfy the choosier diner, plus a ten-dish tofu section for vegetarians (although somewhat perplexingly several have fish in them). Slow-cooked lamb cubes with galangal, lemongrass and coconut milk comes in a curiously light-coloured sauce, but the lamb is tender. There are also unusual dishes such as stir-fried kohlrabi with shiitake mushrooms and black fungi, and stir-fried sweet gourd with bean sprouts and spring onions. And, of course, there's stir-fried morning glory.

Huong Viet

An Viet House, 12–14 Englefield Road, N1 ▪ 020 7249 0877 ♿

⊖ BR Dalston Kingsland

🍽 Vietnamese

🕐 Mon to Fri 12.00 to 15.30 & 17.30 to 23.00, Sat 12.00 to 16.00 & 17.30 to 23.00

🖥 Mastercard, Visa ▪ 10% optional service rising to 12% for parties of 8 or more

££ starters £3.30–£5.50 ▪ mains £3.50–£6.70 ▪ desserts £1–£3 ▪ set menu (for 4) meat or vegetarian £13pp ▪ lowest bottle price £7.45

✪ Vietnam HQ

This former council bathhouse is a rather four-square and solid-looking building that has been reborn as Huong Viet – the canteen of the Vietnamese Cultural Centre. The resto has long had a reputation for really good, really cheap food, and regulars have stuck with it through a couple of general refurbishments. But, despite acquiring a drinks licence, this place is never going to turn into a trendy bar restaurant. The food has stayed fresh, unpretentious, delicious and cheap, although prices are creeping upwards. The service is still friendly and informal. Start with the spring rolls – small, crisp and delicious. Or the fresh rolls, which resemble small, carefully rolled-up table napkins. The outside is soft, white and delicate-tasting, while the inside teams cooked vermicelli with prawns and fresh herbs – a great combination of textures. Ordering the prawn and green leaf soup brings a bowl of delicate broth with greens and shards of tofu. Pho is perhaps the most famous Vietnamese 'soup' dish, but it is really a meal in a bowl. The pho here is formidable, especially the Hanoi noodle soup, filled with beef, chicken or tofu. Hot, rich and full of bits and pieces, it comes with a plate of herbs, crispy bean sprouts and aromatics that you must add yourself at the last moment so none of the aroma is lost. The other dishes are excellent, too. Look out for mixed seafood with pickled veg and dill, which works exceptionally well. You should also try the noodle dishes – choose from the wok-fried rice noodle dishes, or the crispy-fried egg noodles.

Istanbul Iskembecisi

9 Stoke Newington Road, N16 ■ 020 7254 7291

⊖ BR Dalston Kingsland

🍴 Turkish

🕐 daily 12.00–05.00

🗠 all major credit cards ■ no service added

££ starters £3–£4.50 ■ mains £7–£9 ■ sides £2.50–£3 ■ desserts £3
■ lowest bottle price £9.50

✪ Stay up late at this most Turkish of Turkish restos

**Despite being named after its signature dish – iskembe is a limpid
tripe soup –** the Istanbul is a Turkish grill house. Admittedly it is a
grill house with chandeliers, smart tables and upscale service, but it
is still a grill house. And because it stays open until late into the early
morning it is much beloved by clubbers and chefs – they are just
about ready to go out and eat when everyone else has had enough
and set off home. The grilled meat may be better over at Mangal II
(which is just across the road, or on page 220), but the atmosphere
of raffish elegance at the Istanbul has real charm. The iskembe, or
tripe soup, has its following. Large parties of Turks from the snooker
hall just behind the restaurant insist on it, and you'll see the odd
regular downing two bowlfuls of the stuff. For most people, however,
it's bland at best, and even the large array of additives (salt, pepper,
chilli – this is a dish that you must season to your personal taste at
the table) cannot make it palatable. A much better bet is to start with
the mixed meze, which brings a good houmous and tarama, a superb
dolma, and the rest drawn from the usual suspects. Then on to the
grills, which are presented with more panache than usual. Pirzola
brings three lamb chops; shish kebab is good and fresh; karisik isgara
is a formidable mixed grill. For a more interesting option there's
arvnavaut cigeri-sicak – liver Albanian style. Isn't it sad that they no
longer serve kelle sogus (roasted head of lamb)?

→ For branches, see index

Mangal II

4 Stoke Newington Road, N16 ■ 020 7254 7888

⊖ BR Dalston Kingsland

🍴 Turkish

🕐 Mon to Fri 17.00–01.00; Sat 14.00–01.00; Sun 12.00–01.00

🖥 cash or cheque only ■ no service added

££ starters £2.75–£3.95 ■ mains £7.95–£8.95 ■ desserts £3.25 ■ menus (for 2) £29.50pp ■ lowest bottle price £10.75

✪ Cheap, cheerful and magnificent grilled meats

It is time to be led by your nose … The first thing to hit you at Mangal II is the smell. The fragrance of spicy, sizzling chargrilled meat is unmistakably, authentically Turkish. This, combined with the relaxing pastel décor, puts you in holiday mood before you've even sat down. The ambience is laid-back, too. At slack moments, the staff shoot the breeze around the ocakbasi, and service comes with an ear-to-ear grin. All you have to do is sit back, sink an Efes Pilsener and peruse the encyclopedic menu. Prices are low and portions enormous. Baskets of fresh bread are endlessly replenished and there's a vast range of tempting mezeler (starters). The 25 options include simple houmous and dolma; imam bayildi, aubergines rich with onion, tomato and green pepper; thin lahmacun, meaty Turkish pizza; and karisik meze, a large plate of mixed dishes that's rather heavy on the yogurt. The main dishes (kebablar) themselves are sumptuous, big on lamb and chicken, but with limited fish and vegetarian alternatives. The patlican kebab is outstanding – melt-in-the-mouth grilled minced lamb with sliced aubergines, served with a green salad, of which the star turn is an olive-stuffed tomato shaped like a basket. The kebabs are also superb, particularly the house special, ezmeli kebab, which comes doused in Mangal's special sauce. On rare occasions the grilled quails listed on the menu are actually available, and are a 'must have' item. They are very good indeed. After that you might just be tempted by a slab of toothachingly sweet baklava. Alternatively, round off the evening with a punch-packing raki.

The Real Greek

14–15 Hoxton Market, N1 ■ 020 7739 8212

⊖ Old Street

|◉| Greek

🕒 Mon to Sat 12.00–15.00 & 17.30–22.30

🖰 www.therealgreek.co.uk

🗗 all major credit cards except AmEx ■ 12.5% optional service added

££ mezedes £10–£20 ■ fagakia £8–£9.50 ■ desserts £5.50 ■ lowest bottle price £12.50

⭐ The best Greek food on London

This particular Real Greek is called Theodore Kyriakou. And showing off the authentic dishes of his homeland is the difficult mission Kyriakou has embarked upon. Next door to the restaurant is what was once the Hoxton Mission Hall, but now the lofty room has been converted into a busy Mezedopoliou, a bar where you can order a few meze (they are sold singly by the plateful and the bar is open from noon to 22.30) and try a dozen stunning Greek wines by the glass or carafaki. It's a relaxed way to sample some seriously good food. Then Real Greek went on to set up a third establishment, which has become the template for a small chain – The Real Greek Souvlaki & Bar (see p. 196). The senior restaurant goes from strength to strength. The menu changes with the seasons. The first section is 'Mezedes' and each platter has three or four components. One such might include chicken sofrito; courgettes stuffed with mince; tzatziki; and beetroot with yogurt and walnuts. Or there may be a combination of a scallop; a salad of lakerda (a preserved fish); fava; and horta – warm seasonal greens. On to 'Fagakia': these small dishes could be either starters or sides, such as grilled squid served with a leek and lemon pilaff. Main courses are a revelation. Try duck stuffed with cinnamon spinach; roast pork with smoked sausage; or kakavia – a full-on fish soup served with mayonnaise. Then there is a whole range of Greek cheeses and desserts: the Kymian fig and chocolate pot is outstanding. Wine lovers will find an amazing list of superb Greek wines – real quality at bargain prices.

→ For branches, see index or website

Rivington Grill, Bar, Deli

28–30 Rivington Street, EC2 ■ 020 7729 7053

⊖ Old Street

🍴 British

🕐 Mon to Fri 08.00–11.00 (breakfast), 12.00–14.30 & 18.30–23.00; Sat 12.00–23.00; Sun 12.00–22.30

🖱 www.rivingtongrill.co.uk

🗗 all major credit cards ■ 12.5% service added

££ breakfast £1.50–£7.50 ■ starters £4.95–£7.75 ■ mains £8.50–£24.50 ■ desserts £5.50–£7.75 ■ Sunday set menu £22.50 (3 courses) ■ lowest bottle price £14.50

✪ Seasonal British food at its best

The Rivington Grill, Bar, Deli has a very long name indeed, and it's the kind of name that hedges its bets. This place has an elegant, high-ceilinged, white-painted dining room, a comfortable bar with high stools for solo diners, and plenty of sofas. The Deli part is to be found in a separate shop just around the corner. The restaurant menu is seasonal and interesting. This food is not Italian, it is not French, it is not fancy and it is not formal. The dishes don't even answer to Modern British. If there is such a cuisine as Ordinary British, then this is it. On the face of it everything looks simple, but someone in the kitchen has given the dishes some thought and the combinations work well together. There may be Scotch broth; a beetroot and goats' cheese salad with walnuts; devilled kidneys on toast – lamb's kidneys cooked perfectly and with a well-made sharp sauce. Or deep-fried skate cheeks with tartare sauce. Main courses also satisfy. There's hamburger and chips; honey-baked ham with mustard sauce; haddock fish fingers and chips with mushy peas; roast suckling pig with pumpkin and quince sauce. Puddings veer from blood orange trifle, to steamed chocolate pudding and trad numbers like banana custard. The wine list starts steadily but then skitters on through a handful of pricey bottles to Vosne-Romanée and the like. Stick with the middleweights for the best value. Ask about the 'feasts' served on platters for a large table – whole suckling pig, or a huge roast fish. Good food on a grand scale.

Santa Maria del Buen Ayre

50 Broadway Market, E8 ■ 020 7275 9900   ♿

⊖ Bethnal Green

🍽 Latin American

🕐 Mon to Fri 18.00–22.30; Sat 10.00–22.30; Sun 12.00–22.30

🖥 www.buenayre.co.uk

🖇 all major credit cards except AmEx ■ 12.5% optional service added for parties of 6 or more

££ starters £4–£4.50 ■ mains £8–£15 ■ sides £3–£3.50 ■ desserts £4 ■ lowest bottle price £9.50

✪ Significant meat mountain, sizzling at your table

When that meat itch needs scratching Santa Maria etc. is a pretty good place to do it. This resto seeks to recreate an Argentine 'Parrilla' – a kind of grill house. There is a nod to vegetarians, but as a guideline start thinking meat. Start with empanadas – there are three kinds on offer: beef, chicken, and spinach with cheese. These small pastries are made with a good, light, crisp shortcrust pastry. The main courses are split into two sections – first there are the 'platos principas' and then there are the 'parrilladas'. The platos are simple – an 8oz or a 14oz prime Argentine sirloin steak; or rib-eye steak; or fillet steak; or rump steak. Also good home-made sausages, and 'vacio de ternera', which is an Argentine speciality – veal flank steak. The 'Parrilladas' (or brazier) is a small table-top griddle plate over a charcoal fire. It ensures that your grub stays warm, pretty vital should you order a parrillada (for a minimum of two), because parrillada should be translated as meat mountain. Order the 'Buen Ayre' and you are faced with two large sausages, well-seasoned and meaty; black pudding, very decent, floral and not too fatty; sweetbreads, marginally overcooked; kidneys, ditto; short ribs, excellent crispy bits; and flank steak, very close-grained and fatty. The side order of chips is a worthwhile addition – very crisp, very fluffy. Service is sound and the wine list un-grasping. Pud-wise the famous and ultra sweet dulce de leche turns up in flans and cheesecakes. Best to opt for the moody coffees – 'bombon' is a shot glass with a thick layer of condensed milk that has an espresso floating on top of it.

Sông Quê

134 Kingsland Road, EC2 ▪ 020 7613 3222

⊖ Old Street

🍽 Vietnamese

🕓 Mon to Sat 12.00–15.00 & 17.30–23.00; Sun 12.00–23.00

🔲 all major credit cards except AmEx ▪ no service added

££ starters £2.90–£6.90 ▪ mains & noodles £4.80–£12.20 ▪ sides £1.70–£2.20 ▪ desserts £1.50–£2 ▪ lunch menu £3.80–£4.20 ▪ lowest bottle price £7.50

✪ Pho Central

Sông Quê has made something of an impact among the cluster of Vietnamese eateries strung out along this section of the Kingsland Road. It's a garish place inside, but proximity to other restos means that if you make the journey and can't get a table here (it's best to book), there are several other establishments offering Vietnamese cooking within walking distance, including Viet Hoa (see opposite). Sông Quê offers a staggering 170 dishes. There are 28 starters, 21 noodle dishes, 10 rice dishes, 28 seafood, 13 vegetable dishes and 19 pho or traditional Vietnamese noodle soup dishes – each a meal in itself. Try bo nuong la tot: grilled slices of beef wrapped in betel leaf, or goi cuon, fresh rolls of rice paper with zingy fresh herbs. Larger dishes include diep xao hanh gung, scallops with ginger and spring onions, and the essential rau muong xao loi; translated, but still a puzzle, as 'stir-fried-ong choy with garlic', it's a dish of the most delicious iron-tasting vegetable, a.k.a. water morning glory. Pho is a must. Each kind comes with rice noodles, shredded onion and coriander simmered in fresh broth with a separate plate of raw bean shoots, a bunch of basil leaves, Vietnamese parsley and sliced red chillies. You dunk the additional raw vegetables in the hot broth, taking great care with the red chillies. Of the nineteen varieties, pho ga is chicken, tai nam is rare sliced steak and well done flank, while hu tiu my tho is mixed pork and prawn. Good simple flavours. If in awe of the complex menu, go for vit chien don cuon banh trang – crispy duck with the trimmings.

Viet Hoa Café

72 Kingsland Road, E2 ■ 020 7729 8293

....

⊖ Old Street

....

🍽 Vietnamese

....

🕘 Mon to Fri 12.00–15.30 & 17.30–23.30; Sat & Sun 12.30–23.30

....

🗔 all major credit cards ■ 12.5% optional service added (dinner only)

....

££ starters 90p–£6.50 ■ mains £3.50–£8.90 ■ sides £1.70–£5.50
    ■ desserts £2.20–£2.95 ■ lowest bottle price £8.50

....

✪ Friendly family business

The Viet Hoa dining room is large, clean, light and airy, with an impressive golden parquet floor. The café part of the name is borne out by the bottles of red and brown sauce that take pride of place on each table. The brown goop turns out to be hoisin sauce and the red stuff a simple chilli one, but they have both been put into recycled plastic bottles on which the only recognisable words are 'Sriracha extra hot chilli sauce – Flying Goose Brand'. Apparently this has made all but the regulars strangely wary of hoisin sauce. For diners wanting to go as a group and share, an appetiser called salted prawn in garlic dressing is outstanding – large prawns marinated and fried with chilli and garlic. From the list of fifteen soups, pho is compulsory. Ribbon noodles and beef, chicken or tofu are added to a delicate broth that comes with a plate of mint leaves, Thai basil and chillies, your job being to add the fresh aromatics to the hot soup – resulting in astonishingly vivid flavours. Main courses include shaking beef, cubes of beef with a tangy salad, and drunken fish, fish cooked with wine and cloud ear mushrooms. Both live up to the promise of their exotic names. There are a good many salad and tofu dishes, including tofu with chilli and black bean. Bun tom nuong is a splendid one-pot dish of noodles with chargrilled tiger prawns. Also in one-pot-with-vermicelli territory, you'll find bun nem nuong, which features grilled minced pork, and that old favourite, Singapore noodles. Among the desserts you'll find 'fried ice cream' – the connoisseur's choice.

Zen Satori

40 Hoxton Street, N1 ■ 020 7613 9590 ♿

⊖ Old Street

🍴 Indian/Chinese/Thai

🕐 Mon to Fri 12.00–15.00

🖰 www.zen-satori.co.uk

🖨 all major credit cards ■ no service added

££ starters £2.85–£5 ■ mains £5.95–£9.95 ■ sides £3 ■ desserts £3.95 ■ set lunch £4.95 & £6.95 ■ lowest bottle price £8.50

✪ Catering school bargain

Zen Satori is the training restaurant of the Asian and Oriental School of Catering, but do not be deceived into thinking that you might end up with an amateurish meal. Granted, the service may be friendly and charming rather than super-slick, but it is easy to prefer it that way. Running down one side of the dining room is a gleaming modern, open kitchen full of bustling cooks – some are students, some are lecturers. Prices are dirt-cheap. The food is fresh, well cooked and well presented. There are four different set lunches: pick Thai and enjoy chicken and mushroom tom yum, chicken and coriander cakes, and then beef with lemongrass and French beans, plus a choice of rice or noodles. Order Chinese and get wonton soup, vegetable spring roll, and lemon chicken, plus either rice or noodles. For vegetarians there is a soup, spring roll and green curried vegetables combo. The Indian option teams mulligatawny soup, samosas, South Indian chicken curry, and rice. The curry is a good one – authentically hot, with well-balanced spices and a complex array of tastes. There is also an à la carte menu where you'll find starters such as sesame prawn toast or chicken tikka – juicy, fresh, large chunks. The wine list tops out while still eminently affordable and there are several decent beers on offer. If you are too mean for the set lunch, you'll appreciate the range of 'special one-plate lunch options', which are an even bigger bargain, either way the school deserves your support so leave a big tip.

North

Camden Town, Primrose Hill and Chalk Farm

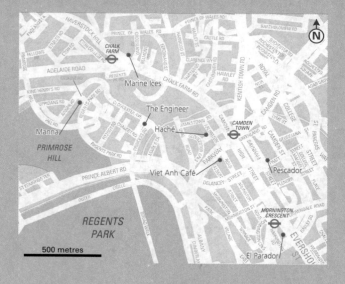

The Engineer

65 Gloucester Avenue, NW1 ■ 020 7722 0950

⊖ Chalk Farm

🍴 Modern British/gastropub

🕐 Mon to Fri 09.00–11.30, 12.00–15.00 & 19.00–22.30; Sat & Sun 09.00–12.00

🖰 www.the-engineer.com

🗗 all major credit cards except AmEx ■ 12.5% optional service added

££ breakfast £2.25–£9.50 ■ starters £4–£6.75 ■ mains £11.75–£16.75 ■ desserts £5.50–£7 ■ lowest bottle price £13

✪ Gastropub with a great back yard

The Engineer is now one of London's senior gastropubs, and eating places are spread throughout the building and garden. Wherever you end up sitting, you'll get offered the same menu (which changes every two weeks) and you'll pay the same price. The cooking is accomplished, with good strong combinations of flavours, and a cheerful, iconoclastic approach to what is fundamentally Mediterranean food. The opening move is home-made bread and butter, the bread is warm from the oven, with a good crust, and the butter is beurre d'Isigny, and they will even refill the basket after you've scoffed the lot. Starters are simple and good. There's soup and that price includes the bread mentioned earlier. There may be hommus with warm flatbreads and spicy lamb kofta, or something more exotic like tequila-cured salmon with blinis, horseradish cream and cucumber. At lunchtime there are one or two simpler mains than in the evening: toad in the hole with mash and sugar snap peas; huevos rancheros with tortilla and black beans. For dinner, expect dishes such as grilled swordfish with lemon-scented fennel and bloody Mary sauce; risotto cake with butternut squash and feta cheese; or red braised belly pork with steamed baby gem lettuce. A side order of baker fries brings thick wedges of baked potato fried until crispy. Desserts include banana Pavlova, or custard tart. There is always a decent pint of beer to be had and the coffee is excellent. The garden always gets mobbed in good weather – book early.

Haché

24 Inverness Street, NW1 ■ 020 7485 9100

⊖ Camden Town

⦿ Burgers

🕒 Mon to Sat 12.00–22.30; Sun 12.00–22.00

🖱 www.hacheburgers.com

🖶 all major credit cards ■ 12.5% optional service added

££ burgers £4.95–£9.95 ■ sides £1.95–£2.50 ■ desserts £2.95–£4.50 ■ lowest bottle price £12.95

✪ Steak haché – French for posh burger

They may be made from Angus beef, or chicken, or vegetables or even tuna, but they are still burgers. Haché is a very modern kind of burger place, and within the limits of a burger restaurant it does a very good job. The dining room looks good, with small chandeliers and comfortable seating, and ingredients are signwritten along the walls (think back a decade to the design of the original Belgo). This whole place asserts that it is not a burger place; but steak haché looks like a burger, tastes like a burger and costs about the same as a premium burger. The burgers are good; the quality of meat is good, and they are cooked as requested. The ciabatta buns are good. The fries are good. The chunky chips are good. The onion rings are suitably greasy and disgusting. When you tire of permutations of an Angus beef hamburger with chorizo, or Stilton, or Portabella mushrooms, or sweet cure bacon, you could opt for the 'chicken Spanish' – chicken, sweet roast red pepper and goats' cheese; the 'veggie blue cheese' – fresh vegetables and chickpeas topped with Stilton; or even the tuna Haché burger. There are also seasonal specials, such as 'Mexicain' (sic), with Cajun spices and salsa. The desserts are eminently missable – ice cream and cake masquerading as brownie; and there is a sensibly short wine list. Service is sound. The true 'Haché experience' is to tuck into a well-made burger that doesn't cost the earth. Experience it soon.

Manna

4 Erskine Road, NW1 ■ 020 7722 8028

⊖ Chalk Farm

🍴 Vegetarian

🕐 Mon to Sat 18.00–23.00; Sun 12.30–15.00

🖰 www.manna-veg.com

🖃 Mastercard, Visa ■ 12.5% optional service added for parties of 6 or more

££ starters £4.95–£6.95 ■ mains £9.25–£12.95 ■ salads £3.95–£6.50 ■ desserts £3.50–£6.95 ■ lowest bottle price £10.50

✪ Veggie heaven

If your new film – the one where a beautiful American businesswoman meets a tongue-tied but cute Brit aristo … you know the kind of thing – needed an authentic 1970s veggie restaurant for a crucial hand-holding scene, Manna would fit the bill perfectly. This time-warp sometimes extends to the service, so don't pitch up here in a hurry, or without a serious appetite – there is no whimsy about the portions here. The cooking is very sound, and if there is such a thing as a peculiarly 'veggie' charm, this place has plenty. And there's even a menu code (v) = vegan dishes; (vo) = vegan option; (org) = organic dish; (n) = contains nuts; and (g) = gluten free. You can order a selection of any three salads or starters as the 'Manna meze', which is a pretty good option given the huge portions. The menu changes regularly, but may include starters such as organic Gorgonzola pizzette with red onion confit and walnuts, or a tortilla tower – spinach, red pepper and potato omelettes layered with smoked Cheddar. Or how about potato bondas stuffed with pink chilli coconut chutney? Salads are complex – grapefruit and avocado, green pea shoots, watercress and baby mustard leaves, or perhaps organic warm white bean salad with sage oil and crisp sourdough. Mains are an eclectic bunch: whiskey barbecue marinated tofu on roast-garlic mash, or Majorcan baked aubergine stuffed with onions and topped with Romanesco sauce. Puds are serious: organic chocolate ooze pudding and organic fruit crumble are a challenge to all but the stoutest appetites.

Marine Ices

8 Haverstock Hill, NW3 ■ 020 7482 9003

⊖ Chalk Farm

🍴 Italian/ice cream

🕐 Tues to Fri 12.00–15.00 & 18.00–23.00; Sat 12.00–23.00; Sun 12.00–22.00

🗗 all major credit cards except AmEx ■ no service added

££ starters £3–£5.20 ■ mains £7.95–£11.95 ■ sides £2–£4.50 ■ desserts £1.50–£4.95 ■ lowest bottle price £10.35

✪ Old-time Italian, old-time ice cream

Marine Ices is a family restaurant from a bygone era. In 1947 Aldo Mansi rebuilt the family shop along nautical lines, kitting it out in wood with portholes (hence the name). In the half-century since, while the family ice-cream business has grown and grown, the restaurant and gelateria has just pottered along. That means old-fashioned service and home-style, old-fashioned Italian food. It also means that Marine Ices is a great hit with children, for in addition to the good Italian food there is a marathon list of stunning sundaes, coupes, ice creams and sorbets. The menu is long: antipasti, salads, pastas and sauces, vitello, fegato, carne, pollo, pesce, specialities and pizzas. Of the starters, you could try selezioni di bruschetta. Or go for the chef's salad, a rocket salad with pancetta and splendid croûtons made from eggy bread. Pasta dishes are home-made: mix and match various sauces with various pasta – starters, mains, 'oven' dishes such as cannelloni and lasagne, then the menu lists nearly every old-style Italian dish you have ever heard of. Onwards to a host of pizzas – immense, freshly made and very tasty. When you've had your meal, demand the gelateria menu. There are sundaes, from peach Melba to Knickerbocker Glory. There are bombe, coppe, cassate and, best of all, affogati – three scoops of ice cream topped with hot chocolate or, even nicer, espresso coffee. Or run amok among fourteen ice creams and eight sorbets. A takeaway tub of the Mansis' ice cream has been the making of many a dinner party.

El Parador

245 Eversholt Street, NW1 ■ 020 7387 2789

⊖ Mornington Crescent

▮◉▮ Spanish/tapas

🕑 Mon to Thurs 12.00–15.00 & 18.00–23.00; Fri 12.00–15.00 & 18.00–23.30; Sat 18.00–23.30; Sun 18.30–21.30

🖶 all major credit cards ■ 10% optional service added for parties of 5 or more

££ tapas £3–£6 ■ desserts £4 ■ lowest bottle price £13

✪ Tasty tapas, tasty prices

A small, no-frills Spanish restaurant and tapas bar, El Parador seems to be somewhat stranded in the quiet little enclave around Mornington Crescent, between King's Cross and Camden. It serves very tasty tapas at very reasonable prices and has a friendly, laid-back atmosphere, even on busy Friday and Saturday nights. Try a glass of the dry Manzanilla to start or accompany your meal. It's a perfect foil for tapas. As ever with tapas, the fun part of eating here is choosing several dishes from the wide selection on offer, and then sharing and swapping with your companions. Allow at least two or three tapas a head – more for a really filling meal – and go for at least one of the fish or seafood dishes, which are treats. Highlights include chipirones salteados, baby squid pan-fried with sea salt and olive oil, or salteados de gambas, nice fat tiger prawns pan-fried with parsley, paprika and chilli. Carnivores shouldn't miss out on the jamón serrano – delicious Spanish cured ham, or the morcilla de Burgos, sausages that are a cousin of black pudding. The vegetarian tapas are particularly good here. Try pure de patatas del Parador, mash with pan-fried pepper and Manchego, or tortilla Española, a classic Spanish omelette. Desserts keep up the pace: marquesa de chocolate is a luscious, creamy, home-made chocolate mousse, while flan de naranja is a really good orange crème caramel. The al fresco tables hidden behind the resto are sought after and should be booked in advance. It's worth checking out El Parador's strong selection of Spanish wines as there are some good-value bottles.

Pescador

23 Pratt Street, NW1 ■ 020 7482 7008

⊖ Camden Town

🍽 Portuguese/fish

🕐 Mon to Fri 18.00–23.00; Sat 13.00–23.00.

🗗 all major credit cards except AmEx ■ no service added

££ starters £2.50–£6 ■ mains £8.80–£25 ■ sides £2.50 ■ desserts £3
■ lowest bottle price £9.80

⭐ Fine fish, with a Portuguese accent

**Venture into Pescador and you might as well be in Portugal,
which is a good thing,** always presuming that you like fish. The
dining room is a plain, cream-painted room that is slowly being
overwhelmed by a tidal wave of knick-knacks themed around fish
and fishermen. The tables are small and close together and, while
the lady of the house takes charge of the till behind the bar, a flotilla
of waiters bustles about. This is a busy place and you should book.
Starters range from the simple – pasteis de bacalhau, a dish of small,
fluffy, fried rissoles of potato and salt cod, is very good indeed, to
all manner of luxurious seafood – giant prawns, clams, mussels.
One attractive option is to share a main course portion of sapateira
between two: this is billed as 'a crab served with toast', and that's
what you get – spread the toast with the brown meat. As is the way
with good fish restaurants, there is always a daily special and this
might be a large, fresh sea bream that is priced according to the
market and can be served in fillets or left on the bone, depending
how confident you are feeling. Plainly grilled, very fresh fish is always
delicious, and there is also halibut, scabbard fish, squid, sea bass
and skate. If you like rich food and plenty of it, opt for the arroz de
marisco. You get a large casserole full of shellfish chowder thickened
with rice but left sloppy like a very loose risotto. Tremendous. The
Portuguese wines repay investigation, particularly the crisp, dry
Alvarino vinho verde.

→ For branches, see index

Viet-Anh Cafe

41 Parkway, NW1 ■ 020 7284 4082

⊖ Camden Town

🍴 Vietnamese

🕐 daily 12.00–14.00 & 17.30–23.00

🖯 all major credit cards except AmEx ■ 10% optional service added

££ starters £1–£3 ■ mains £3.95–£13 ■ lowest bottle price £10

✪ Cheap, cheerful and Vietnamese

Authentic, it says on the card, and authentic it tastes on the plate.
Viet-Anh is a bright, cheerful café with oilcloth-covered tables, run by
a young Vietnamese couple. They cook and give service that's beyond
helpful. In complete contrast to the occasionally intimidating feel
of some of the more obscure Chinese restaurants, this is a friendly
and welcoming place. If there is anything puzzling or unfamiliar, you
have only to ask. Vietnamese vegetarian spring rolls and Vietnamese
chicken pancake are classic starters. The former are crisp, well
seasoned, and flavoured with fresh coriander; the latter are a delight
– two large, paper-thin, eggy pancakes stuffed with vegetables and
chicken, and served with large lettuce leaves. You take a leaf, add
a slice of the pancake, roll it up, then dip it in the pungent lemony
sauce and eat. Hot and cold, crisp and soft, savoury and lemony
– all in one. Ordering prawn sugar-cane stick brings large prawns
skewered on a piece of sugar cane. Eat the prawn, then chew the
cane. Pho chicken soup is made with slices of chicken and vegetables
plus flat rice-stick noodles in broth. Slurp the noodles and lift the
bowl to drink the soup. Lemongrass chicken on boiled rice is a more
fiery dish – seriously hot. There are over a hundred items on the
menu, and most are satisfying one-plate meals. Wines are priced
sensibly, or you could try the Shui Sen tea – more fragrant than
jasmine tea and just as refreshing.

Crouch End and
Wood Green

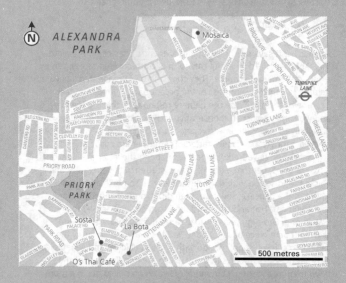

La Bota

31 Broadway Parade, Tottenham Lane, N8 ■ 020 8340 3082

⊖ Finsbury Park/Turnpike Lane

|●| Spanish/tapas

⏰ Mon to Thurs 12.00–14.30 & 18.00–23.00; Fri 12.00–14.30 & 18.00–23.30; Sat 12.00–15.00 & 18.00–23.30; Sun 12.00–23.00

🖻 all major credit cards except AmEx ■ no service added

££ tapas £2–£4.50 ■ mains £7.50–£12.95 ■ desserts £2.75 ■ lowest bottle price £8.95

⭐ N8 Tapas zone

This bustling tapas bar and restaurant enjoys a healthy evening trade, and with good reason. It's a Galician (north-west Spanish) place, and that's always a plus sign, particularly for seafood. Your first decision is a crucial one: do you go all out for tapas (there are 30 on the menu, plus 17 vegetarian ones, plus another 18 or so daily specials chalked on a blackboard)? Or do you choose one of the main courses – Spanish omelette, paellas, steaks, chicken, fish and so forth? Perhaps the best option is to play to La Bota's strengths and order a few tapas, then a few more, until you have subdued your appetite and there's no longer a decision to make. In the meantime enjoy the air conditioning – and the house wine at a very reasonable price. Start with simple things. Boquerones en vinagre brings a plate of broad, white anchovies with a pleasant vinegar tang. Jamón serrano is thinly sliced, ruby-red and strongly flavoured – perfect with the basket of warm French bread that is on every table. Then move on to hot tapas: mejillones pescador is a good-sized plate of mussels in a tomato and garlic sauce; chistorra a la sidra is a mild sausage cooked in cider; riñones al Jerez is a portion of kidneys in a sherry sauce, rich and good. Alas de pollo barbacoa is an Iberian take on chicken wings. Then there's arroz al campo – rice cooked with saffron and vegetables; chicken riojana; and patatas bravas, the tasty dish of potatoes in a mildly spicy tomato sauce. Just keep them coming …

Mosaica

Building C, The Chocolate Factory, Clarendon Road, N22

■ 020 8889 2400   &

⊖ BR Wood Green

⊖| Modern British

⊕ Tues to Fri 12.00–14.30 & 19.00–22.00; Sat 18.30–22.00; Sun 12.30–15.00

⌐ www.mosaicarestaurants.com

⊟ all major credit cards ■ 10% optional service added for parties of 6 or more

££ starters £4.95–£9.95 ■ mains £6–£15 ■ desserts £6 ■ lowest bottle price £11.95

✪ Good food in a moody location

Up in the high pastures of Wood Green there is a straggle of large, run-down buildings called The Chocolate Factory that has been colonised by artists, potters, designers and anyone arty needing cheap, no frills space. You'll find Mosaica hidden at the heart of Building C, and it is an amazing place – spacious, stylish and comfortable. There is a long bar made up of cinder blocks, topped with a twenty-foot sheet of glass. There's a huge open kitchen. And for once they've got the atmosphere dead right – stylish but informal, neighbourhood but sharp. The food is a complete surprise. It's terrific. The menu at Mosaica is short and changes daily – all is seasonal and all is fresh; starters might include charred asparagus with fried duck egg and Parmesan; grilled squid with grilled lime; a rabbit terrine with olives; and tuna carpaccio with spring onion and lemongrass dressing. Mains range from sea bass fillet with warm potato salad and baby aubergines, to grilled rib-eye steak with garlic mash and fine beans – the rib-eye sliced and meltingly tender, the mash rich and not over-gluey. Or perhaps there's an epic dish such as veal T-bone with wild mushroom port wine jus. Notable puds: chocolate and amaretti biscuit mousse. The wine list is short and the service more enthusiastic than polished, but the food is great and the prices are forgiving.

O's Thai Café

10 Topsfield Parade, N8 ■ 020 8348 6898

⊖ Finsbury Park

|● Thai

⏲ Mon 18.30–23.00; Tues to Sat 12.00–15.00 & 18.30–23.00; Sun 12.00–22.30

🖰 www.oscafesandbars.co.uk

🖰 Mastercard, Visa ■ 10% optional service added for parties of 5 or more

££ starters £1.95–£8.95 ■ mains £5.95–£12.95 ■ sides £4.25 ■ desserts £1.95–£2.50 ■ set lunch & dinner £6.50 & £13.95 ■ lowest bottle price £9.95

✪ Friendly neighbourhood Thai

O's Thai Café is young, happy and fresh, rather like O himself. With his economics, advertising and fashion-design background, and a staff who seem to be having fun, O brings a youthful zip to Thai cuisine. His café is fast and noisy, and the music is played at high volume. But that's not to say the food is anything less than excellent, and it's very good value, too. Order from the comprehensive and well-explained menu or from the blackboard of specials, which runs down an entire wall. Of the many starters satays are tasty, prawn toasts and spring rolls are as crisp as they should be, and paper-wrapped thin dumplings really do melt in the mouth. Tom ka chicken soup is hot and sharp, with lime leaf and lemongrass. Main courses include Thai red and green curries – the gaeng kiew wan, a spicy, soupy green curry of chicken and coconut cream, is pungently moreish – as well as an interesting selection of specials such as yamneau, a.k.a. weeping tiger – sliced, spiced, grilled steak served on salad with a pungent Thai dressing. If you like noodles, there is a selection of pad dishes – stir-fries with a host of combinations of vegetables, soy sauce, peanuts, spiciness, chicken, beef, pork, king prawn or bean curd. Puddings may include khow tom mud, banana with sticky rice wrapped in banana leaf, or Thai ice cream. There's a wide and varied wine list, with Budweiser, Budvar, Gambrinus and Leffe beers on draught.

Sosta

14 Middle Lane, N8 ■ 020 8340 1303

⊖ Highgate/Finsbury Park

🍴 Italian

🕐 Mon 18.30–22.45; Tues to Sat 12.00–15.00 & 18.30–22.45; Sun 12.00–22.15

🖥 www.sosta.co.uk

🗗 all major credit cards ■ 10% optional service added

££ starters £3.95–£5.95 ■ mains £8.95–£14.50 ■ desserts £2.50–£4.25 ■ menus: Mon 'regional' £10.95; Tues to Fri nights & Sat lunch 'degustazione' £11.95; Tues to Sun lunch £8.95 & £10.95 ■ lowest bottle price £9.95

✪ Old-school Italian, old-school value

During the 1970s Silvano Sacchi was at the helm of two of London's more fashionable eateries, the Barracuda (a smart Italian fish restaurant in Baker Street) and San Martino (an Italian tratt in St Martin's Lane). Having sold out to a plc, Sacchi retired to Italy with his money and memories. Then a few years ago he dived back into the maelstrom of the London restaurant scene and opened Sosta – it seems to have been busy from day one. The antipasti include insalata tricolore – a mozzarella, avocado and tomato salad; carpaccio di spada – fresh swordfish; or tomato bruschetta. Onwards to 'primi', where you'll find pasta e fagioli alla Veneto, a thick pasta and borlotti bean soup; and pasta dishes such as gnocchi all'aragosta – in lobster sauce; papardelle al ragu; and tagliolini alla rusticana. Pasta dishes incur a small supplement when taken as a main course. 'Secondi' offers five fish and five meat dishes. Orata alla plancia is grilled sea bream. Then there's piccata di vitello al tartufo nero – escalopes of veal with black truffle, or tagliata di Angus – fillet steak. Puds are sound: semi freddo; panna cotta; tiramisù. The wine list has some trad Italian bottles that appeal greatly. At Sosta the service is slick and the tables are close together. The huge pepper mill of the 1970s may have been replaced by a natty modernist Parmesan grater, but everyone is attentive in what now seems like an old-fashioned way.

Hampstead, Golders Green and Belsize Park

L'Artista

917 Finchley Road, NW11 ■ 020 8731 7501

⊖ Golders Green

🍽 Italian/pizza

🕒 daily 12.00–24.00

💳 Mastercard, Visa ■ 10% optional service added

££ starters £4–£7.10 ■ mains £4.90–£13.80 ■ sides £1.80 ■ desserts £3.80 ■ lowest bottle price £9.90

✪ Busy and buzzy – pizza and pasta

Don't worry about the intermittent Vesuvian tremors – it's merely the Northern Line. L'Artista is situated opposite the entrance to Golders Green tube, and occupies an arch under the railway lines. With its pavement terrace, abundant greenery and umbrellas, this is a lively, vibrant restaurant and pizzeria that exercises an almost magnetic appeal to the young and not so young of Golders Green. Inside, the plain décor is enhanced by celebrity photographs; the waiters are a bit cagey if asked just how many of them have actually eaten here, but the proximity of the tables ensures that you'll rub shoulders with whoever happens to be around you, famous or not. The menu offers a range of Italian food with a good selection of main courses such as fegato Veneziana, a rich dish of calf's liver with onion and white wine. The trota del pescatore is also good, teaming trout with garlic. But L'Artista's pizzas are its forte. They are superb. As well as traditional, thin-crust Capricciosa with anchovies, eggs and ham, or Quattro Formaggi, there are more unusual varieties such as Mascarpone e rucola, a plain pizza topped with mascarpone cheese and heaps of crisp rocket, which is actually very good. The calzone, a cushion-sized rolled pizza stuffed with ham, cheese and sausage and topped with Napoli sauce, is wonderful. Pastas are varied and the penne alla vodka, made with vodka, prawns and cream, is well worth a try. For something lighter, try the excellent insalata dell'Artista, a generous mix of tuna, olives and fennel, with an equally good garlic pizza bread.

→ For branches, see index

Bloom's

130 Golders Green Road, NW11 ■ 020 8455 1338

⊖ Golders Green

|◉| Jewish

🕘 Mon to Thurs & Sun 12.00–23.00; Fri 10.00–14.00 (15.00 in summer)

⌐🖰 www.blooms-restaurant.co.uk

🖪 all major credit cards ■ no service added

££ starters £3.20–£4.50 ■ mains £7.20–£17.90 ■ sides 90p–£2.20 ■
desserts £2.90–£3.50 ■ lowest bottle price £15.50

✪ Trad Jewish deli-diner

Bloom's goes way back to 1920 when Rebecca and Morris Bloom
first produced their great discovery – the original veal Vienna. Since
then 'Bloom's of the East End' has carried the proud tag as 'the most
famous kosher restaurant in the world'. Setting aside the indignant
claims of several outraged New York delis for the moment, given its
history it's a shame that the East End Bloom's was forced to shut,
and that they had to retrench to this, their Golders Green stronghold,
in 1965. Nonetheless, it's a glorious period piece. Rows of sausages
hang over the takeaway counter, there are huge mirrors and chrome
tables, and you can expect inimitable service from battle-hardened
waiters. So, the waiter looks you in the eye as you ask for a beer.
'Heineken schmeineken,' he says derisively. At which point you opt for
Maccabee, an Israeli beer, and regain a little ground. Start with some
new green cucumbers – fresh, crisp, tangy, delicious – and maybe
a portion of chopped liver and egg and onions, which comes with
world-class rye bread. Or go for soup, which comes in bowls so full
they slop over the edge: there's beetroot borscht and potato, which
is very sweet and very red; lockshen, the renowned noodle soup; or
kreplach, full of dumplings. Go on to main courses. The salt beef is
as good as you might expect, and you can try it in a sandwich on rye
bread. There are also solid and worthy options like liver and onions,
and you can still order extra side dishes like the dreaded, heart-
stopping fried potato latke.

Jin Kichi

73 Heath Street, NW3 ■ 020 7794 6158

⊖ Hampstead

🍴 Japanese

🕐 Tues to Fri 18.00–23.00; Sat 12.30–14.00 & 18.00–23.00; Sun 12.30–14.00 & 18.00–22.00

🖰 www.jinkichi.com

🖨 all major credit cards ■ no service added

££ skewers £1.30–£1.90 ■ mains £10.60–£12.80 ■ sides £3.20–£3.40 ■ desserts £2.90–£3.30 ■ set lunch £7.30–£13.80 ■ lowest bottle price wine £18, sake £6.60

✪ Charming Japanese grill house

Unlike so many Japanese restaurants, where the atmosphere can range from austere to intimidating, Jin Kichi is a very comfortable place. It's cramped, rather shabby and has been very busy for over a decade (tables are booked up even on the quiet nights of the week). It differs from sushi-led establishments in that the bar dominating the ground floor with the stools in front of it is home to a small and fierce charcoal grill, where an unhurried chef cooks short skewers of this and that. By all means start with sushi. Ordering the nigiri set brings seven pieces of fresh fish for an eminently reasonable price. But then go for the 'grilled skewers'. Helpfully enough there are two set meals offering various combinations, and each delivers seven skewers. These make for a very splendid kind of eating, since each skewer comes hot off the grill. Be adventurous – grilled skewer of fresh asparagus and pork rolls with salt is a big seller. Grilled skewer of chicken wings with salt is simple and very good, but grilled skewer of duck with spring onion is even better. Grilled skewer of chicken gizzard with salt is chewy and delicious, while the grilled skewer of chicken skin with salt is crisp and very moreish. But the top skewer must be grilled skewer of ox tongue with salt. Drink ice-cold Kirin beer served in a frosted glass. The remainder of the menu leads off to fried dishes, tempura, different noodle dishes, soups and so forth, but the undoubted star of the show is the little grill.

Kimchee

887 Finchley Road, NW11 ■ 020 8455 1035

⊖ Golders Green

🍽 Korean

🕒 Tues to Sun 12.00–15.00 & 18.00–23.00

🔁 all major credit cards ■ 10% optional service added

££ starters £1.90 ■ mains £6.50–£7.90 ■ lowest bottle price £9.80

✪ A neighbourhood star – but Korean

Times have changed in Golders Green and the opening of a bright
and modern Korean restaurant on the Finchley Road is one of the
more obvious signs. It's a charming place with a well-mannered
clientele split fifty-fifty between homesick Koreans and adventurous
Golders Greenites. Korean food majors in strong flavours, and in
dishes that are finished at the table (each table has a barbecue built
into the middle of it and your waitress will cook at least part of your
meal in front of you). Start with some pickles: kimchee, fermented
cabbage with loads of salt and fierce chilli-hot red bean paste, is the
most famous. The sliced radish with vinegar is milder and the pickled
cucumbers are very good indeed. There is also yuk whe, the Korean
equivalent of steak tartare – shredded raw beef bound together with
egg yolk and slivers of pear. This unlikely-sounding combination is
improbably good. Koon mandoo, large pan-fried dumplings, have
very good crispy bits. For main course try one of the table-grilled
dishes. There's bulgogi, marinated beef cooked on the metal plate
in front of you; or sliced pork; or seafood. The 'pot dishes' are also
interesting: a stone pot is heated up until it is sizzling, a layer of rice is
then added and on top of that are placed some meat, vegetables and
an egg yolk. When it arrives at table your waitress mixes it all together
and you get dol bibim bab – instant fried rice cooked by the hot pot.
To drink, either stick to Korean beer, or try 'soju', a clear spirit served
on ice from a mini-bottle.

No. 77 Wine Bar

77 Mill Lane, NW6 ■ 020 7435 7787

● West Hampstead

🍽 Modern British

🕒 Mon & Tues 12.00–23.00 (no food Mon); Wed to Sat 12.00–24.00; Sun 12.00–22.30

🗄 all major credit cards except AmEx ■ 12.5% optional service added

££ lunch options £4.75–£7.75 ■ snacks £2.50 ■ starters £3.95–£6.25 ■ mains £7.95–£12.95 ■ lowest bottle price £11

✪ A friendly, casual, party place

This rowdy and likable North London wine bar has survived its first couple of decades and learnt only too well how to match velocities with its clientele. Drawing a veil over a disastrous episode when there was an attempt to take the cuisine upmarket, things now run more smoothly. The food is a kind of refined comfort food and is backed up by a long and informed wine list that offers great value. The 'bits on the side' make great bar nibbles – crispy whitebait; houmous; grilled chorizo; Cajun spiced chips with aioli olives. For lunch there is a range of one-hit dishes – risotto; a Caesar salad; roast chicken in foccacia served with chips. In the evening starters include steamed mussels in white wine; sesame tempura tiger prawns on stir-fried vegetables with oyster sauce; duck liver and Grand Marnier pâté with balsamic red onions and foccacia; crostini; or simple home-made soups. Mains range from a roast breast of goose on savoy cabbage with chestnuts, baby potatoes and juniper berries; to a mixed wild mushroom risotto; or fish of the day. But such smarter dishes are underpinned by stalwarts like the shepherd's pie; a sound sirloin steak; and the No. 77 beefburger, large and sassy coming with Applewood cheddar, sautéed onions and fries. Like the menu, the wine list changes as whim and stocks dictate, but the pricing encourages you to try something new. Patriotically enough, there are usually a couple of rather good English wines on the list here.

Solly's Exclusive

146–150 Golders Green Road, NW11 ■ 020 8455 2121

⊖ Golders Green

🍽 Jewish

🕐 Mon to Thurs 18.30–22.30; Sat (winter only) one hour after sundown to 01.00; Sun 12.30–22.30

🛱 all major credit cards except AmEx ■ no service added

££ starters £3.50–£4.00 ■ mains £10.50–£16.00 ■ desserts £3.50–£4.00
■ set dinner & Sunday lunch £24 ■ lowest bottle price £16

⭐ Jewish restaurant, Jewish bling

What makes Solly's Exclusive so exclusive is that it is upstairs.
Downstairs is Solly's Restaurant, a small, packed, noisy place
specialising in epic falafel. You'll find Solly's Exclusive by coming
out of Solly's Restaurant and going around the side of the building.
Upstairs, a huge, bustling dining room accommodates 180
customers. The décor is interesting – tented fabric on the ceiling,
multi-coloured glass, brass light fittings – while waitresses, all of
them with 'Solly's Exclusive' emblazoned across the back of their
waistcoats, maintain a brisk approach to the niceties of service. The
food is tasty and workmanlike. Start with the dish that pays homage
to the chickpea – hoummus with falafel, which brings three crispy
depth charges and some well-made dip. Even the very best falafel
in the world cannot overcome the thunderous indigestibility of
chickpeas, but as falafel go these are pretty good. Otherwise, you
could try Solly's special aubergine dip, or the Moroccan cigars, made
from minced lamb wrapped in filo pastry and deep-fried. Solly's
pitta, a fluffy, fourteen-inch disc of freshly baked bread, is closer to
a perfect naan than Greek-restaurant bread. Pittas to pine for. For
mains, the lamb shwarma is very good: nicely seasoned and spiced,
and served with excellent chips and good salad. The barbecue roast
chicken comes with the same accompaniments, and is also sound.
Steer clear of the Israeli salad, however, unless you relish the idea
of a large bowl of chopped watery tomatoes and chopped watery
cucumber. This is a kosher restaurant, so if you're not fully conversant
with the Jewish calendar, check before setting out.

The Wells

30 Well Walk, NW3 ■ 020 7794 3785

⊖ Hampstead

🍽 Modern British/gastropub

🕙 daily 12.00–15.00 & 19.00–22.00

🖰 www.thewellshampstead.co.uk

🗗 all major credit cards ■ 12.5% optional service added

££ lunch £14.95 (2 courses) & £15.95 (3 courses) ■ dinner £26.50 (2 courses) & £30 (3 courses) ■ sides £3 ■ lowest bottle price £13.50

✪ A very Hampstead kind of gastropub

As the gastropub revolution rolled over London discussions inevitably gravitated toward defining just what makes a gastropub, and one of the places most often used as a focus is The Wells. This establishment is smack in the middle of old Hampstead, and recently solidified its position by a gentle re-positioning of menu and cooking to introduce some more gastropubby dishes and ease up on the formality. Dinner here still carries a pretty restauranty price tag, but the kitchens now cook more accessible food. There are a couple of dining rooms, lofty and elegant. The menu changes to take account of the seasons, but starters might include cream of cauliflower soup with truffle oil and poached free-range egg; spring roll of goats' cheese and spinach with beetroot and apple chutney; or a well-made terrine of foie gras and Bayonne ham, served with toast and sauce gribiche. The short list of main courses touches all the bases – roast halibut with pearl barley risotto and buttered chestnuts; tournedos of venison with braised red cabbage, creamy mash and roast parsnips; or how about cassoulet of duck confit, Alsace bacon, brioche crumbs and parsley? Puds range from pear tarte Tatin with vanilla ice cream, to sticky chocolate pecan pie. The wine list is user friendly, service is slick and (as befits a gastropub) the cuisine just about stays on the comfort side of restaurant dishes.

Harrow and Wembley

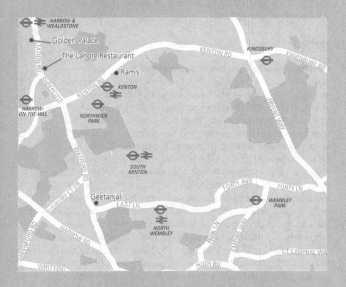

Cinnamon Gardens

42–44 Ealing Road, Wembley, Middx ■ 020 8902 0660

⊖ Wembley Central

🍽 Sri Lankan

🕐 daily 11.00–23.00

🖰 cash only ■ no service added

££ starters £1.25–£5.25 ■ mains £4–£6.95 ■ desserts £2.50–£3.95
   ■ lowest bottle price £9.99

✪ Large and laid-back Sri Lankan

Cinnamon Gardens is a bright and modern restaurant at the
Wembley end of Ealing Road. The dining room is all minty green
and apricot with a tiled floor and some ostentatiously modern
chairs, which thankfully prove comfortable. The walls are also home
to a virulent series of murals. This is a Sri Lankan restaurant, and
things proceed at a Sri Lankan pace. Don't worry – simply relax and
assess the relative merits of Lion lager and Lion stout; soon you will
be in just the right mood. Starters include most of the Sri Lankan
favourites. There are mutton rolls, crab claws, and chicken 65. There
is also a section on the menu devoted to 'fried specials', any of which
make a great starter when teamed with some bread – try fried lamb
or fried squid. Another section features devilled dishes, ranging all
the way from a devilled potato to devilled king prawn. There's a
whole host of hoppers, or rice pancakes, including egg and jaggery
– the latter rich with unrefined sugar. The Cinnamon special biryani is
stunning: dark and richly flavoured, it comes with a bit of everything,
including a lamb chop and a hard-boiled egg. It is also worth noting
that the rotis are very good here, light and flaky. The sambols are also
top stuff. The seeni sambol is a relatively mild, sweet onion jam, while
the katta sambol is an incredibly wild chilli concoction. The service is
friendly if a little dozy. Try the Portello, a lurid-purple soft drink with
an almost radioactive glow.

Dadima

228 Ealing Road, Wembley, Middx ■ 020 8902 1072 ♿

🔆 Alperton

🍴 Indian/vegetarian

🕐 Mon to Fri 12.00–15.00 & 17.00–22.00; Sat & Sun 12.00–22.00

🗐 all major credit cards except AmEx ■ no service added

££ starters £2–£4 ■ mains £3–£4 ■ sides £2.50–£3 ■ desserts £2
■ thalis: lunch £2.99, dinner £4.99 & £5.99 ■ lowest bottle price
£2.20 for 180ml

⭐ Good veggie food, easy-going atmosphere

There's something very charming about these small Gujarati cafés
that quietly go about their business feeding lots of people: their
food is wholesome, prices are spectacularly low, and the atmosphere
invariably cheery. Inside Dadima is clean and businesslike; what's
more it's fully licensed so you can add a healthful glass of red wine to
your vegetarian dinner. The starters and snacks are very good. Panni
puri are small, crunchy, and savoury, with flavours well-balanced:
simply load a teaspoon of the sharp sauce into each small flying
saucer and devour them whole. For something a bit spookier try the
khichi. This is a strange dish, with a strange texture – it is basically
a very solid rice flour sludge, you dress each mouthful with a little
oil and then some finely ground hot red pepper. Kachori are much
more accessible, small balls, crisp outside and with a core of spicy
lentil mix – very satisfying with a dollop of the sweet sharp tamarind
sauce. Onwards towards main courses, which are also very good:
palak paneer is a smooth spinach purée with a few chunks of chewy
cheese scattered through it; or try the dal makhni, a rich stew with
black lentils and kidney beans – floating on the top is the makhani
part, a large lump of butter. Stir the butter into the gravy, enjoy! It
is really rich and really fattening. With your meal pile into the breads
which are very well done here. The wine is also worthy of a mention
as it comes in those little airline bottles, so no more drinking up sour
leftovers.

Geetanjali

16 Court Parade, Watford Road, Middx ■ 020 8904 5353

⊖ Wembley Central

🍽 Indian

🕐 daily 12.00–15.00 & 18.00–24.00

🏷 all major credit cards ■ 10% optional service added

££ starters £2.50–£4.50 ■ mains £5.90–£10.50 ■ sides £4–£5 ■ desserts £2.90–£3.50 ■ lowest bottle price £11.50

✪ Best-ever tandoori chops

There are a good many Indian restaurants in Wembley and it would be easy to write off Geetanjali as just one more of the same. On the face of it, sure, the menu is pretty straightforward, with a good many old, tired dishes lined up in their usual serried ranks – chicken tikka masala, rogan josh and so on and so forth. But Geetanjali has a secret weapon, a dish that brings customers from far and wide. Word on the street is that this place serves the best tandoori lamb chops in North London. This chop lover's haven has a large, roomy dining room, and the service is attentive, if a little resigned when you pitch up and order a raft of beers and a few portions of chops – or, as the menu would have it, lamb chopp. Of course, the chops are good. Very good. Thick-cut, exceedingly tender and very nicely spiced. Accompany them with a luccha paratha, warm and flaky and presented in the shape of a flower with a knob of butter melting into its heart. The alternative is the intriguingly named bullet nan, which promises to be hot and spicy, and delivers in good measure. Even if you're not a complete chopaholic, you can also do well here. Go for starters such as the good chicken tikka, made with chicken breast. Rashmi kebab is also good, made from minced chicken and spices. Main courses include mathi chicken, which is chicken with fenugreek, and lamb badam pasanda. And should this emphasis on meat leave you craving some of the green stuff, there's sag aloo or karahi corn masala.

Golden Palace

146–150 Station Road, Harrow, Middx ■ 020 8863 2333

⊖ Harrow & Wealdstone

🍴 Chinese/dim sum

🕔 Mon to Sat 12.00–23.30; Sun 11.00–22.30; dim sum until 17.00 every day

🗄 all major credit cards ■ 10% optional service added

££ dim sum £2.20–£3.50 ■ starters £3.50–£5 ■ mains £5.20–£10 ■ sides £2.80–£5 ■ desserts £1.50–£3.50 ■ lowest bottle price £10.50

✪ Excellent dim sum

You would class the Golden Palace as a seriously busy restaurant even if it were in the heart of Chinatown, but to find a sophisticated dim sum specialist packing in hundreds of eager customers for a weekday lunch in suburban Harrow is a shock. Inside all is chic and slick, and large tables of young Chinese ladies-who-lunch sit happily alongside families with babies in highchairs. Everyone is eating dim sum and waiters and waitresses rush through with towering steamers. The dim sum here are very good indeed and there's a bustle in the atmosphere that is infectious. The best strategy is to order several dim sum – some familiar and some exotic – and then repeat those you like best. All the dumplings are keenly priced. Bear in mind that most of the dumplings come in threes. Standouts are the crystal prawn dumplings – a thin, steamed dumpling full of fresh, almost crunchy prawn, and the prawn and chive dumplings, which are similar but with the green of fresh chives showing through the translucent pastry. Deep-fried shredded squid is quite simply the best, tenderest, crispest 'Calamari' you have ever eaten. And try the truly amazing mini lotus-wrapped glutinous rice with meat – two in a portion, open the lotus leaves and there's a stunning sticky rice ball with a centre of slow-cooked pork, rich, delicious and intense. The sheer variety of the dishes on offer is impressive, but it is even more unusual to find them all done so well, and at such a reasonable price. Service is brisk but friendly, and the tea is … well, tea.

The Lahore Restaurant

45 Station Road, Harrow, Middx ▪ 020 8424 8422

⊖ Harrow & Wealdstone/Harrow on the Hill
---
⑩ Indian

◔ daily 11.30–23.30

🗗 cash or cheque only ▪ no service added

££ starters £1.50–£9.50 ▪ mains £2.75–£9.50 ▪ sides £3.75–£8 ▪
desserts 75p–£3 ▪ unlicensed, BYO (no corkage)

✪ Rough and ready Pakistani grill house

The Lahore Restaurant has a BYO drinks policy and an open kitchen, but that's where the trendiness stops. This homely and unpretentious Pakistani eatery serves grilled meats and karahi dishes. The service is friendly, the food fresh and the prices are extremely reasonable. The room is plain, and a couple of ceiling fans struggle to disperse the fierce heat coming off the grills. There have been some queries about the chilli heat of some dishes – sometimes 'hot' doesn't translate as more than 'medium' and sometimes it means 'eye-watering'. To start, order a couple of rotis and some grilled meats. Chicken tikka is sound – a good portion, and tandoori chicken wings are great. They're well marinated, perfectly cooked and spicy. Tandoori lamb chops are outstanding – thick-cut, heavy with spice and juicy. Seek kebabs have a welcome belt of fresh chilli and green herbs. It would be quite feasible to make a decent meal of starters and bread, but the curries are very good, too, with simple dishes full of flavour, such as karahi jeera chicken. The star turn is the karahi karela gosht – the tender, slow-cooked lamb has a rich sauce balanced by the addictive taste of bitter melon. The breads are very good indeed. For an interesting contrast, order a tawa paratha and an onion kulcha. The paratha is wholemeal, thick, filling and fried until the outside is flaky-crisp. The onion kulcha is doughy but stuffed with a rich onion mix that includes fresh coriander. Beware, the off-licence next door shuts at 21.00 on weekday evenings.

Ram's

203 Kenton Road, Harrow, Middx ■ 020 8907 2030   &

⊖ Kenton

🍽 Indian/vegetarian

🕐 daily 12.00–15.00 & 18.00–23.00

🗗 Mastercard, Visa ■ 10% optional service added

££ starters £2.10–£4.80 ■ mains £3.30–£5 ■ desserts £1.60–£2.50 ■ lunch menu £4.99 ■ lowest bottle price £9.25

✪ Stunning Indian veggie food

Anyone in downtown Mumbai will tell you that India's best vegetarian food comes from the state of Gujarat. And one of the leading contenders for the best of Gujarati food is the city of Surat. Hurrah! London has its very own Surti restaurant – Ram's. The staff rush around, eager and friendly; their pride in both the menu and their home town is obvious and endearing. The menu is a long one and the food is very good. Gujarati snacks make great starters. Petis are small balls of peas and onions coated in potato and deep-fried. Kachori are the same kind of thing, but with mung daal inside a pastry coat. Patras are made by rolling vegetable leaves with a 'glue' of chickpea flour batter; the roll is then sliced across, and each slice becomes a delicate and savoury pinwheel. Stuffed banana bhaji is a sweet and savoury combo. The kand is a Surti special – slices of purple potato in a savoury batter. Sev khamni is a sludge of well-spiced chickpeas with coconut, served topped with a layer of crisp sev. Flavours are clear and distinct, and some dishes have a welcome chilli heat. Mains do not disappoint. The famous undhiu – a weekend special – is a complex dish of vegetables 'stuffed' with a Surti spice paste. It combines aubergines with three kinds of potatoes (purple, sweet and white), as well as bananas and peas. The peas pilau is simple and good. The methi parathas are dry and tasty. The puris are fresh, hot and as self-indulgent as only fried bread can be.

Sakoni's

127–129 Ealing Road, Alperton, Middx ■ 020 8903 1058

⊖ Alperton

🍴 Indian/vegetarian

🕐 Mon to Thurs & Sun 11.00–23.00; Fri & Sat 11.00–23.30

🗄 Mastercard, Visa ■ 10% optional service added

££ starters £2.75–£4.60 ■ mains £4.95–£5.50 ■ desserts £2–£3 ■ set menus: Sat & Sun breakfast buffet/lunch & dinner buffet £6.50 ■ unlicensed

✪ Top-notch Indian veggie food factory

Crowded with Asian families, all of whom seem to be having a seriously good time, the bunfight at Sakoni's is overseen by waiters and staff in baseball caps, and there's even a holding pen where you can check out the latest videos and sounds while waiting your turn. From a décor point of view, the dining area is somewhat clinical: a huge square yardage of white tiling, but the Indian vegetarian food here is terrific. It's old hat to many of the Asian customers who dive straight into the 'Chinese' dishes. These tend to be old favourites such as chow mein and haka noodles, cooked with Indian spicing. Unless curiosity overwhelms you, stick to the splendid South Indian dishes. Sakoni's is renowned for its dosas. These are pancakes, so crisp that they are almost chewy, and delightfully nutty. They come with two small bowls of sauce and a filling of rich, fried potato spiced with curry leaves. Choose from lain dosa, masala dosa and chutney dosa, which has spices and chilli swirled into the dosa batter. Try the farari cutlets, not cutlets at all, in fact, but very nice, well-flavoured dollops of sweet potato mash, deep-fried so that they have a crisp exterior. Also worth trying are the bhel puri, the pani puri and the sev puri – amazingly crisp little taste bombs. Pop them in whole and the flavour explodes in your mouth. Some say that the juices at Sakoni's are the best in London, and while that may be hyperbole they certainly are very good indeed. Try madaf, made from fresh coconut.

→ For branches, see index

Holloway and Highgate

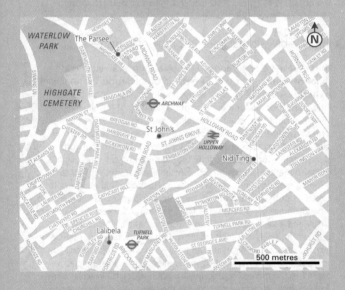

Lalibela

137 Fortess Road, NW5 ■ 020 7284 0600

⊖ Tufnell Park

🍽 Ethiopian

🕐 daily 18.00–24.00

🗗 all major credit cards ■ 10% optional service added

££ starters £3.50 ■ mains £7.50–£8.50 ■ sides £3.50–£3.75 desserts £2.50–£3 ■ lowest bottle price £10

✪ Implausibly laid-back service, Ethiopian dishes

The Lalibela is a 12th-century Ethiopian church carved in the shape of a cross, from a huge outcrop of solid rock. The restaurant is equally remarkable for serving uncompromisingly authentic Ethiopian food and for a genuine understanding of hospitality. There's a slightly harassed but still laid-back feel to the place that's a great comfort to the diner. The unwary can end up seated on low, carved, wooden seats around traditional low tables (so that you can eat with your hands). If your knee joints won't take that kind of punishment, plead for an ordinary table and resign yourself to dripping sauce down your shirt front. There is a limited number of starters, but they banish any inkling you may have about being in an odd kind of curry house. The lamb samosas have very dry, papery pastry and a savoury, spicy filling – delicious. The Lalibela salad is potatoes and beetroot fried together with a spicy sauce and served hot. Main courses are served traditionally, that is to say as pools of sauce set out on a two-foot-diameter injera bread. Injera is cold, made from fermented sourdough, and thin; tear off a piece and use it to eat with. Portions are small, but the flavours are intense. If you prefer, you can have the dishes with rice or mashed potato. What goes on the injera? Wot, that's what. Doro wot is a piece of chicken and a hard-boiled egg in a rich sauce, while begh wot is lamb with a bit more chilli. Fried fish tibs is a dish of fried fish marinated in rosemary and lemon juice served with a mild chilli and garlic sauce. Try the Ethiopian traditional coffee, which is not only delicious, but comes with its own mini-ceremonial.

Nid Ting

533 Holloway Road, N19 ■ 020 7263 0506

⊖ Archway

🍽️ Thai

🕐 Mon to Sat 18.00–23.30; Sun 18.00–22.15

🗄️ all major credit cards ■ no service added

££ starters £3.95–£4.95 ■ mains £5.95–£8.95 ■ desserts £2.50 ■ set dinner £15 ■ lowest bottle price £10.50

✪ Neighbourhood value, neighbourhood Thai

What are restaurants for? Some pundits would have you believe that restaurants are for posing in, some that their mission is to entertain. Nid Ting is a place that feeds people. Lots of them. And it feeds people well, serving good, unfussy Thai food. The dishes here have not been tamed to suit effete Western palates, and you'll get plenty of chilli heat and pungent fish sauce. You'll also get good value and brisk service – both of which obviously appeal, as the place is usually packed. This is a genuine neighbourhood restaurant at ease with its surroundings. The starters are neat platefuls of mainly fried food: chicken satay is sound, although the sauce is a bland one; a much better bet is the 'pork on toasted' – a smear of rich, meaty paste on a disc of fried bread. The prawns tempura are large and crisp, and the peek ka yas sai is very successful – stuffed chicken wings, battered and deep-fried. The menu then darts off into numerous sections: there are hot and sour soups, clear soups, salads, curries, stir-fries, seafood, rice, noodle dishes, and a long, long list of vegetarian dishes – all before you get to the chef's specials. From those specials, try the lamb Mussaman curry, which is rich and good, made with green chillies and coconut milk. From the noodles, try pad see ew, a rich dish made with thick ribbon noodles and your choice of chicken, beef or pork. As a side order, try the som tum, which is a pleasingly astringent green papaya salad.

The Parsee

34 Highgate Hill, N19 ■ 020 7272 9091

⊖ Archway

🍴 Indian

🕐 Mon to Sat 18.00–22.45

🖱 www.theparsee.co.uk

🗐 all major credit cards ■ 10% optional service added

££ starters £3.50–£6.75 ■ mains £9.75–£12.50 ■ sides £4.25–£4.50 ■ desserts £3.50–£4.50 ■ set dinner £20, £25 & £30 ■ lowest bottle price £13.90

✪ Local Indian restaurant, exotic Parsee cuisine

London has had an acclaimed Parsee chef for some years now. His name is Cyrus Todiwala and his main restaurant is Café Spice Namaste (see p. 177). Since the opening of The Parsee, however, London has also had what may be the world's best Parsee restaurant and Todiwala is its godfather. Parsees are renowned for their love of food – and for being the most demanding of customers. They start from the admirable standpoint that nothing beats home cooking and complain vehemently if everything is not exactly to their liking. They will be at home in this part of North London. The food here is very good. Honest, strong flavours – rich and satisfying. Start with the admirable home-style akoori on toast – splendid, spiced, scrambled egg. Or try the masala ma murgh ki kalaeji, chicken livers in a typical Parsee masala, cooked quickly and served with a roti. Or maybe go for something from the grill, such as dhana jeera ni murghi, a superior chicken 'tikka' made with ginger and cumin. Main courses include that most famous of Parsee dishes, the dhaansaak, a rich dish of lamb and lentils. Then there's the murghi ni curry nay papeto – a distinctive curry made with chicken and potato, cashew nuts, sesame seeds and chickpeas. The breads – rotli – are very good, nutty and moreish. The vegetable dishes are good too: koru nay motta murcha is a simple dish made with cubed pumpkin. This is a small, 'family' restaurant serving delicious and unfamiliar Indian food. An adventure well worth having.

St John's

91 Junction Road, N10 ■ 020 7272 1587

⊖ Archway

🍴 Mediterranean/gastropub

🕐 Mon to Thurs 18.30–23.00; Fri 12.00–15.30 & 18.30–23.00; Sat 12.00–16.00 & 18.30–23.00; Sun 12.00–16.00 & 18.30–21.30

💳 all major credit cards ■ 12.5% optional service added for parties of 5 or more

---

££ starters £5.25–£6.50 ■ mains £9.50–£14.50 ■ desserts £5–£5.50 ■ lowest bottle price £11.50

✪ Great gastropub

The Junction Road is rather unprepossessing and makes an unlikely setting for this fine establishment, which was one of the earlier gastropubs to get established. The emphasis is firmly on the gastro, and the food is broadly Mediterranean, with a passion for all things rich, earthy and flavoursome. Not only that, but the dining room, which lies beyond the pub itself, looks fabulous – all louche, junk-store glamour with its high, gold-painted ceiling, low chandeliers and plush banquettes. There's an open kitchen at one end of the room, while at the other a giant blackboard displays the long menu. As an opening move, the friendly staff bring fresh bread and bottles of virgin olive oil and balsamic vinegar. The menu changes day by day, but there will probably be a soup – perhaps carrot and orange, or ham, chickpea and spinach broth. Other starters might be a chicken, pork and black pud terrine, or chargrilled squid with chorizo. The food is robust and mercifully unpretentious. Main courses range from the traditional – lamb rump with champ and greens, to the more adventurous – such as monkfish, paella rice, spinach and chilli. You'll need to take a breather before venturing into pud territory. Pannetone with ice cream; pineapple Pavlova; or a chocolate pistachio and date tart. The intelligent wine list includes a dozen by the glass, with a notable Cava. St John's gets more crowded and more convivial as the night goes on, but it is possible to have a dîner à deux; just make sure you're ready to be romantic by 19.30, when you might get a table.

Islington and Highbury

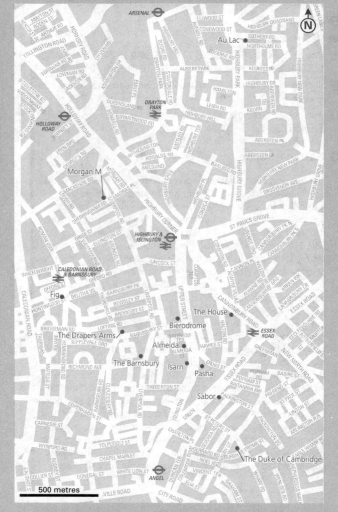

Almeida

30 Almeida Street, N1 ■ 020 7354 4777   &

⊖ Highbury & Islington

🍴 French

🕐 daily 12.00–14.30 & 17.30–23.00; (Terrace) May to October 09.00–12.00 & 12.00–14.30

🔗 www.conran.com

🗁 all major credit cards ■ 12.5% optional service added

££ starters £5.50–£12.50 ■ mains £14–£21 ■ sides £3–£5 ■ desserts £4.50–£7 ■ menus: £26 & £29.50; regional lunch & pre-/post-theatre £14.50 & £17.50 ■ lowest bottle price £14.50

✪ Haven for Francophiles

It may be located in oh-so-trendy Islington opposite the home base of the Almeida Theatre, and it may be yet another outpost of Sir Terence Conran's sprawling London empire, but spiritually Almeida is stuck in some faintly remembered rural France. The menu at Almeida manages to be a distillation of all that is good about an old-fashioned, gently familiar kind of French cooking and eating. On top of which, the large dining room is comfortable and the service is slick without being oppressive. There is a comprehensive wine list, with a good selection available by the glass. This is a place to overdose on nostalgia. Bisque de homard is the genuine article; six or twelve escargots à la Bourguignon provide garlic heaven; there's poireaux vinaigrette, truffes noires; cuisses de grenouilles persillées; and best of all, the trolley of charcuterie. This chariot is wheeled round to your table and you can pig out on well-made terrines, pâtés and rillettes to your heart's content. Mains carry the theme forward triumphantly: cassoulet Toulousain; steak au poivre; whole roast sea bass au pastis. Pukka pommes frîtes. For pud there's the tantalisingly named 'trolley of tarts', or petit pot au chocolat. With such a single-minded menu, Almeida could have ended up as something of a French resto theme park, but the kitchen is passionate about the classic dishes, and the mood ends up affectionate rather than reverential. No wonder it is busy enough to make booking for dinner a prudent idea.

Au Lac

82 Highbury Park, N1 ■ 020 7704 9187

⊖ Arsenal

🍽 Vietnamese

🕐 Mon to Wed 17.30–23.00; Thurs to Fri 12.00–14.30 & 17.30–23.00; Sat & Sun 17.30–23.00

🗗 Mastercard, Visa ■ 10% optional service added

££ starters £2.20–£5.50 ■ mains £4–£8 ■ desserts £1.50–£2.50 ■ set dinner £11–£15 ■ lowest bottle price £8.50

✪ Informal neighbourhood Vietnamese

Vietnamese restaurants in London tend to divide into two camps. On the one hand there are the spartan canteens – no frills, no nonsense and no concessions to non-Vietnamese speakers. And on the other there is a sprinkling of glossy, West End establishments. This branch of Au Lac is hidden away in Highbury and has a dining room that is comfortable in an informal, shabby sort of way, with knick-knacks on the walls. There's now a newer, flashier branch on the Kingsland Road. Start with goi cuon. These are soft rice-flour pancakes wrapped around crunchy veg and large grilled prawns, and they're fresh and light. Then there's goi tom – you get large steamed prawns, a small pot of hot and spicy sauce, and several large iceberg lettuce leaves. Take a leaf, add sauce and prawn, wrap, eat, enjoy. The deep-fried monkfish with garlic and chilli is very good and there are good soups, too. The noodle soups – pho, bun bo, and tom hue – come in large portions. They are cheap and tasty, good for eating when alone. For a more sociable, sharing meal, try the chicken with lemongrass and chilli. The noodles are also very good – pho xao do bien is a grand dish of stir-fried rice noodles with fresh herbs and seafood, providing a good combination of flavours and textures. Another very impressive dish is the 'minced pork with aubergine in hot pot'. Ordering this brings a small casserole whose contents appear almost black. Very dark, very rich, very tasty. If offered special 'Vietnamese sake' beware – this clear hooch is very ferocious indeed.

→ For branches, see index

The Barnsbury

209–211 Liverpool Road, N1 ■ 020 7607 5519

⊖ Highbury & Islington

🍽 Modern British/gastropub

🕐 Mon to Fri 12.00–15.00 & 18.30–22.00; Sat 12.00–16.00 & 18.30–22.00; Sun 12.00–16.00 &18.00–21.00

🖥 www.thebarnsbury.co.uk

🖨 all major credit cards ■ 12.5% optional service added

££ starters £3.50–£6.50 ■ mains £10.50–£14.50 ■ sides £3 ■ desserts £4.50 ■ early menu (pre-19.30) £12 ■ lowest bottle price £13

✪ Very sound, very pubby, gastropub

Over the years the site that is now The Barnsbury has gone through a number of less agreeable incarnations, including a spell as a really dodgy bar, but now no. 209 Liverpool Road has settled into a new role as a pleasant, informal, pubby type pub with good food. And wonder of wonders, it serves pub food rather than restaurant food. The management have got the menu right, the prices right, the service right and the ambience right. The Barnsbury deserves its success. The menu changes day to day and offers seven starters, seven mains and half a dozen puds; the proprietors must be congratulated for not succumbing to the lure of fancy dishes. In the colder months starters will probably include a couple of soups – French onion soup or spinach and broccoli soup. Other starters may be a warm Puy lentil salad, chorizo and poached egg; a prawn and crayfish cocktail, with pumpernickel bread; or a smoked duck, walnut and pickled cucumber salad – good complementary flavours. Mains are 'in-your-face-ordinary' and none the worse for that. Steak and Guinness pie; chargrilled chump of English lamb, aubergine and coriander pâté; or grilled whole plaice, garlic, oregano and lemon juice. Puddings are also satisfying: chocolate cheesecake; rice pudding brûlée; Seville orange cake. The blackboard wine list steers a sensible course between good value at the bottom of the price range and interesting bottles at the top. As gastropubs get ever fancier and pricier, it is refreshing to see somewhere that emphasises the solid and dependable.

Bierodrome

173–174 Upper Street, N1 ■ 020 7226 5835 ♿

⊖ Highbury & Islington

🍽 Belgian

🕐 Mon to Fri 12.00–15.00 & 18.30–22.00; Sat 12.00–16.00 & 18.30–
22.00; Sun 12.00–16.00 &18.00–21.00

🔗 www.belgorestaurants.co.uk

🗗 all major credit cards ■ 12.5% optional service added

££ starters £4.50–£6.95 ■ mains £7.25–£17.95 ■ desserts £4.25
■ menus: lunch £5.95 & evening meal deal (18.00–19.30) £7.50
■ lowest bottle price £11.75

✪ HQ Belgian beers

Bierodrome is part of the Belgo organisation (see p. 20) and shares
its emphasis on modernist design. Here a recent refurb has replaced
the stark concrete floor with wood and things are a tad more cuddly
than formerly. This place is a temple to beer, and with that beer you
can eat if you wish. It is no surprise that when the Bierodrome first
opened they found that the customers were walking off with the
beer and wine list. It makes stunning reading, with more than seventy
beers to pore over and ultimately pour out. As you work your way
through a series of delicious glassfuls, what you will need is some
food. Unsurprisingly, the beeriness spreads through the menu, which
introduces a change of pace from the other branches – yes, there is
life after mussels! Here there are sausages, along with steaks, duck
confit, croquettes and frîtes. Wild boar sausages are made with dark
Chimay beer and are served with stoemp, a superior kind of mashed
potato indigenous to Belgium. Then there are the famous Belgo
mussel pots that can be enjoyed marinière, Provençale, Portuguese or
even Thai – the latter cooked with creamed coconut and coriander. Or
there's a range of gourmet burgers. Steaks include a 6oz sirloin with
frîtes, salad, tomatoes and garlic butter. There is an 'express' lunch
bargain that lumps together mussels, frîtes and a drink. As you'd
expect from a 'beer-driven' establishment, this place can get lively.

→ For branches, see index

The Drapers Arms

44 Barnsbury Street, N1 ■ 020 7619 0348

⊖ Highbury & Islington

🍴 Modern British/gastropub

🕐 Mon to Fri 12.00–15.00 & 19.00–22.30; Sat 12.00–15.00 & 19.00–
22.30; Sun 12.00–15.00 & 18.30–21.30

🗗 all major credit cards ■ 12.5% optional service added

££ starters £5.50–£9 ■ mains £11.50–£16 ■ desserts £6 ■ sides £3
■ lowest bottle price £13

✪ Friendly gastropub

**The Drapers started life as an old-fashioned, double-fronted
Georgian pub** and that is pretty much how it has remained,
despite the gastropub makeover. There's a bar downstairs and a
dining room upstairs, and out the back is a large walled yard that
has been paved over and kitted out with tables and chairs, and a
pair of huge awnings in case of rain. This 'extra dining room' seats
another 45 hungry customers, and when the weather is sunny it is
a thoroughly charming place. The menu changes twice daily and
reflects the seasons, but starters may include pea soup; caramelised
onion and goats' cheese tart with rocket and Parma ham; roast
artichoke, sun-blushed tomatoes with feta and piquillo peppers; or
a foie gras parfait with quince jelly and toasted sourdough. Or how
about a salad of chicken livers, pancetta, frisée and soft-poached
egg? Mains might include slow-cooked rabbit with black olives and
sherry vinegar; deep-fried plaice with pea purée and chips; a 10oz
sirloin with chips and Béarnaise; or monkfish and scallop skewer with
cardamom rice. The chips are stellar, and side dishes include welcome
combos such as wilted spinach and lemon oil. Puds are sound, and
sensibly the kitchen sticks to favourites like sticky toffee pudding and
custard; double chocolate brownie, hot chocolate sauce and crème
fraîche; or nougat glacé with mango and basil. Good sandwiches
and bar snacks mean that this is a good place for more 'pubby' than
'gastro' manoeuvres.

The Duke of Cambridge

30 St Peter's Street, N1 ■ 020 7359 3066

⊖ Angel

🍴 Modern British/gastropub

🕐 Mon to Fri 12.30–15.00 & 18.30–22.30; Sat 12.30–15.30 & 18.30–22.30; Sun 12.30–15.30 & 18.30–22.00

🖱 www.singhboulton.co.uk

🖃 all major credit cards ■ 12.5% optional service added for parties of 5 or more

££ starters £3–£9 ■ mains £9–£17 ■ desserts £5.50 ■ sides £3 ■ lunch special £6.75 ■ lowest bottle price £13

✪ Organic pioneer and gastropub

In the canon of organic, things don't get much holier than this, the first gastropub to be certified by the Soil Association. Game and fish are either wild or caught from sustainable resources, and the 40-strong wine list is 95 per cent organic. As 'organic' becomes every supermarket's favourite adjective, it is hard to remember that it was tough going in the beginning, and the Duke was there at the start. There's a small, bookable restaurant at the back, but most diners prefer to share the tables in the noisy front bar. The blackboard menu changes twice daily and is commendably short; you order from the bar. Robust bread with good olive oil and grey sea salt is served while you wait. Starters may include leek and potato soup; a pork liver and sage parfait with pickles and toast; or smoked mackerel, beetroot and caper salad. Main courses are an eclectic bunch: a 7oz chickpea burger comes with grilled bread, tomato salad and yogurt dressing, while roast cod is teamed with spinach, a mangetout risotto and mussel cream sauce. Grilled pork chop comes with horseradish Dauphinoise, savoy cabbage, and grilled venison steak is served with braised lentils, green beans, bacon and fig jam. Puddings include pear crumble with cream, and a chocolate soufflé cake with crème fraîche and kumquat compôte. The wines are well chosen and varied, but must compete with the splendid Eco Warrior ale brewed by the Pitfield Brewery.

Fig

169 Hemingford Road, N1 ■ 020 7609 3009

⊖ Caledonian Road/BR Caledonian Road & Barnsbury

◉ Modern European

⏱ breakfast & brunch Thurs to Sat 09.00–14.00 & Sun 09.00–16.00;
dinner Tues to Sat 19.00–22.30

⌂ www.figrestaurant.co.uk

🖅 all major credit cards except AmEx ■ 12.5% optional service on dinner

££ starters £3.80–£6.20 ■ mains £10.20–£15 ■ desserts £4.80 ■ lowest
bottle price £12.50

✪ Friendly, if eccentric, local resto

This place is small, unpretentious, informal, and the food is very
good. There are about thirty covers at Fig (plus a handful more in
the garden at the rear when the season and weather cooperate) and
the dining room is painted a restful mushroomy sort of brown. The
kitchen performs wonders with a pared-down kitchen brigade who
sensibly concentrate on a short menu – five starters, five mains and
five puds. Dishes are confident and hearty with upfront flavours.
Starters may include a rabbit, chorizo, saffron and artichoke paella;
blackened mackerel, roast sweet potato and gingered spinach; or
a salad of persimmon, avocado, pomegranate, feta with a Manuka
honey yogurt dressing. These are well-considered combos that
are good to eat. Mains follow the same themes – grilled marlin,
courgette onion bhaji, pineapple relish and pea shoots; roast lamb
with Brussels tops, roast squash and caponata; calves' liver with puy
lentils, grilled piquillo peppers, halloumi and cranberry argan oil;
or monkfish with wild mushroom ravioli, Jerusalem artichoke purée
and chardbow chard. Once again these are considered assemblies of
taste and texture and are well made. Puds are equally fine – raspberry
jellies with ice cream and Turkish delight. At Fig everything is seasonal
and they cook with passion. The wine list is strong at the gentler
price levels; service is friendly, and bearing in mind the very few staff
involved, the restaurant spins along merrily. A local hero.

The House

63–69 Canonbury Road, N1 ▪ 020 7704 7410 ♿

⬡ Highbury & Islington/BR Essex Road

🍽 Modern British/gastropub

🕐 Mon 17.30–22.30; Tues to Fri 12.00–14.30 & 17.30–22.30; Sat 12.00–15.30 (brunch) & 17.30–22.30; Sun 12.00–15.30 (brunch) & 18.00–21.30

🖱 www.inthehouse.biz

🗄 all major credit cards except AmEx ▪ 12.5% optional service added

££ starters £5.50–£12.50 ▪ mains £12.95–£22.50 ▪ desserts £3.50 ▪ desserts £5–£8.50 ▪ menu du jour Tues to Fri £14.95 & £17.95 ▪ lowest bottle price £14

✪ A restaurant masquerading as gastropub

As befits a location in one of Islington's smarter enclaves, The House seems more gastro than pub. But what is most unusual about this N1 establishment is that for once aspirations on the menu seem matched by real talent in the kitchen. The House emerged after a lengthy (and seriously expensive) transformation from dodgy local to chic eating and has been busy ever since; service is friendly and unstuffy. The kitchen is an open one and before you even get to your food the signs are good – the chefs work quickly, quietly and neatly. On the top of the grill there is an imposing piece of meat warming through: the chargrilled rib of Buccleuch beef, shallot crust, gratin Dauphinoise, green beans, jus gras. Whoever gets to share this particular rib will be thankful that it wasn't straight from fridge to grill. From the starters a parfait of foie gras, chicken livers and Armagnac comes with toasted brioche. There's a tatin of red onion, with grilled goats' cheese. Mains also hit the spot: braised spiced pork with ginger and pommes cocotte; roast sea bass with piperade; the house shepherd's pie. When talking shepherd's pie, a price tag as large as you will find here takes some living up to, but this shepherd just about delivers. Large chunks of lamb, good gravy, unctuous mash, crisp top. Puds are good – warm gingerbread with clotted cream; Valrhona hot chocolate pudding. Brunch is big here.

Isarn

119 Upper Street, N1 ■ 020 7424 5153

♿ Angel

🍽 Thai

🕐 Mon to Fri 12.00–15.00 & 18.00–23.00; Sat 12.00–23.00; Sun 12.00–22.00

🖱 www.isarn.co.uk

🖨 all major credit cards ■ 12.5% optional service added

££ starters £3.50–£5 ■ soup £4.50–£5.90 ■ mains £6.50–£12.50 ■ sides £1.50–£2.90 ■ desserts £4.50–£6 ■ lowest bottle price £16

✪ Chic Thai fits Islington collar

Tina Juengsoongneun must have a real problem signing within that little box on the back of credit cards. How she must yearn for her maiden name – Yau. The name Yau is enough to make any foodie pay attention because Alan Yau is the man behind a range of splendid restaurants – most notably Hakkasan (see p. 7) – and Tina is Alan's sister. With her Thai husband, Krish Jueng-etc., Tina has set up a very good, very modern Thai restaurant and the Islingtonites have fallen on it with cries of delight. The room is long, and fashionably austere, service is attentive (if sometimes a little clumsy) and the food is fresh tasting with good strong flavours and plenty of contrasting textures. Starters include the ubiquitous Thai fish cake – chewy and agreeably musty; chicken satay – good peanut sauce; and prawn and coconut dumplings – very dim sum. The curries range from monkfish green curry with kuchai and basil, to a beef massaman curry, which is suitably rich. Then there is an array of seafood dishes such as seared lobster tail with tamarind sauce, and various poultry and meat dishes, including some good stir-fries – chicken and green aubergine comes with yellow bean and sweet basil. The trad noodle dishes like pad Thai turn out well – pad thai with prawns, Chinese chives and tofu is particularly successful. Puds are trad and interesting – in the spirit of adventure you should opt for 'Tago with taro and lotus seed'. There's a wine list that touches the right bases for N1. Isarn is a new restaurant that is already perfectly at ease with its surroundings.

Morgan M

489 Liverpool Road, N1 ■ 020 7609 3560

⊖ Highbury & Islington

🍴 French

🕘 Tues 19.00–22.00; Wed to Fri 12.00–14.30 & 19.00–22.00; Sat
19.00–22.00; Sun 12.00–14.30

🖱 www.morganm.com

🖃 all major credit cards except AmEx ■ 12.5% optional service added

££ lunch £19.50 (2 courses) & £23.50 (3 courses); ■ dinner £32 &
dégustation menu £39 ■ menus: garden menu £36 & menu du jour
Tues–Fri £14.95 & £17.95 ■ lowest bottle price £15

✪ French and very classy

Morgan Meunier is a short, passionate Frenchman. He is also
a chef and a very good one. Morgan M is very much his baby:
he painted the pictures displayed on the walls, and the large and
accomplished front-of-house team have all worked with him before.
The restaurant is in a converted Watney's pub and it is now dark
green outside with mint green within. On the wall is a bookshelf
displaying a complete set of Michelin guides. Foodies are already
making this resto a place of pilgrimage, and in the main they are
right to do so. The style of the place is very French, very haute cuisine;
dishes are complex and elegant on the plate; but the seasoning
is spot on and the dishes work well. Pricing is straightforward: at
dinner you opt for the three courses, or get stuck into the six-course
dégustation. Starters may include a ravioli of snails in Chablis with
poached garlic, or a carpaccio of gently smoked scallops with
asparagus coulis and fromage blanc sorbet – very delicate, very fresh
flavours. Onwards to a pavé of turbot topped with a crayfish raviolo,
cream of celeriac, champagne velouté; grilled Anjou squab pigeon;
or roast fillet of veal with sweetbreads, kidney and a splendidly rich
cream and morels sauce. Puds are featured – there's a dark chocolate
moelleux (you get to specify dark or plain chocolate) and a raspberry
soufflé. The wine list scampers up to some very fine wines indeed,
but there are enough bottles on the lower slopes to slake the thirst of
mere mortals.

Pasha

301 Upper Street, N1 ■ 020 7226 1454

⊖ Angel

🍽 Turkish

🕐 Mon to Thurs 12.00–15.00 & 18.00–23.30; Sat 12.00–15.00 & 18.00–24.00; Sun 12.00–23.00

🖪 all major credit cards ■ 10% optional service added

££ starters £3.50–£5.95 ■ mains £7.95–£14.95 ■ sides £2.95–£3.95 ■ desserts £3.95–£4.50 ■ healthy lunch £6.95 ■ menus (min 2): £13.95 (12 meze) & Pasha Feast £19.95 ■ lowest bottle price £12.50

✪ Turkish, but up-to-date

If you picture Turkish food as heavy and oil-slicked, think again. Pasha is dedicated to producing fresh, light, authentic Turkish food that's suited to modern tastes. Dishes are made with virgin olive oil, fresh herbs, strained yogurts and fresh ingredients prepared daily. Pasha doesn't look like a traditional Turkish restaurant either, being open and airy with only the odd brass pot for decoration. For anyone new to Turkish cooking the menu is helpful, and so are the staff, who will encourage you to eat in Turkish style – with lots of small 'meze' dishes. Set menus are popular (minimum two people): there's a simple twelve-meze option and the 'Pasha Feast' (which means ten meze, plus main courses, dessert and coffee). Meze may include hummus, tarama, cacik, kisir (a splendid bulghur wheat concoction), falafel, courgette fritters, meatballs and a host of others. Main courses are more familiar, but the choice is better than usual. Try kilic baligi, which is fillet of swordfish marinated in lime, bay leaf and herbs, and served with rice; shish kebab, which is the standard lamb kebab; or Izmir kofte, meat balls in tomato sauce. Alternatively, try yogurtlu iskender – a trio of shish, kofte and chicken on pitta bread soaked in fresh tomato sauce with fresh herbs and topped with yogurt. Though meat undeniably dominates the menu, there are five vegetarian and three fish selections. Puddings include the usual Turkish stickies, but are light and freshly made. Wines are priced fairly, and there is Efes beer from Turkey.

Sabor

108 Essex Road, N1 ■ 020 7226 5551 &

⊖ Angel

🍽 Latin American

🕐 Mon to Fri 17.00–23.00; Sat & Sun 11.00–23.00

🖰 www.sabor.co.uk

🗗 all major credit cards except AmEx ■ no service added

££ starters £3.25–£4.95 ■ mains £9.50–£16 ■ sides £2.50 ■ desserts £4.50 ■ dinner Mon to Thurs £15 & £17.50 ■ lowest bottle price £11

✪ Nuevo Latino, for nuevo Islington

While Upper Street was busily turning itself into restaurant gulch, nearby Essex Road was glumly dragging its feet. It's as if Upper Street has embraced the café society while all that was left to Essex Road were the greasy spoons. Sabor is a new, light, bright, modernist restaurant with food that is 'inspired by the flavours of countries across Latin America, including Colombia, Brazil, Peru and Argentina'. The menu may read South American, but flavours are pin sharp, and dishes are both light and elegant. Among the starters you'll find empanadas – miniature half-moon-shaped pasties, usually solid and unforgiving, but at Sabor they are light and crisp. There are two ceviches listed – monkfish or mushroom. The monkfish is stunning, the fish has been 'cooked' thoroughly by the high acidity, and the flavours of the grapefruit, blood orange, chilli and lots of fresh coriander sing out. Really good. Main courses are well presented and well-crafted: tiny, pink lamb chops sit on a delicious pile of orange-flavoured quinoa and there's a relish made from papaya, rosemary and garlic. Or how about red snapper cooked in a banana leaf and served with a salad made with palm hearts? The rib-eye steak comes with chimichurri and grilled plantains: the steak is accurately cooked, the plantains are sweet/sharp, and the chimichurri is a revelation – a thick and chunky sauce made from parsley and garlic bound together with oil. Light and green and delicious. The wine list majors in South America.

Kilburn, Queens Park and Willesden

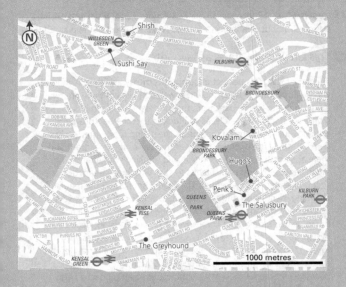

The Greyhound

64–66 Chamberlayne Road, NW10 ■ 020 8969 8080

⊖ Kensal Green

|●| Modern British/gastropub

🕑 Mon 18.30–22.30; Tues to Sat 12.30–15.00 & 18.30–22.30; Sun 12.00–18.00

🗗 all major credit cards ■ 12.5% optional service added

££ starters £4.50–£7 ■ mains £8.50–£14 ■ sides £2.50 ■ desserts £4.50 ■ lunch 'Famous Five' specials Mon to Fri £5 ■ lowest bottle price £11

✪ This Greyhound starts as favourite

This bit of NW10 is perfect gastropub territory and the Greyhound was quick out of the traps. Now it is well established; there are two long rooms stretching back from the pavement and each has its own front door. On the left, as you look at it, is the bar (previously a rugged Irish bar) and to the right is the dining room (previously a derelict shop). The open kitchen is to the rear of the restaurant and there are a couple of large doors linking drinking with dining. The menu changes monthly, but tends to stick with mainstream dishes, simply executed and presented. The food is sound and the regularly changing menu short and to the point. Starters range from sweet potato and coconut soup, to a well-made risotto of morcilla and broad beans. Seared tuna comes with a ginger dressing; deep-fried oysters come with a Bloody Mary salsa; and gnocchi comes with tomato, rocket and goats' cheese. The short list of mains ranges from roast cod with confit potatoes and Brittany artichokes, to poached smoked haddock with bubble and squeak, poached egg and Hollandaise. Fillet of pork is served with a gratin and cabbage; poached gilthead bream is teamed with olive oil mash; and a grilled rib-eye steak with green beans, chips and green peppercorn sauce. The wine list is user-friendly and avoids merciless smash and grab, while the service is friendly and things run pretty smoothly. Unsurprisingly, the owners of this place used to own the handsome racing greyhound in the painting.

Hugo's

25 Lonsdale Road, NW6 ■ 020 7372 1232

⊖ Queens Park

🍴 British

🕐 Mon to Fri 09.30–23.00; Sat & Sun 10.00–23.00

🔲 Mastercard, Visa ■ 12.5% optional service added

££ breakfast/brunch £3.50–£8.80 ■ starters £2.50–£9.70 ■ mains
   £11.80–£15.80 ■ sides £3.80 ■ desserts £5.50 ■ daily specials £10
   ■ lowest bottle price £12.80

⭐ Comfortable neighbourhood stalwart

For many years this resto was known as the Organic Café and then
it changed hands and was renamed Hugo's. But it would take a very
perceptive person to pinpoint any differences other than the name.
The kitchen ticks all the right boxes: organic, seasonal, local produce,
non-endangered fish, traditional methods, eco-friendly practices.
Breakfast and brunch are given their own place in the scheme of
things. Overall this place qualifies as a genuine neighbourhood
gem in a quiet, semi-private road with a light and airy dining room
decorated with twisted fig branches and reclaimed chicken-wire light
fittings. The menu changes sporadically and is divided traditionally
into starters, mains and puds, with the addition of one-course dishes
consisting of salads and pastas. But you can mix and match as you
wish. The cooking is reasonably classical and well grounded, with
little that is unnecessarily fancy. Expect a soup – butternut squash and
coconut perhaps – or a mixed crostini platter. Or grilled goats' cheese
with aubergine caviar, or maybe an organic smoked salmon platter.
For main course artichoke risotto comes with smoked mozzarella and
vies for attention with pan-fried fillet of bream with crayfish risotto.
Braised shank of lamb competes with a stunning steak – organic
chargrilled 8oz rib-eye steak, served with hand-cut chips and glazed
shallots. Puddings are on the heavy side: glazed lemon tart with
honey crème fraîche, or Jack Daniel's pecan chocolate cake. The
drinks list is short, but there is a large enough range of wines, beers,
spirits and juices to accommodate all but the most picky customers.

Kovalam

12 Willesden Lane, NW6 ■ 020 7625 4761

⊖ BR Brondesbury Park

|◐| Indian

🕓 Sun to Thurs 12.00–14.30 & 18.00–23.00; Fri & Sat 12.00–14.30 & 18.00–24.00

🕭 www.kovalamrestaurant.co.uk

🖶 all major credit cards ■ no service added

££ starters £1.95–£5.95 ■ lunchtime thali £5.95 (£4.95 vegetarian)
■ mains £4.25–£7.95 ■ sides £2.95–£3.10 ■ desserts £1.75–£3.95
■ set meal £14.50 & £12 (vegetarian) ■ lowest bottle price £8.50

✪ From Kovalam beach to NW6

In the 1960s and 1970s Willesden Lane was something of a magnet for curry lovers as it boasted a couple of London's first authentic South Indian vegetarian establishments. These places shocked diners, who at that time were 'curry and chips at closing time' sort of folk, by serving cheap and honest veggie food. Now Willesden Lane is no longer the cutting edge of curry, but that did not dissuade some South Indian entrepreneurs from taking over the curry house at no. 12 and re-launching it as 'Kovalam – South Indian cuisine'. Kovalam is a brightly lit if traditionally decorated restaurant where the best dishes are the specials rather than the curry house staples that creep onto the list. Start with the ghee-roast masala dosa, which is large, crisp and buttery, and has a suitably chilli-hot potato heart. The paripu vada with chutney are very good – crisp lentil cakes with coconutty chutney. For your main courses, look closely at the vegetable dishes and the specials: aviyal is creamy with coconut; kaya thoran is green bananas with grated coconut, shallots and mustard. The koonthal masala is worth trying – it's squid in a very rich sauce sharpened with tamarind. Also try the aaterechi fry – dry-fried cubes of lamb with onion, curry leaves and black pepper; it's very tender and very tasty. Or perhaps the kadachaka kootan? This is a dish of curried breadfruit, heavy with coconut. The breads are good, as are the scented plain rices – lemon and coconut.

Penk's

79 Salusbury Road, NW6 ■ 020 7604 4484

⊖ Queens Park

|⊕| French

🕘 Mon to Thurs 12.00–15.00 & 19.00–23.00; Fri 12.00–15.00 &19.00–23.30; Sat 10.30–15.00 & 19.00 to 23.30; Sun 10.30–22.30

🖥 www.penks.com

🗗 all major credit cards except AmEx ■ no service added

££ brunch Sat & Sun £5.45–£6.95 ■ starters £3.95–£6.95 ■ mains £8.95–£15.95 ■ sides £2 ■ desserts £5.45–£7.45 ■ lowest bottle price £12

✪ Bistro is as bistro does

Penk's is very much a family resto – mum makes the puds, step-dad does the wine list, and sis helps front-of-house. After abandoning a lucrative job as a land buyer for a property company (and doing a stint at Kensington Place, see p. 100, to learn his trade), the eponymous Penk decided to open a 'good honest bistro', and it has turned into a model of what a neighbourhood restaurant should be. Penk's is all about bold strokes. The décor is all primary colours, a bright blue exterior giving way to a long, thin room painted sunflower-yellow, with space for just 30 diners at wooden tables. Another 20 can fit in a back room suitable for parties, which is hidden at the end of a corridor lined with wonderful black-and-white prints of the restaurant. The dinner menu keeps things simple with starters such as spiced roast tomato soup before moving on to monkfish gratin, while 'confit aromatic duck with crispy toast and plum chutney' brings a hint of Peking to a taste of France. Salads are similarly simple yet inventive: pot-roasted tuna teamed with white beans, parsley, lemon, soft-boiled egg, aioli and rocket screams Provence. For main course, poached sea bass is an Italianate affair with salsa verde, roast tomatoes and asparagus, served on crostini. Or there's a casserole of cauliflower, pumpkin and spinach with cheesy polenta that should gladden any veggie heart. Puds range from sticky toffee pudding with ice cream to the caramelised lemon tart with clotted cream.

The Salusbury

50–52 Salusbury Road, NW6 ■ 020 7328 3286

⊖ Queens Park

🍴 Italian

🕐 Mon 19.00–22.15; Tues to Sat 12.30–15.30 & 19.00 –22.15; Sun 12.30–15.30 & 19.00–22.00

🗄 Mastercard, Visa ■ 12.5% service added for parties of 5 or more

££ starters £4.50–£11.50 ■ mains £9.50–£16 ■ sides £2.74–£4
■ desserts £4.50 ■ lunch special £5 ■ lowest bottle price £11

✪ The gastropub goes to Italy

The Salusbury has worked hard for its reputation and is now one of London's better gastropubs. Broadly speaking, the pub is a U-shaped space. You go in one door through the bar and continue round the bar to come out in the dining room – a quieter room filled with the kind of tables your mum had in her living room, stripped and scrubbed, and a display of eclectic art lining the walls. If there's one niggle, it's that portion sizes can be daunting. In Yorkshire they call it being 'over-faced', but if sound, Italian-accented cooking coupled with excellent value is what rings your bell, you'll like The Salusbury a lot. The varied menu follows a mainly modern Italian theme rather than the more predictable Modern British bias of so many gastropubs. Starters (and a wave of dishes that could either be starters or mains) may include sautéed prawns with chilli and garlic; red onion soup with Pecorino Romano; smoked goose breast with mushroom tartare; pappardelle with swordfish, black olives and fresh oregano; or artichoke risotto with pesto. There's a practical emphasis on pasta and risotto. Main courses may include monkfish cartoccio with roast peppers and mussels, or confit leg of duck with lentils. Moving on to pud territory, Amaretto, ricotta and almond pudding vies with sgroppina – a soft lemon sorbet doused in grappa – and pure chocolate tart. The wine list is not large, but it is well chosen; service is friendly and un-pushy. And there is the Salusbury Foodstore at no. 56 – good deli, and pizzas to go.

Shish

2–6 Station Parade, NW2 ■ 020 8208 9290 &

⊖ Willesden Green

🍴 Middle Eastern

🕐 Mon to Fri 11.00–24.00; Sat 12.00–24.00 (brunch 10.30–16.00); Sun 10.30–23.00 (brunch 10.30–16.00)

🖱 www.shish.co.uk

🖱 all major credit cards ■ 12.5% optional service added

££ brunch £3.50–£5.25 ■ mezze £2–£3.45 ■ shish £5.95–£8.45 ■ desserts £2.50–£3.95 ■ kid's menu £4.25 ■ lowest bottle price £11.50

⭐ The new face of the kebab

A large, curved-glass pavement frontage displays a sinuous bar counter that snakes around the dining room, leaving grills, fridges and chefs' stations in the centre. Shish is pretty slick. Diners take a stool at the counter; it is for all the world like being at a modernist sushi bar. This place owes a debt to Israeli roadside eateries, with its falafel and shish kebabs, but the 'concept' (all fast-food missions have to have a suitable 'concept') is much more inclusive. The inspiration for Shish is the food of the Silk Road. Starters are divided into lots of cold mezze and a shorter list of hot mezze. The tabbouleh needs a bit more coriander and parsley. The cucumber wasabi is pleasant pickled cucumber. The red and green falafel are well made – the red variety is engagingly spicy. The hot bread is as delicious as only freshly baked hot bread can be. Kebabs are served in two different ways: either plated with rice, couscous or French fries, or in a wrap. The shish kebabs are really rather good. Mediterranean lamb comes up very tender; apricot and ginger teams chicken with good tangy apricot flavour; the Persian kofta is made from minced beef and lamb; or there is king prawn shish. The portions all seem decent-sized and there are further fish and vegetarian options. Die-hard kebabbers can even insist on a satisfactorily fierce squelch of chilli sauce. This food benefits from being freshly cooked and eaten hot from the grill. It's relatively cheap, too.

→ For branches, see index

Sushi Say

33b Walm Lane, NW3 ■ 020 8459 2071   &

⊖ Willesden Green

🍴 Japanese

🕐 Tues to Fri 12.00–14.30 & 18.30–22.30; Sat 13.00–15.30 & 18.00–23.00; Sun 13.00–15.30 & 18.00–22.00

🍽 all major credit cards ■ no service added

££ starters £3.90–£5.90 ■ assorted sushi £12.10–£20.10 ■ assorted sashimi £16.50 ■ mains £6–£12 ■ desserts £1.95–£4.45 ■ set lunch £8.80–£13.50 ■ set dinner £19.50–£30.30 ■ lowest bottle price £10.50; 200ml carafe sake £8

✪ Expert sushi for novice diners

Yuko Shimizu and her husband Katsuharu run this small but excellent Japanese restaurant and sushi bar. It has a very personal feel, with just ten seats at the bar and twenty in the restaurant, plus a private booth for five or six. *Shimizu* means pure water, and the cooking is pure delight. The menu offers a full classical Japanese selection, making it a difficult choice between limiting yourself to sushi or going for the cooked dishes. Perhaps adapting the European style, and having sushi or sashimi as a starter and then main courses with rice, brings you the best of both worlds. Sitting at the sushi bar allows you to watch Katsuharu at work. With a sumo-like stature and the widest grin this side of Cheshire, his fingers magic nigiri sushi onto your plate. In the lower price brackets you'll find omelette, mackerel, squid and octopus. At the top end there's sea urchin, fatty tuna and yellowtail. In between there is a wide enough range to delight even the experts. Nigiri toku brings you eleven pieces of nigiri and seaweed-rolled sushi, and it's a bargain – heavy on the fish and light on the rice. Cooked dishes do not disappoint. Ordering ebi tempura brings you crispy battered king prawns, the batter so light it's almost effervescent. It's worth trying the home-made puddings, such as goma (sesame) ice cream. For experts, there's half-frozen sake – Akita Onigoroshi – not so much a slush puppy, more of a slush mastiff.

Maida Vale, Swiss Cottage and Finchley Road

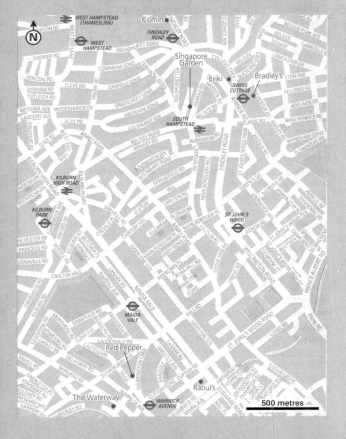

Bradley's

25 Winchester Road, NW3 ■ 020 7722 3457

⊖ Swiss Cottage

🍽 Modern British

🕐 Tues to Fri 12.00–15.00 & 18.00–23.00; Sat 18.00–23.00; Sun 12.00–15.00

🗗 all major credit cards ■ 12.5% optional service added

££ starters £6–£8 ■ mains £11–£16.95 ■ sides £2 ■ desserts £6–£7.50 ■ set menu £9.95 & £13.95 ■ Sunday lunch £18 & £22 ■ lowest bottle price £12.90

✪ Comfortable neighbourhood star

Bradley's has been an open secret in North London for years – secret in that it's damn hard to find. Make the effort for a great-value set lunch, an innovative à la carte menu and an unusually presented wine list. The set menu is admirably straightforward. A typical three-course choice could include grilled asparagus, warm jersey potatoes with samphire and lemon dressing; seared beef with Asia spiced salad; then raspberry and orange crème brûleé. Excellent value and good training for an attack on the à la carte menu in the future. Cooking is sound and dishes tend to be classic flavour combinations with very well judged twists. For example, there's roasted peaches with Bayonne ham, mascarpone and basil; tian of Cornish crab with avocado and tomato vinaigrette; and chargrilled squid with Piedmont pepper. Mains include wild salmon with balsamic strawberries, watercress and herb couscous; Barbary duck breast with cherry compôte, cabbage and turnip Dauphinoise; or wild sea bass fillet with peperonata and fennel purée. Purists might question strawberries with salmon, or cabbage and turnip in a Dauphinoise, but they work well. Bradleys' wine list is divided into quaint sections like 'aromatic', 'medium weight', 'clean and fresh', 'heavyweight', 'old ones' and 'blockbusters'. In the latter section you can find a Vosne Romanée 1er Cru, a bottle of Château Talbot and other fine wine bargains. Bradley's is a mature and successful neighbourhood restaurant, the kind of place we would all like just at the end of our street.

Cumin

O2 Centre, 255 Finchley Road, NW3 ■ 020 7431 0151   &

⊖ Finchley Road

🍽 Indian

🕐 Sun to Wed 12.00–23.00; Thurs to Sat 12.00–24.00

🖰 www.cumin.co.uk

🖻 all major credit cards ■ 10% optional service added

££ starters £3.50–£5.45 ■ mains £5.95–£9 ■ sides £2.50–£3.85
   ■ desserts £2.65–£3.75 ■ daily lunch deal £6 ■ lowest bottle price
   £11

✪ Sound Indian food – fast

It's not often that you get to go to dinner in a shopping mall. At
the O2 Centre you'll find an array of cinemas and an imposing line-
up of fast food joints. Make your way up to the 'Second Level', and
you'll find Cumin (a modernist Indian restaurant) wedged between
Yo! Sushi and Ed's Easy Diner. The dining room is large and industrial,
well lit with broadly spaced, heavy, wooden tables. Orders are taken
and the starters arrive in a matter of minutes – we are not talking
painstakingly cooked-to-order here. But such is the forgiving nature
of Indian food that the dishes survive really well. Murg malai tikka
– chicken tikka but with a yogurt marinade – is tender and not dried
out. The dum ke kebab, a rolled kebab made with lamb mince and
ginger that is finished in the pan with plenty of fresh mint, is very
good with well-balanced spicing. A tandoori roti to mop up with is
fresh and well made. Main courses come plated and include either
naan or rice, which makes for good value. A 'Kashmiri roganjosh'
is sound. A chicken jalfrezi is chilli warm rather than chilli hot and
comes with a very tomatoey, sweet and sharp sauce that will jar
with anyone more accustomed to the more widespread oniony
interpretation of the dish. There is a good range of veggie dishes,
although the cumin aloo – new potatoes with cumin seeds and fresh
coriander – seems light on both cumin and seasoning. Puds round up
the usual suspects. The service is brisk and friendly. Overall, Cumin is a
restaurant that is trying hard.

Eriki

4–6 Northways Parade, Finchley Road, NW3 ▪ 020 7722 0606

⊖ Finchley Road

🍽 Indian

🕐 Fri 12.00–15.00 & 18.00–23.00; Sat 18.00–23.00

🖱 www. eriki.co.uk

🗗 all major credit cards ▪ 12.5% optional service added

££ starters £3.95–£5.95 ▪ mains £7.95–£12.95 ▪ sides £2.25–£5.95
   ▪ desserts £3.75–£3.95 ▪ lowest bottle price £13.95

✪ Slick Indian, ambitious menu

Eriki is an ambitious, new-style Indian restaurant. This means that
attention has been paid to the design (glowing, richly coloured walls,
heavy wood chairs, blond wood floor), to the menu, which includes
a few less familiar regional dishes, and to the prices, which are a tad
higher than you might expect – presumably to keep out riffraff. This
place is determined to distance itself from run-of-the mill High Street
curry houses. Service is slick and overall Eriki achieves its objective
and delivers a polished (if pricey) night out. The food is good and
commendably unfussy, although the starters do get a fairly elaborate
presentation. Scallops hariyali arrives in a scallop shell like an old-
style coquilles St Jacques – two accurately cooked scallops in a mild
creamy sauce. Or there's calamari mirch fry; stir-fried squid; or masala
dosa. (There is a healthy representation of South Indian dishes on the
menu, including a good range of veggie options.) Classic mains such
as koh-e-rogan josh are well spiced and with a good coarsely ground
sauce. Murgh Xacutti is, again, well spiced. The duck with tamarind
and pink pepper is light and almost a fusion dish. Kumb palak, young
spinach leaves teamed with a few button mushrooms, tastes very
fresh. And the kali dal – although carrying a pretty fierce price tag for
a lentil dish – is well made, with mixed pulses and a hefty tempering
of butter. Breads are sound, the Malabari tawa paratha being the
pick: very flaky, very self-indulgent. Eriki is better than your average
High Street Indian by a long way.

Raoul's

13 Clifton Road, W9 ▪ 020 7289 7313

⊖ Warwick Avenue

🍴 European/deli

🕐 Mon to Sat 08.30–22.15; Sun 09.00–22.15

🖰 www.raoulsgourmet.com

🖶 Mastercard, Visa ▪ 12.5% service added for parties of 5 or more

---

££ breakfast £4.25–£6.50 ▪ starters £4.25–£8 ▪ mains £8.25–£15
   ▪ sides £1.95 ▪ desserts £2.20–£4.75 ▪ lowest bottle price £12.95

✪ A comfortable neighbourhood institution

Raoul's certainly looks like a café (although a stylish, film-setty, modern café) and it is certainly open for long hours each day. But this establishment is something more, it's a very W9 affair and as a result Raoul's is more of a restaurant that thinks it's a café, than the other way around. The waiters are unhurried without seeming world-weary. The room is modern without being aggressively designery. And the menu offers all things to all customers and is backed up by a blackboard listing daily specials. No wonder it is full of people waiting out the day. The breakfast dishes are good. For a café this place is more eggs Benedict than fried bread, but the full English comprises scrambled or fried eggs, bacon, sausage, grilled tomatoes and toast; the American and modernist influences don't become apparent until further down the page – bagels with smoked salmon and cream cheese, French toast and maple syrup. Sandwiches are modernist on the one hand – ciabatta roll with melted mozzarella, grilled peppers, rocket and sun-dried tomatoes, and trad on the other, with Croque Monsieur. Good quality, very fresh ingredients, well presented, exemplary. If you dock here during a main-meal time turn to the blackboard; there may be starters such as grilled spareribs and spinach salad; then mains such as fettucine with fresh asparagus and truffle oil, or a Scotch rib-eye steak with garlic butter and French fries. There's a short wine list with economical house wines, and service is cheerful. A very comfortable place.

→ For branches, see index

Red Pepper

8 Formosa Street, W9 ■ 020 7266 2708

⊖ Warwick Avenue

🍽 Pizza/Italian

🕒 Mon to Fri 12.00–15.00 & 18.30–23.00; Sat 12.00–23.00; Sun 12.30–22.30

🗗 Mastercard, Visa ■ 12.5% optional service added

££ starters £5–£8.50 ■ mains £8–£16 ■ sides £4.50 ■ desserts £4.50 ■ lowest bottle price £11

✪ Terrific pizzas, tiny resto

The Red Pepper may not be the largest restaurant in Maida Vale and it certainly isn't the most elegant. The service hovers on the edge of brusque, and for what is a neighbourhood pizza joint the prices would be high enough to raise an eyebrow anywhere less sleek than W9. But it is packed. Over the years every review of Red Pepper has opened with a complaint that the tiny tables are crammed in too tightly, the tables jostling together so that the waiters have to combine an aptitude for slalom skiing with the skills of a limbo dancer. No matter. There are half a dozen starters, a few pasta dishes, some specials and the list of pizzas. The starters are light and fresh; a spiced crab salad with baby spinach leaves looks pretty on the plate and is good on the fork as well. Or there's pan-fried goats' cheese with green beans and sun-dried tomato dressing, or a bowl of green pea soup with a chargrilled tiger prawn bobbing in it. There are specials, but you should turn your attention to the pizzas. They are large, flat and thin, but not too thin. Toppings are top quality. As well as the usual suspects – Margherita, Napoli, stagioni – the 'rossi' is worthy of special mention. The redness comes from tomatoes, red peppers and chilli oil and the gooey top is nicely piquant. The 'primavera' is also very good, topped with San Daniele ham, Parmesan and a handful of rocket. The all-Italian wine list has some interesting bottles at gentle prices – check out the Sardinian reds.

Singapore Garden

83a Fairfax Road, NW6 ▪ 020 7328 5314

⊖ Swiss Cottage

🍽 Singaporean

🕐 Sun to Thurs 12.00–14.45 & 18.00–22.45; Fri & Sat 12.00–14.45 & 18.00–23.15

🖫 all major credit cards ▪ 12.5% optional service added

££ starters £5.20–£10 ▪ mains £6.50–£32.50 ▪ sides £2–£7 ▪ desserts £4.50–£6.50 ▪ lowest bottle price £15

✪ Large, sprawling, jolly, family restaurant

Singapore Garden performs a cunning dual function. A good deal of the cavernous dining room is filled with well-heeled, often elderly, family groups from Swiss Cottage and St John's Wood, treating the restaurant as their local Chinese and consuming crispy duck in pancakes. The other customers, drawn from London's Singaporean and Malaysian communities, are tucking into the Teochew braised pig's trotters. So there are both cocktails and Tiger beer. It's a busy restaurant, so don't even think of turning up without a reservation, but there is persistent talk of an extensive re-modelling, which will raise the number of seats. The food is interesting and good. Start with a chiew yim soft-shell crab, which is lightly fried with garlic and chillies rather than annihilated in the deep fryer, like the fresh crab fried in the shell, which does offer exceptional crispy bits. If you're feeling adventurous, follow with a real Singapore special – the Teochew braised pig's trotter, which brings half a pig's worth of trotters slow-cooked in a luxurious, black, heart-stoppingly rich gravy. Or try the claypot prawns and scallops, which delivers good, large, crunchy prawns and a fair portion of scallops, stewed with lemongrass and fresh ginger on glass noodles. Very good indeed. From the Malaysian list you might pick a daging curry – coconutty, and not especially hot. Or the squid blachan, rich with the strange savoury taste of prawn paste. Or a simple dish such as archar, which is a plate of crunchy pickled vegetables sprinkled with ground peanuts. Good food, happy place.

The Waterway

54 Formosa Street, W9 ■ 020 7266 3557

⊖ Warwick Avenue

🍽️ Modern British/gastropub

🕐 Mon to Fri 12.30–15.30 & 18.30–22.15; Sat & Sun 12.30–16.00 & 18.30–22.15

🖱️ www.thewaterway.co.uk

🗄️ all major credit cards ■ 12.5% optional service added

££ starters £5–£6.50 ■ mains £8.50–£14 ■ sides £3–£4 ■ desserts £5–£5.50 ■ lowest bottle price £13

❂ Loud and proud, pubby gastropub

Once upon a time the Waterway was marooned at the extreme end of the rough boozer spectrum, after which it was taken over by new management. After a shaky start, the dining room towards the rear has developed into a very sound gastropub, with comfortable leather banquettes and friendly service. It is still primarily a canal-side venue with plenty of room for drinking outside, and both the music and the crowd are loud. But at least now there is decent food to be had. The menu went through a period of studied eccentricity, but the incumbent chef has gone back to basics and there is now a balance between comfort food specials and trad French favourites. So starters run the gamut from goats' cheese parfait, to citrus-cured salmon, chicken rillettes, or steamed mussels – nothing very shocking there, commendably accessible. Then there is a section headed the 'Classics' where you'll find a decent burger, the rather coyly named 'Londoner sausage sandwich', and the 'classic Caesar salad', which includes a rather un-classic grilled chicken breast. Mains range from pan-roast cod with a fricassee of ham hock and ratte potatoes, to braised pork belly with hispy cabbage, lardons and mashed potatoes. The puds include a warm chocolate fondant; a pear compôte; and apple tarte Tatin. You have to admire anywhere that matches the food served to the clientele and the surroundings so accurately. The Waterway has tried a few approaches over the years, but it looks as if this one just might work.

Stoke Newington

ABNEY PARK CEMETERY
STOKE NEWINGTON

Rasa Travancore

CLISSOLD PARK

Rasa

Anglo Anatolyan

Testi

La Belle Époque

DALSTON KINGSLAND

CANONBURY

500 metres

Anglo Anatolyan

123 Stoke Newington Church Street, N16 ■ 020 7923 4349

⊖ BR Stoke Newington

🍽 Turkish

🕐 daily 18.00–23.00

🖨 all major credit cards ■ no service added

££ starters/mezze £2.95–£5.50 ■ mains £6.90–£10.99 ■ sides £1.50–£2
■ desserts £2.50–£3 ■ set menu Sun to Thurs £7.95 ■ lowest bottle
price £9.50

✪ Small, functional, cheap and Turkish

The food is sound at the Anglo Anatolyan, the bills are small,
and the tables are so crowded together that you get to meet all
the other diners. But the most intriguing feature of the restaurant
is the large and impressive royal crest engraved in the glass of the
front door. Under it an inscription reads, 'By Appointment to Her
Majesty Queen Elizabeth II, Motor Car Manufacturers'. Why? Do the
Windsors slip up to Stoke Newington when they feel a new Daimler
coming on? Predictably, asking the waiters for provenance doesn't
help much: they look at you seriously and confide that they 'got
the door secondhand'. The food at the Anglo Anatolyan is usually
pretty decent. The bread in particular is amazing: large, round, flat
loaves about two inches deep, cut into chunks, soft in the middle
and crisp on the outside; it is baked at home by a local Turkish
woman. To accompany it, start with ispanak tarator, which is spinach
in yogurt with garlic, and a tremendous, coarse tarama. And also
sigara borek, crisp filo pastry filled with cheese and served hot, and
arnavut cigeri, cubes of fried lamb's liver. The main courses are more
easily summarised: sixteen ways with lamb, one with quails, two with
chicken, one with prawn, and two vegetarian dishes. Kaburga tarak
is crisp, tasty lamb spareribs; iskender kebab is fresh doner on a bed
of cubed bread, topped with yogurt and tomato sauce; kasarli beyti
is minced lamb made into a patty with cheese and grilled. They are all
pretty good. Printed across the bottom of each bill is 'Another cheap
night out.' True enough.

La Belle Époque

37 Newington Green, N1 ■ 020 7249 2222

⊖ BR Canonbury

🍽 French café/pâtisserie

🕐 Tues to Fri 08.00–18.00; Sat 09.00–18.00; Sun 09.00–17.00

🖰 all major credit cards except AmEx ■ no service added

££ croissants & cakes £1–£3.25 ■ lunch dishes £4.30–£5.25 ■ 'Belle Époque' mousse £3.25 ■ tea/coffee £1–£1.65 ■ unlicensed

✪ Parisian quality delights Stoke Newington

An authentic French café in Stoke Newington? Formidable! Overlooking Newington Green, La Belle Époque showcases the skills of proprietor Eric Rousseau, a prodigious pâtissier-chocolatier-confiseur-glacier. Before opening La Belle Époque, he trained in Paris and worked all over the world. Eric is the first baker in Britain to receive France's official 'Artisan Boulanger' certificate. He makes fortnightly trips across the Channel to buy the twenty types of flour that produce dozens of different loaves, including that elusive 'proper' baguette, as well as supplies of chocolate and gourmet goods, including cassoulet and confitures, truffles, foie gras and escargots. Weekends always see queues of Stokies waiting to take home the hand-made croissants and other Viennoiserie. But 'eating in' at one of the tables in the light and airy shop area, or in the darker back room, will show Eric's obsessive attention to detail. Croissants come with Beurre d'Isigny and miniature pots of French jam. Accompany them with a genuine café au lait. Lunch brings a daily changing choice of quiches (with or without a green salad); mixed salads; Bouchées à la Reine, vol au vents stuffed with mushrooms; and Croques Monsieur, made with the classic béchamel filling, rather than being the usual ham-and-cheese toastie. At tea time, cakes, tarts and gateaux are extravagant in both design and engineering. Eric's signature creation is the 'Belle Époque' itself: Cuban chocolate mousse with a crème brûlée centre filled with Grand Marnier and orange fondant. You can even sign up for one of the regular courses and polish up your own baking skills.

Rasa

55 Stoke Newington Church Street, N16 ■ 020 7249 0344

⊖ BR Stoke Newington

🍴 Indian/vegetarian

🕐 Mon to Fri 18.00–22.45; Sat & Sun 12.00–15.00 & 18.00–23.30

🖰 www.rasarestaurants.com

🗗 all major credit cards ■ 12.5% optional service added

££ starters £3 ■ mains £3.70–£5.95 ■ sides £2.25–£4 ■ desserts £2–£3
■ Kerala Feast £16 ■ lowest bottle price £9.95

✪ South Indian veggie – the original and genuine

**Rasa has built up a formidable reputation for outstanding South
Indian vegetarian cooking,** but as well as great food, you'll find that
the staff are friendly and helpful, and the atmosphere is uplifting.
Inside, everything is pink (napkins, tablecloths, walls), gold ornaments
dangle from the ceiling, and a colourful statue of Krishna playing
the flute greets you at the entrance. Rasa's proprietor and most
of the kitchen staff come from Cochin in Kerala. As you'd expect,
booking is essential. This is one occasion when the set meal – or
'Kerala feast'– may be the best, as well as the easiest, option. But
however you approach a Rasa meal, everything is a taste sensation.
Even the pappadoms are a surprise: try the selection served with six
home-made chutneys. If you're going your own way, there are lots
of starters to choose from. Mysore bonda is delicious, shaped like
a meatball but made of potato spiced with ginger, coriander and
mustard seeds; or there is kathrikka, slices of aubergine served with
fresh tomato chutney. The main dishes are good, too. Cheera parippu
curry is made with fresh spinach, and toor dal with a touch of garlic;
moru kachiathu combines mangoes and green bananas with chilli
and ginger. Or go for a dosa (paper-thin crisp pancakes). Masala dosa
is packed with potatoes and comes with lentil sauce and coconut
chutney. Puddings sound hefty, but arrive in mercifully small portions;
the pal payasam is a rice pudding made with cashew nuts and raisins.
A fine end to a meal.

→ For branches, see index

Rasa Travancore

56 Stoke Newington Church Street, N16 ■ 020 7249 1340

⊖ BR Stoke Newington

🍽 Indian

🕐 Mon to Sat 18.00–23.00; Sun 12.00–15.00 & 18.00–23.00

🖱 www.rasarestaurants.com

🗃 all major credit cards ■ 12.5% optional service added

££ starters £2.60–£5.25 ■ mains £3.90–£7.95 ■ sides £2–£3.45
■ desserts £5.50 ■ lowest bottle price £9.95

✪ Exploring Syrian Christian cuisine

Rasa Travancore is painted glow-in-the-dark Rasa pink, just like
the original Rasa, which faces it across the roadway. Rasa Travancore
moves the spotlight onto a particular facet of Keralan cuisine:
Syrian Christian cooking, and a very welcome move it is, too. All the
South Indian flavour notes are there – coconut, curry leaves, ginger,
chillies, mustard seeds, tamarind – but as well as veggie specialities,
Syrian Christian dishes feature fish, seafood, mutton, chicken and
duck. The menu is a long one and great pains have been taken to
explain every dish. Apparently the king prawns in konjufry have been
marinated in 'refreshing spices'. Or there's Kerala fish fry, a large
steak of firm-fleshed kingfish dusted with spice and pan-fried. Very
delicious. Travancore kozhukkatta is a sort of ninth cousin to those
large, doughy Chinese dumplings – steamed rice outside with spiced
minced lamb inside. The main course dishes are fascinating and
richly flavoured. Kozhy olthu curry – billed as 'a famous recipe from
Sebastian's mum' – is a rich, dryish, oniony, chicken curry. Lamb stew
is a simple and charming lamb curry. Duck fry is dry-fried chunks of
duck with curry leaves and onion. Kappayyum meenum vevichathu is
a triumph – a soupy fish curry, delicately flavoured and served with
floury chunks of boiled tapioca root dusted with coconut. Excellent
accompaniments are the tamarind rice, which has an amazing depth
of flavour, and the flaky, buttery Malabar paratha. This place has all
the charm of the original veggie haven over the road with the added
pluses of some rare and interesting meat and fish dishes.

Testi

38 Stoke Newington High Street, N16 ■ 020 7249 7151

⊖ BR Stoke Newington

🍴 Turkish

🕐 daily 12.00–01.00

🗂 all major credit cards except AmEx ■ no service added

££ starters/mezze £3.50–£3.95 ■ mains £5–£10.95 ■ sides £2.50
■ desserts £3 ■ lowest bottle price £9.50

✪ Honest Turkish grill house

Testi is a large and bustling Turkish restaurant, and, somewhat disappointingly, the testi from which it takes its name is not testicles (as the rumour would have it), but testi as in the Turkish word for water jug. At the centre of the dining room is the obligatory open grill and the design theme is frills, rustic implements, terracotta-coloured plasterwork, and a red ceiling splattered with fine white squiggles. The staff manages to be both efficient and friendly, prices are low and the grill chef is significantly gifted. The starters are very sound – humus is nutty and smooth; ali nazik is a dish of aubergine in creamy yogurt; kisir is stunning… bulghur wheat, plus very finely chopped tomatoes and peppers. The sucuk izgara is grilled Turkish sausage, discs of pleasantly musty-spicy sausage, very distinctive. The hot bread is wonderful. For main course you should order what are billed on the menu as 'Thesticals' – koc yumurtasi – and to avoid confusion subtitled 'lamb testicles marinated and char-grilled'. They are delicious. A soft texture, crisp outside, yielding within, smoky from the grill. And while you're at it, the grilled kidneys are good, the liver is good, and the grilled quail is good. The 'kaburga', lamb spare ribs, is outstandingly good – chewy, crispy and salty all at the same time. But if you cannot bring yourself to grab dinner by the thesticals, the menu lists all the old favourites: shish kebab, chicken wings, lamb chops. And all the grills here are served with some very fine accompaniments, including a dish of charred sweet onions that comes in a sauce made from sumac and lemon juice.

South

Battersea, Clapham and Wandsworth

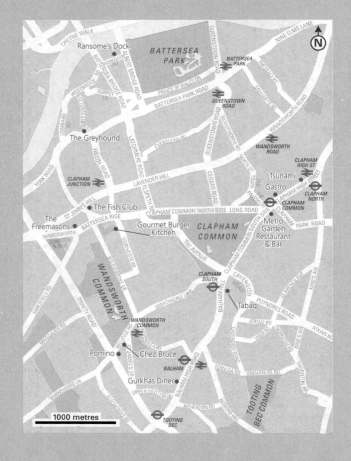

Chez Bruce

2 Bellevue Road, SW17 ■ 020 8672 0114

BR Wandsworth Common

French

Mon to Thurs 12.00–14.00 & 19.00–22.30; Fri 12.00–14.00 & 18.30–22.30; Sat 12.30–14.30 & 18.30–22.30; Sun 12.00–15.00 & 19.00–22.30

www.chezbruce.co.uk

all major credit cards ■ 12.5% optional service added

££ lunch Mon to Fri £23.50 (3 courses), Sat & Sun £30 (3 courses) ■ dinner Mon to Sun £30 (3 courses) ■ lowest bottle price £18.50

A national treasure

Bruce Poole's comfortable little restaurant has weathered the storm attendant on being singled out for Michelin stardom with admirable aplomb. Chez Bruce still stands for honest, unfussy, earthy, richly flavoured food. The menu boasts old-fashioned dishes that never pander to the latest gastro-trend and make use of less fashionable ingredients – like pig's trotters, rabbit or mackerel. Prix fixe three-course menus and truly amazing cooking combine to make this place bargain HQ. The menu changes from day to day. The kind of starters you can expect are cream of fennel soup with wild mushroom pastillas; Middle White pig's head croquettes with sauce gribiche and red wine jus; grilled mackerel with smoked eel, savoy cabbage and mustard. Or there might be a classic lurking – perhaps vitello tonnato. Main course dishes are deeply satisfying. You might find pot au feu of duck with bread sauce and foie gras; crisp fillet of bream with artichokes, gnocchi and red pepper compôte; or rolled pork belly with glazed root vegetables and aligot. This is one of the last strongholds of offal (perhaps the reason why this restaurant is the favourite haunt of so many off-duty chefs?). Look out for sweetbreads, or perhaps calf's liver. The Michelin star has led to the wine list being extended and refined and it now wins prizes of its own. The sweets here are well-executed classics: proper crème brûlée, or rhubarb and champagne trifle. No wonder Chez Bruce is heavily booked every evening. Go for lunch instead – it'll make your day.

The Fish Club

189 St John's Hill, SW11 ■ 020 7978 7115 &

⊖ BR Clapham Junction

🍴 Fish

🕓 Tues to Sat 12.00–22.00; Sun 12.00–21.00

🖥 www. thefishclub.com

🗗 all major credit cards ■ no service added

££ starters £2.95–£7.95 ■ mains £5.75–£12.75 ■ sides £2.50–£4.50
■ desserts £2.50–£3.95 ■ lowest bottle price £12.95

✪ The future of fish and chips

The Fish Club isn't a club, it's something much more intriguing.
This resto departs from the normal run of fish and chip shops in that
it is run by chefs, not 'fryers'. For once the food is given top priority.
As you walk in you'll spot a large chilled counter playing host to
plenty of spanking fresh fish; there's an open kitchen; there is a fryer,
but there is also a grill. The blackboard lists what is on offer and
everything is cooked to order. The fish and chips to go is served up
in a cardboard box (like an oversize pizza box), but if you eat in you
get real china and cutlery at the large refectory tables to the rear.
The menu always includes one classic battered fish – often this fish is
from a less fashionable species like coley; the proprietors make every
effort to wean their customers off endangered fish like cod. Starters
range from oysters to smoked sprats or potted shrimps. For mains, if
you don't fancy battered fish with chips, how about a pair of small
'slip' soles grilled with butter? Or a whole Royal Bream chargrilled? Or
a perfectly cooked wing of skate? And to go with your fish, choose
from chips (very good, crisp outside, fluffy within); or sweet potato
chips (as good as the chips, but with a caramelised sweetness); or
a decent feta salad. Even the sauces are pukka – try the salsa verde
or the tartare sauce. The prices tend to be at restaurant levels rather
than competing with the chippies, but for fresh fish cooked carefully
that seems just.

The Freemasons

2 Northside, Wandsworth Common, SW18 ■ 020 7326 8580

⊖ BR Clapham Junction

🍴 Modern British/gastropub

🕐 Mon to Sat 12.00–15.00 & 18.30–22.00; Sun 12.30–16.00 & 18.30–21.30

🖱 www. freemasonspub.com

🗗 all major credit cards ■ no service added

££ starters £4–£7 ■ mains £8–£13 ■ sides £2–£4 ■ desserts £4 ■ lowest bottle price £12

✪ Gastro balanced by pub

This pub has gone full circle. First The Freemasons became a bar called the Roundhouse; then it was a Livebait fish restaurant; and now it is The Freemasons once again. Inside, the décor is 'standard-gastropub': sofas, mis-matched dining chairs, big pictures, the familiar scruffy-comfortable look. You can eat anywhere in the pub, but the dining area is somewhat raised and overlooks the open kitchen. The food is good, dishes avoid most of the horrors of elaborate presentation, flavours are strong and there are some interesting combinations of taste and texture. Start with the plate of decent home-made hommus with bread to take the sting out of your appetite while you study the menu. Starters might include tempura soft-shell crab on crisp polenta with avocado and pickled radicchio; a whole buffalo mozzarella – very good milky mozzarella – with plum tomatoes, rocket and pesto; a salt cod and cassava fishcake – a competitive fishcake, but it's hard to spot any cassava. Mains are substantial and well thought out: a grilled lamb steak comes with a light and fluffy herb couscous and chickpeas in a ratatouille sauce; pan-fried wasabi salmon comes with egg noodles and a tamarind sauce; a large piece of roast pork belly arrives very crisp and gnarled, pleasantly chewy, with a dollop of decent mash and some chilli sauce. The lemon and vanilla cheesecake does its job. The Timothy Taylor's Landlord bitter is well kept, and there is a short, gently priced wine list. Service is friendly.

Gastro

67 Venn Street, SW4 ■ 020 7627 0222

⊖ Clapham Common

🍴 Very French

🕘 daily 08.00–24.00

🖪 cash or cheque only ■ no service added

££ starters £3.95–£12.95 (lobster £45) ■ mains £10.95–£19.50 ■ sides £2.95–£4.30 ■ desserts £4.50–£6.50 ■ menus: lunch Mon to Fri £9.95; Cous Cous night Tues £12.45 ■ lowest bottle price £11.95

✪ French to the coeur

Gastro was a pathfinder as Cla'am scampered headlong towards trendiness. And where once all was favouritism for regulars, and a no-bookings policy, now you may need a reservation to get in. The food is still unabashed about its Frenchness, but there are competing eateries up and down Venn Street, and Gastro is no longer streets ahead. The staff are French and the menu lists all the Gallic favourites, which tend to be inexpensive and generously portioned. Think yourself back to your last French holiday and enjoy. Under hors d'oeuvres you'll find a pukka soupe de poisson with the classic trimmings. Ordering seafood is straightforward: oysters are sold in sixes; mussels arrive à la marinière; and crabe mayonnaise is exactly that – a whole crab and mayonnaise. No arguments there. The mains will also cosset any Francophile tendencies you may have: carré d'agneau grillé au pain d'épice, rack of lamb with gingerbread crust; andouillette frîtes sauce moutarde – that deadly French sausage made from pigs' chitterlings; or an authentic entrecôte grillé, sauce Béarnaise, frîtes. And there is always boudin noir pommes purées, black pudding, apples and mash. Fish dishes are well represented: try lotte et ventrêche, monkfish with bacon. For puds think pâtisserie, and good pâtisserie at that. The wine list has perked up of late. and Gastro offers a 'cous cous menu' on Tuesday night – couscous, salad, pichet of wine 'Tout compris'.

Gourmet Burger Kitchen

44 Northcote Road, SW11 ■ 020 7228 3309

BR Clapham Junction

Burgers

Mon to Fri 12.00–23.00; Sat 11.00–23.00; Sun 11.00–22.00

www.gbkinfo.co.uk

all major credit cards ■ no service added

££ burgers £3.95–£7.40 ■ sides £2.25–£4.45 ■ lowest bottle price £10.95

✪ The acceptable face of the hamburger

On the face of it, the words 'gourmet burger kitchen' do not make easy bedfellows. 'Gourmet' contradicts 'burger', and 'kitchen' has an unnervingly homely ring to it. But taken as a whole phrase, you can see the intention. 'There are burgers here', the proprietors seem to want us to know, 'but not those thin, mass-produced ones. Our burgers have flair and originality, but they are not high-falutin' burgers; everything is hand-made and good.' Anyway, GBK will do for now. The room is cramped and dominated by a large counter behind which there seem to be serried ranks of waitresses and chefs. Everything is pretty casual – you go up to the bar, order and pay, and then your meal is brought to the table. The menu starts at the 'classic – 100 per cent Aberdeen Angus Scotch beef, salad and relish'. It also offers the blue cheese burger, which adds the tang of Stilton to the main event; the chilli burger; the avocado and bacon burger; the Jamaican – with mangoes and ginger sauce; the pesterella – with fresh pesto and mozzarella; lamb; venison; chicken, bacon and avocado; chorizo; or for vegetarians there is even a 'burger' made from Portabella mushroom; or aubergine and goats' cheese; or falafel. The fries are good and the side salad is excellent, with good fresh leaves and a perky dressing. The Gourmet Burger Kitchen has a good feel to it, and the food is top-quality. Despite the dread word 'gourmet', prices are not out of reach.

→ For branches, see index or website

The Greyhound

136 Battersea High Street, SW11 ■ 020 7978 7021   ♿

⊖ BR Clapham Junction

🍽 Modern British/gastropub

🕐 Tues to Sat 12.00–14.30 & 19.00–22.00; Sun 12.00–15.00

🖥 www.thegreyhoundbattersea.co.uk

💳 all major credit cards ■ 10% optional service added

££ à la carte lunch only £4–£4.50 ■ mains £6.50–£7.50 ■ desserts £3.50 ■ dinner £26 (2 courses) & £29.50 (3 courses) ■ Sunday lunch £15 (2 courses) & £18.50 (3 courses) ■ lowest bottle price £12

✪ Shock-and-awe wine list

Radical and foodie menu hits Battersea. The Greyhound may represent the latest turning point in the history of the gastropub. This hound looks like a gastropub; is as comfortable and as friendly as a gastropub. But you are in a restaurant. The prices are resto prices and the wine list is long enough, and considered enough, to grace any top-flight dining room. The menu is commendably short – four starters, four mains, four puds – and the kitchen has real passion. 'Argentine beef tartare' combines chopped fillet with popcorn and space dust so that it crackles in your mouth – good fun, and a good flavour; it's served with blobs of foie gras cream, red chard and an oyster beignet. Another starter may be the Golden Valley goats' curd salad – this comes fried with golden beetroot and artichoke heart. The main course options may range from duck breast, to mutton, tuna, and pasta. The duck is well cooked and comes with fluffy black pudding. The mutton sits on a bed of houmous. The veggie option is triumphant – three different pastas, three different sauces: cheese (good); salsa verde (better); wild mushroom (best). Puds are equally complex and delightful. Overall, the elegance and complexity of the dishes means that service can be a tad ragged, but it is hard to worry. The Greyhound delivers good and passionate cooking, you'll see original ideas and even if the bill is on the high side, on balance it will be worth it.

Gurkhas Diner

1 The Boulevard, Balham High Road, SW17

■ 020 8675 1188   ♿

⊖ Balham

🍽 Indian

🕐 Mon to Sat 12.00–14.30 & 18.00–23.00; Sun 12.00–22.00

🗄 all major credit cards ■ 10% optional service added

££ starters £2.90–£4.25 ■ mains £5.50–£9.50 ■ sides £3.50–£4.50
■ desserts £3–£3.50 ■ lunch menu £7.50 & £10.50 ■ lowest bottle
price £10.95

✪ Nepali dishes at unpretentious resto

Once an electrical goods shop on the Boulevard, no. 1 is now a
restaurant that offers something a bit different – Nepalese food. But
when it comes down to it, 'Gurkhas' is anything but a diner. The light
and spacious room has a parquet floor and this is a restaurant where
your napkin comes in a stylish napkin ring and there are over-size
wine glasses. Great efforts have also been made with the presentation
of the dishes on the plate and there's a good deal of 'arranging'
and 'sauce drizzling' going on, which is largely superfluous given
the interesting and well-cooked food. From the starters dayalu is a
simple potato cake made with lentils, and served with a fine-grained,
spicy, sesame sauce. The nakasee is also good – a bamboo skewer
of chicken with another delicious sauce. Or there's bhutuwa, which
is a stir-fry made with chunks of highly seasoned chicken liver. Main
courses include a series of dishes made in the 'chuli', a charcoal-
fuelled beehive oven. Gurkhali chicken is very good, with a green
marinade and strong flavours. Khasi tang is a large lamb shank served
on the bone with rich gravy, while 'sherpa hot' is a dish that looks as
if it has come from Lancashire – lamb curry is topped with discs of
potato, giving a new credibility to the term hotpot. Vegetable dishes
are also attractive; rato farsi is a mild curry made with pumpkin.
Gurkhas Diner deserves your support for daring to do something
different, and for the genuine smiley welcome.

Metro Garden Restaurant & Bar

9 Clapham Common South Side, SW4 ■ 020 7627 0632

⊖ Clapham Common

🍽 Modern British

🕐 Mon to Fri 18.00–23.00; Sat 12.00–23.00; Sun 12.00–22.30

🖰 www.metromotel.co.uk

🗗 all major credit cards except AmEx ■ 12.5% optional service added

££ starters £3.95–£6.95 ■ mains £10.95–£14.50 ■ sides £1.95–£3.25 ■ desserts £3.50–£8.95 ■ set dinner £23.50 & £27 ■ lowest bottle price £12.50

✪ Your own secret garden

As you emerge from the southern exit of Clapham Common tube station, Metro is facing you – which is presumably how the place came by its name. Over the last couple of years the charming 'secret' garden has become such a widely known secret that the proprietors finally bit the bullet and changed the name to include it. As you'd expect of any establishment thoughtful enough to provide blankets for the dogs of Sunday brunchers lingering over the newspapers in the secluded garden, the Metro Garden Restaurant has become something of a neighbourhood favourite. The food is interesting, but mercifully wholehearted. Start with sautéed lambs' livers, sage and thyme polenta, caramelised baby onions, balsamic reduction, or pan-roast scallops, butterbean and sage purée and crisp pancetta. Or perhaps the deep-fried salt and pepper squid on wilted greens appeals? Main courses include enough brave combinations of taste and texture for the adventurous diner, and the kitchen casts the net widely for inspiration – rare tuna fillet may come with a lemon thyme and pink peppercorn crust, plus rocket and Parmesan mash; or a Moroccan-style merguez stew may be teamed with apricot couscous; or roast duck breast with pak choi, juniper and honey jus. Puds are mainstream: ginger and caramel cheesecake with candied orange; coffee panacotta with mint pesto; lemon tart with raspberry coulis; the renowned and over-indulgent chocolate nemesis – the chocoholic's dish of choice. The service is slick but friendly, the wine list sound rather than adventurous.

Pomino

35 Bellevue Road, SW17 ■ 020 8672 5888

⊖ BR Wandsworth Common

🍽 Italian

🕘 Mon to Fri 11.00–15.30 & 17.00–23.00; Sat & Sun 11.00–16.00 (brunch) & 17.00–23.00 (22.30 Sun)

🔗 www.pomino.com

🖥 all major credit cards except AmEx ■ 12.5% 'optional' service added

££ starters £4–£7.50 ■ mains £7.50–£12.50 ■ sides £2.75–£3 ■ desserts £4–£6.70 ■ lowest bottle price £9

✪ Chic neighbourhood Italian

This place was once the Surrey Tavern until it got a well-judged makeover from the group behind Christopher's (see p. 178). Now it's Pomino, a middleweight Italian restaurant, and they deserve our congratulations for not banging out yet another stereotype gastropub. The décor is sledgehammer subtle, lots and lots of blue and white tiles; there is a stainless steel open kitchen and some high tables with stools; otherwise it is all reassuringly restauranty. And so is the menu. Starters include ribolita – the hearty Tuscan bean and veg soup; carpaccio of beef with rocket and pecorino; a salad of octopus with cannellini beans, tomato and basil. The antipasto Pomino is made up from very decent charcuterie cut to order. There is also bruschetta – tomatoes and olive oil, and a salad of rocket and bitter leaves with sweet raisins, pecorino and balsamic dressing. The home-made pasta is very sound: rigatoni comes with tomato, buffalo mozzarella and basil – good mozzarella and the pasta cooked suitably al dente. The main courses touch all the comfort bases; there are grilled Tuscan fennel sausages with cannellini beans – good meaty sausages, good beans, this plateful could pose as a pin-up entitled 'hearty fare'. Then there's roast leg of duck with olives and braised endive, or roast red snapper with cherry tomatoes, celery and saffron sauce. Puds are sound. The wine list goes from plonk to super-Tuscan fairly briskly and service is slick.

Ransome's Dock

35–36 Parkgate Road, SW11 ■ 020 7223 1611 &

⊖ BR Battersea Park

🍴 British

🕐 Mon to Fri 12.00–23.00; Sat 12.00–24.00; Sun 12.00–15.30

🖰 www.ransomesdock.co.uk

🗗 all major credit cards ■ 12.5% optional service added

££ starters £5.25–£8.50 ■ mains £10.50–£21.50 ■ sides £3–£4
■ desserts £5–£7 ■ set lunch £14.75 ■ lowest bottle price £12.50

✪ A British restaurant with notable wine list

Ransome's Dock is a versatile restaurant, both formal enough
for those little celebrations or occasions with friends, and informal
enough to pop into for a single dish at the bar. The food is good,
seasonal and made with carefully sourced ingredients. Dishes are
well cooked, satisfying and unfussy; the wine list is encyclopedic; and
service is friendly and efficient. All in all, Martin Lam and his team
have got it just right. Everything stems from the raw ingredients: the
bread may be from Poilâne; the potted shrimps from Morecambe
Bay; they dicker with the Montgomerys over prime Cheddar cheeses.
The menu changes monthly, but the philosophy behind it does not.
There's an extensive brunch menu at the weekend. Before rampaging
off through the main menu, make a pit stop at the daily specials;
if nothing tempts you, turn to the seven or eight starters. If it's
on, make a beeline for the grilled Norfolk smoked eel, with warm
buckwheat pancake and crème fraîche. It's very rich, very good
and very large. Or there may be Perroche goats' cheese with pear
and roast pepper salad, or Morecambe Bay potted shrimps with
wholemeal toast. Main courses are well balanced – Dutch calf's liver
may come with spinach and roast garlic mash. Or there's Trelough
duck breast with Oloroso sherry-braised vegetables. Or there may be
a 'shorthorn' sirloin steak with piquillo pepper butter and big chips.
Puddings run from the complicated – a hot prune and Armagnac
soufflé with Armagnac custard, to the simple – rhubarb fool.

Tabaq

47 Balham Hill, SW12 ▪ 020 8673 7820

⊖ Clapham South

🍽 Indian

🕑 Mon to Sat 12.00–14.45 & 18.00–23.30

🖰 www.tabaq.co.uk

🖶 all major credit cards ▪ no service added

££ starters £2.95–£6.25 ▪ mains £5.50–£12.50 ▪ sides £1.50–£5.95
▪ desserts £2.75–£6 ▪ lowest bottle price £9.95

✪ Sophisticated Pakistani cooking

The owners of Tabaq used to drive up from the suburbs to work in a smart West End restaurant and on the way they would travel along Balham Hill and past Clapham Common. They had set their sights on having a restaurant of their own, smarter than the usual curry house, somewhere they could serve traditional Pakistani specialities. They took over no. 47 and named it after the tabaq – a large serving dish. Over a decade later they have a shelf full of awards and a restaurant full of loyal customers to show for it. The menu comes with a multitude of sections: starters, grills, seafood, chicken curries, specialties, rice, breads and natural vegetables. To start, go straight for the tandoor and grill section, which features some of the best dishes on the menu. Seekh kabab Lahori is made from well-seasoned minced lamb. Or try the masala machli Lahori – fish in a light and spicy batter. As an accompaniment, order a naan-e-Punjabi – a heavy, butter-rich bread from the tandoor – with kachomer, a kind of coarse-cut Asian salsa. At this stage of your meal you may well be tempted to choose simply from the salan, or chicken curries. There's murgh taway ka makhani – this sauce is thought to be a buttery ancestor of chicken tikka masala, or murgh palak, chicken and spinach. Desserts include one item you do not immediately associate with Pakistani cuisine – baked Alaska, which serves two and must be ordered in advance.

Tsunami

Unit 3, 1–7 Voltaire Road, SW4 ■ 020 7978 1610

⊖ Clapham North

🍴 Japanese

🕐 Mon to Fri 18.00–23.00; Sat 12.30–23.30

🖱 www.tsunamijapaneserestaurant.co.uk

🗗 all major credit cards ■ 12.5% optional service added

££ starters £3.50–£9.95 ■ mains £7–£16.50 ■ sides £2 ■ desserts £3.95–£5.95 ■ lowest bottle price £12

✪ Neighbourhood Japanese – but more so

The dining room at Tsunami is surprisingly large and elegant in a minimalist, Japanesey sort of way. All the staff are helpful and friendly, and the kitchen bustles away in full view through a long serving hatch. The restaurant is at the end of Clapham High Street that is nearest to Brixton, which is very much an area in transition. Scruffy shops gave way to trendy bars and in turn these are gradually being supplanted by ambitious restaurants, of which Tsunami is the perfect example. The food is very good, the presentation on the plate is quite outstanding, and the bill is not over-the-top. For once all those pretty-as-a-picture arrangements seem to stem from a genuine love of the beautiful. Order a few starters to share. The kataifi prawns with creamy spicy sauce is very good – plump prawns in crispy overcoats. Or there's sunkiss sashimi – seared with hot olive oil and dressed with ponzu: salmon or scallop. Or the kawari age – tempura made with black cod. Best of all is the tuna tataki, which is a sashimi made with seared tuna and dressed with a sharp ponzu dressing. Each slice is raw in the middle and firm around the edge – very delicious indeed. The tempura is light and crisp – asparagus, carrot, pumpkin. From the main dishes, an old favourite, hira unagi – grilled marinated eel – comes with rice and miso soup; 'prime Scottish fillet beef' comes with balsamic teriyaki soy; and the now ubiquitous black cod comes with sweet miso. Puds are accessible and service friendly.

Bermondsey and Borough

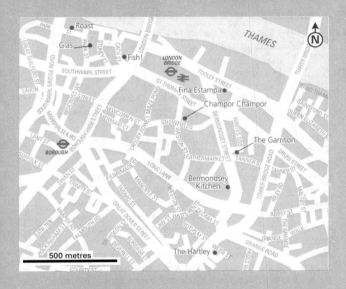

Bermondsey Kitchen

194 Bermondsey Street, SE1 ■ 020 7407 5719   ♿

⊖ London Bridge

🍴 Modern British

🕐 Mon to Fri 12.00–15.00 & 18.30–10.30; Sat 09.30–23.00; Sun
09.30–15.30

🖰 www. bermondseykitchen.co.uk

🗐 all major credit cards ■ 12.5% optional service added

££ brunch Sat & Sun £6–£9 ■ starters £4.50–£6 ■ mains £9–£13 ■ sides
£2.95 lowest bottle price £12.95

✪ Comfortable eating

**When all the old pubs in a neighbourhood have been converted
into gastropubs,** the next logical development is to start building
gastropubs, from scratch. The Bermondsey Kitchen was at the
forefront of this trend, but it still clings stubbornly to the gastropub
ethos – there is a daily changing (and commendably short) menu,
prices are very reasonable and the bar is busy with local trade. The
presentation of the dishes here is gratifyingly straightforward; there
is a welcome absence of towers and complication, and plenty of
strong flavours. Among the starters you may find poached mussels
with anchovy aïoli; a bruschetta featuring wild mushrooms sautéed
in garlic butter; or a plateful of fine charcuterie – Serrano ham,
lomo, chorizo and salchichon. Main courses split two fish, veggie,
and two meat. There may be Longhorn rib-eye steak with cinnamon
and pumpkin mash; chicken breast with braised chicory, vine
tomato and basil sauce; grilled tuna with warm pepper, mangetout,
black olive salad and salsa verde. The kitchen buys well: look out
for the stunning rare-breed meats from the 'Ginger Pig' farm. The
imaginative vegetable accompaniments and side dishes are worthy
of special mention – sprout tops with Seville orange butter; harissa-
fried potatoes; celeriac remoulade. Puds are trad and satisfying – hot
chocolate pudding or tiramisù; and there are carefully chosen British
cheeses on offer. The wine list here will please almost everybody, since
bottles range from sound and cheap to mid-range and interesting.

Champor Champor

62 Weston Street, SE1 ■ 020 7403 4600   ♿

⊖ London Bridge

🍴 Asian eclectic

🕐 Mon to Sat 18.15–22.15 (lunch by appointment for 6 or more)

🖥 www.champor-champor.com

🗄 all major credit cards ■ 15% optional service added

££ menus: £22 (2 courses) & £26.50 (3 courses); tasting menu £39.50 (7 courses) ■ lowest bottle price £13

✪ Glam décor and glam cooking

You are unlikely to stumble into Champor Champor by accident, as this brightly painted, genuinely eccentric, little restaurant is marooned on the barren shores of Weston Street. The two proprietors describe the food as 'creative Malay-Asian' and the chef, Adu Amran Hassan, not only handles the presentation of the dishes, but also the interior design. Despite various expansions and revamps the resto still only seats 40, but there is a 'members' lounge' downstairs. The food is tough to categorise, but the presentation is sophisticated and stylish and all the flavours are agreeably up-front. The menu changes with the seasons. To start, there may be baked pigeon breast in roti chanai parcel with a Malay curry sauce; steamed tilapia with turmeric leaf; crab and coconut bisque; or cassava cake with banana crisps and a wild mushroom sauce. Do not be disheartened by the unfamiliarity of these dishes – ingredients are carefully matched and flavours work well. Main courses are equally eclectic: masala lamb fillet is served with an aubergine mousse and an onion and wasabi sauce, or how about duck wontons served with a mandarin and palm sugar sauce and a duck liver sambal? This is well-judged adventurous cookery and makes a pleasant change. Even the desserts are suitably exotic – 'chocolate slice, roast parsnip and honey ice cream' touches several bases. The wine list is also refined, but fairly priced, and there is a range of moody Asian beers.

Fina Estampa

150 Tooley Street, SE1 ■ 020 7403 1342　　　　　　　　&

⊖ London Bridge

⦿ Peruvian

🕐 Mon to Fri 12.00–22.30; Sat & Sun 18.00–22.30

🖰 www.finaestampa.co.uk

🖬 all major credit cards ■ 10% optional service added

££ starters £3.90–£9.50 ■ mains £10.95–£15.95 ■ sides 50p–£2
　■ desserts £3.95 ■ lowest bottle price £13.50

★ Trad Peruvian food hits town

While London is awash with ethnic eateries, Fina Estampa's
proud boast is that it is the capital's only Peruvian restaurant (if you
discount Nobu, p. 87). The husband-and-wife team running this
place certainly tries hard to enlighten the customers, and bring a
little downtown Lima to London Bridge. With its fresh cream-, gold-
and coffee-coloured interior, Fina Estampa has a warm and bright
ambience and upbeat music, and the attentive, friendly staff add
greatly to this vibe. The menu is traditional Peruvian, which means
there's a great emphasis placed upon seafood. This is reflected in
the starters, with such offerings as chupe de camarones, a succulent
shrimp-based soup; cebiche, a dish of marinated white fish served
with sweet potatoes; and jalea, a vast plate of fried seafood. Ask for
the salsa criolla – its hot oiliness is a perfect accompaniment. There
is also causa rellena, described as a 'potato surprise' and it is exactly
that: layers of cold mashed potato, avocado and tuna fish served
with salsa – the surprise being how something so straightforward
can taste so good. Main courses – the fragrant chicken seco, chicken
cooked in a coriander sauce, or the superb lomo saltado, tender strips
of rump steak stir-fried with red onions and tomatoes – are worthy
ambassadors for this simple yet distinctive cuisine. Perhaps most
distinctive of all is the carapulcra, a spicy dish made of dried potatoes,
pork, chicken and cassava – top choice for anyone seeking a new
culinary adventure.

Fish!

Cathedral Street, SE1 ■ 020 7407 3803   ⅌

⊖ London Bridge

🍴 Fish

🕐 Mon to Sat 11.30–23.00; Sun 12.00–22.00

🖥 www.fishdiner.co.uk

🗄 all major credit cards ■ 12.5% optional service added

££ starters £4.95–£8.95 ■ mains £9.95–£16.95 ■ sides £1.50–£3.95 ■ desserts £4.25–£5.95 ■ children's menu £6.95 ■ lowest bottle price £13.95

✪ Fish! it says, and fish is what it does

The Fish! Group of restaurants has been through a turbulent time. The majority of the chain has fallen by the wayside, but this restaurant (which was the first site) is still plugging away trying to convert Brits into fish-lovers. The feel is large and airy due to the glass walls and there's a courtyard for alfresco eating, plus bar seating for armchair chefs who like to watch the real ones at work. The good intentions of the place, however, are still apparent. The restaurant is a 'GM free-zone', and the claim is that all cod comes from sustainable fisheries in Icelandic waters. There's a lengthy printed list of fishy contenders, a number of which will be available depending on what the market has come up with. You select your favourite from those available, choose whether you want it steamed or grilled, and then opt for salsa, Hollandaise, herb butter and garlic butter, or red wine fish gravy to go with it. Create your own combo. The choice ranges from organic salmon, through sea bream, to Dover sole, by way of a dozen others. Portions are large and the fish is fresh. The left side of the menu offers starters like prawn cocktail and Thai crabcakes, while main dishes include fishcake; tuna burger with chips; or fish and chips with mushy peas. If you like a traditional approach to fish, Fish! won't disappoint. Puddings include stalwarts like bread-and-butter pudding; apple crumble; or chocolate tart. The house white, a Sauvignon, is light, crisp and fairly priced.

The Garrison

90 Bermondsey Street, SE1 ■ 020 7089 9355 ⛪

⊖ London Bridge

🍴 Modern British/gastropub

🕐 Mon to Fri 08.00–12.00 & 18.30–22.30; Sat 09.00–11.30, 12.00–15.30 & 18.00–22.30; Sun 09.00–11.30, 12.00–15.30 & 18.00–21.30

🖥 www.thegarrison.co.uk

🗔 all major credit cards ■ 12.5% optional service added

££ starters £4.50–£6.70 ■ mains £9.50–£16 ■ sides £2.70–£3 ■ desserts £4.50 ■ lowest bottle price £12.50

⭐ Gastropub and cinema

The Garrison may be unique in that it is a gastropub that opened on a site that was formerly … a gastropub! This place was previously The Honest Cabbage before it was reborn under new management as The Garrison. There is now a row of cramped banquettes plus some tall counters with bar stools. It's a lively place and the menu divides into three sections – good-value bar snacks such as Welsh rarebit or whitebait, a brunch menu at the weekends, and the pukka menu, which is short and to the point. You'll get to pick from four starters (unless you import a fish finger sarnie from the bar snacks list) and half a dozen mains. They will probably be fairly ambitious dishes like seared foie gras, roasted mango brioche and aged balsamic; shellfish bisque, crab and tarragon wonton; or a game terrine with toast and pickles. But you could also look under the heading 'salads' – feta with spiced breadcrumbs, or Gorgonzola, pear, pink grapefruit and chicory. Mains are equally sophisticated – grilled bream, roast fennel, ratatouille dressing; roast magret of duck, spiced apricot, shallot and thyme jus, fondant potato; or twice-baked goats' cheese soufflé, shallot and Parmesan cream. For pud there is a cheeseboard (from Neal's Yard); sticky toffee pudding; chocolate fudge brownie with crème fraiche; and rather good home-made ice creams – the caramel ice cream gets three stars as does the malted milk, with the white peach sorbet getting an honourable two stars.

Glas

3 Park Street, SE1 ■ 020 7357 6060

⊖ London Bridge

🍴 Swedish

🕒 Tues to Sat 12.00–14.30 & 18.30–22.00

🖰 www.glasrestaurant.com

🖶 all major credit cards ■ 12.5% optional service added

££ cold dishes £3.95–£8.95 ■ hot dishes £4.95–£9.95 ■ dessert £3.95–£6.95 ■ lowest bottle price £14.95

✪ Swedish showcase

The Borough Market is something of a honeypot for foodies and as well as the stalls and shops there's an increasing portfolio of restaurants. Glas is on Park Street, directly under the rumbling railway line, and offers a well-judged combination of Swedish cooking, a grazing menu and fair prices. It's a light, bright restaurant where the décor verges on pale: light walls, bleached wood floor, white tables. The staff are pleasant and will help you through the intricacies of the 'grazing' menu. The best ordering strategy is to fire an opening salvo, and then a couple of follow ups – that way you can reprise any dish you particularly enjoy. At the front of your order you should include some herring. Swedes are obsessed with herring and if all herrings were as good as these perhaps we would be, too. Vodka and lime herring is meaty, fresh and delicious; but then so is the glamastar herring – a gentle pickle; the curry herring is also good. You could also select white bean soup; duck foie gras terrine; roast reindeer. The more complex dishes show off the talent in the kitchen: scallops are teamed with sweetbreads and served with salsify and trout roe – surprisingly successful. Or there's roast venison with liquorice sauce and curly kale, or hot smoked salmon. Puds don't appear to be wildly Swedish – chocolate and orange mousse. Service is sound and the wine list accessible – but it is easy to plump for a beer named 'Kronlein's Crocodile'.

The Hartley

64 Tower Bridge Road, SE1 ■ 020 7394 7023

⊖ Bermondsey

🍽 Modern British/gastropub

🕐 Mon to Fri 12.00–15.00 & 18.00–22.00; Sat 11.00–16.00 & 18.00–22.00; Sun 12.00–21.00

🖰 www.thehartley.com

🖻 all major credit cards ■ 12.5% optional service added

££ starters £4–£7 ■ mains £8–£14 ■ sides £2.50–£3 ■ desserts £4.50–£6.50 ■ lowest bottle price £11.50

✪ Gastropub deserves to be jammed

Hartley, as in the famous jam maker. The Hartley company's old jam factory is on the other side of Tower Bridge Road and has been redeveloped into expensive loft apartments. So in this instance it's a case of where once there was jam there's now plenty of bread. This gastropub aims at the newer, richer locals, the food is very good indeed, and prices are competitive. The chef knows his stuff: big flavours, brave combinations of ingredients, unfussy dishes, unpretentious food. The blackboard features the daily specials and the menu itself changes from time to time. Setting aside the merits of 'tripe, chorizo and chips', go straight for the smoked eel, horseradish and rocket – inch-square cubes of fried potato make a perfect foil for fluffy horseradish cream, rocket and a melted butter and chive sauce. This is stunning, a truly great combo. There will be a terrine on the menu – perhaps made from confit duck and Toulouse sausage. Skilful stuff and good to eat. Mains run from macaroni cheese, truffle, poached egg and baby spinach, to a salt cod fishcake, green salad, fat cut chips and aioli. The tartlet of veal sweetbreads, ox tongue, black pudding and grain mustard is a very confident dish, admirably crisp pastry, the various meats piled on top of a mound of spinach perked up with grain mustard. Puds appeal – hot chocolate tart with vanilla ice cream. The wine list is on a blackboard over the bar and offers sound bottles at sensible prices; service is informal and friendly.

Roast

The Floral Hall, Borough Market, SE1 ■ 020 7940 1300

⊖ London Bridge

🍽 British

🕐 Mon to Fri 07.00–10.00, 12.00–15.00, 17.30–23.00; Sat 07.00–
12.00, 12.00–16.00, 18.00–23.00; Sun 12.00–16.00

🗗 www.roast-restaurant.com

🗄 all major credit cards ■ 12.5% optional service added

££ starters £6–£12.50 ■ mains £10.50–£18 ■ sides £2.80–£3.50
■ desserts £5.50 ■ pre-/post-theatre £18 & £21 ■ lowest bottle price
£14

✪ Stunningly beautiful space, resolutely British food

Borough Market provides an essential focus for all London foodies
and Roast aims to make sure that in this welter of gourmet activity
British cooking gets a fair shout. As an objective this is so worthwhile,
so long awaited and so deserving of your support that you should
make a booking now without worrying about the fine detail like food,
service and ambience. But you need not worry – the dining room is
outstandingly beautiful, a glazed box 'hanging' over the busy food
market. By day the sunshine streams in (when there is any) and by
night your view may be of floodlit St Paul's in all its glory. The menu
at Roast is rewritten twice a day to make the most of the advantages
of having a kitchen at the heart of the market. Starters range from
grilled Cornish pilchards; to Golden Cross goats' cheese with pickled
pears and spiced breadcrumbs; and Dublin Bay prawns with cook's
salad cream. Then there's a section of roasts and grills – Dover sole
fillet with chickweed and melted butter, or a roast lamb leg stuffed
with apricots. And main courses like hake with melted potted shrimps
and crab butter; steak and kidney pudding; or Northfield farm beef
and mustard sausages. The ingredients are fresh and the cooking
good. Puds are trad, service is charming and the wine list has some
Brit wines and a good many Brit beers.

Brixton, Dulwich and Herne Hill

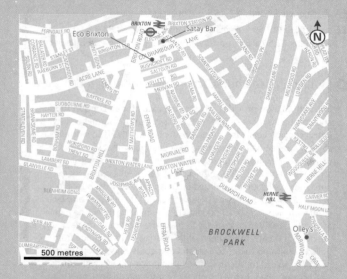

Eco Brixton

4 Market Row, Brixton Market, Electric Lane, SW9

■ 020 7738 3021

⊖ Brixton

🍽 Pizza

🕐 Mon & Tues, Thurs to Sat 08.00–17.00

🖰 www.ecorestaurants.com

🖰 all major credit cards except AmEx ■ no service added

££ starters £2–£4 ■ mains £5.20–£7.90 ■ sides £3.20 ■ desserts £4.50
■ unlicensed, BYO (no corkage)

✪ Top-notch pizzas

If you're in Brixton Market around noon, Eco is a must for your
lunch break. You may have to share a table (and then after queuing
among the shuffling shoppers), but you can always study the menu
while you wait. Formerly Pizzeria Franco, now Eco Brixton, this place
has the same menu as its sister, Eco, on Clapham High Street, but
the Brixton branch closes at 17.00. It's small and popular, so things
can get hectic. Still, the service is friendly, the pizzas crisp and the
salads mountainous. Plus there is an identically priced takeaway
menu. All the famous pizzas are here, including a pleasingly pungent
Napoletana with the sacred trio of anchovies, olives and capers, and
quattro stagioni, packed full of goodies. But why not try something
less familiar, such as aubergine and sun-dried tomato? Or enjoy
la dolce vita, where rocket, mushrooms and Dolcelatte all vie for
attention? Or even the amore, with its French beans, artichoke,
pepper and aubergine? Or one of the calzone? It's a difficult
choice. For a lighter meal – lighter only because of the absence of
carbohydrate – try a salad. Tricolore is made with baby mozzarella,
beef tomato, avocado and olives. Side orders like the melted
cheese bread and mushroom bread are highly recommended. For
sandwiches, Eco also impresses. Focaccia is stuffed with delights like
Parma ham and rocket, or mozzarella and avocado. You could also
go for starters, but at lunch they seem a little surplus to requirements.

→ For branches, see index or website

Olley's
67–69 Norwood Road, SE24 ▪ 020 8671 8259   ⚬

⊖ BR Herne Hill

🍴 Fish & chips

🕐 Mon 17.00–22.30; Tues to Sun 12.00–22.30

🖰 www.olleys.info

🗗 all major credit cards except AmEx ▪ no service added

££ tapas £3–£6 ▪ starters £3.70–£4.05 ▪ mains £6.45–£16.45 ▪ sides
£1–£2.75 ▪ desserts £3.25–£5.95 ▪ daily lunch special £5 ▪ lowest
bottle price £10.95

✪ Prize-winning fish and chips

Olley's is single-minded: this is a famous fish and chip shop. It is
famous partly because it has won various awards, and partly because
it mounts a tireless publicity offensive. Olley's is just across the road
from Brockwell Park, and gently expands to take over one shop front
after another until the dining room is now a whopping 90-seater.
There is a separate area devoted to takeaway. The list of starters is
to the point. You can opt for fresh grilled sardines; prawn cocktail;
or battered calamari. On to more serious matters – the chips are
good here. Niazi believes in pre-blanching, and when done well this
technique guarantees chips that are fluffy inside and crisp outside.
The mushy peas are commendable and so are the wallys – which
non-Londoners will know better as gherkins. The fish is a triumph:
fresh, white and flaky inside, crisp and golden outside – obviously
the fryer knows his craft. Setting aside the matter of chips, the leader
board reads as follows: cod, plaice, haddock, salmon, monkfish,
swordfish, halibut and hake. You can also choose to have your fish
grilled or steamed, which is the best way when it comes to sea bass
or Dover sole. Desserts are steady, and there is a whole menu of
liqueur coffees. If you have the temerity to ask for a fish and *large*
chips, the plateful that arrives is so large that the staff must be taking
the proverbial.

Satay Bar

447 Coldharbour Lane, SW9 ■ 020 7326 5001   &

⊖ Brixton

▮⊙▮ Indonesian

⏲ Mon to Fri 12.00–17.00 & 18.00–23.00; Sat & Sun 13.00–17.00 &
18.00–23.00

⌁ www.sataybar.co.uk

🗗 all major credit cards ■ 12.5% optional service added

££ starters £3.45–£6.45 ■ mains £4.95–£7.65 ■ sides £4.95 ■ desserts
£3.25–£3.75 ■ set lunch & dinner £13.95 ■ lowest bottle price
£11.95

❂ Loud bar, loud Indonesian food

Tucked away behind the Ritzy cinema, the Satay Bar is a lively resto
and bar (or perhaps that should be bar and resto). Be warned that the
background music is foreground music, so – party, party, party! If you
are old and grizzly this may not appeal, but otherwise settle in, relax
and take a look at the art. Should you like one of the many paintings
adorning the walls, buy it – they are for sale. Dishes are Indonesian
with the chilli factor toned down (for the most part) to accommodate
European taste buds. The menu is a testing one – at least when it
comes to pronouncing the names of the dishes – but the food is well
cooked, service is friendly and efficient, and the prices are reasonable.
Your waiter will smile benignly at your attempt to say udang goreng
tepung – lightly battered, deep-fried king prawns served with a sweet
chilli sauce. Obvious choices, such as the chicken or prawn satay, are
highly rated. Or try the chicken wings with garlic and green chilli.
The hottest dishes are to be found among the curries. Even though
styled 'medium', kari ikan, a red snapper-based, Javanese fish curry,
packs a punch, while the rendang ayam, a spicy chicken dish, is only
cooled by the addition of a coconut sauce. For something lighter, the
mee goreng is a satisfying dish of spicy egg noodles fried with lamb,
prawns and vegetables, or there's gado-gado, a side dish of bean
curd and vegetables with spicy peanut sauce, which is almost a meal
in itself.

Kennington and Vauxhall

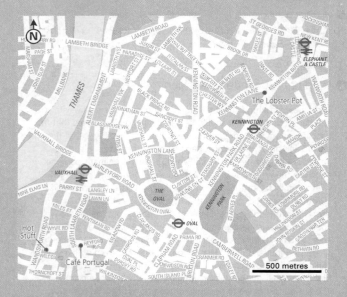

Café Portugal

Victoria House, South Lambeth Road, SW8 ■ 020 7587 1962 ♿

⊖ Vauxhall

🍽 Portuguese

🕐 Mon to Sun 06.30–23.00

🔗 www.cafeportugal.com

🗟 all major credit cards ■ no service added

££ starters £3.50–£5.20 ■ mains £7–£12.50 ■ desserts £2.60 ■ lowest
bottle price £9

⭐ Portugal on every channel

**The first item on any proud new Portuguese restaurateur's
shopping list must be the telly.** All the televisions in South Lambeth
Road seem to be turned up loud, and the one in the bar of Café
Portugal is no exception (thankfully, the one in the restaurant-half of
the operation is not always switched on). Portuguese entrepreneurs
have all mastered the trick of integrating their establishments with
the community and Café Portugal is a laid-back, easy-paced kind
of eatery with distinctly dodgy mud-orange décor. The food is
workmanlike and appears authentically Portuguese. To start with, you
can opt for calamares fritos, and sopa do día, the soup of the day. Or
more interesting dishes like ameijoas a Café Portugal, which are clams
and must be a step up on that trusty old Portuguese special, avocado
with prawns. Then there are a dozen fishy options, including lobster,
sea bass, Dover sole, monkfish and salt cod. Bacalhau à Gomes de
Sá turns out to be a stunning and gloriously simple dish of salt cod
cooked in the oven with potatoes, onions and chunks of hard-boiled
egg. For the meat-eater there's carne de porco à Alentejana, another
all-in-one, home-cooked kind of meal in which small chunks of pork
are served with some clams, chorizo and chopped pickled vegetables,
with small cubes of crisp-fried potato scattered over the top. At
Café Portugal puddings are largely pastries and you are doomed if
you don't like eggy confections. Reasonably priced and interesting
Portuguese wines.

Hot Stuff

19 Wilcox Road, SW8 ■ 020 7720 1480

⊖ Vauxhall/Stockwell

|●| Indian

⏱ Mon to Fri 12.00–22.00; Sat 15.00–22.00

🖑 www.eathotstuff.com

🖰 all major credit cards ■ no service added

££ starters 85p–£6 ■ mains £2–£7 ■ sides £2.50–£3 ■ desserts £1.50–£2 ■ unlicensed, BYO (no corkage)

✪ Small, Indian and hot stuff

Run by the Dawood family, this tiny restaurant is something of an institution. Despite expansion and full use of the pavement in the summer, it has only a few seats and offers simple and startlingly cheap food to an enthusiastic local following. The food is just what you would expect to get at home – assuming you were part of Nairobi's Asian community. Trade is good and the dining room, though unprepossessing, is welcoming: all soft blues and orange with an array of different-coloured chairs. The starters are sound rather than glorious, so it's best to dive straight into the curries. There are various chicken curries and lamb curries, all keenly priced. It is hard to find any fault with such a cheap dinner. The most expensive option is in the fish section: king prawn biryani, which costs about the same as you would pay for a curried potato in the West End. The portions aren't monster sized, and the spicing isn't subtle, but the welcome is genuine and the bill is tiny. Try the delights of the stuffed paratha – light and crispy with potato in the middle, they taste seriously delicious. Chickpea curry, daal soup and mixed vegetable curry all hit the spot with vegetarians. For meat-eaters, the chicken Madras is hot and workmanlike, while the chicken bhuna is rich and very good. Hot Stuff closes prudently before the local pubs turn out, and part of the fun here is to watch latecomers – say, a party of three arriving at 21.50 and seeking food. Promising to eat very simply and very quickly may do the trick.

The Lobster Pot

3 Kennington Lane, SE11 ■ 020 7582 5556

⊖ Kennington

🍽 Very French/fish

🕐 Tues to Sat 12.00–14.30 & 19.00–23.00

🖥 www. thelobsterpotrestaurant.co.uk

🖥 all major credit cards ■ 12.5% optional service added

££ starters £8.50–£12.50 ■ mains £15.50–£18.50 ■ desserts £5.30
   ■ menus: lunch (weekdays only) £11.50 & £14.50; dinner £21.50
   ■ lowest bottle price £12.50

⭐ Very French, very fishy

You have to feel for Nathalie Régent. What must it be like to be
married to – and working alongside – a man whose love of the
bizarre verges on the obsessional? Britain is famed for breeding
dangerously potty chefs, but The Lobster Pot's chef patron, Hervé
Régent, originally from Vannes in Brittany, is well ahead of the field.
Walk down Kennington Lane towards the restaurant and it's even
money as to whether you are struck first by the life-size painted
plywood cutout of Hervé dressed in oilskins, or the speakers relaying
a soundtrack of seagulls and melancholy Breton foghorns. These
clues all point towards fish. The fish here is pricey, but it is fresh and
well chosen. Starters range from well-made, very thick, traditional
fish soup, to a really proper plateau de fruits de mer. The main course
specials sometimes feature strange fish that Hervé has discovered at
Billingsgate. As well as classics like l'aile de raie au beurre noisette
(skate with brown butter), there are good spicy dishes, such as filet
de thon à la Créole, which is tuna with a perky tomato sauce. Simpler,
and as good in its way, is les crevettes grillées à l'ail, big prawns in
garlic butter. The accompanying bread is notable, a soft, doughy pain
rustique, and for once le plateau de fromage à la Française doesn't
disappoint. The Lobster Pot's weekday set lunch makes lots of sense.
It could get you smoked salmon pâté, followed by pan-fried plaice
goujons, and crêpe sauce à la mangue.

Putney

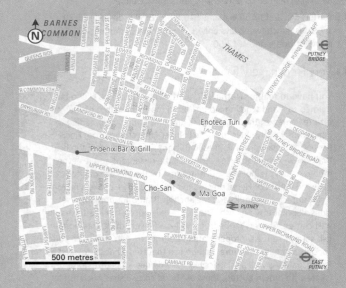

Cho-San

292 Upper Richmond Road, SW15 ■ 020 8788 9626

⊖ BR Putney

🍴 Japanese

🕐 Tues to Fri 18.30–22.30; Sat & Sun 12.00–14.30 & 18.30–22.30

💳 Mastercard, Visa ■ 12.5% optional service added

££ sushi £3–£5.90 (for 2 pieces) ■ mains £7–£10 ■ desserts £2.60–£4.50
■ sashimi/sushi boat £19.90 ■ lowest bottle price £12.50; sake £3.50

✪ Neighbourhood Japanese restaurant

Too many Japanese restaurants use extremely high prices and
ultra-swish West End premises to keep themselves to themselves. As
a European adventurer basking in the impeccably polite and attentive
service, it's hard not to feel a little anxious. What should you order?
How do you eat it? Will it taste nice? How much does it cost? If you
have ever been assailed by these worries you should pop along to
Cho-San in Putney. This is your chance to try all those dishes you have
never had, without wounding your pocket. The sushi is good. The
sashimi is good. And a giant boat of assorted sushi and sashimi, with
miso soup and dessert, is both good and good value. But why not
try some more obscure sushi? The price of even the fancier items is
reasonable here. Or, if you prefer your fish cooked, choose the perfect
tempura cuttlefish – a stunning achievement, its batter light enough
to levitate. And then there are always the kushiage dishes, where
something is put onto a skewer, gets an egg and breadcrumb jacket
and is treated to a turn around the deep-fryer. Ordering tori kushiage
gets you two skewers, chicken and a chunk of sweet onion. Delicious.
Or opt for tempura king prawn. Then there are the meat dishes, the
fish dishes, the rice dishes, the soba noodles, and the hot sakes, cold
sakes and beers. You could eat your way to a good understanding of
Japanese food here. Ask the charming, helpful staff and get stuck in.

Enoteca Turi

28 Putney High Street, SW15 ■ 020 8785 4449 &

⊖ Putney Bridge

|O| Italian

🕐 Mon to Sat 12.30–14.30 & 19.00–23.00

🖯 www.enotecaturi.com

🖶 all major credit cards; no cheques ■ 12.5% optional service added

££ starters £6.50–£10.50 ■ mains £10.50–£17.50 ■ sides £3–£3.50
■ desserts £5.50–£6.50 ■ lunch menu £13.50 & £16.50 ■ lowest
bottle price £12.50

✪ Italian wines, a long list and a strong list

**If you like your Italian food a little more adventurous than the
usual,** then it is worth making the journey to Putney and Giuseppe
Turi's pretty little restaurant. It offers a very genuine and personal
version of Italian regional cooking – Turi himself hails from Apulia,
and many dishes are based on recipes from this area. Enoteca takes
its name from the Italian term for a smart wine shop and there's
a monumental list of more than 90 specialist Italian wines and a
separate by-the-glass menu offering 11 Italian regional wines – an
excellent way to educate the palate. As for the food, at lunch there
is a shortened version of the dinner menu and dishes are a couple of
pounds cheaper. You'd do well to start with asparagus served with
Parmesan-coated, deep-fried egg, or perhaps a plate of antipasto
Pugliese – marinated, grilled vegetables served with a fava purée.
Among pasta dishes may be ravioli di castagne e ricotta, or fettuccine
with Pachino tomatoes. Main courses may include stinco d'agnello
con purée di patate e cipolline, which is lamb shank with spring
onion and potato purée, or petto d'anatra – duck breast served with
new season vegetables and dry marsala sauce. Desserts will test your
mettle – go for the torta di cioccolata con nocciole, a blockbusting
chocolate and hazelnut cake, or perhaps the particularly good,
authentic tiramisù. Booking essential, even midweek. More of a wine
bluff than a wine buff? Check out the wines recommended alongside
each dish.

Ma Goa

244 Upper Richmond Road, SW15 ▪ 020 8780 1767

⊖ BR Putney/East Putney

🍴 Indian

🕐 Mon to Sat 18.30–23.00; Sun 13.00–16.00 & 18.00–22.00

🖱 www.ma-goa.com

🗗 all major credit cards ▪ 12.5% optional service added

££ starters £3.75–£5 ▪ thali £9.95 ▪ mains £7.85–£13.50 ▪ sides £1–£4
  ▪ desserts £3.75–£4 ▪ Sunday lunch buffet £10 ▪ Early Bird (pre-
  20.00, not Sun) £10 & £13 ▪ lowest bottle price £10.95

✪ Goan home cooking

It seems that every year sees a further expansion of this family-run business, but despite the stylish décor, despite the café-style chairs and tables, and the computer system to handle bills and orders, the overwhelming impression you are left with when you visit Ma Goa is of eating in somebody's home. This place is as far as you can possibly get from the chuck-it-in-a-frying-pan-and-heat-it-through school of curry cookery. The food is deceptively simple, slow-cooked and awesomely tasty. The menu is fairly compact: half a dozen starters are followed by a dozen mains, while a blackboard adds a couple of dishes of the day. Shrimp balchao is a starter made from shrimps cooked in pickling spices and curry leaves. Sorpotel is made from lamb's liver, kidney and pork in a sauce rich with roast spices, lime and coriander. The Ma Goa chorizo is rich, too, with palm vinegar, cinnamon and green chillies. Main courses are amazing. The spices are properly cooked out by slow cooking, which makes lifting the lids of the heavy clay serving pots a voyage of discovery. Porco vindaloo, sharp with palm vinegar, is enriched with lumps of pork complete with rind. Ma's fish caldin is a kind of fish stew with large chunks of fish in a coconut-based sauce. Vegetarians are equally well served. Bund gobi is stir-fried, shredded cabbage with carrots, ginger and cumin, while beringella is an aubergine dish made with pickling spices. The rice here is excellent.

Phoenix Bar & Grill

162–164 Lower Richmond Road, SW15 ■ 020 8780 3131   ♿

⊖ BR Putney

🍽 Italian

🕑 Mon to Thurs 12.30–14.30 & 19.00–23.00; Fri & Sat 12.30–15.00 & 19.00–23.30; Sun 12.30–15.00 & 19.00–22.00

🖱 www. sonnys.co.uk

🖯 all major credit cards ■ 12.5% optional service added

££ starters £5.50–£7.50 ■ mains £9.50–£16.50 ■ sides £2.50 ■ desserts £4.50–£6 ■ menus: lunch Mon to Sat £9.50, £13.50 & £15.50 3; dinner Sun to Thurs £10.50, £15.50 & £17.50 ■ lowest bottle price £11.95

✪ Adding tone to the neighbourhood

This restaurant is a member of London's leading family of neighbourhood restaurants and is related to Sonny's (see p. 355). Anyone fancying their chances in what is a cut-throat marketplace would do well to study these establishments. They are all just trendy enough, the service is just slick enough and the cooking is marginally better than you would expect – with competitive pricing. There's a large, white-painted room inside and a large, white-painted courtyard out front where you can eat alfresco. Starters may include a salad of chicory, pears, walnuts and gorgonzola; home-cured bresaola with rocket and shaved Parmesan; grilled scallops with organic leaves, tomato and herb oil; or pumpkin ravioli with sage cream and Parmesan. The famous vincisgrassi maceratesi – an epic eighteenth-century truffled lasagne – is on the menu it is a 'must have' indulgence. Mains range from gnocchi with roast butternut squash and girolles; through roast rump of lamb with grilled sweet potato and glazed shallots; to spiedino of monkfish and scallops on Piedmontese peppers. Among the puds are chocolate cake with toasted almond ice cream; spumone Amaretto; and apple fritters. Service is friendly and the wine list has bottles for most circumstances.

Tooting, Balham and Wimbledon

Balham Kitchen & Bar

15–19 Bedford Hill, SW12 ■ 020 8675 6900   ♿

⊖ Balham

🍽 Modern British

🕐 Mon to Thurs 08.00–23.00; Fri & Sat 08.00–01.00; Sun 08.00–22.30

🖰 www.balhamkitchen.com

🗗 all major credit cards ■ 12.5% optional service added

££ breakfast £2–£12 ■ starters £5–£9.50 ■ mains £9–£25 ■ sides £3
■ desserts £5–£6.50 ■ lunch menu Mon to Fri (12.00–17.00) £10 &
£13 ■ lowest bottle price £12.95

✪ West End slick, transplanted to local resto

As a locale, SW12 is moving up the social scale so fast that you
half expect to see an outbreak of nosebleeds. Perhaps it's all a
response to the Balham Kitchen and Bar? The name may be prosaic,
but this place is part of the SoHo House Club group – we are talking
svelte member's club in Soho, and another SoHo House Club in New
York, somewhere so blisteringly trendy that it featured on *Sex in the
City*. The Balham Kitchen is a large bar, but the size doesn't make the
slightest difference. Even midweek the place is packed. The menu is
carefully constructed along Brasserie lines. The starter section goes
from watercress soup, to moules marinière, and on to hand-carved
Serrano ham. There's a 'small plates' section featuring a skewer
of black pudding and cheese, or perhaps a plate of crispy squid
appeals? Then there's 'salad and sandwiches', which offers a decent
cheeseburger and a well-made Caesar salad, unfussy and dressed
with a cold, soft-boiled egg – very classical. Main courses flirt with
retro: chicken Kiev, or smoked haddock with a rarebit crust. A grilled
rib-eye steak is served with well-made Béarnaise sauce and chips. A
duck pot pie with broad beans is wholly successful, the duck leg sticks
up through the pastry crust and the gravy is very decent. The wine
list is rather shaded by the array of cocktails, but carries on manfully.
Service is crisp.

The Earl Spencer

260 Merton Road, SW18 ■ 020 8870 9244

⊖ Southfields

|●| Modern British/gastropub

🕐 Mon to Sat 12.30–14.30 & 19.00–22.00; Sun 12.00–15.00 & 19.00–21.30

🖰 www.theearlspencer.co.uk

🖶 Mastercard, Visa ■ no service added

££ starters £5–£7.50 ■ mains £7.50–£13 ■ sides £2.50 ■ desserts £4.50–£6.50 ■ lowest bottle price £10

✪ Good pub, good gastro

The Earl Spencer is a cracking gastropub and it is no surprise that it is a past winner of Pub of the Year. There are few design fripperies, the room is plain, large and bare. The bar serves decent beer. Portions are large, prices are very reasonable. Service is friendly, and the wine list offers sound value. The menu is an ever-changing one: things run out, dishes are seasonal. The standard of cooking is always very high. 'Mulligatawny soup, coriander and raita' is a real blast from the past, but a welcome one for all oldies who remember the hot sweet taste of the Heinz tinned version. Even the most pricey starter turns out to be stunning value: you get a plate of sound Caesar salad with two large, perfectly cooked scallops, each wrapped in crisp bacon. There's no pretentious presentation, no towering mounds of rocket, no artfully balanced scallops. You get good, fresh, well-cooked food. There's a game terrine served with toast and spiced crab apples, or deep-fried squid, ox tongue, black bean sauce. If anything, the main courses are even more satisfying: slow-roasted shoulder of lamb, sweet potato Dauphinoise, purple sprouting broccoli; a pork, peanut and coconut curry is served with sticky rice and pak choi; or for vegetarians a gratin of Munster, new potato and melted onions. Puds range from the straightforward sticky toffee pudding, to the downright self-indulgent – deep-fried ice cream with dulce de leche. This is how gastropub food should be.

The Fire Stables

27–29 Church Road, SW19 ■ 020 8946 3197

⊖ Wimbledon

🍴 Modern British/gastropub

🕐 Mon to Sat 12.00–16.00 & 18.00–22.30; Sun 12.00–16.00 & 18.00–22.00

🗗 all major credit cards except AmEx; no cheques ■ no service added

££ starters £4.75–£7.50 ■ mains £8.50–£18 ■ sides £3.50 ■ desserts £5–£6 ■ lowest bottle price £12

✪ Gastropubnormal

By gastropub standards The Fire Stables is now something of a veteran, and it is a veteran that has won its share of awards. Even in busy Wimbledon the bar does good trade, and the spacious restaurant also prospers. The chairs are comfortable and the tables big enough, the high ceiling and large windows give a spacious feel, the floor is made of painted floorboards – in short everything is 'gastropubnormal'. The menu changes daily and the food is well presented and reasonably priced. Starters range from fennel and potato soup to a foie gras and chicken liver parfait <u>w</u> red onion marmalade. You may have spotted the typographical idiosyncrasy, which wears pretty thin pretty quickly. They don't write 'with' at The Fire Stables; what they put is '<u>w</u>'. So you get duck spring rolls <u>w</u> teriyaki dressing – this could get irritating by the time you get to farmhouse cheeses <u>w</u> Bath Olivers. Other starters may include smoked chicken and mango salad, or tomato, mozzarella and red onion tart. Among the main courses may be pumpkin risotto; slow-roast belly pork <u>w</u> mash; stuffed leg of rabbit wrapped in prosciutto <u>w</u> new potatoes; spaghettini <u>w</u> smoked salmon and chervil cream; and sea bass <u>w</u> roast fennel and potato salad. Puds are desirable if predictable numbers: bread-and-butter pudding; sticky toffee pudding <u>w</u> vanilla ice cream; pear and almond tart <u>w</u> crème fraîche; and baked cheesecake <u>w</u> raspberry coulis.

Jaffna House

90 Tooting High Street, SW17 ■ 020 8672 7786

⊖ Tooting Broadway

|O| Sri Lankan

🕘 daily 12.00–24.00

🖰 www.jaffnahouse.co.uk

🖰 Mastercard, Visa ■ no service added

££ starters 50p–£1.50 ■ mains £3.50–£9 ■ sides £1.25–£3.50 ■ desserts £1.25–£1.50 ■ lunch menu £4 (vegetarian) & £5 (non-vegetarian) ■ lowest bottle price £7

✪ Glorious food, glorious prices

Jaffna House is a charming, simple, scruffy place. The food is Sri Lankan, very good, often very spicy and implausibly cheap. At the front there is a basic café and takeaway area, while at the back (the entrance is actually on Coverton Road) you'll find the dining room, which is not that much smarter than the café. Service is friendly, but there is one trap: in the smart bit there are two menus, one for starters and one for main courses – it is easy to get carried away and order your whole meal from the starters menu. The starters are good, even if there is an emphasis on frying (but thankfully the fried food is well done, dry and crisp). Vadai are small patties of mixed lentils, fried. Mutton rolls are delicious – filled pancakes, breadcrumbed and deep-fried. Vaaipan are hand grenade-sized balls sweetened with mashed banana and fried. Fish cutlets are similarly shaped, subtly spiced fishcakes. Bridging the gap to the main courses are the 'devilled' dishes – mutton or beef. These are strongly flavoured, dry curries and they are hot. Among the curry leaves and onions there are enough green chillies to make the lips sting. Then the menu romps on through hoppers to various kotthu, which are made with chopped up rotis; a strange Sri Lankan speciality called pittu, a kind of rice flour stodge; dosas and a few curry house staples; plus a long list of tandoori specials. Best to stick with the Sri Lankan dishes and drink cold Lion beer.

Kastoori

188 Upper Tooting Road, SW17 ■ 020 8767 7027

⊖ Tooting Broadway

|●| Indian vegetarian

⏱ Mon & Tues 18.00–22.30; Wed to Sun 12.30–14.30 & 18.00–22.30

🗗 Mastercard, Visa ■ no service added

££ starters £2.75–£4.25 ■ mains £4.75–£5.75 ■ sides £2.25–£2.75
■ desserts £3.25–£3.50 ■ lowest bottle price £8.95

✪ Veggie food with real class

Anyone who is genuinely puzzled that people can cope with and indeed enjoy a diet of vegetables alone should try eating at Kastoori. Located in a rather unpromising-looking bit of town, Kastoori is a Gujarati 'Pure Vegetarian Restaurant'. The food they serve is leavened with East African influences, and the large and cavernous restaurant is run by the admirably helpful Thanki family – do be sure to ask their advice, and act on it. First onto the waiter's pad (and indeed first into the mouth, as they go soggy and collapse if made to wait) must be dahi puri – tiny crispy flying saucers filled with a sweet-and-sour yogurty sauce, potatoes, onions, chickpeas and so forth. You pop them in whole; the marriage of taste and texture is a revelation. Samosas are excellent and the onion bhajia are also a revelation – bite-sized and delicious, a far cry from the ball-of-knitting served in most High Street curry emporia. Then make sure that someone orders the vegetable curry of the day, and others the outstanding cauliflower with cream curry and special tomato curry – a hot and spicy classic hailing from Katia Wahd. Leave room for the chilli banana – bananas stuffed with mild chillies (an East African recipe), and mop everything up with generous helpings of puris and chapatis. The smart move is to ask what's in season, as the menu is littered with oddities that come and go. For example, there's a 'beans curry' subtitled 'Chef's Choice'.

Lahore Karahi

1 Tooting High Street, SW17 ▪ 020 8767 2477

🚇 Tooting Broadway

🍽 Indian

🕐 daily 12.00–24.00

🖥 www.lahorekarahi.co.uk

🖪 all major credit cards ▪ no service added

££ starters 60p–£2.20 ▪ mains £2.50–£4.95 ▪ sides 60p–£2.25
▪ desserts £1.60–£1.95 ▪ unlicensed, BYO (no corkage)

✪ Fast food, but good food

Though the bright neon spilling onto the pavement beckons you from Tooting High Street, spiritually speaking, the Lahore Karahi is in the curry gulch of Upper Tooting Road. It's a busy place, and behind a counter equipped with numerous bains-marie stand rows of cooks, distinguishable by their natty Lahore Karahi baseball caps, turning out a daily twelve-hour marathon of dishes. Prices are low, food is chilli-hot and service is speedy. Don't be intimidated: just sit down (don't worry if you have to share a table) and start ordering. Regulars bring their own drinks or stick to the exotic fruit juices – mango, guava or passion. Unusually for what is, at bottom, an unreconstructed grill house, there is a wide range of vegetarian dishes 'prepared under strict precautions'. Karahi karela is a curry of bitter gourds; karahi saag paneer teams spinach and cheese; and karahi methi aloo brings potatoes flavoured with fenugreek. Meat-eaters can plunge in joyfully – the chicken tikka, seekh kabab and tandoori chicken are all good and all spicy-hot, the only fault being a good deal of artificial red colouring. There are also a dozen chicken curries and a dozen lamb curries, along with a dozen 'specialities'. Those with a strong constitution can try the dishes of the day, like nihari, which is lamb shank on the bone in an incendiary broth, or paya, which is sheep's feet cooked until gluey. Breads are good here: try the methi naan, or the tandoori roti. Great for takeaway. Try the biryanis.

Light House

75–77 The Ridgeway, SW19 ■ 020 8944 6338　　　&

◎ Wimbledon

◎ Modern European

◷ Mon to Sat 12.00–14.30 & 18.30–22.30; Sun 12.30–15.00

⌨ www. lighthousewimbledon.com

⊟ all major credit cards ■ 12.5% optional service added

££ starters £5–£10.50 ■ mains £13–£22 ■ sides £3 ■ desserts £5.20–£7
　　■ lunch menu Mon to Sat £14 & £16.50 ■ lowest bottle price £12.50

✪ Sophisticated local resto

Light House is a strange restaurant to find marooned in leafy suburbia – you would think that its modern, very eclectic menu and clean style would be more at home in a city centre than in a smart, quiet, respectable neighbourhood. Nevertheless it continues to do well. First impressions always count, and a light, bright interior – cream walls and blond wood – plus genuinely friendly staff make both arriving and eating at Light House a pleasure. At first glance, the menu is set out conventionally enough in the Italian style: antipasti, primi, secondi, contorni and dolci. But that's as far as the Italian formality goes – the influences on the kitchen here are truly global. Starters may range from black bean marinated mozzarella with pickled carrots, to celeriac soup with rocket and almond purée. It would be very easy to get this sort of cooking wrong, but in fact Light House makes a fair job of succeeding. Among the 'primi', dishes like tempura soft-shell crab with soba noodle salad jostle with combinations like broccoli and Taleggio ravioli with asparagus and rocket. Mains range from sea bass with wild garlic leaves, salsa verde and olive oil mash, to red roast duck with sweet potato, bok choy and smoked chilli jam. Puddings have a retro note but can still delight – fudge and vanilla semifreddo with chocolate sauce or lemon tart with crème fraîche. The wine list features twenty each of whites and reds, and crosses as many frontiers as possible.

Masaledar

121 Upper Tooting Road, SW17 ■ 020 8767 7676

⊖ Tooting Bec/Tooting Broadway

⑩ Indian

⏱ daily12.00–24.00

🖰 www.masaledar.co.uk

🖰 Mastercard, Visa ■ no service added

££ starters £1.95–£3.25 ■ mains £5.25–£8.95 ■ sides £3.50–£3.95
■ desserts £1.50–£2.95 ■ lunch special £2.95 ■ no alcohol

✪ Good food, great value

What can you say about a place that has two huge standard lamps, each made from an upturned, highly ornate Victorian drainpipe, topped with a large karahi? When it comes to interior design, Masaledar provides plenty of surprises, and a feeling of spaciousness. This establishment is run by East African Asian Muslims, so no alcohol is allowed on the premises, but that doesn't deter a loyal clientele, who are packing the place out. Along with several other restaurants in Upper Tooting Road, Maseladar has had to expand, and has added another 25 covers. The food is fresh, well spiced and cheap – vegetable curries and meat curries are sound and at bargain prices – and, to cap it all, you eat it in an elegant designer dining room. For starters there are samosas – meat or vegetable. Or try the chicken wings from the tandoor, or the delicious lamb chops. You might move on to a tasty, rich chicken or lamb biryani, or try a classic dish like methi gosht – this is strongly flavoured and delicious, guaranteed to leave you with fenugreek seeping from your pores for days to come. Then there's the rich and satisfying lamb Masaledar, which is disarmingly described as 'our house dish cooked to tantalise your taste buds'. The breads are terrific, especially the thin rotis. Look out for the various deals that range from 'All day lunch platter' to 'birthdays, parties, conferences … private parties of up to 120'.

Sarkhel's

199 Replingham Road, SW18 ■ 020 8870 1483

⊖ Southfields

|●| Indian

🕐 Tues to Thurs 12.00–14.30 & 18.00–22.30; Fri & Sat 12.00–14.30 & 18.00–23.00; Sun 12.00–14.30 & 18.00–22.30

🔗 www.sarkhels.com

🖃 all major credit cards except AmEx ■ no service added

££ starters £4.25–£11 ■ mains £5.95–£10 ■ sides £2.95–£5.95 ■ desserts £2.95–£3.50 ■ menus: Sunday buffet £9.95 (adults), £6.95 (children); Express lunch £5; thali lunch £9.95 (not Sun) ■ lowest bottle price £11.90

✪ Top-flight Indian

Sarkhel's is a large, elegant restaurant that serves well-spiced food with a number of adventurous dishes scattered through the menu – the hot, fresh Chettinad dishes are particularly fine. Moreover, this is a pleasant, friendly, family-run place offering good cooking at prices that, though not cheap, certainly represent good value. Booking is recommended. Start by asking if there are any 'specials'. These are dishes that change according to what is available at the markets. You might be offered a starter of Tareli macchi, fish cooked in a spicy batter – a famous Bombay Parsee dish, or murg ke chaap sixer, andhra-style fiery hot chicken 'lollipops'. The seekh kebab is as good as you'll find anywhere. For main course dishes, check the specials again – it might be something wonderful such as a kolmi nu Patia, a spicy Parsee prawn dish. On the main menu, try the galina cafreal, a rich Goan chicken dish, or perhaps the jardaloo ma gosht, a sweet-and-sour lamb dish made with apricots. All are delicious, without even a hint of surface oil slick. Be sure to add some vegetable dishes – perhaps the baigan patiala, which is a dish of cubed aubergine and cashew nuts stewed with a touch of ginger and chilli. The menu also has frequent regional festivals – if you're puzzled by strange dishes, ask for help, as you'll get good advice and fabulous food.

→ For branches, see index

Tower Bridge

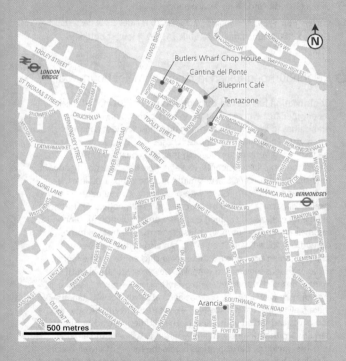

Butlers Wharf Chop House
Cantina del Ponte
Blueprint Café
Tentazione

Arancia

500 metres

Arancia

52 Southwark Park Road, SE16 ■ 020 7394 1751   ♿

⊖ Bermondsey

|◉| Italian

🕒 Tues to Sat 12.30–14.30 & 19.00–23.00

🌐 www.arancia-uk.co.uk

💳 all major credit cards ■ no service added

££ starters £3.75–£4.50 ■ mains £9.25–£9.75 ■ sides £3 ■ desserts
£3.25–£3.50 ■ lunch menu £7.50 & £10.50 ■ lowest bottle price
£10.50

✪ Neighbourhood Italian in changing neighbourhood

Gentrification has spread through this part of town, and this is
yet another area where house prices have climbed beyond reason.
Arancia has to live with these changing times. Ten years ago this
patch was all pie and mash and car chases. The proprietors of Arancia
are to be congratulated on keeping the food cheap enough to
attract the long-term residents, while at the same time good enough
to ensnare newcomers. Starters might include zuppa di spinaci, a
spinach and mint soup served with bruschetta. Or you might find
insalata di baccalà, a salad of salt cod and roast peppers. Or tortino
di polenta e cipolla, a winning combination of polenta cake and
caramelised onions. For main course there may be trota al forno,
baked trout spiked with Strega. You can also bank on dishes such
as pollo al Marsala, boned, stuffed roast chicken; salsicce e fagioli,
Italian sausages served with cannellini beans; or stufato al frutti di
mare, a mixed seafood stew with everything in it from mussels to
monkfish by way of squid, scallops and cuttlefish. For vegetarians
there may be torta al basilico e olive – a tart made with ricotta, basil
and olives and served with spinach. The puddings are adventurous:
perhaps a rather good chocolate semifreddo, or pear and almond
tart. The pursuit of bargain prices is also the theme of the all-Italian
wine list. They are certainly inexpensive wines, and they are all just
about drinkable.

Blueprint Café

Design Museum, Shad Thames, SE1 ■ 020 7378 7031

⊖ Tower Hill

🍴 British

🕐 Mon to Sat 12.00–15.00 & 18.00–23.00; Sun 12.00–15.00

🖰 www. conran.com

🖰 all major credit cards ■ 12.5% optional service added

££ starters £5–£10 ■ mains £12.50–£19.50 ■ sides £3.50 ■ desserts
£5–£7.50 ■ set meal £19.50 & £29.50 ■ lowest bottle price £16.50

✪ Seriously good cooking, splendid view

**The Blueprint Café is one of those restaurants that has been
quietly going about its business for so long** that it has merged
imperceptibly into the background. If the Blueprint had opened in the
last year or so it would be attracting rave reviews and people would
be mobbing the place. Consider just two points: there's a great-value
set menu, and a secondary wine list that offers twenty decent wines
at knockdown prices. The dining room is modern but unthreatening,
and occupies a glass-fronted box jutting out towards the river – the
views of Tower Bridge are amazing. The food is very good indeed. The
menu changes every day and is market-driven. How about nettle and
celery soup? Or beetroot, soft-boiled egg and horseradish? Or there
might be preserved garlic, tapenade and goats' cheese – light and
lemony goats' cheese on toast, with coarsely chopped olive tapenade,
and a whole head of garlic softened and sweetened by slow cooking.
Or maybe smoked eel with Jersey Royals and mint appeals? The
mains carry on the theme with fresh seasonal dishes: halibut with
parsley and anchovy sauce; a tart made with Durrus cheese, potatoes
and rosemary; beef and parsley pie – slow-cooked beef in gravy rich
with parsley butter. What a good pie! Poached turbot with morels
successfully teams a huge chunk of plain steamed fish with a cream
sauce. Puds range from almond tart to crème brûlée, by way of a very
rich choco-laden gateau, the St Emilion.

Butlers Wharf Chop House

36e Shad Thames, SE1 ▪ 020 7403 3403   ♿

⊖ Tower Hill

|◉| British

⏱ Mon to Sat 12.00–15.00 & 18.00 –23.00, Sun 12.00 –15.00

⌂ www. conran.com

▱ all major credit cards ▪ 12.5% optional service added

££ starters £6–£24 ▪ mains £14–£26 ▪ sides £2.75–£3.50 ▪ desserts £4.50–£7.50 ▪ lunch menu £22 & £26 ▪ lowest bottle price £15.75

✪ Flying the flag for Brit producers

Butlers Wharf Chop House really deserves everyone's support, for this is a restaurant that makes a genuine attempt to showcase the best of British produce. There's superb British meat, splendid fish, and simply epic British and Irish cheeses. What's more, the Chop House wisely caters for all, whether you want a simple dish at the bar, a well-priced set lunch, or an extravagant dinner. The dining room is spacious and bright, and the view of Tower Bridge a delight, especially from a terrace table on a warm summer's evening. The lunch menu changes regularly, but tends to feature starters such as potted duck, brandied prunes and toast, or Loch Fyne smoked salmon. Mains will include dishes like fish and chips, and steak and kidney pudding as well as the house specialities such as a flawless roast rib of beef with Yorkshire pudding and gravy. After that you just might be able to find room for a pud like rhubarb crumble tart with vanilla ice cream, even if the sticky toffee pudding is a dish too far. Dinner follows the same principles, but is priced à la carte. Thus, there may be starters such as cock-a-leekie soup, and half a lobster mayonnaise. Mains might include steak, kidney and oyster pudding; charcoal-grilled veal with butter beans; or halibut with mussel and saffron broth. There's also steak and chips, priced by size so you can eat to your wallet's content.

Cantina del Ponte

Butlers Wharf, Shad Thames, SE1 ■ 020 7403 5403

⊖ Tower Hill

🍴 Italian

🕐 Mon to Sat 12.00–15.00 & 18.00–23.00; Sun 12.00–15.00 & 18.00–22.00

🖱 www. conran.com

🖥 all major credit cards ■ 12.5% optional service added

££ starters £7 ■ mains £9.50–£14.50 ■ sides £2.75 ■ lowest bottle price £14.50

✪ Unstressed Italian bolt hole

The Cantina del Ponte jostles for attention with its considerably pricier next-door neighbour, the upscale Pont de la Tour. Thankfully, it does not try to keep up, but instead offers a different package. Here you are greeted with the best earthy Italian fare, presented in smart Conran style. The floors are warm terracotta, the food is strong on flavour and colour, the service is refined, and the views are superior London dockside. Book ahead and bag a table by the window or, better still, brave the elements in summer and sit under the canopy watching the boats go by. The seasonal menu is a gentle meander through all things good, Italian-style, with a tempting array of first courses, and mains that include pizza, pasta and risotto, not to mention side orders, puddings and cheeses. Simple, classic combos like Mozzarella with aubergines always appeal. Or there's grilled squid with chilli and rocket. Veggie dishes such as gnocchi with cherry tomatoes and basil are good, or how about a classic like risotto primavera? The pizzas are well made and feature all the old favourites, like quattro formaggi, Margherita and Napoletana. Main courses range from sea bass with rosemary, through lamb steak with courgettes, to scallops with pancetta and broad beans. Puds veer from tiramisù, through torta di cioccolata and noci, to pannacotta with rhubarb. It's worth noting that you can order pizzas 'to go' from the Cantina, which is certainly a boon for locals.

Tentazione

2 Mill Street, SE1 ■ 020 7237 1100 &

⊖ Bermondsey

|O| Italian

🕔 Mon to Sat 12.00–15.00 & 18.00–23.00; Sun 12.00–15.00 & 18.00–22.00

🖱 www.tentazione.co.uk

🗗 all major credit cards ■ 12.5% optional service added

££ starters £7–£10 ■ mains £12–£20 ■ desserts £6–£8 ■ menus: £28 & £36; degustazione £38 & £60 ■ lowest bottle price £15

✪ Cosy Italian local

This small, busy and rather good Italian restaurant has crept up behind Sir Terence Conran's Thameside flotilla of eateries and given them a terrific run for their money. The food is simple, high-quality peasant Italian, with strong, rich flavours. The pasta dishes are good here, as are the stews, and the wine list is interesting. This place has a flexible attitude – most of the starters can be turned into main courses, and the menu changes to reflect the seasons and the markets. You may find choices such as the ravioli – filled with pumpkin and amaretti, and served with butter and sage; or green pappardellle with rabbit and olives; fresh gratinated mussels on a spicy sauce with garlic crostini; or a simple-sounding dish such as minestrone di verdura con riso. Main courses offer hammer blows of flavour: fillet of lemon sole with mustard grains, porcini mushrooms and smoked oysters; venison stew with juniper, cabbage and bacon; honey-glazed duck breast, green tea lasagna with foie gras and spring onions. Or maybe steer toward a risotto made with beetroot and Prosecco. For pudding it is hard to better the sformatino di ricotta con salsa al caffè, a delicious ricotta pudding with coffee sauce, although the 'chocolate ecstasy' has many fans. Italian cheeses are also featured – pan-fried Ovinford cheese comes with Abbamele Sardo and Sardinian cassarrau bread. There is an interesting wine list that caters to most pockets … especially deep ones.

West

Barnes, Sheen and Kew

Escale

94 Kew Road, Richmond, Surrey ▪ 020 8940 0033

⊖ Richmond

🍽 Turkish

🕐 daily 12.00–23.00

🕙 www.escale-richmond.co.uk

🗗 all major credit cards ▪ 12.5% optional service added

££ starters £3.95–£5.50 ▪ mains £9.50–£14.50 ▪ sides £3–£8 ▪ desserts £4.25–£4.95 ▪ menus: set meze £23.50 (for 2); Chef's special £21.50 ▪ lowest bottle price £12.95

✪ Neighbourhood Turkish

Among the ever-increasing number of restaurants crowding into this area, Escale adds a Turkish option to the repertoire. It has established a reputation as a popular 'local' – good, unpretentious food with amiable, efficient service and wallet-friendly prices certainly attracts the regulars. Booking is essential most nights, but you will never be hurried on your way should you linger longer than planned. Weather permitting, there are pavement tables at the front. Small samplers of meze with very moreish bread are served on arrival: a ploy that usually results in the mixed cold meze starter being the first entry on the waiter's pad. Hot starters include patates kôftesi, which are Turkish potato croquettes; particularly delicious felafel; or perhaps kiymali börek, little filo parcels filled with minced lamb and herbs. Main course dishes are substantial; the mixed grill – consisting of lamb, chicken, lamb shish, kofte and lamb's liver, served with bulghar wheat and salad – will satisfy the healthiest of appetites, while the chicken shish is plentiful and perfectly chargrilled. The deep-fried sardines are served in a sharp lemon marinade and there is grilled sea bass on a bed of spinach. A small selection of vegetarian dishes is also available and includes veggie moussaka; mushroom Stroganoff; or mücver (courgette and feta cheese fritters). Puddings include all the usual suspects including rice pudding, ice cream, and cheesecake. Escale is a pleasant local that has got both its atmosphere and pricing about right.

The Glasshouse

14 Station Parade, Kew Gardens, Surrey ■ 020 8940 6777

⊖ Kew Gardens

|●| Modern British

⏱ Mon to Sat 12.00–14.30 & 19.00–22.30; Sun 12.30–15.00 & 19.30–22.00

🖰 www.glasshouserestaurant.co.uk

🖃 all major credit cards ■ 12.5% optional service added

££ lunch £18.50 (2 courses) & £23.50 (3 courses) ■ dinner £35 (3 courses) ■ tasting menu Mon to Fri £45 (7 courses) ■ lowest bottle price £15

✪ Elegant restaurant, elegant cooking

The Glasshouse has settled into its dual role, part local hero and part Michelin-starred destination restaurant. Chef Anthony Boyd honed his craft at the much decorated Square (see p. 90) and Chez Bruce (see p. 299). At The Glasshouse he has developed a style of his own. What's more, the restaurant is on the doorstep of Kew Gardens underground station, which makes it easily accessible. The interior has a clean-cut, modern feel to it and the comfortable chairs are worthy of a special mention. The food is good. Very good. The menu changes daily offering eight selections for each course. The set lunch is a 'snatch-their-hand-off' bargain. For the full Michelin experience there's a multi-course tasting menu. The imaginative and straightforward cooking owes much to French cuisine. Starters range from a warm salad of wood pigeon with deep-fried truffled egg; to Spanish white bean soup with chorizo; or a pave of foie gras with candied carrot. Mains may include fillet of beef with mashed potato, girolles, shallots and garlic ragout; slow-roast pork belly with morteau sausage; or poached halibut in red wine with globe artichokes and field mushrooms. Puddings have a deft touch and include favourites like petit pot au chocolat blanc with chocolate truffles; a sour red cherry sorbet with olive oil biscuit; or a ginger financier with orange buttermilk sorbet. The wine list is short and thoughtfully drawn up, with one or two unusual selections.

Redmond's

170 Upper Richmond Road West, SW14 ■ 020 8878 1922

⊖ BR Mortlake

🍴 Modern British

🕐 Mon to Sat 18.30–22.30; Sun 12.00–14.30

🖰 www.redmonds.org.uk

🖱 all major credit cards ■ no service added

££ 'Early menu' (to 19.45) £12.50 (2 courses) & £15.50 (3 courses)
■ dinner £32.50 (3 courses) ■ Sunday lunch £18.50 (2 courses) &
£23.50 (3 courses) ■ lowest bottle price £14.95

✪ Neighbourhood stalwart

**When Redmond and Pippa Hayward opened this small
neighbourhood restaurant** it was head and shoulders above
anything else the locale had to offer. A few years down the line and
'Barnes, Sheen & Kew' may not quite be a match for Soho, but there
is an increasing number of decent places to eat. Redmond's is one
of the best, propelled by a telling combo of very good cooking and
reasonable prices. They tweak the menu on a daily basis, so it reflects
the best of what the season and the markets have to offer. The dinner
menu is not particularly short – about six or seven starters and mains
– and proves astonishing value. There is also a very competitive 'early'
menu running until 19.45. What's even more agreeable is an absence
of supplements. And the food here really is very good indeed: well
seasoned, precisely cooked, presented elegantly. If the 'pork Hors
d'oeuvres' is available when you visit, pounce. Redmond's charcuterie
is accomplished; or there may be curried parsnip soup; or a galette of
Jerusalem artichokes and shallots. Main courses combine dominant
flavours with elegant presentation – roast fillet of organic salmon
with wild mushrooms; pan-fried sea bass with crushed new potatoes
sauce vierge; or slow-braised oxtail with parsnip mash. The puddings
also impress: crème brûlée; banana tarte Tatin with vanilla ice cream;
or bread and butter pudding with rum and cinnamon. The wine list
is littered with interesting bottles at accessible prices – and some
particularly good halves.

Riva

160 Church Road, SW13 ■ 020 8748 0434   ♿

⊖ BR Barnes Bridge

|O| Italian

🕐 Mon to Fri 12.00–14.30 & 19.00–23.00; Sat 19.00–23.30; Sun 12.00–14.30 & 19.00–21.30

🗗 all major credit cards ■ 12.5% optional service added

££ starters £7–£11.50 ■ mains £12–£19.50 ■ sides £3 ■ desserts £6–£7 ■ lowest bottle price £14.50

✪ Authentic Italian food

Andrea Riva has always been something of a darling of the media and his sophisticated little restaurant exerts a powerful pull, strong enough to convince even fashionable folk to make the dangerous journey to the south bank of the Thames. When they get there they find a rather conservative-looking restaurant, with a narrow dining room decorated in dull greens and faded parchment, and chairs that have clearly seen service in church. As far as the cuisine goes, Riva provides the genuine article, so most customers are either delighted or disappointed, depending on how well they know their Italian food. The menu changes regularly with the seasons. Starters are good. The frittelle is a tempura-like dish of deep-fried Mediterranean prawn, salt cod cakes, calamari, sage and basil, with a balsamic dip. Serious Italian food fans, however, will find it hard to resist the sapori Mediterranei, which gets you grilled scallop and langoustines; baccalà mantecato and polenta; eel and lentils; mussels in tomato pesto; and grilled oysters. Among the main courses, rombo al rucola is a splendid combination of tastes and textures – a fillet of brill with a rocket sauce and boiled potatoes. Fegato and polenta unta – calf's liver served with garlic polenta and wild mushrooms – delivers a finely balanced blend of flavours. The house wines are all priced at a very accessible level. Of the whites, the pale-coloured Tocai is crisp, light and refreshing.

Sonny's

94 Church Road, SW13 ■ 020 8748 0393

⊖ BR Barnes Bridge

🍴 Modern British

🕐 Mon to Sat 12.30–14.30 & 19.30–23.00; Sun 12.30–15.00

🖰 www.sonnysrestaurant.co.uk

🖿 all major credit cards ■ 12.5% optional service added

££ starters £4.75–£9.50 ■ mains £11.50–£16.50 ■ sides £2.50–£3
■ desserts £5–£7.50 ■ Menus: set lunch Mon to Sat £13.50 & £16.50
■ set dinner Mon to Thurs £17.50 & £19.50 ■ Sunday lunch £21.50
■ lowest bottle price £10.95

✪ The outlook is sunny

**Perceptive Barnes-ites have been supporting Sonny's since
Modern British cuisine** was just a twinkle in a telly chef's eye. The
interior of the resto is modern but gratifyingly unthreatening and
there is a busy, casual feel about the place. Sonny's shop next door
sells a good many of those little delicacies that you would otherwise
have to journey to the West End to secure. But do not be deceived
into thinking that the cooking here is suburban. The menu changes
to reflect the seasons, so you might find starters like velouté of
sweet potatoes with goats' cheese mousse; or a pressé of rabbit and
baby vegetables with pistachio duxelles; a salad of Bayonne ham
and black pudding with potatoes and confit shallots; or pan-fried
scallops with oyster beurre blanc. Main courses may team John Dory
with choucroute, carrots and pancetta, or pan-fried calves' liver with
creamy polenta. There is even room for a retro classic like Tournedos
Rossini, and something simple but good like shoulder of 'Middle
White' pork served with Brussels sprouts and wild mushrooms. The
service is welcoming and the wine list provides some sound bottles
at sound prices. Puddings are comfortable: sorbets, jellies, raspberry
brûlée, served with biscotti. There's also a decent set dinner Monday
to Thursday. Sonny's is the kind of restaurant we would all like to
have at the end of the road, friendly, good food, comfortable.

The Victoria

10 West Temple Sheen, SW14 ■ 020 8876 4238

⊖ BR Mortlake

◐ Modern British/gastropub

🕘 Mon to Fri 12.00–14.30 & 19.00–22.00; Sat 12.00–15.00 & 19.00–
22.00; Sun 12.00–15.00 & 19.00–21.00

🖰 www.thevictoria.net

🖰 all major credit cards ■ 12.5% optional service added

££ starters £4.95–£8.95 ■ mains £8.95–£19.95 ■ sides £2.50 ■ desserts
£2.95–£5.95 ■ lowest bottle price £12.95

✪ Good, accommodating gastropub

It would be nice to live in West Temple Sheen. The name has
a good ring to it. The houses are palatial and pricey, both Sheen
Common and Richmond Park are close at hand, and then there's The
Victoria, a fine gastropub. Since the turn of the century The Victoria
has flaunted the obligatory conservatory, squashy sofas and painted
floorboards. But what you're paying for is restaurant cooking in an
informal setting, plus a restaurant wine list and restaurant service,
and although prices have been creeping up, what you pay seems
pretty reasonable. The menu changes daily – or even more frequently
than that, should dishes run out – and features half a dozen starters
and the same number of mains and puds. Starters may offer a
sophisticated soup of white almond gazpacho with steeped raisins; or
a classic like salade Lyonnaise; or smoked haddock and bacon quiche.
There is also the Victoria tapas plate – very popular. Mains are steady
dishes well executed: Appleton pork chop with black pudding potato
pancake and choucroute; Charolais sirloin steak with onion gravy and
chips; grilled wild salmon with roasted new potatoes, chorizo and
aioli. These are all examples of those special, simple-sounding dishes
that are hard to get right. Desserts are top stuff. It's a pleasure to
watch punters savouring buttermilk pudding with poached Yorkshire
rhubarb, or taunting chocoholics with white and dark chocolate
truffle cake. B&B? There are seven simple but comfortable bedrooms.

Chelsea and Fulham

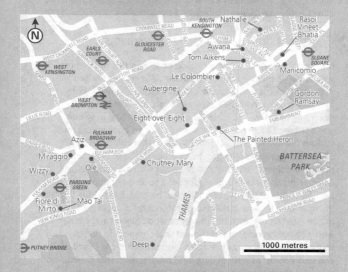

Aubergine

11 Park Walk, SW10 ■ 020 7352 3449

⊖ South Kensington

🍽 French

🕒 Mon to Fri 12.00–14.30 & 19.00–23.00; Sat 19.00–23.00

🖪 all major credit cards ■ 12.5% optional service added

££ lunch £34 (3 courses inc. wine) ■ dinner £60 (3 courses) ■ gourmand
£74 (7 courses) ■ lowest bottle price £14

✪ Good cooking based on quality ingredients

**It's hard to imagine it, but a decade or so ago this neck of the
woods was a bleak-ish place to eat out.** Aubergine changed all
that, and it merits the accolade 'old-established'. Now it is both
familiar enough, and light and airy enough, for even the most
discerning of ladies who lunch. The best of everything in season
and a talented kitchen make for a busy place, so booking is a must.
William Drabble is a very able chef. A lunch that comprises terrine
of confit chicken and foie gras, followed by breast of duck, braised
turnips and thyme, and then coffee parfait with mascarpone ice
cream, with all the bells and whistles of a serious restaurant and half
a bottle of decent wine, makes for a real bargain. Even at full throttle
the main dinner menu is still priced reasonably for cooking of this
calibre. Starters may include Pithivier of wood pigeon and Parma ham
with wild mushrooms, or tortellinis of snails, garlic and parsley. Main
courses include dishes such as roast John Dory with cod brandade
and mushrooms; assiette of duck with prunes; roast veal sweetbread
cassoulet of white beans and foie gras. These are well-conceived
and well-executed dishes, beautifully presented. Desserts are equally
accomplished – chocolate mousse with bottled cherries, or poached
pear in red wine. The service is accomplished and unobtrusive;
the wine list can test the bravest wallet. The Menu Gourmand will
spin the experience out by presenting seven pixie portions, a grand
gastronomic treat.

Awana

85 Sloane Avenue, SW3 ■ 020 7584 8880 &

⊖ Knightsbridge/Sloane Square

▯●▯ Malaysian

⊕ Mon to Wed 12.00–15.00 & 18.00–23.00; Thurs to Sat 12.00–15.00 & 18.00–23.30; Sun 12.00–15.00 & 18.00–22.30

⌐ᴑ www.awana.co.uk

⊟ all major credit cards ■ 12.5% optional service added

££ starters £6.50–£10.50 ■ satay bar from £2.50 ■ mains £9.50–£25 ■ sides £2–£3.50 ■ desserts £6–£7.50 ■ lowest bottle price £19

✪ Full-on Malaysian opulence

There is more highly polished hardwood here than even the trendiest restaurant designers could have dreamt of. Awana is a London representative of an international restaurant group and we are talking slick and Ritzy rather than cheap and cheerful. Which makes a change, as most of London's Malaysian restaurants fall into the latter category. The 'Satay Bar' dishes up a gently spicy peanut sauce with a broad array of little skewers – salt water tiger prawns, scallops, corn-fed chicken, rump of lamb; there's even a veggie option: 'aubergine and mushroom'. In the main, the satay is well done. Other notable starters are rusuk kambing pangang, which are grilled lamb ribs, and the rojak buah, which is a Malaysian sour fruit salad. Then there are traditional soups – sup kambing is a thick lamb soup not dissimilar to a Welsh cawl, but with the flavour sharpened by Malay herbs. The classic curries such as rendang daging, slow-cooked beef, are well handled. And there are also various stir-fries and rice dishes – the udang galah cha kuew teow is a luxurious assembly based around lobster tail. Service is very friendly and this restaurant is unusual in that it is a Malay resto with a sommelier and a lengthy wine list. Desserts include those famously bizarre Malay concoctions that team cooked beans with shaved ice, but the home-made ice creams are the best option – jack fruit, tamarind.

Aziz

24–32 Vanston Place, SW6 ■ 020 7386 0086 &

⊖ Fulham Broadway

|●| Middle Eastern

⏲ Mon to Sat 12.00–24.00; Sun 10.00–24.00

🗄 all major credit cards ■ 12.5% optional service added

££ mezze £3–£7.50 ■ mains £7.50–£18 ■ desserts £5 ■ menus: lunch £12.50; dinner £17.50 ■ lowest bottle price £12.50

✪ Comfortable Middle Eastern eating

Aziz has a very large and dominant site on Vanston Place, partly because it is neighbour to del'Aziz, which is a shop and deli (and, it must be admitted, what is virtually another restaurant) – they are all part of the same operation. Proximity to counters laden with good things benefit the vibe, which is helpful, as the restaurant known formally as Aziz looks very posh. There is no hint of Middle Eastern scruffiness here, all is modern, and all is elegant. This presentation carries onto the plate where dishes show up looking very polished. Thankfully, flavours are upfront, and prices are not that fierce. The menu splits into a number of sections – you'll find hot, cold and dessert mezze, then starters and main course dishes as well. From the mezze, trad dishes like houmous and marinated baby aubergine with sumac and chilli are done well, while the hot dishes are fresh and good. 'Starters' such as the pastilla of chicken with almonds, or the pan-fried marinated chicken livers with cumin and lime are elegant and delicious, though it is hard to say why they are not mezze. Main courses split into tagines, kebabs and fish – monkfish tagine, shellfish broth, saffron, potato and confit of baby fennel is a complex dish well put together. Desserts are particularly fine: chocolate fondant, and Moroccan mint tea ice cream. The wine list has a good spread and gentle prices. At Christmas del'Aziz does a good trade in cooked turkeys to carry home. Scrooge would be pleased.

Chutney Mary

535 King's Road, SW10 ■ 020 7351 3113

⊖ Fulham Broadway

🍴 Indian

🕐 Mon to Fri 18.30–23.00; Sat 12.30–14.30 & 18.30–23.00; Sunday 12.30–15.00

🔗 www.realindianfood.com

🔲 all major credit cards ■ 12.5% optional service added

££ starters £5.25–£10.50 ■ mains £13.50–£25.50 ■ sides £1.50–£4.50 ■ desserts £5.50 ■ menus: Sat & Sun brunch £16; children's menu £9 ■ lowest bottle price £16.50

✪ Elite Indian restaurant

Chutney Mary is an elegant place to eat and the dramatic look of the dining room owes a good deal to an able theatrical lighting designer. But the men in the kitchen (headed by chef Rubinath) know their job and turn out refined Indian food. This is not a cheap restaurant, but the quality of cooking is such that it comes under the heading of 'justifiable extravagance'. Start with the crab cake – spankingly fresh crab, loosely bound and top-and-tailed with a potato rosti. Delicious. Or there's the tokri chaat, which is an edible basket filled with various street-food treats and topped with yogurt and chutney. Or the Konkan crab claws with garlic – huge tender claws swimming in a sea of garlic butter. Vegetarians will enjoy the platter of teen tikki – lotus root and sago, figs and green peas, spiced yogurt. Mains are equally impressive. Mangalore jheenga are giant prawns, chilli-hot and tamarind-tangy. There's a Goan green chicken curry, or there's Kerala pepper roast duck with a cinnamon coconut sauce. The side dishes are worth noting: methi palak saag teams spinach with fenugreek and lotus root. Breads are good here – lacchi paratha. The dessert menu is also inspired – there is a garam masala brûlée, or a dark chocolate fondant served with orange blossom lassi. Service is attentive and there is a book-sized wine list backed by a wine cellar that would put many French establishments to shame.

Le Colombier

145 Dovehouse Street, SW3 ■ 020 7351 1155

⊖ South Kensington

🍽 Very French

🕐 Mon to Sat 12.00–15.00 & 18.30–22.30; Sun 12.00–15.30 & 18.30–22.00

🔲 all major credit cards ■ 12.5% optional service added

££ starters £5.20–£12.50 ■ mains £13.50–£19.90 ■ sides £2.50
■ desserts £5.80 ■ lowest bottle price £13.90

✪ The Parisian quartier of Chelsea

Viewed from the pavement outside on Dovehouse Street you can see that Le Colombier was once a classic, English, street-corner pub. But now it's a pub that has a small, glassed-in area in front, covered with tables and chairs. How very Parisian, you might think, and you would be right. This is a French place. It is run by Monsieur Garnier, who has spent most of his career in the slicker reaches of London's restaurant business. With his own place he has reverted to type and everything is very, very French. The menu is French, the cooking is French, the service is French and the décor is French. The cooking is about as good as you would have found in a smart Routiers in rural France during the 1970s. Starters include such bistro classics as oeufs pochés meurette; soupe de poissons; and feuilleté d'escargots à la crème d'ail. And there are oysters; goats' cheese salad; duck liver terrine; and tomato and basil salad. Listed under 'les poissons' there is flétan sauce beurre blanc (halibut), and coquilles St Jacques à la crème de morilles, which is scallops with morel cream sauce. Under 'les viandes' there is steak tartare with pommes frîtes; filet de boeuf au poivre; and saucisses de Toulouse aux lentilles. Under 'les grillades' are the steaks and chops. Puddings include crêpes Suzette. Both the service and the approach to wine are as French as the menu.

Deep

The Boulevard, Imperial Wharf, SW6 ■ 020 7736 3337

⊖ Fulham Broadway/BR Wandsworth Town

¶O¶ Fish/Scandinavian

🕐 Tues to Fri 12.00–15.00 & 19.00–23.00; Sat 19.00–23.00; Sun 12.00–16.00

🕙 www.deeplondon.co.uk

🗗 all major credit cards ■ 12.5% optional service added

££ starters £6.50–£9.75 ■ mains £13.50–£19.75 ■ desserts £5 ■ set lunch £12.50, £15.50 & £19.50 ■ lowest bottle price £14.50

✪ Modern fish restaurant with a conscience

Deep stepped into the deep end when it opened at Imperial Wharf. The Wharf is teetering on the brink of being a trendy new gastro destination, having a flock of restaurants and blocks of chic apartments with the obligatory river views. When the development is thriving and all the flats (sorry, apartments) have been sold, Deep will be sitting pretty. Until then it is an elegant restaurant that is something of a hidden gem. The mainsprings of the place are a couple called Sandefeldt: he is the chef and she runs the front of house. The food is broadly Scandinavian and heavily fish-orientated. Sandefeldt is passionate about fish and it shows in the dishes; he is also keen on using only sustainable fish and has an annual charity – when he opened, his diners were each asked to make a £1 donation to the World Wildlife Fund. Some dishes even have the Marine Stewardship Council logo. But underneath all the worthy stuff is some accurately cooked, ultra-fresh fish. Starters may include a creamy mussel soup with a centrepiece of a dollop of crab meat and a quail's egg; the selection of herrings is stunning; there's an octopus salad. Mains range from a plain grilled Dover sole; to lemon smoked tuna; pan-fried fillet of bream; or steamed fillet of salmon. The cooking is accomplished and presentation very elegant. The wine list has reasonably priced bottles and whizzy ones, but be very wary of the twenty or so different aquavits on offer.

Eight over Eight

392 King's Road, SW3 ■ 020 7349 9934

⊖ Sloane Square

|●| Asian eclectic

🕐 Mon to Fri 12.00–15.00 & 18.00–23.00; Sat 12.00–16.00 & 18.00–23.00; Sun 18.00–22.30

⊖ www.eightovereight.nu

🗗 all major credit cards ■ 12.5% optional service added

££ starters £6–£8 ■ mains £9–£21.50 ■ sides £3.75 ■ desserts £5.50 ■ set lunch Mon to Sat £15 ■ lowest bottle price £14

✪ Oriental inscrutability, Chelsea style

The name Eight over Eight derives from some obscure tenet of Oriental numerology – the East seems to have taken the art of 'lucky numbers' to another level. This establishment is part of Will Ricker's expanding empire that also includes E&O (see p. 98), which performs a very similar service for the denizens of Notting Hill. The front part of Eight over Eight is dedicated to a large and busy bar where chic cocktails predominate, while the rear is the dining room and is edged with booths. The cuisine is described as 'Pan Asian', so dim sum jostles futo maki rolls, tempura, sashimi and curries, before the menu leads on to salads, then barbecued and roasted meats. It is an eclectic selection and there is something on the menu to whet any appetite. Start with old favourites like chilli-salt squid; or pork spare ribs; or prawn and chive dumplings, none of which are cheap, but all of which are presented very elegantly. The sashimi and roll sushi is fresh, good and sometimes groundbreaking – seared tuna with miso aïoli, or beef fillet sashimi, wasabi dressing. The curries are well spiced, and the salads most interesting – how does duck, watermelon and cashew salad appeal? Then maybe lotus leaf chicken, shiitake mushroom and sweet chilli soy. Service is slick and drinks range from cocktails to cold beer by way of a serious wine list. But do beware, picking lots of dishes can mean ending up with lots of middling price tags and a rather grown-up bill.

Fiore di Mirto

839 Fulham Road, SW6 ■ 020 7736 3217/020 7751 0448

⊖ Parsons Green

⦿ Sardinian

🕒 Mon to Sat 12.00–14.30 & 18.30–23.00

🖪 all major credit cards ■ 10% optional service added

££ starters £4–£7.20 ■ mains £7–£13.95 ■ sides £3 ■ desserts £4–£6 ■ lowest bottle price £12.50

✪ Neighbourhood Italian, but it's Sardinian

Fiore di Mirto is a small, light, friendly restaurant with a Sardinian heart but Metropolitan manners. The menu doesn't feature quite as many regional dishes as Sardo (see p. 15), but the food is fresh and good, and it fits right in on this stretch of the Fulham Road, which is awash with small neighbourhood restaurants. The wine list has a strong contingent of Sardinian bottles, but casts its net widely. Service is friendly and professional. The menu runs through antipasti, pasta, carne e pesce, to dessert. Starters range from pan-fried pecorino cheese with tomatoes, to squid with aubergine fregola and mint – fregola is a variety of pasta, the size and shape of a grain of sweetcorn. Or there's antipasto Sardo, which is a plate covered in pan carasau (a Sardinian bread the same dimensions and texture as a pappadom), topped with various hams, salamis and cheeses. The pasta choices are interesting: nettle ravioli with new potatoes, thyme and pecorino; spaghetti with bottarga; or a well-made risotto with plenty of razor clams – very delicious, and with a perfect texture. Main courses are well presented. Sea bream comes baked in Vernaccia wine with olives and green beans; there are marinated sardines with bay leaf and pine nuts served with baked new potatoes; a rack of lamb comes with roast endive. Puds round up biscotti; sebadas; and a tiramisù made with pistachios. Beware the eponymous Mirto, a Sardinian liqueur that tastes better in Sardinia.

Update! Restaurant closed at time of going to press – future plans not known

Gordon Ramsay

68–69 Royal Hospital Road, SW3 ■ 020 7352 4441   ♿

⊖ Sloane Square

🍴 French

🕐 Mon to Fri 12.00–14.00 & 18.30–23.00

🖰 www.gordonramsay.com

🖳 all major credit cards ■ 12.5% optional service added

££ set lunch £40 (3 courses) ■ à la carte £70 (3 courses) & £90 (7 courses) ■ lowest bottle price £20

✪ Temple to gastronomy

The Gordon Ramsay empire continues to expand, but even with the increasing television workload and the seemingly annual addition of yet more restaurants, head office in Chelsea continues to be packed. Thankfully, the prices are not as high as you might fear for such Michelin-endorsed gastronomy. As ever, the set lunch is a bargain and well worth any detour – as long as you can get a booking. The menu here evolves gently. On the main menu, look out for a ravioli of lobster and langoustine poached in a lobster bisque and served with a lemongrass and chervil velouté; or a carpaccio of pigeon from Bresse with shavings of confit foie gras, baby artichokes and a Parmesan salad – this is a stunning dish of unusual delicacy; or caramelised slices of pig's foot with veal sweetbreads and a celeriac rémoulade and a salad of green beans – as robust and delicious as you could wish for. And those are just starters! Mains intrigue: fillet of turbot poached in red wine with radicchio and celeriac risotto; saddle of Scottish venison with creamed cabbage, beetroot fondant and sautéed wild mushrooms. Even the desserts fascinate – hot chocolate fondant with milk mousse and ice cream. To order successfully here, just pick a dish or an ingredient you like and see how it arrives; you won't be disappointed. They claim that reservations can only be made a month in advance. So you must either book ahead or at the last minute.

Manicomio

85 Duke of York Square, SW3 ∎ 020 7730 3366   ♿

⊖ Sloane Square

🍴 Italian

🕐 Mon to Fri 12.00–15.00 & 18.30–22.30; Sat 12.00–17.00 (brunch) &
18.30–22.30, Sun 12.00–16.00 (brunch) & 18.30–22.00

🖥 www.manicomio.co.uk

🖪 all major credit cards ∎ 12.5% optional service added

££ starters £7–£13 ∎ mains £12.25–£22.50 ∎ sides £3–£5 ∎ desserts
£6–£7.50 ∎ lowest bottle price £13.50

✪ Comfortable, neighbourhood Italian

**Manicomio is an easy-going restaurant that manages to bring off
a difficult trick.** Despite being a new project, it gives the impression
of being long established, due to genuine brickwork and middle-of-
the-road décor. The dining room was carved out of one end of the
Duke of York barracks. There are some seats outside, which is great
if the weather is clement, dodgy when relying on the space heaters.
Service is slick and Italian, which description accurately sums up most
of the wine list as well. The cooking is good and the menu broadly
seasonal. Manicomio is not a place to look for gentle, peasant Italian
fare, as there is an edge of chic to even the simplest dishes here – but
this is Sloane Square after all. Starters such as a salad of broad beans
and peas with pecorino is as fresh, as green and as good as you
could wish for. Beef carpaccio is very tender, and with a grand zigzag
of mustardy dressing. The pasta dishes are sophisticated: spaghetti
with crab, chilli and garlic, or rabbit and Tuscan sausage ravioli – silky
pasta. Main courses are solid: calves' liver with Swiss chard and
balsamic; pan-fried halibut with ratte potatoes, tomato and black
olives; or grilled leg of lamb with aubergine and pepperonata. Puds
are trad: tiramisù, or lemon tart with pistachio and iced milk. The
brunch menu that is served at weekends is a cut-down version of the
à la carte.

Mao Tai

58 New King's Road, SW6 ■ 020 7731 2520

☻ Parsons Green

🍴 Chinese

🕐 Mon to Fri 12.00–15.00 & 18.15–23.30; Sat & Sun 12.30–15.00 & 18.15–23.00

🔗 www.maotai.co.uk

🗗 all major credit cards ■ 12.5% optional service added

££ dim sum £3.50–£5 ■ starters £3.50–£11 ■ mains £8.50–£24.50 ■ sides £3–£8.50 ■ desserts £4.70–£5 ■ lowest bottle price £13.50

✪ Polished, local, Chinese resto

Mao Tai is much more Chelsea than Chinatown, both in appearance and in the kind of food it serves. It's a pretty restaurant, cleverly lit, well decorated and with brisk, efficient service. The menu has evolved over the years and the ground has shifted away from the fiery Sichuan influences to something more suave. Such surroundings – and, to be fair, such food – do not come cheap. Still, you'll leave well fed and well looked after, as both the cooking and service are slick and chic. Start with steamed scallops – these are usually a pretty good indication of things to come, and at Mao Tai they are well cooked. Salt and pepper prawns are very fresh. Dumplings feature: try pork and ginger; prawn, chive and chilli; mushroom and spinach; and pea shoot and prawn (served until 20.00). The salt and pepper Chesapeake Bay soft-shell crabs in the starters section are good. From the fish section, choose Tianjin turbot steamed on the bone – these are serious restaurant dishes at serious prices. Or perhaps sirloin strips with lemongrass and cracked black pepper appeals? Dishes here are made with free-range Angus beef. Onwards to sautéed chicken with orange blossom honey and pineapple, or rabbit with lemongrass and garlic. In the vegetable section there's broccoli in oyster sauce, and seasonal pea shoots. In the face of all these rather exalted prices, the Mao Tai boast may make sense. 'Mao Tai does not use M.S.G.'

→ For branches, see index or website

Miraggio

510 Fulham Road, SW6 ■ 020 7384 9774

⊖ Fulham Broadway

🍴 Italian

🕐 daily 12.30–15.00 & 18.00–23.00

🖱 www.miraggio.co.uk

🖪 all major credit cards ■ 10% optional service added

££ starters £2.50–£10 ■ mains £6–£18 ■ sides £3 ■ desserts £4 ■ lowest bottle price £10

✪ Friendly, no-fuss, neighbourhood Italian

Bright café-style tables and a simple rustic air belie the quality behind this family-run establishment. Your first sign of this is the appetising choice of antipasti. There are mouthwatering, wafer-thin strips of chargrilled courgette and aubergine; nutty little boiled potatoes with virgin olive oil and roughly chopped flat-leaf parsley; strips of grilled peppers; small and large mushrooms; and an aubergine and tomato bake with tiny melted mozzarella cheeses. It's enough to stop even the most jaded foodie in their tracks. For starters, choose the antipasti della casa and you'll get the best the next door deli has to offer. Otherwise, try beef carpaccio with truffle oil, or melanzana alla Parmigiano, baked aubergine rich with cheese. Pastas include the usual suspects: lasagna, and fettuccine with fresh seafood in tomato sauce. There are plenty of meat and fish choices too, including spigola al forno, baked sea bass; calamari fritti, a dish of perfectly cooked deep-fried squid; and abbacchio al forno, roast lamb. If you're not already having spinach with your main course, try a side order of spinaci burro e Parmigiano. Popeye would faint with pleasure. Puddings include what is claimed to be the best tiramisù in the area; champagne or fruits of the forest sorbets; and zoccolette, a home-made profiterole with a Nutella filling. Service is efficient but friendly and the kitchen is to the rear, which is good if you like watching cooks at work.

Nathalie

3 Milner Street, SW3 ■ 020 7581 2848

⊖ Sloane Square/South Kensington

🍽 French

🕐 Tues to Sat 12.00–14.00 & 19.00 –22.00

🖰 www.nathalie-restaurant.co.uk

🖬 all major credit cards ■ 12.5% optional service added

££ starters £6.50–£11.50 ■ mains £14.50–£18.50 ■ sides £3.25
■ desserts £5.50–£6.50 ■ French bento box lunch £14.50 ■ lowest
bottle price £12.50

✪ Long on Gallic charm

**What kind of chance does a local restaurant stand in a street like
this?** Stumble off in any direction and there are smart restaurants
aplenty, but (to use the vernacular) no. 3 Milner Street has been a
restaurant for yonks. Eric Chatroux, the latest incumbent, merely
called in the builders and decorators and now you walk into a cleaner,
more modern-looking dining room. Designer-paint effects on the
walls, modish chandeliers, stylish chairs. Starters include chicken
consommé with chicken oyster ravioli; a game terrine; crayfish with
red and black radish salad and Bayonne ham; or a tart of smoked
haddock and leeks. But when the food arrives it is plain upon the
plate, skilfully cooked, and well seasoned. A 'duck and potato crêpe
Vonnassienne, foie gras sauce' comes with a very light, almost
souffléed, pancake atop the duck. Jolly good eating. A stuffed quail
looks lonely perching in a forest of rocket, but is a neat parcel with
good flavours. Main course dishes work on the principle of taking
non-scary ingredients – sea bream, bass, beef, duck, chicken – and
cooking them Gallic-style. Thus turbot is poached in court bouillon
and served with seasonal vegetables – nice fish, perfectly cooked and
still firm. Puds are good – a dish of three 'petits pots' is presented in
three small saucers, one containing vanilla cream, one dark chocolate,
and, the star, an intense, green pistachio cream. Service is friendly,
and the wine list winds its merry way through a thicket of serious
clarets at serious prices.

Olé

Broadway Chambers, Fulham Broadway, SW6 ■ 020 7610 2010

⊖ Fulham Broadway

🍴 Spanish/tapas

🕐 Mon to Thurs 17.00–23.00; Fri & Sat 12.00–15.00 & 17.00–23.00; Sun 17.00–22.30

🖰 www.olerestaurants.com

🖰 all major credit cards ■ no service added

££ tapas £1.65–£6.55 ■ desserts £3.15–£3.95 ■ lowest bottle price £11.10

❂ Small, but busy, tapas haven

You can't miss Olé. It's bright and modern with blond wood everywhere, and right opposite Fulham Broadway tube. Olé is a combination bar and restaurant. The bar is open for drinks if you're not hungry and there's the restaurant at the back if you are. This is the sort of place where you may start by going for a drink, and end up eating and being pleasantly surprised by the food. The menu, which changes monthly, is modern Spanish and geared to tapas-style sharing. It is divided into Frias (cold dishes), Calientes (hot dishes), and Ensaladas (salads). For the conventional, there are favourites such as jamón Serrano; boquerones; patatas bravas; chorizo al vino blanco; and gambas al ajillo. The gambas are sweet and hot, with garlic, chilli and olive oil. Tortillas abound here. Instead of just tortilla Española, there are four more: with pimentos, with chorizo, with tuna, and with a spinach cream filling. All are freshly made, and all make pretty good options. Meat-eaters can enjoy tapas such as solomillo de cerdo on verduras al vapor, a la esencia de mostaza, which is fillet of pork with steamed vegetables and mustard essence; carne de buey a la plancha con verduras y salsa de tomate y datiles, beef fillet with vegetables and date sauce; or pollo a la plancha con surtido de pimientos y crema de ajo, grilled chicken with peppers and cream of garlic. For the sweet of tooth there are eight puddings. The all-Spanish wine list is worth checking out.

→ For branches, see index or website

The Painted Heron

112 Cheyne Walk, SW10 ■ 020 7351 5232

⊖ Fulham Broadway

🍽 Indian

🕐 Mon to Fri 12.00–14.30 & 18.00–23.00; Sat 18.00–23.00; Sun 12.00–14.30 & 18.00–21.30

🖰 www. thepaintedheron.co.uk

🖬 all major credit cards ■ 12.5% optional service added

££ starters £5–£8 ■ mains £11–£15 ■ sides £4 ■ desserts £4 ■ lunch platter £15 ■ lowest bottle price £13

✪ Sophisticated restaurant, sophisticated flavours

The Painted Heron has got the balance between authenticity and modernist reinvention about right. The food here is honest, well spiced, and not too fussily presented. The room is cool and elegant, no flock wallpaper, nothing over the top. Service is sound and, as in so many modern Indian establishments, a lot of effort has gone into the wine list. The standard of cooking is high and it is no wonder that the Heron has skewered a very long list of awards. Lunches are quiet, but in the evening this is a busy place, so you should book. The à la carte menu changes gradually as dishes come and go. Among the starters may be crab with red onions and chilli in dosa pancake; pigeon breasts roast in the tandoor; and calves' liver in a tandoor marinade with mango – a seriously good dish, with melty liver and a grand spike of chilli. Mains are well conceived. The spicing is upfront and enjoyable, and although they are Indian dishes, they are described in European terms – chicken tikka with almonds in tomato and cream curry; scallops in a spiced yogurt curry with mushrooms and spring onions; or topside of beef in a Rajasthani red-chilli paste – chunks of pleasantly chewy meat in a rich gravy. From the veg dishes, 'asparagus, green peas in a fenugreek curry' is a belter – crunchy greenstuff and creamy methi-flavoured sauce. Breads are terrific. Delicious European style puds – apple pie with rose syrup.

→ For branches, see index or website

Rasoi Vineet Bhatia

10 Lincoln Street, SW3 ■ 020 7225 1881

⊖ Sloane Square

🍽️ Indian

🕐 Mon to Fri 12.00–14.30 & 18.00–22.30; Sat 18.00–22.30

🔗 www.vineetbhatia.com

🗄️ all major credit cards ■ 12.5% optional service added

££ starters £9–£16 ■ mains £14–£27 ■ sides £4–£6 ■ desserts £9–£12 ■ menus: lunch £19 & £24; menu gourmand £58 & £69; veg gourmand £49 & £58; degustation lunch £30 ■ lowest bottle price £18

✪ Indian superstar

This restaurant belongs to Vineet Bhatia and his wife. It is small (eight tables at the back and half a dozen in front), it is classy, and 'this time it's personal'. For the first time, Bhatia is self-employed and he is on tiptop form. The food is Michelin two-star level (if only we could rely on their Francophile inspectors agreeing!). This is Indian food at its finest – simple, intensely flavoured, well-spiced dishes with inspired combinations of colour and texture. Service is friendly (this is a family business) and there is a buzz of excitement about the place. The Menu Gourmand is a long multi-course affair, full of surprises, delicious and wholly satisfying. Starters include 'assorted sea scallops' – three scallops, one with chilli and sesame, one with onion seed, and one that's particularly fine with a spice crust. Or there's a duck platter: duck kebab, samosa, salad, and soup. There's an amazing lobster dish that is either starter or main – Ginger and chilli lobster, spiced lobster jus, curry leaf and broccoli khichdi … and then the plate is dusted at the table with sour spices and cocoa. It's a perfectly cooked lobster tail, the khichdi is like a spicy risotto, and there's the added perfume of cocoa. Other mains include lamb shank roganjosh cooked on the bone, and a biryani of pickle-flavoured chicken baked under a flaky pastry lid. The wine list is Chelsea and zips up towards the Château Latour. There's a pudoholics dessert platter.

Tom Aikens

43 Elystan Street, SW3 ■ 020 7584 2003

⊖ South Kensington

🍽 Modern British

🕐 Mon to Fri 12.00–17.00 & 19.00–23.00

🖥 www.tomaikens.co.uk

🖩 all major credit cards ■ 12.5% optional service added

££ set lunch £29 (3 courses) ■ à la carte £60 (3 courses) ■ tasting menu £75 (7 courses) ■ lowest bottle price £18

✪ Fine dining, top cooking

Taking a bit of a punt, Tom Aikens set up his eponymous restaurant in Chelsea, the restaurant opened busy and was promptly deluged with a shedload of awards and the thumbs up from Michelin. All of which would have been more surprising if he hadn't been the same Tom Aikens who previously gathered a hatful of awards at Pied à Terre. This is a very personal restaurant; it is not open on Saturday and Sunday, but when it is Tom tends to be in the kitchen. Service is silky and the food is sophisticated and considered. A very rewarding place to eat. Setting aside (and you shouldn't) the set lunch, there's an à la carte option and the full tasting menu – seven courses and coffee. All dishes are imaginative, well presented and with good assertive flavours. From the starters – braised snails come with snail beignets, red wine cassonade, potato soup and garlic, while a roast langoustine comes with truffle macaroni, braised chicken wing, pork belly and haricot beans – a very good dish indeed, the different elements working well together. For main course, braised veal shin comes with roast veal sweetbreads, pommes purées, braised onion and caper and rosemary sauce, and John Dory fillets are served with a fennel purée, bouillabaisse potatoes and basil sauce vierge. Puds are also complex and rewarding – chocolate negus with pistachio mousse, pistachio parfait, and pistachio and milk ice cream, or pineapple roast with vanilla and rum, pineapple jelly. The wine list is extensive, but the charming sommelier is particularly helpful. You should eat here soon, you're worth it!

Wizzy

616 Fulham Road, SW6 ■ 020 7736 9171

🚇 Parsons Green

🍽 Korean

🕐 daily 12.00–24.00

🔗 www.wizzyrestaurant.co.uk

🗐 all major credit cards ■ 10% optional service added

££ starters £5.50–£6 ■ mains £8.50–£15 ■ desserts £2.50–£5.50 ■ set lunch £7.90 & £15 ■ lowest bottle price £12.50

✪ Wizzy gets busy

'**Contemporary Korean Cuisine'** – three words you don't often see gracing the same sentence, but this is the tag line that Wizzy uses to describe her very individual dishes. The menu blurb thrashes around trying to define the food: 'authentic', 'modern', 'sophisticated', 'progressive', 'phenomena' and 'gastronomical experiences', but you are unlikely to end up any the wiser. Best to resign yourself to the fact that Wizzy (both the place and the diminutive lady chef in a white baseball cap) is a one-off. The food is recognisably Korean, but then it is also stylish and modern with well-balanced flavours and textures. Service is attentive, friendly and rather anxious. The food is good. Start with the beef tartar, which is topped with caviar and seasoned with sesame oil – the Naju pears add a contrasting crunch and everything sits in a bowl of ice. The dumplings are very good. The 'pancakes' are good – an array of fried bits and bobs like strange tempura. The 'salad' is a tour de force, crunchy pear again, plus fresh herbs, bean sprouts and mango and a mandarin dressing. Mains come with rice and accompaniments – the 'Wizzy style' beef rib stew is ultra slow-cooked, very tender and with a superb and rich broth. Ginseng chicken is a chicken breast stuffed with ginseng, garlic and dates – a dish that works well. Prices are Fulham prices, but this is distinctive food and well worth trying.

Ealing and Acton

The Ealing Park Tavern

222 South Ealing Road, W5 ■ 020 8758 1879

⊖ South Ealing

|O| Modern British/gastropub

⏲ Mon 18.00–22.30; Tues to Sat 12.00–15.00 & 18.00–22.30; Sun 12.00–16.00 & 18.00–21.00

🖶 all major credit cards ■ no service added on parties of 5 or less

££ starters £5–£6.50 ■ mains £9–£14 ■ desserts £5–£7.50 ■ lowest bottle price £11.50

✪ Comfortable neighbourhood gastropub

It doesn't seem very long ago when this place was a lager and football hovel. Then it reverted to its original name, the Ealing Park Tavern, and settled into a new role as a tidy pub serving rather good food. It should be no surprise, as the owners are the people behind another fine gastropub, St John's (see p. 261). The Tavern is a handsome place and, like its North London sibling, is founded on the simple premise that hospitality is important. The bar has two or three decent real ales and the wine list is short, but gives a fair choice at accessible prices. The dining room has a tall counter separating it from an open kitchen and the menu is chalked up on a blackboard. The menu is a short one, but it is thoughtfully written, changes daily and there is something for everybody. Starters may include a spiced parsnip soup; spaghetti vongole; fishcakes with chive crème fraîche; or a hearty country terrine – all sound stuff. Main courses are well presented, substantial and seem pretty good value. There may be fish pie; braised lamb shank with a tomato and white bean stew; or slow roast Gloucester Old Spot pork belly with apple sauce. Fish dishes tend to be a good option: how does a whole lemon sole with new potatoes and Hollandaise sauce sound? Puds are comforting and comfortable – orange crème brûlée; treacle tart with clotted cream; chocolate brownie with vanilla ice cream.

Monty's

54 Northfield Avenue, W13 ■ 020 8567 6281   ♿

⊖ Northfields

🍽 Indian

🕐 daily 12.00–14.30 & 18.00–23.30

🖰 www.montys.uk.com

🖃 all major credit cards ■ no service added

££ starters £2.50–£5.95 ■ mains £6–£13.75 ■ sides £3.90 ■ desserts
£2–£3.50 ■ set dinner £15.95 ■ lowest bottle price £12.45

⭐ Stellar curry house

Once upon a time, a very long time ago, the Ealing Tandoori held West London curry lovers in thrall – it was the undisputed first choice. Then, in the late 1970s, the three main chefs left to open their own place, which they called Monty's, on South Ealing Road. As business boomed, two of the chefs moved on to set up independently. But as all three co-owned the name 'Monty's', they all use it, and that is why there are now several different Monty's, all fiercely independent, but each with the same name and logo. Unlike many small Indian restaurants, these are 'chef-led', which is why the cooking is classy, the portions are good and prices are fair. The trad tandoori dishes are fine, like the tandoori chicken. Or there is hasina – lamb marinated in yogurt and served on an iron plate as a sizzler. Breads are delicious – pick between nan and Peshwari nan. But the kitchen really gets to shine with simple curry dishes like methi gosht – tender lamb (and plenty of it) in a delicious sauce rich with fenugreek; chicken jalfriji; or the very rich moglai chicken. Vegetable dishes are also good – both brinjal bhaji and sag panir are delicious. Monty's is one of very few local curry houses to serve perfectly cooked, genuine basmati rice. So the plain boiled rice – nutty, almost smoky, with grains perfectly separate – is worth tasting on its own. Monty's is the archetype of the perfect neighbourhood curry house.

→ For branches, see index

North China Restaurant

305 Uxbridge Road, W3 ■ 020 8992 9183

⊖ Ealing Common

🍴 Chinese

🕐 Mon to Thurs & Sun 12.00–14.30 & 18.00–23.30; Fri & Sat 12.00–
14.30 & 18.00–24.00

🖰 www.northchina.co.uk

🖰 all major credit cards ■ 10% optional service added

££ starters £4.50–£6.50 ■ mains £5.50–£12 ■ sides £2.20–£3.80
■ desserts £3.80–£4.20 ■ set dinners £14.50–£20.50 ■ lowest bottle
price £12.20

✪ Duck from Peking arrives in Acton

**The special Peking duck, which always used to require 24 hours'
advance notice,** is now so popular that the restaurant cooks a few
ducks every day regardless. So you don't always have to pre-order.
But then you do, because it is so popular that they cannot guarantee
that you'll get one unless you order it. The North China has a 24-carat
local reputation; it is the kind of place people refer to as 'being as
good as Chinatown', which in this case is spot-on, and the star turn
on the menu doesn't disappoint. Unlike most other – upstart, deep-
fried – crispy ducks, the Peking duck here comes as three separate
courses. First there is the skin and breast meat, served with pancakes,
shreds of cucumber and spring onion, and hoisin sauce. Then a fresh
stir-fry of the duck meat with bean sprouts, and finally the meal ends
with a giant tureen of rich duck soup with lumps of the carcass to
pick at. It is awesome. So what goes well with duck? At the North
China familiar dishes are well cooked and well presented. You might
start with barbecued pork spare ribs, or the lettuce wraps, made with
prawn and chicken. For a supplementary main course, prawns in chilli
sauce, although not very chilli, is teamed with fresh water chestnuts
and tastes very good. Singapore fried noodles is powered by curry
powder rather than fresh chilli, but fills a gap.

Rasputin

205 High Street, Acton, W3 ▪ 020 8993 5802

⊖ Acton Town

▮◉▮ Eastern European

🕘 daily 18.00–23.30

🖻 all major credit cards except AmEx ▪ 10% optional service added

££ starters £2.95–£9.95 ▪ mains £6.50–£12.95 ▪ desserts £2.50–£3.50
   ▪ lowest bottle price £9.95

✪ Ra, Ra, Rasputin – neighbourhood eatery

Rasputin is up at the Ealing end of Acton High Street. Formerly a
dark cave-like sort of room, a series of refurbs later it is now, in the
words of the proprietors, 'modern'. The menu has moved gently
away from what was hitherto an all-Russian affair. All this must
be noted before you have made any inroads into the 25 different
vodkas, which come both as single shots and – take care here – 'by
the carafe'. With the menu comes a plate of cucumber, cabbage,
green tomatoes and peppers, all markedly salty and with a good
vinegary tang. For a starter, try pierogi – rich little dumplings that
come stuffed with a choice of potato and cheese, meat, or sauerkraut
and mushrooms. The blinis – small buckwheat pancakes – are also
good, with smoked trout or, if you fancy a bargain, with Sevruga
caviar. The Moscovite fish platter is also delicious. If they're on offer
opt for the cabbage parcels, which is a simple but satisfying dish of
cabbage leaves stuffed with meat and rice, or chicken Kiev made
with tarragon butter. Fish fans may want to try the salmon fillets in
dill sauce. Desserts are rather staid – crème brûlée, or pancakes filled
with a choice of chocolate, walnuts or fruit preserve. Also interesting
is the Russian tea served in a glass and holder. It is made with tea,
lemon and a splash of vodka, with a small bowl of honey alongside
for sweetening.

The Rocket

11–13 Churchfield Road, W3 ■ 020 8993 6123

⊖ BR Acton Central

🍴 Italian/gastropub

🕒 Mon 19.00–22.00; Tues to Sun 12.30–15.30 & 19.00–22.15

🖲 www.therockettw3.co.uk

🖬 all major credit cards ■ no service added

££ starters £5–£7 ■ mains £10–£16 ■ sides £3.50–£4.50 ■ desserts
£4.50–£5.50 ■ lunch specials £7 ■ lowest bottle price £11

✪ Good gastropub with an Italian accent

**The Rocket was once a scuzzy bikers' pub where pool tables were
the only kind of tables that mattered.** Fast forward a handful of
years and there is a spacious and comfortable bar to the front, and
a spacious terrace for drinking outside in front of it. This Victorian
boozer now looks pretty good with light-coloured wood floors and
deep red walls. The dining room is to the rear and the food is full-
on and very good. The cuisine is Italian and the menu follows the
convention of listing starters, then pasta and risotti, mains, and finally
puds. The menu changes monthly and may include starters like a
confit duck leg terrine with winter vegetables. Good as this is, it is
almost eclipsed by 'frico'– a fry-up of new potatoes, Asiago cheese
and mushrooms served under a pile of rocket. Crispy, melty, rich,
self-indulgent, a gloriously simple plateful. There's a good-tempered
risotto made with porcini and truffle oil, scattered through with small
chunks of potato to soak up the flavours. Pasta dishes are good here.
The mains range widely – grilled marlin with sautéed cima di rapa;
chicken breast stuffed with Montasio cheese and served with a leek
and mushroom risotto; grilled veal chop with noisette potatoes. The
wine list has some decent bottles at sensible prices – look for the
vibrant Madiran. The dessert menu rounds up the usual suspects,
from amaretto tiramisù to ice creams and sorbets.

Sushi-Hiro

1 Station Parade, Uxbridge Road, W5 ■ 020 8896 3175

⊖ Ealing Common

🍴 Japanese

🕐 Tues to Sun 11.00–13.30 & 16.30–21.00

🗗 cash only ■ no service added

££ sushi 60p–£12 ■ sashimi platter £40 ■ sake & beer £2.20

✪ Best-ever sushi

Sushi-Hiro is a very self-effacing sort of restaurant. The sign
outside says 'Sushi-Hiro, Japanese Gourmet Foods' and it is absolutely
true. When you push open the door you find that half the room is
given over to a waiting area for takeaway customers, there's a sushi
counter with stools, a handful of tables and that's about it. The menu
offers sushi in various guises. You are given a miniature clipboard
with a small form to fill in your order and that's when it all gets tricky,
as there are 50 or so boxes to tick. The best strategy is to start with
the chef's selection of superior nigiri, which brings ten pieces of sushi
– tuna, salmon, herring roe, turbot, bass, red clam, scallop, salmon
roe, red bream and sweet shrimp. Try them all and then repeat the
ones you like the most. The sushi here is very good: the rice is soft
and almost warm, the balance between the amount of rice and
amount of topping is just about perfect, and the fish is squeakily
fresh and very delicious. Or try a piece of eel – very rich, or mackerel
– a revelation: it's light and not oily at all. Alternatively, go for pickled
plum roll – made with rice, pickled plum and shiso leaves, which have
an addictive flavour, or salmon roe – salty and sticky. Then round
things off with a small bowl of rather splendid miso soup, which
comes with a couple of little clams lurking in the depths.

Earls Court and South Kensington

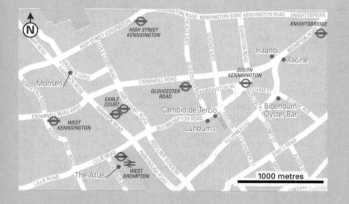

The Atlas

16 Seagrave Road, SW6 ■ 020 7385 9129

⊖ West Brompton

🍴 Modern British/gastropub

🕐 Mon to Sat 12.30–15.00 & 19.00–22.30; Sun 12.30–15.00 & 19.00–22.00

🖰 www.theatlaspub.co.uk

🗗 all major credit cards except AmEx ■ no service added

££ starters £5–£7.50 ■ mains £8–£12.50 ■ desserts £4–£5 ■ lowest bottle price £10.50

✪ Solid and reliable gastropub

Greybeards at the Atlas must look back fondly on the gastropub revolution. It is old-hat now, but when the Atlas opened it was one of only a few places that accurately judged the mood. Success has bred success and this is now the first link in a gradually increasing chain. The flavours come mainly from Italy with the occasional North African and Spanish diversion, plenty of upfront flavours, and an identical tone is adopted in all the pubs. The menus are seasonal, so starters may include asparagus and leek soup with olive oil and shaved Parmesan, and a serious antipasti plate – goats' cheese frittata, pea purée crostini, and roast ox tongue with onion marmalade. There are a couple of midway dishes that could either be starter or main, such as conchiglie with slow roast vine tomatoes. Main courses include grilled Tuscan sausages, with fennel and black pepper and baked polenta; salt roast loin of pork with thyme and honey; and 'Caldeirada', a Portuguese seafood stew served with mint and lemon rice. The afters selection is short and to the point – a decent chocolate cake vies with 'Montgomery's Cheddar and Gorgonzola' served with pear and grilled bread. The wine selection is also chalked up, and there are some unusual offerings served by the glass, which makes The Atlas a good venue for wine lovers in search of a bit of impromptu tasting. This is a busy, noisy, friendly and young place, and the food is good into the bargain.

Bibendum Oyster Bar

Michelin House, 81 Fulham Road, SW3 ■ 020 7589 1480

⊖ South Kensington

🍽 Seafood

🕔 Mon to Sat 12.00–22.30; Sun 12.00–22.00

🖰 www.bibendum.co.uk

🖯 all major credit cards ■ 12.5% optional service added

££ starters £5.75–£18 ■ mains £8–£31 ■ sides £4.50–£7 ■ desserts £6–£6.50 ■ lowest bottle price £14.50

✪ Seafood and eat it

Bibendum Oyster Bar is one of the nicest places to eat shellfish in London. The 1911 building, a glorious tiled affair that was a former garage for the French tyre people, is Conranised throughout, but the oyster bar is in what looks like the old ground-floor workshop, and they've done precious little to it. On the forecourt stand two camionettes: one a shellfish stall, selling lobsters, oysters and crabs to the smart set; the other a flower stall, with lilies, ginger flowers and roses rather than carnations. Upstairs is Bibendum proper – a very grown-up restaurant. The menu is a shellfish lover's heaven. Here you'll find three different types of rock oyster – you can choose your favourite or order a selection to find out the difference. The crab mayonnaise comes in the shell, giving you the enormous fun of pulling it apart and digging through the claws. Or you can have it done for you in a crab salad – probably just as good, but not nearly so satisfying. If you're really hungry, there's a particularly fine plateau de fruits de mer (for minimum two people), which has everything: crab, clams, langoustines, oysters, prawns and shrimps, as well as winkles and whelks. There is plenty of choice for those allergic to claw-crushers, simple combinations such as Szechuan chicken salad, or grilled tuna with marinated tomatoes. Desserts are simple and delicious – petit pot au chocolat; cheese; and the inevitable crème brûlée.

Cambio de Tercio

163 Old Brompton Road, SW5 ▪ 020 7244 8970

⊖ Earls Court/South Kensington

🍽 Spanish

🕐 Mon to Fri 12.30–14.30 & 19.00–23.30; Sat 12.30–15.00 & 19.00–
23.30; Sun 12.30–15.00 & 19.00–23.00

⌂ www.cambiodetercio.co.uk

🗗 all major credit cards ▪ no service added

££ starters £6–£14.75 ▪ mains £14.50–£16.75 ▪ sides £3.50–£5
▪ desserts £4.75–£7 ▪ lowest bottle price £17

✪ Exceptional Spanish cooking

One of the big surprises of the past decade has been the rise and
rise of Spain as a gastronomic force. Spanish restaurants were always
known for obsessively hunting down the very best ingredients, but
recently they have somehow added flair, excitement and invention
to the mix and it is very welcome. Cambio de Tercio manages to
showcase all these virtues at once. The cooking is very good here.
You can start with a plate of 'Joselita Gran Reserva' – 100g of Iberico
ham made from the famous pata negra acorn-fed pig, a very princely
and pricey porker indeed. Or there's a red tuna tartare that comes
with pistachio mustard and salmon caviar – delicious and with several
complementary textures; or sardines marinated in cider vinegar; or
Serrano ham croquetas – crisp outside, melting within. Or how about
a new take on the famous Galician dish, at Cambio the octopus
comes with three kinds of potato – purple potato crisps, cubes of
new potato, and a silky mash, it's very good indeed. Main courses
are also inspired and inspiring – suckling pig with good crackling;
monkfish dressed with a crisp sprinkling of deep-fried Iberico ham fat;
a dish of oxtail cooked slowly and gently until the juices caramelise.
The wine list is a monster – take your pick of sixteen fine wines from
the Ribera del Duero, or explore other lesser-known Spanish regions.
Service is formal and helpful, and the restaurant buzzes along until
late – very much as it would in Spain.

→ For branches, see index or website

Haandi

136 Brompton Road, SW3 ■ 020 7823 7373

⊖ Knightsbridge/South Kensington

🍴 Indian

🕐 Mon to Fri 12.00–15.00 & 18.00–23.00; Sat & Sun 12.00–15.00 & 18.00–23.30

🖰 www.haandi-restaurants.com

🖬 all major credit cards ■ 12.5% optional service added

££ starters £3.75–£12.50 ■ mains £6–£12.90 ■ sides £2.80–£7.50 ■ set lunch from £7.95 ■ lowest bottle price £11.95

✪ Honest, spicy food

East African Punjabi restaurants are famous for simple dishes, rich, intense sauces and a welcome belt of chilli heat – the kind of food that hitherto has meant a trek to Southall or Tooting. Which makes Haandi something of a brave initiative. The management decided to expand an empire based on successful establishments in Nairobi and Kampala by adding the long and narrow space that, in a bygone age, was a Sloaney haven known as the Loose Box. The décor is curry house-smart, but the menu and chefs have been flown in from East Africa. The curries are incredibly rich and become so by being reduced gradually rather than thickened with powdered nuts. Start with some kebabs. Tandoori fish tikka is made with tilapia. The chicken malai tikka is also very good. Another star turn from the tandoor is the lamb tandoori chops, which are implausibly tender chops, richly spiced, with good crispy bits to gnaw. The curries are also very satisfying. Try the tawa prawn masala – good-sized prawns, which are cooked firm and retain some bite, and inhabit a very rich, very strongly flavoured, almost dry masala. Or how about the kake di lamb curry? This is a trad lamb curry, served on the bone. The vegetable dishes are equally good. Dum aloo Kashmiri is made with potatoes that have been stuffed with cashew nuts, curd cheese and sultanas – implausible but delicious. The breads are excellent – look out for the chilli naan.

→ For branches, see index or website

Lundum's

119 Old Brompton Road, SW7 ■ 020 7373 7774 &

⊖ Gloucester Road/South Kensington

|O| Danish

⏱ Mon to Sat 09.00–16.00 & 18.00–23.00; Sun 12.00–16.00 (brunch)

🖰 www.lundums.com

🖻 all major credit cards ■ 12.5% optional service added

££ lunch £13.50 (2 courses) & £16.50 (3 courses) ■ dinner £17.25 (2 courses) & £22.50 (3 courses) ■ Sunday brunch buffet £21.50 ■ lowest bottle price £14

✪ London's Danish HQ

There are four Lundums working in this business, so for once the claim to be a genuine family business seems to hold up. There's nothing particularly Danish about the room, which is pleasantly light and airy with huge mirrors and a skylight, and over the years the restaurant has spread into the adjacent shop front. The staff proudly produce interesting (and delicious) dill-flavoured aquavit, which they import specially, along with Danish hams, cheeses and all manner of other delicacies. The food is elegantly presented, competently handled and … Danish. At lunchtime it's trad Danish; in the evening, modern Danish. You cannot help but be swept along by the tidal wave of commitment and charm. At dinner the menu, which changes seasonally, reads like a lot of other menus – smoked salmon gravadlax, roast lamb, pan-fried cod. Best, then, to visit at lunch, when there are more Danish dishes on offer. Go à la carte and try the shoal of herrings – simply marinated, or spicy, or lightly curried, or sour with dill. As well as classic open sandwiches you can also choose a smorrebrod m/lunt of fiskefrikadeller (fish meatballs), or frikadeller (meat meatballs). There are also platters: the Danish comprises herrings, meatballs, plaice and salad, or there's an all-fish platter. Or try the Medisterpolse – Danish sausage with red cabbage. Desserts are indulgent and the aquavit deadly, but best of all this restaurant gives you a window into a different cuisine and the Lundum family make charming guides.

Mohsen

152 Warwick Road, W14 ■ 020 7602 9888

⊖ Earls Court

|⊙| Iranian

⊙ daily 12.00–24.00

⊟ cash or cheque only ■ no service added

££ starters £3–£4 ■ mains £12–£15 ■ desserts £3–£4 ■ dish of the day
£7 ■ unlicensed, BYO (no corkage)

✪ Thrilling grilling, the Iranian way

**Just suppose that you are visiting Homebase on the Warwick
Road.** As the traffic thunders past, spare a thought for the people
who still live here. For, indeed, across the road you will see signs of
habitation: two pubs – one a Young's house, the other selling Fuller's
beer; and between them Mohsen, a small, busy Iranian restaurant.
For somewhere in such an obscure location, Mohsen tends to be
gratifyingly busy. In the window is the oven, where the bread man
works to keep everyone supplied with fresh-from-the-oven sheets
of bread. The bread is terrific and the waiters conspire to see that it
arrives in relays and never has a chance to get cold. The starters list
is largely made up of things to go with the bread. You must have
sabzi, a basket containing fresh green herbs – tarragon, flat parsley
and mint – plus a chunk of feta. Eat it with your bread. Or there's
maast o mouseer, which is a dish of yogurt and shallots. Or chicken
livers cooked with mushrooms. The main courses tend to revolve
around grilled meat – joojeh kabab, for example, is a poussin, jointed,
marinated, grilled and served on rice. Then there is chello kabab-e-
barg, which is outstanding – a tender fillet of lamb flattened and
grilled. It's traditionally accompanied by an egg yolk. Look out for
the dish of the day; on Wednesday it is kharesh badenjan, a stonking
stew of lamb and aubergines. Drink aromatic Iranian tea from tiny,
gilded glasses.

Racine

229 Brompton Road, SW3 ■ 020 7584 4477

⊖ Knightsbridge/South Kensington

🍴 French

🕐 Mon to Fri 12.00–15.00 & 18.00–22.30; Sat 12.00–15.30 & 18.30–
22.30; Sun 12.00–15.00 & 18.00–22.00

🏷 all major credit cards ■ 14.5% service added

££ starters £5.25–£12.50 ■ mains £12.50–£21 ■ sides £2.75–£5.50
■ desserts £5.75–£6.95 ■ set lunch & dinner £15.50 & £17.50
■ lowest bottle price £15

✪ Homage to traditional French food

Racine goes from strength to strength. It fields something of a
foodie 'dream team' – chef Henry Harris and front-of-house Eric
Garnier – and the food is French. Not just any old French, but familiar,
delicious, nostalgic dishes from the glory days of French cooking. The
dining room at Racine is dark brown and comfortable. The service is
friendly and Gallic. The prices are reasonable, and haven't crept up
too much year on year. It's no surprise that this place is busy enough
to make booking an imperative. Henry Harris is a very good cook
and his menus are invariably skilfully written. Everything tempts,
everything is priced reasonably, and he takes a great deal of trouble
to source and buy top-quality seasonal ingredients. To start with,
expect simple but glorious combinations such as jambon de Bayonne
with celeriac rémoulade; pâté de foie de volaille et fines herbes;
melted Raclette, shallot and cornichons salad; or a truly wonderful
warm garlic and saffron mousse with mussels – light and airy, with a
triumphant texture and a delicate taste. Mains continue the 'classical'
theme: roast skate with braised endive and green peppercorn sauce;
tête de veau with a well-made sauce ravigote; plus chicken, chops,
steak and fish. The dessert menu deals in classics: petit pot au
chocolat; strawberries in Beaujolais; and Mont Blanc, which is a rich
chestnut purée with meringue and chocolate sauce. The wine list is
Francocentric, but merciful – even the smart bottles seem reasonably
priced.

Hammersmith and Chiswick

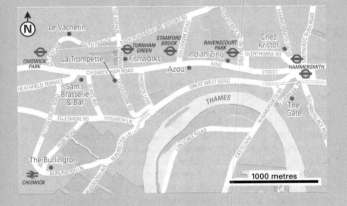

Azou

375 King Street, W6 ■ 020 8563 7266

⊖ Stamford Brook/Ravenscourt Park

🍽 North African

🕐 Mon to Fri 12.00–14.30 & 18.00–23.00; Sun 18.00–23.00

🗄 all major credit cards ■ 12.5% optional service

££ starters £3.50–£5.50 ■ mains £9.50–£14.50 ■ sides £2.50–£2.70
■ desserts £3.50 ■ lowest bottle price £10.50

✪ North African food, warm welcome

Azou is a small, comfortable, informal North African restaurant
where you can enter into the spirit and end up sitting on the floor
on a cushion. It is run by husband and wife team Chris and Chris
Benarab. The kitchen knows its business, and the classics – tagines,
couscous, grills – are presented with some panache. The menu is
split into various sections. First there is a list of kemia, by way of
starters. These are the North African equivalent of tapas and include
all the favourites, from dips such as hummus and baba ganoush
to bourek – those little pastries filled with cheese or mince, and
'briks' from Tunisia, which are deep-fried filo parcels of potato, tuna
and egg. One classic that should not be missed is the méchouia,
which is a salad of grilled tomato and pepper. The main courses are
arbitrarily divided up. Under 'couscous', vegetarian teams vegetables
and chickpeas; 'fish' combines fish, shellfish and prawns, or there's
'royale', which brings lamb shank, chicken breast and Merguez
sausage. Under 'Tagines' there's the tagine el ain, lamb shank with
prunes, apricots and almonds. From the 'Azou Specialities', the tagine
romanne appeals – chicken in sweet and tangy pomegranate sauce
with almonds, raisins and caramelised onions. These dishes are well
made and fairly priced. Even the extravagant 'Mechoul' (a whole
lamb to feed twelve) which must be ordered in advance, is fairly
priced. To drink, there's a sound Moroccan wine and an interesting
beer from Casablanca.

The Burlington

1 Station Parade, Burlington Lane, W4 ■ 020 8995 3344

⊖ BR Chiswick

🍽 Modern British

🕐 Mon to Sat 18.30–22.30; Sun 12.00–14.30

🕸 www.theburlington.org.uk

🗗 all major cards except AmEx ■ 10% service

££ starters £4.75–£7.95 ■ mains £7.50–£14.50 ■ sides £2.50 ■ desserts £5.50–£6.95 ■ menus (18.30–19.45) £12.50 & £15 ■ lowest bottle price £10

✪ A grand local, bistro

This bistro in affluent Grove Park is a first step across the river for Redmond and Pippa Hayward – who run Redmond's (see p. 353) in Sheen. The look here isn't aggressively designery, but the room is clean and fresh. There are 30 or so seats in the main dining room, bolstered by a few tables in a conservatory out the back, and an area of pavement in front of the restaurant that will take a few outdoor tables. The service is friendly and efficient. The food is very good. Strong flavours, quality ingredients, well presented. The king of the starters is the Burlington platter, which is a one-plate antipasti trolley: roast peppers/olives/salt cod brandade/creamy celeriac remoulade/ slow-roast belly pork/chorizo/a coffee cup mushroom and rosemary soup/black pudding/smoked salmon/duck liver parfait/gravlax. Simple and excellent. Or there may be a salad of artichokes and green beans with wild mushrooms and hazelnut dressing. Mains range from pan-fried bream fillet with fennel and orange salad, new potatoes and tarragon sauce; to perfectly cooked calves' liver with a lemon and thyme risotto; or a grandstand dish like roast marinated pigeon breasts, soft thyme polenta, black pudding, caramelised endive, seared foie gras and Port jus – a very good, very rich combo. Hayward has a knack for bringing out light, bright herbal flavours – the thyme polenta is stunning. Puds are stalwart – dark chocolate tart with rosemary and caramel ice cream; blood orange and vodka jelly with coffee madeleines.

Chez Kristof

111 Hammersmith Grove, W6 ■ 020 8741 1177 &

⊖ Hammersmith

🍽 French

🕐 Mon to Fri 12.00–15.00 & 18.00–23.15; Sat 12.00–16.00 & 18.00–
23.15; Sun 12.00–16.00 & 18.00–22.30

🖰 www.chezkristof.co.uk

🖯 all major credit cards ■ 12.5% optional service added

££ starters £5–£9 ■ mains £12.50–£17 ■ sides £3.50 ■ desserts £5
■ lunch & pre-theatre £12 & £15 ■ lowest bottle price £13.50

✪ French food, French atmosphere

Named after his father's first London restaurant, Chez Kristof
is a solidly retro French establishment opened by Jan Woroneki
(proprietor of Wòdka in Kensington and Baltic in Southwark). Chez
Kristof is busy, probably due to the comfortable French dishes on
the menu and accessible pricing. The menu is old-fashioned in the
nicest possible way, littered with cosy French dishes – boudin noir
is served with apple: good black pudding with a pleasant contrast
from tart apple, all presented in a very hot cast iron dish. There's
a ragout of snails in garlic butter; salad of fines herbes with truffle
oil; a Savoyarde vegetable soup; moules à la Normande. The mains
also feature comfort classics – coq au vin comes to table in an iron
casserole dish, and while the chicken concerned was rather too
small (it seems indelicate to speculate that it was more likely a young
hen than an old cock) the gravy has the body that comes from long
and slow cooking. Other stalwarts from the list include cassoulet;
an entrecôte steak served with Marchand de vin sauce and frîtes;
and confit of duck with olives and potatoes. A daube of ox cheeks
is suitably rich and gluey. The puds are in character – chocolate
fondant, crème brûlée, pain perdu with apples, and there is always
the option of a 'selection of French cheeses'. Chez Kristof is a cheerful
place with familiar dishes and the bread is good, all of which bolsters
its French credentials.

Fishworks

6 Turnham Green Terrace, W4 ■ 020 8994 0086

⊖ Turnham Green

🍴 Fish

🕐 Tues to Fri 12.00–14.30 & 18.00–22.30; Sat 12.00–15.00 & 18.00–22.30; Sun 12.00–15.00

🖰 www.fishworks.co.uk

🖫 all major credit cards ■ no service added

££ starters £6.90–£12.90 ■ mains £10–£24.90 ■ sides £1.95–£8.50 ■ desserts £4.95–£6.50 ■ fruits de mer £12.50–£45pp ■ children's menu £4.95 ■ lowest bottle price £15

✪ Fresh fish and wet fish

There's something spooky about this part of Chiswick – the last few years have seen it turn from middle-class respectable to restaurant gulch. Fishworks is the London end of a chainlet that links branches in Bath, Bristol and Christchurch, and the vibe is right. Inside is a pretty, modern dining room with a gardeny bit at the rear. Service is friendly and attentive, the wine list is interesting and not too rapacious; all in all, a very satisfying place. There's a longish menu and a very long list of specials on a blackboard. From the starters, perhaps the roast shellfish with garlic and olive oil appeals. Or there may be fresh Dartmouth crab salad with tarragon mayonnaise. Or how about steamed River Fowey mussels with wine and parsley? Or grilled tuna? Alternatively, try the 'skate with black butter and capers'. There is a serious fruits de mer. And there are 'whole fish – for the table', such as a wild sea bass for two. Vegetables are simple and good; a dish of buttered spinach leaves is outstanding. The bread is good. This is a comfortable place where the fish are both skilfully chosen and skilfully cooked. The wine list is eclectic and there are some interesting bottles at accessible prices. Start with half a bottle of cold Manzanilla San Leon, and look out for the unusual Pazo Ribeiro, from Galicia – dry, white and zingy. Note – the fishmonger's counter is open 08.30–22.30.

→ For branches, see index or website

The Gate

51 Queen Caroline Street, W6 ■ 020 8748 6932

⊖ Hammersmith

🍴 Vegetarian

🕐 Mon to Fri 12.00–14.45 & 18.00–22.45; Sat 18.00–23.00

🖰 www.thegate.tv

🗗 all major credit cards ■ 12.5% optional service added

££ starters £4.50–£6 ■ mains £8.50–£13 ■ sides £2.95 ■ desserts
£4.50–£6 ■ lowest bottle price £11

❂ Veggie heaven

**The extraordinary thing about The Gate (which is tucked away
behind the Hammersmith Apollo)** is that you hardly notice that it's
a vegetarian restaurant. This is enjoyable dining without the meat. It's
not wholefood, it's not even healthy; indeed, it's as rich, colourful,
calorific and naughty as anywhere in town. The clientele is a quiet and
appreciative bunch of locals and pilgrims – it's unlikely that anyone
could just stumble across this hidden-away, former artists' studio.
The airy décor and the high ceiling give it a serene, lofty feel, which
may be The Gate's only nod to veggie solemnities. The short menu
changes regularly, but starters are always well balanced and attractive.
There's usually a tart, like the leek and trompette tart. Also excellent
are the sweetcorn fritters, which are served with a sweet chilli sauce.
Portions are hearty, so it's a good idea to share starters in order to
pace yourself and sample all the courses. The mains are generally
well executed. Butternut, basil and goats' cheese ravioli is pan-fried
in sage butter and served with purple sprouting. Or perhaps there's a
chipotle-glazed artichoke – poached in chilli and lime-leaf stock before
being filled with avocado and feta cheese. Puddings are splendid:
vanilla crème brûlée served with strawberry and rose salsa. Those
without a sweet tooth should go for the cheese plate. The drinks list is
extensive, and the wine section has something for everyone.

Indian Zing

236 King Street, W6 ■ 020 8748 5959

⊖ Ravenscourt Park

🍽 Indian

🕐 Mon to Sun 12.00–15.00 & 18.00–23.00

🖰 www.indianzing.co.uk

🖯 all major credit cards ■ 12.5% optional service added

££ starters £2.50–£5.50 ■ mains £7–£11 ■ sides £2–£3.60 ■ desserts £3.60–£4 ■ lowest bottle price £12

✪ A modern Indian with vibrant spicing

It is hard to live up to a name like Indian Zing, but chef-proprietor Manoj Vasaikar manages it. Vasaikar (who was well reviewed for his last restaurant) is not only a good cook, but also a thoughtful one, blending India's regional recipes and traditional ingredients with modern techniques and presentation. Starters include dahi kachori, little pastries filled with a spicy mixture and topped with sprouted beans and yogurt. Or chapli kebab – this interleaves slices of lamb with slices of aubergine. The patrani macchi is a real star, a fillet of fish cooked with green herbs and coconut and rolled in a banana leaf. There is even chicken peppercorn malia tikka, an upmarket chicken tikka, the chicken pieces marinated with green peppercorns and cheese. The main courses are also well done, for once there is a splendid vegetarian dish 'tandoori artichoke and paneer in mahi khaliyaa sauce', which is a skewer from the tandoor that features chunks of paneer cheese with a decent chilli rub, baby artichokes, onions – the gravy is heavy with cashew nuts and tomatoes. There's a Malabar chicken curry billed as chilli hot, but coming to table medium, plenty of coconut milk, mustard seed and curry leaves. The dhansaak is made with dill, pumpkin and lentils and has a good depth of flavour. The kitchen gets the spicing just about perfect in every dish – Indian Zing is what it's called and Indian zing is what you get.

Sam's Brasserie & Bar

11 Barley Mow Passage, W4 ■ 020 8987 0555   ♿

⊖ Chiswick Park

🍽 Modern European

🕐 Mon to Sat 09.00–23.00; Sun 09.00–22.30

🖰 www.samsbrasserie.co.uk

🖫 all major credit cards ■ 12.5% 'optional' service added

££ starters £4.75–£7.50 ■ mains £9.50–£16.50 ■ desserts £6–£7 ■ set lunch Mon to Fri £9.95 ■ lowest bottle price £12.50

✪ Beware the bloody Mary

Rick Stein is one of the backers of this bright new brasserie, and since it opened, Chiswickians have taken to Sam's like ducks to water. Sam was formerly manager at the Seafood Restaurant in Padstow and he has obviously learnt a thing or two about matching the ambience to the customers. The Barley Mow centre is the new name for an old paper factory and the large spaces lend themselves to a modern, comfortable, informal Brasserie, which is exactly what they have been turned into. There is a small gallery that seats 25, which does duty as a private room, and the dining room proper has a window to the kitchen. The head chef is Rufus Wickham and his menu manages to combine comfortable with interesting. A fish soup comes with classic trimmings and is rich and smooth. Roast figs are served with pancetta and balsamic vinegar. A combination of grilled leeks, soft-boiled egg, sherry vinegar and Parmesan works very well. Main courses range from crisp sea bass with pickled cucumber and sauce Vierge; to rump of lamb with creamed flageolet beans; and a very large, but still tender, basted magret of Gascon duck served with orange sauce and braised turnips. The puds are sound – chocolate tart; crème brûlée; poached apricots with Greek yogurt. Service makes light of the large numbers and is informal without being slack. The wine list ambles through the familiar regions with plenty to drink at reasonable prices.

La Trompette

5–7 Devonshire Road, W4 ■ 020 8747 1836   ♿

⊖ Turnham Green

🍴 French

🕐 Mon to Sat 12.00–14.30 & 18.30–22.30; Sun 12.00–15.00 & 19.00–22.00

🖱 www.latrompette.co.uk

▱ all major credit cards ■ 12.5% optional service added

££ lunch £23.50 (3 courses) (£27.50 on Sunday) ■ dinner £35.50 (3 courses) & £40.50 (with cheese) ■ lowest bottle price £16

✪ Seriously good cooking

La Trompette is already securely embedded in the hearts of Chiswickians. This state of affairs isn't a great surprise as Trompette is a thoroughbred from the same stable as Chez Bruce (see p. 299), The Glasshouse (see p. 352) and The Square (see p. 90). The dining room is comfortable with a good deal of light oak and chocolate leather on show. The kitchen knows its stuff, so the food is very good, the wine list is comprehensive, the pricing is restrained and the service is on the ball. The prix fixe arrangements are straightforward – it is always comforting to know what kind of bill you are in for as you set off; just about the only supplement is when you add an extra cheese course – something that is well worth while. The menu changes daily. Presentation is simple, but elegant. Starters may include such delights as thinly sliced rump of veal with chips cooked in duck fat, rocket and meat juices; or grilled red mullet with aïoli, chorizo and saffron beurre blanc; or cream of leek and potato soup. Mains are rich and satisfying. In the appropriate season you might be offered crisp sea bream with olive oil mash, red peppers and aged balsamic vinegar; or sauté of calf's sweetbread and kidney with shallot purée, salsify, garlic and parsley; or duck magret with foie gras, parsnips, griottine cherries and port sauce. Puds range from classics such as citrus fruit trifle, to indulgent chocolate profiteroles. Enjoy!

Le Vacherin

76–77 South Parade, W4 ■ 020 8742 2121

⊖ Chiswick Park

🍴 French

🕐 Mon 18.00–24.00; Tues to Sun 12.00–15.00 & 18.00–24.00

🖥 www.levacherin.co.uk

🗂 all major credit cards except AmEx ■ 12.5% optional service added

££ dinner menu: starters £4.95–£11 ■ mains £11.85–£16 ■ desserts £5.50–£7 ■ lunch menu: starters £5.95 ■ mains £9.90 ■ dessert £4.95 ■ lowest bottle price £13.40

✪ Francophile English chef does excellent job

It's hard to know how to pigeonhole Le Vacherin. Despite having an English chef, this is a defiantly French restaurant and the menu is littered with nostalgic, rustic dishes – very Elizabeth David. The cooking is good here, well-balanced dishes, intense flavours, good seasoning and a healthy dollop of real passion. The dining room décor is something of a French cliché – it certainly looks the part. And perhaps there's some lingering memory of 1970s fondue, but the starter of a whole baked Vacherin is immensely popular and the kitchen gets through 40 to 50 a week. Setting aside its merits, various other opening moves appeal: old-style Burgundy snails with pungent garlic butter; a warm salad of scallops, black pudding and Alsace bacon; a goats' cheese tart with endives and a walnut salad. There are a dozen main courses: steak frîtes; pork belly and lentils; a Provençal fish stew; duck cassoulet. 'Joue de boeuf braisée à la Bourguignonne' is jolly good, a rich wine-dark stew, hyper-intense gravy with a few chunks of bacon and the ox cheek cooked until melting point. Or there are old favourites like blanquette de veau, or grilled lemon sole, chips and tartare sauce. The wine list has some sensibly priced, straightforward bottles on it – note those from the South West of France. If you get to the dessert course still unswayed by the merits of molten cheese, then opt for one of the classics – petit pot au chocolat; profiteroles; crème brûlée; prune and Armagnac tart.

Richmond and Twickenham

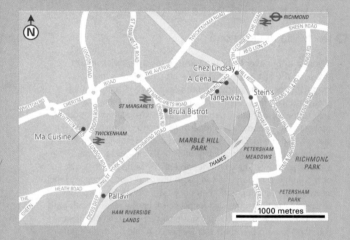

A Cena

418 Richmond Road, Twickenham, Middx ■ 020 8288 0108

⊖ Richmond/BR St Margaret's

🍽 Italian

🕐 Tues to Sat 12.00–14.30 & 19.00–22.30; Sun 12.00–14.30

🖪 all major credit cards ■ no service added

££ starters £5–£9.50 ■ pasta/risotto £6.50–£11.50 ■ mains £13.75–£19
■ sides £3 ■ desserts £5–£6.50 ■ lowest bottle price £12.95

✪ Dolce vita in Richmond

If you stumble over Richmond Bridge towards Twickenham,
A Cena is the first restaurant on the left. This place is more
Knightsbridge than Richmond, but seems to have survived that
always difficult first couple of years in some style. There is a bar
area to the front that aims to tempt streetwise locals with modish
cocktails; all is trendy, all is modern. The menu changes to suit the
seasons and the markets, and the food is good – simple in the best
kind of way, with clever combinations of flavour and texture. These
are straightforward Italian dishes and all the better for that. The
only caveat is that portions can be on the small side, especially when
viewed in conjunction with their price tags. Dishes are admirably
seasonal – start with the wild fennel soup, or veal sweetbreads with
artichokes and Marsala. Simple starters like mozzarella di bufala with
squashed tomato bruschetta, or Dorset crab salad with almond aioli
always appeal. The pasta of the day and the risotto are well made;
dishes such as leek risotto with prosciutto vie with fusilli with tomato,
basil and Parmesan. Main courses read and eat well: baked sea bass
with lemon, capers, anchovy and new potatoes; veal chop with
roast cherry tomatoes and wild greens; polenta fritters with tomato,
spinach and Parmigiano. The puds are good. The zuppa Inglese
– Italian for trifle – and the baked ricotta cheesecake are seriously
rich, and so they should be.

Brula Bistrot

43 Crown Road, St Margaret's, Twickenham, Middx ■ 020 8892 0602

⊖ BR St Margaret's

|◉| French

🕓 Mon to Sat 12.30–14.30 & 19.00–22.30; Sun 12.00–15.00

🖰 www.brulabistrot.com

🖰 Mastercard, Visa ■ no service added

££ starters £4.50–£5 ■ mains £11–£18 ■ sides £2.75 ■ desserts £4.75 ■ menus: lunch £11 & £13.50; Sunday lunch £13.50 & £15; menu rapide (lunch daily) £15 ■ lowest bottle price £12.50

✪ The French quarter of St Margaret's

At the turn of the century, two friends chose St Margaret's as a locale and, as they were called Bruce Duckett and Lawrence Hartley, opened a restaurant called Brula. Pretty soon the business become so successful that they had to move across Crown Road into larger premises. Now the Brula Bistrot (the name was enlarged, in keeping with the new premises) is no longer a cramped affair. There are large windows with a profusion of rather elegant stained glass. Thankfully, the food and philosophy have endured – well-cooked French bistro food, limited choice, low, low prices. Lunch is a particular bargain. The menu changes weekly, so you might choose between dishes such as marinated squid salad, or braised leeks with hard-boiled egg. Then on to fish of the day with haddock purée, or jambonneau with parsley sauce. Finally, you get your pick of the puds. All very French. Running alongside is 'the Bistrot Offers' list, informal à la carte – nine snails with garlic butter; celeriac remoulade, poached egg and ham; roast lamb chump with pissaladière; king scallops with artichoke purée and pancetta. The Frenchness even extends to the list of suggested apéritifs at the top of the evening menu: kir, or kir royale. And, should you spurn these blandishments, the wine list is short and agreeably priced with a good showing at the cheaper end.

Chez Lindsay

11 Hill Rise, Richmond, Surrey ■ 020 8948 7473

⊖ Richmond

🍴 Very French/pancakes

🕘 Mon to Sat 12.00–23.00; Sun 12.00–22.00

🗗 Mastercard, Visa ■ 12.5% optional service added

££ starters £3.95–£10.75 ■ mains £4.75–£15.75 ■ sides £3.50
■ desserts £3–£5.95 ■ menu du midi £6.75 ■ lowest bottle price
£8.50 cider, £12 wine

✪ Breton through and through

**At first glance, Chez Lindsay looks rather like Chicago in the
1920s** – all around you people are drinking alcohol out of large
earthenware teacups. The cups are, in fact, traditional Breton drinking
vessels known as bolées, the drink is cider, and Chez Lindsay lists a
trio of them, ranging from Breton brut traditionnel to Norman cidre
bouché. Most people are attracted to this small, bright restaurant by
the galettes and crêpes, though the menu also includes a regularly
changing list of hearty Breton dishes – especially fish. It's a place for
Francophiles – both the kitchen and the front of house seem to be
staffed entirely by Gauls, which in this instance means good service
and tasty food. Start with the moules à la St Malo, which are cooked
with shallots, cream and thyme. Then you must decide between
the galettes or more formal main courses. The galettes are huge
buckwheat pancakes, large and lacy, thin but satisfying. They come
with an array of fillings: egg and ham; scallops and leeks; Roquefort
cheese, celery and walnuts; and 'Chez Lindsay', cheese, ham and
spinach. The other half of the menu features a good steak frîtes and
lots of fish and shellfish. The 'gratin de Camembert, vivanneau et
crevettes' is an interesting dish – a gratin containing red snapper,
prawns and Camembert. Or there's the bar grillé – a whole grilled
sea bass with salad and new potatoes. Real pud enthusiasts will save
themselves for the chocolate and banana crêpe.

Ma Cuisine

6 Whitton Road, Twickenham, Middx ■ 020 8607 9849

BR Twickenham

Very French

Mon to Sat 12.00–14.30 & 18.30–23.00

all major credit cards ■ 10% optional service added

££ starters £4–£6 ■ mains £10–£15 ■ desserts £4 ■ lunch £12.95 & £15.50 ■ lowest bottle price £12

Very cheap, very sound, very French

Ma Cuisine is sibling to its near neighbour McClement's, and while McC's is upscale and wins Michelin stars, Ma Cuisine is cheerful and wins the tyre people's medal for special value. This is an old-fashioned, bistroey sort of place, even down to the gingham-look table covers and French staff, whose first priority is to ensure that you are kept supplied with baguette and butter. The menu is made up of unrepentantly old-school French favourites. So saying, the cooking is adequate and the atmosphere buzzes along. You don't often see a starter that includes a hunk of foie gras and is still priced so favourably: 'Yorkshire pudding, topped with sautéed foie gras and onion gravy'. The foie gras is fine, but the rather leathery pudding wouldn't do in Yorkshire. There may also be French onion soup; or grilled sardines with garlic butter; a rather good rillette of skate with olive oil dressing; or a risotto of wild mushrooms. Mains continue the theme – blanquette of rabbit with tarragon sauce; coq au vin, slow-cooked chunks of what was once an impressively large bird; cassoulet suffers from a few shortcuts, but is suitably filling; sea bream with red wine glaze. Puds include a tolerable tarte Tatin, and a chocolate pot with coffee cream. Amazingly enough, the wine list also keeps faith with the mood and a Cab. Sauv. from the Languedoc is workmanlike enough. A deal like this gladdens the hardest heart.

→ For branches, see index

Pallavi

1st Floor, 3 Cross Deep Court, Heath Road, Twickenham, Middx
- 020 8892 2345

BR Twickenham

Indian

Mon to Sun 12.00–15.00 & 18.00–23.00 (24.00 Sat & Sun)

www.mcdosa.com

all major credit cards ■ 10% optional service added

££ starters £1.95–£5.95 ■ dosai £2.95–£4.95 ■ mains £4.50–£7.95
■ sides £2.50 ■ desserts £2–£3.50 ■ lowest bottle price £10.95

✪ The soul of Kerala in the heart of Twickenham

This is a small outpost of an extensive Indian restaurant empire.
Pallavi is one of the simplest and the cheapest, and started its days
as a large takeaway counter with just a few seats, then moved over
the road from the original site to smarter premises. The cooking
has travelled well, and still deserves the ultimate compliment – it is
genuinely home-style, with unpretentious dishes and unpretentious
prices. True to its South Indian roots, there is an impressive list of
vegetarian specialities, but the menu features just enough meat and
fish dishes to woo any kind of diner. Start with that South Indian
veggie favourite, the Malabar masala dosa. This huge, crisp pancake
is made with a mixture of ground rice and lentil flour, and is a
perfect match for the savoury potato mixture and chutney. Or try the
delightfully named iddly, a steamed rice cake made with black gram,
which is eaten as a breakfast dish in India. The main dishes are simple
and tasty, and are served without fuss. For unrepentant carnivores,
chicken Malabar or keema methi both hit the spot. But there are
also some interesting fish dishes, including the fish moilee. Veggies
are good, too: try parippu curry, split lentils with cumin, turmeric,
garlic, chillies and onions, or the cabbage thoran, sliced cabbage with
carrots, green chillies and curry leaves. The pilau rice, lemon rice and
coconut rice are tasty, and the parathas are even better – try a green
chilli, or a sweet coconut paratha.

Stein's

The Tow Path, rear of 55 Petersham Road, Surrey

■ 020 8948 8189

◉ BR Richmond

🍴 German

🕐 May–mid-October (depending on weather) daily 12.00–22.00; rest of year: Fri to Sun 12.00–22.00

🖰 www.stein-s.com

🗐 all major credit cards except AmEx ■ no service added

££ starters £2.75–£6 ■ mains £7–£8 ■ sides £3 ■ desserts £3–£4 ■ lowest bottle price £14.60

✪ Bavarian beer garden on Thames towpath

This must be the only restaurant in London that has no indoor seating of any kind. In front of the hut that lies 'to the rear of no. 55 Petersham Road' there are enough tables and benches to seat 200. The idea is that Stein's is open until 22.00, with lunch served between noon and 15.00; breakfast, dinner, or just coffee and cake all fit into the day as relevant. This place has a restaurant licence so you can only drink alcohol when you order food and then it is limited to beer and wine. The two main draught beers are Paulaner Helles (the golden lager-style one) and Erdinger Weissbier (the cloudy wheat beer one) and are very good. The 'Bavarian specialities' on the menu revolve around sausages and very good they are, too. The Nuernberger wurst are small and well-spiced cousins to our own chipolatas. The Thuringer bratwurst is a larger, meaty, porkier number. The Muenchner weisswurst is a white veal sausage that is boiled rather than grilled – it's the traditional accompaniment to wheat beer at breakfast time. Sausages come with decent sauerkraut and mash, or really stunning pretzels in the case of the weisswurst. And some are teamed with bratkartoffeln, which translates as chunky sauté potatoes with attitude. Stein's is an eccentric, jolly sort of place to eat and seems to get the thumbs-up from the students at the nearby London German School in Petersham.

Tangawizi

406 Richmond Road, East Twickenham, Surrey ■ 020 8891 3737

⊖ BR Richmond

|●| Indian

⏱ Mon to Sat 18.30–23.00

🖏 all major credit cards ■ no service added

££ starters £4.50–£9.95 ■ veg mains £6.50–£7.50 ■ non-veg mains £7.50–£12.50 ■ sides £1.95–£2.95 ■ desserts £3.25–£4.95 ■ lowest bottle price £10.95

✪ Modernist Indian restaurant, modernist prices

Tangawizi is the Swahili word for ginger, but despite East African ownership, this restaurant seems conservative menu-wise. You won't find any of the great East African-Asian dishes on a list that in the main confines itself to North Indian favourites. The décor is certainly modern enough, with low lights and mauve walls, angular tables and comfortable chairs. Service is friendly and there is live music on Friday nights. Starters range from chowk ki tikki, potato cakes served with chutneys, to murgh malai kebab, a very tender, cheesy chicken tikka; or ajwaini jhinga, large prawns marinated with carom seeds before being cooked in the tandoor, or there are plenty of old favourites like seekh kebab. Portions are large, but perhaps not quite large enough to compensate for prices that would be more at home in the West End than Richmond. Main courses are sound and the spicing is well balanced, although there is an occasional lack of seasoning. Methi wala chicken is a grand dish, rich and simple. Tanghai lamb comes to table in a hollowed-out coconut, the sauce made from curry leaves and coconut (a South Indian excursion). The breads – notably the onion kulcha and the mint paratha – are well done. Tangawizi is an ambitious Indian restaurant, determined to stand out from the late-night curry houses, and the food is good, but you do wish that they would throw caution to the winds and add some more interesting East African dishes to the menu.

Shepherd's Bush and Olympia

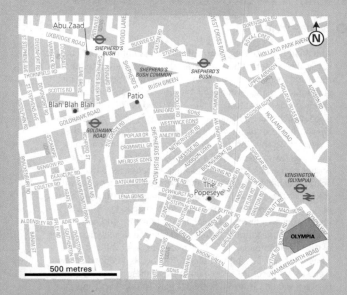

Abu Zaad

29 Uxbridge Road, W12 ∎ 020 8749 5107

⊖ Shepherd's Bush

🍴 Syrian

🕐 daily 11.00–23.00

🗗 all major credit cards except AmEx ∎ no service added

££ starters £2–£3 ∎ mains £4.90–£11 ∎ desserts £2 ∎ no alcohol

⭐ Damascus in W12

Abu Zaad bears the trappings of its success lightly. Slowly but surely, this restaurant has expanded, the bar has moved to the back room and there are now a few more tables. It still serves as a pit stop for coffee and pastries and the cooking arrangements are still dominated by a charcoal grill and a full-sized bread oven. Abu Zaad is a busy place and a friendly one – the food is good and awesomely cheap. The décor teams rich greens with decorative metal panels – very Damascene. This may be the cheapest place in London to experiment with meze. Here, a trifling sum will get you a large portion of makanic, meaty, chipolata-sized sausages; baba ganouj, delicious aubergine mush; foul medames, boiled fava beans with chickpeas, tomato and lemon juice; or hummus. A stunning haystack of tabbouleh comes with spankingly fresh chopped parsley and mint. Ordering a dish called falafi brings four crisp and nutty falafel. You must try the fattoush, a fresh, well-dressed salad with croûtons of deep-fried flatbread. In fact, all meze you order will arrive with a basket of delicious fresh flatbread. The food is described on the menu as 'Damascene Cuisine', but most of these dishes are claimed by every Middle Eastern chef. Drink a glass of carrot and apple juice and feel healthy. The menu goes on to list dozens of main courses, from rich casseroles to charcoal grills, and they are all reasonably priced. There's a good case for not bothering with a main course here – simply order seven or eight meze between two.

Blah Blah Blah

78 Goldhawk Road, W12 ■ 020 8746 1337

⊖ Goldhawk Road

🍽 Vegetarian

🕓 Mon to Sat 12.30–14.30 & 18.30–23.00

🗂 cash or cheque only ■ no service added

££ starters £3.95–£4.95 ■ mains £9.95 ■ desserts £4.95 ■ unlicensed, BYO (£1.25 corkage pp)

✪ Very sound veggie resto

Blah Blah Blah is an old-time veggie haven, and has décor to match. The floors, tables and chairs are wooden, there are blinds rather than curtains, and the only decorations of note are driftwood and old iron lamps. Add wallpaper music and the echoing noise levels become formidable. Legend has it that an old chap called Paul McCartney was overheard here asking for the music to be turned down. The menu casts its net widely and you can expect dishes with all manner of influences, but all of them reasonably priced and generously portioned. Among the starters might be cream of asparagus soup; plum tomato and mozzarella torte; a Greek salad; and a spicy Indian potato cake filled with curried cauliflower, carrots and peas. Dodging over to the Windies, there may be plantain fritters made with raisins, ginger and sweet potato and served with a tomato, chilli and pineapple sauce. Main courses are similarly eclectic. Stir-fried noodles come with hot Thai sauce; baked tostada is put together with sweet potato gratin, refried beans and a jalapeno cream sauce; a 'Mediterranean' roulade teams baked and rolled potato layers with ricotta and roast peppers and courgettes, served with a creamy spinach sauce and deep-fried leeks; or there could be a Middle Eastern pie filled with new potato, chilli and tomatoes. Puds are rewarding: glazed lemon tart; rhubarb and apple charlotte; roast plum crumble; and the 'wicked' chocolate pot.

Patio

5 Goldhawk Road, W10 ■ 020 8743 5194

🚇 Goldhawk Road

🍽 Polish

🕐 Mon to Fri 12.00–15.00 & 18.00–23.30; Sat 18.00–24.00; Sun 12.00–24.00

💳 all major credit cards ■ no service added

££ starters £3.50–£6.80 ■ mains £8.50–£14.90 ■ desserts £3.50 ■ set menus: lunch & dinner £14.90 ■ lowest bottle price £10.50

✪ Polish hospitality writ large

A former opera singer, the ebullient Eva Michalik, and her husband Kaz have been running this restaurant for more than a decade. At Patio you get good, solid Polish food in a friendly, comfortable atmosphere and for a relatively small amount of money. And this little restaurant is a people-pleaser – you can just as easily come here for an intimate tête-à-tête as for a raucous birthday dinner. There are two floors; downstairs feels a little cosier and more secluded. The set menu (available at lunch and dinner) is Patio's trump card. For a surprisingly small sum, you get a starter, main course, dessert, petits fours … and a vodka. Starters may include plump and tasty blinis with smoked salmon; wild mushroom soup; Polish ham; and herrings with soured cream. Everything is fresh and carefully prepared. For mains, there's a good selection of meat, fish and chicken dishes – the scallops in dill sauce, when available, are outstanding. Or you might try a Polish speciality such as golabki (cabbage stuffed with rice and meat), which is also available as a vegetarian dish, or sausages à la Zamoyski (grilled with sautéed mushrooms and onions). Be prepared, too, for high-octane puds, such as the Polish pancakes with cheese, vanilla and rum – the fumes alone are enough to send you reeling. Also good is the hot apple charlotka with cream. For those after more variety, the à la carte offers further choice, and for not a great deal more money.

The Popeseye

108 Blythe Road, W14 ■ 020 7610 4578

⊖ Hammersmith

🍴 Steak

🕘 Mon to Sat 19.00–22.30

🗗 cash or cheque only ■ 12.5% optional service added

££ steaks £10.45–£45.95 ■ sides £3.45 ■ desserts £4.95 ■ lowest bottle price £11.50

✪ Steak eaters – red in tooth and claw

Just suppose you fancy a steak – a good steak, and perhaps a glass (or bottle) of decent red wine to go with it. You're interested enough to want the best, probably Aberdeen Angus, and you want it cooked simply. The Popeseye is for you. All the meat here is 100% grass-fed Aberdeen Angus and the restaurant is a member of the Aberdeen Angus Society. The dining room is small, and things tend to get chaotic. As to the food, there is no choice: just various kinds of steak and good chips, with home-made puddings to follow. Oh, and the menu starts with the wine list. You choose what you want to drink, and only when that's settled do you choose your steak – specifying, of course, the cut and the size (and they come very big here), and how you want it cooked. Now – about these steaks. Popeseye comes in 6oz, 8oz, 12oz, 20oz and 30oz, as does sirloin, and fillet. You get excellent chips whichever you order and you can add a side salad to assist your vitamin intake. The puddings come from the home-made school of pâtisserie – such delights as apple crumble; sticky toffee pudding; and lemon tart. The wine list is an ever-changing reflection of what can be picked up at the sales and represents good value. There are fine clarets and Burgundies, plus the best of the Rhône, Australia, Argentina, Chile and Spain – and there are also two white wines on offer for people who have lost the plot.

→ For branches, see index

Southall

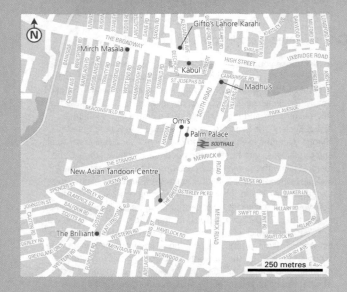

The Brilliant

72–76 Western Road, Southall, Middx ■ 020 8574 1928

⊖ BR Southall

¶⦿¶ Indian

🕒 Tues to Fri 12.00–14.30 & 18.00–24.00; Sat & Sun 18.00–23.30

🖱 www.brilliantrestaurant.com

🖃 all major credit cards ■ 10% optional service added

££ starters £4.50–£16 ■ mains £4.50–£13 ■ sides £6 ■ desserts £3–£4.50 ■ set menus (for parties of 10 or more) £17.40pp ■ lowest bottle price £9

✪ Splendid East African Asian dishes

The Brilliant is a Southall institution. For more than twenty years the Anand family business has been a nonstop success and it is now a bustling 250-seater. For 25 years before that, the family's first restaurant, also called The Brilliant, was the toast of Kenya. The food at The Brilliant is East African-Asian, and very good indeed. Recently there have been some changes; you can see that the Anand family is pulling back slightly and it is to be expected that, as The Brilliant starts hiring chefs from outside, so the menu will go more mainstream. Let's hope that the legendary high standards prevail. To start with, you must try the butter chicken. A half-portion will do for two people as a starter. This dish is an enigma: somehow it manages to taste more buttery than butter itself – really delicious. There's also jeera chicken, rich with cumin and black pepper. And chilli chicken, which is hot, but not quite as hot as it used to be. If you're in a party, move on to the special meal section – these come in two portion sizes, suggested for three people and five people. Methi chicken, masaladar lamb, and palak chicken are all winners. Alternatively, choose among the single-portion curries, which include masala fish, a curry of unimaginable richness with good firm chunks of boneless fish. As well as good rotis, the bread list hides a secret weapon, the kulcha. Hot from the kitchen they are amazing – it's best to order a succession so that they don't go cold.

Gifto's Lahore Karahi

162–164 The Broadway, Southall, Middx ■ 020 8813 8669 ♿

⊖ BR Southall

🍴 Indian

🕐 Mon to Thurs 12.00–23.30; Fri to Sun 12.00–24.00

🖥 www.gifto.com

🗄 all major credit cards ■ no service added

££ starters 90p–£4.90 ■ mains £4.90–£9 ■ sides £1–£2.50 ■ desserts £1–£3.30 ■ unlicensed, BYO (no corkage)

✪ Magnificent Indian food factory

There is no more competitive place for an Indian restaurant than Southall, which makes it all the more remarkable that Gifto has not only been busy for so many years, but continues to expand and add yet more covers. Downstairs is a barn of a room with the open kitchen running along one side and serried ranks of tables on the other. There's a newer room upstairs, but both are busy and there is often a queue at the door on Saturday or Sunday. Gifto's Lahore Karahi specialises in freshly grilled, well-spiced meats and simple curries. The food is good, cheap and takes a minimal time to get from chef to diner. Whatever you add to fill out your order, you should start with bread. The stuffed paratha is good – thin and almost flaky, and both the plain naan and the Peshwari naan are delicious. Accompany them with an order of chicken tikka; the seekh kebab; or the splendid tilapia fish, whole, marinated and cooked in the tandoor. The curries are served in a karahi here and taste very fresh and vibrant. The saag gosht is exemplary, the spinach melting down to make a rich sauce. Also good are the butter chicken, and the karela gosht – lamb and chunks of bitter melon in an intensely flavoured sauce. Either drink the various freshly squeezed juices or bring your own supplies of alcohol. Service is quick and efficient.

Kabul

1st Floor, Himalaya Shopping Centre, The Broadway, Southall, Middx ■ 020 8571 6878

⊖ BR Southall

⦿ Indian/Afghan

🕓 daily 12.00–24.00

🗐 all major credit cards ■ no service added

££ starters £1.20–£4.99 ■ mains £2.50–£9.99 ■ sides 70p–£2 ■ desserts £1.70–£3.50 ■ unlicensed, BYO (no corkage)

✪ Indian food meets Afghani

Find the Himalaya Shopping Centre and wend your way past the silk merchants and the shops selling exotic CDs. Head up the escalator and to the left you'll find the Kabul, which has taken over the space allocated to an entire shop. It's a spacious restaurant with comfortable chairs, dark blue tablecloths and a series of banquettes running along the wall. The menu splits into two sections: Afghan food and Indian food. Curiosity should compel you to try some Afghan dishes. Portions are very large and prices very competitive. Start with dumplings – ordering the Afghan starter called mantu gosht brings a dinner plate covered in large savoury dumplings filled with spiced lamb. Ashak are also dumplings and come in meat and non-meat versions. The vegetarian ones are amazingly good, light dumplings with dough so thin that you can see the green leaves of the filling through the skins. Also notable is the showr-na-kath, a bowl full of chickpeas in a thin, green, herby, chilli-warmed liquid. Eat them with a spoon, or more sensibly with some of the excellent Afghan nan bread. For mains, the quabuli murgh is a large plate of delicious rice pillau made with plenty of sultanas and garnished with shreds of carrot; on top of it is a tender chicken drumstick, and it comes with a bowl of curry with a large minced-lamb cake hidden in its depths. Another winner is the karahi tukham, which is a small karahi full of light, buttery, rich and spicy scrambled eggs.

Madhu's

39 South Road, Southall, Middx ■ 020 8574 1897 &

⊖ BR Southall

¶◎¶ Indian

⏲ Mon & Wed to Fri 12.30–15.00 & 18.00–23.30; Sat & Sun 18.00–23.30

🖰 www.madhusonline.com

🗗 all major credit cards ■ no service added

££ starters £6–£16 ■ mains £7–£10 ■ sides £7 ■ desserts £3.50–£4 ■ menu: lunch & dinner £20 ■ lowest bottle price £9

✪ Very plush resto, very good food

In the past both Sanjay Anand and his restaurant Madhu's collected a hatful of awards. Following a serious fire, it re-opened with chic new décor and a new logo (a red M with a flourish), and things have gone very well indeed. The service is slick, the food is very good and the whole operation is polished, from the smart white asymmetric china to the serried ranks of gleaming cutlery. There is even Louis Roederer Crystal on the wine list. Take heart: the cooking has not lost its way. The food here is predominantly East African-Asian, and is well spiced with good, full-on flavours – thank goodness nothing has been toned down. Starters are pricey, but portions are good. Try the famous butter chicken: very tender, very delicious, but sadly still dyed a lurid orange. Or there are the lamb chops – well spiced and juicy. Main courses also come in large portions. Masala fish is a hunk of tilapia in a rich tomatoey sauce. The simple dishes are well made – sag gosht is a good choice, lamb cooked with fresh spinach and agreeably spicy. The vegetable section hides some treasures: bhune karele, a bitter gourd stuffed and then oven-roasted, is a particularly fine and vibrant dish. Breads are good, particularly the bhatura, which is a fluffy cross between chapati and doughnut. If you can avoid the allure of the Crystal, you'll find Tusker and Whitecap beer. Make sure that they are cold.

Mirch Masala

171–173 The Broadway, Southall, Middx ■ 020 8867 9222 &

⊖ BR Southall

🍴 Indian

🕑 daily 12.00–24.00

🖰 www.mirchmasala.co.uk

🗗 all major credit cards ■ no service added

££ starters £2.50–£8 ■ mains £5.50–£12 ■ sides £2.50–£6 ■ desserts
£2.50–£3.50 ■ unlicensed

✪ Modern restaurant, modern Pakistani food

The original Mirch Masala is still plying its trade in Norbury, South London, and the second branch is busy in Tooting, but this imposing restaurant in Southall has quickly taken over as the flagship. The other branches were the kind of establishments where customers raved about 'food so good' that they could forgive the restaurants any amount of scruffiness. The new resto is a smart affair: new chairs, stone floor, big windows, smart open kitchen. Prices have gone up a little, but the menu is the same and the cooking still tastes fresh and feisty. Be careful to specify how hot you want your dishes to be. As you sit down you get a pappadum and a plate of cucumber and raw onion. From the starters the best choice is to stick to the 'kebabs'. Seek kebabs, chicken tikka and fish tikka are good. The lamb chops are very good – good crispy bits and plenty of fresh bread stuffed with onions. The vegetarian dishes are also good here – look out for the karahi butter beans methi. There is a new range of 'deigi' dishes – a kind of steam-roasting – but the simple karahi curries cooked to order are too good to miss. Very fresh, with plenty of fresh herbs and clean flavours, they include karahi ginger chicken; karahi methi gosht; and, best of, all karella gosht, lamb with bitter melon. The breads are good and the rice dishes sound. Cheap, fresh food, served quickly and without fuss.

→ For branches, see index or website

New Asian Tandoori Centre

114–118 The Green, Southall, Middx ■ 020 8574 2597   ♿

⊖ BR Southall

🍴 Indian

🕐 Mon to Thurs 09.00–23.00; Fri to Sun 09.00–23.30

🗄 cash or cheque only ■ no service added

££ starters 50p–£7 ■ mains £5–£7 ■ sides £2–£3 ■ desserts £1–£3
   ■ lowest bottle price £8

✪ Cheap and cheerful Indian food palace

On the menu at the New Asian Tandoori Centre it states 'Famous
& suitable venue for business & social gathering', and so it is. The
NATC is a large, light and airy place. It is made up from three shop
fronts and splits into three rooms: on the right there's a seriously
busy takeaway operation, in the middle a no-frills canteen, and on
the left a smarter dining room complete with a bar and ornamental
stonework. This is one time when you can stick to the 'middle path'
with confidence. Service is friendly and, except for the tandoori
dishes, the food arrives briskly. The menu offers the kind of strongly
flavoured food you would expect in a Punjabi café. Start with good
jeera chicken, rich with cumin, or simple savoury kebabs: chicken
or lamb. Or there's a vegetable pakora. The boneless fish tikka is
stunning. With the rather good breads in support (chapatis, bhaturas,
naans), a few starters and grilled meats could easily make a meal. But
it would be a pity to miss out on the main course dishes. The menu
is split into two halves: vegetarian and non-vegetarian. There is a
good bhindi dish of fine soggy aubergines; Bombay aloo; chana dal,
a delicious rich yellow chickpea sludge; and a curry made with karela,
bitter melon. Meat-eaters will enjoy the butter chicken; the bhuna
chicken; the economically named lamb curry; and the bhuna lamb
that is served only on Saturday and Sunday.

Omi's

1–3 Beaconsfield Road, Southall, Middx ■ 020 8571 7669 ♿

⊖ BR Southall

🍴 Indian

🕐 Mon to Sat 11.00–23.00; Sun 11.00–21.30

🖥 www.omisrestaurant.co.uk

🗄 all major credit cards ■ no service added

££ starters 70p–£8.50 ■ mains £3.50–£8.50 ■ sides £2.25–£3.50
■ desserts 75p–£1.75 ■ lowest bottle price £10

✪ Charming and cheap

Omi's is a small, no-frills eatery with a kitchen that seems at least as spacious as the dining area. The explanation for this lies down the street, where you'll find one of Southall's larger banqueting and wedding halls (Omi's has a thriving outside-catering operation). But then Omi's has never been purely a restaurant – until some years ago, the food shared a counter with a van-rental business. The restaurant seats 50 with an 80-seat function room upstairs. But you'll still find tasty, Punjabi/Kenyan-Asian dishes, lots of rich flavours and great value. The food is cooked by a formidable line-up of chefs in the back, doubtless knocking up dishes for diners with one hand while masterminding the next Indian wedding for 800 with the other. There's a constant stream of people picking up their takeaways. The starters are behind the counter: chicken tikka is good and spicy, while aloo tikki is a large, savoury potato cake, delightfully crisp on the outside. Or try the masala fish, a large slab of cod thickly encrusted with spices. Go on to sample a couple of the specials. Aloo methi – potatoes cooked with fenugreek – is very moreish indeed, as is the chilli chicken. All the curries are commendably oil-free and thrive on the cook-and-reheat system in operation here. They are best eaten with breads: parathas, rotis and the mega-indulgent, puffy, fried bhaturas are all fresh and good.

Palm Palace

80 South Road, Southall, Middx ■ 020 8574 9209

⊖ BR Southall

🍽 Sri Lankan

🕒 daily 12.00–15.00 & 18.00–23.30

🖥 www. palmpalace.com

🖻 all major credit cards ■ no service added

££ starters £1.50 ■ mains £4.50 ■ sides £4.50 ■ desserts £2.50–£3.50 ■ lowest bottle price £10

✪ Sri Lankan better-than-café

The Palm Palace may be short on palms, and it is not palatial by any manner of means, but the food is great. This is the only Sri Lankan restaurant among the restaurant turmoil that is Southall, and the menu features a great many delicious and interesting dishes. As is so often the case with Sri Lankan food, the 'drier' dishes are particularly appealing, and there is a good deal of uncompromising chilli heat. The dining room is plain but comfortable, service is friendly and attentive. For a starter, try the mutton rolls – long pancake rolls filled with meat and potatoes. Or there's the fish cutlets, which are in fact spherical fishcakes very much in the same style as those you find in smart West End eateries, but better spiced and a tenth of the price. Move on to a 'devilled' dish: mutton, chicken or, best of all, squid – these dishes combine spices with richness very well. There was a time when every curry house in the land featured Ceylon chicken, but here you'll find a short list of real 'Ceylon' curries, including mutton: they're good, if straightforward. Try the chicken 65 – the name is said to refer to the age of the chicken in days: any younger and it would fall apart during cooking; any older it would be tough. The hoppers (Sri Lankan pancakes) are good fun: string hopper, egg hopper, milk hopper. Try a simple vegetable dish as well. Sag aloo brings fresh spinach and thoughtfully seasoned well-cooked potato.

→ For branches, see index or website

Index of branches

Ranoush 48

Lebanese
Branches at:
22 Brompton Road, SW1
 tel 020 7584 6999
86 Kensington High Street, W8
 tel 020 7938 2234
338 King's Road, SW3
 tel 020 7352 0044
Maroush I, 21 Edgware Road, W2
 tel 020 7723 0772
Maroush II, 38 Beauchamp Place, SW3
 tel 020 7581 5434
Maroush III, 62 Seymour Street, W2
 tel 020 7724 5024
Maroush IV, 68 Edgware Road, W2
 tel 020 7224 9339
Maroush V, 4 Vere Street, W1
 tel 020 7493 3030
Gardens, 1 Connaught Street, W2
 tel 020 7262 0222
Deli, 45–49 Edgware Road, W2
 tel 020 7723 3666
Beirut Express, 112–114 Edgware Road, W2
 tel 020 7724 2700
65 Old Brompton Road, SW5
 opening soon
Randa, 23 Church Street, W8
 opening soon

Raoul's 287

European/deli
Branch at:
105–107 Talbot Road, W11
 tel 020 7229 2400

Rasa 294

Indian
Branches at:
Rasa Travancore, 56 Stoke Newington Church Street, N16
 tel 020 7249 1340 (see p. 295)
Rasa Samudra, 5 Charlotte Street, W1
 tel 020 7637 0222 (see p. 12)
Rasa W1, 6 Dering Street, W1
 tel 020 7629 1346
Rasa Maricham, Holiday Inn, 1 Kings Cross, WC1
 tel 020 7833 9787
Rasa Express, 5 Rathbone Street, W1
 tel 020 7637 0222
Rasa Express, 327 Euston Road, NW1
 tel 020 7387 8974

The Real Greek 221

Greek
Branches at:
Souvlaki & Bar, 140–142 St John Street, EC1
 tel 020 7253 7234 (see p. 196)
31–33 Putney High Street, SW15
 tel 020 8788 3270
56 Paddington Street, W1
 tel 020 7486 0466
Units 1 & 2 Riverside House, 2a Southwark Bridge Road, SE1
 tel 020 7620 0162

Rodizio Rico 124

Brazilian
Branch at:
77–78 Upper Street, N1
 tel 020 7354 1076

Riverside Level 1, Royal Festival
  Hall, SE1
  tel 020 7021 0877
1a Bank End, Clink Street, SE1
  tel 020 7403 3659

Wódka 58

Polish
Branches at:
The Baltic, 74 Blackfriars Road, SE1
  tel 020 7928 1111
Chez Kristoff, 111 Hammersmith
  Grove, W12
  tel 020 8741 1177 (see p. 394)

Yi-Ban 206

Chinese/dim sum
Branch at:
5 The Boulevard, Imperial Wharf,
  Imperial Road, SW6
  tel 020 7731 6606

Yo! Sushi 146

Japanese
Branches at:
5th Floor, Harvey Nichols, 109–125
  Knightsbridge, SW1
  tel 020 7201 8641
19 Rupert Street, W1
  tel 020 7434 2724
Selfridges Food Hall, 400 Oxford
  Street, W1
  tel 020 7318 3944
57 Haymarket, SW1
  tel 020 7930 7557
15 Woodstock Street, W1
  tel 020 7629 0051
Fulham Broadway Centre, Fulham
  Road, SW6
  tel 020 7385 6077

02 Centre, 255 Finchley Road,
  NW3
  tel 020 7431 4499
County Hall, Belvedere Road, SE1
  tel 020 7928 8871
95 Farringdon Road, EC1
  tel 020 7841 0790
Whiteley's, Unit 218 Whiteley's
  Shopping Centre, Queensway,
  W2
  tel 020 7841 0790
myhotel, 11–13 Bayley Street,
  Bedford Square, WC1
  tel 020 7636 0076
The Lawn, Paddington Station, W2
  tel 020 7706 9550
N1 Centre, 31 Parkfield Street, N1
  tel 020 7359 3502

Zilli Fish 147

Italian/fish
Branches at:
Zilli Café, 42–44 Brewer Street, W1
  tel 020 7287 9233
Signor Zilli, 40–41 Dean Street, W1
  tel 020 7734 3924

Index of restaurants by cuisine

Vietnamese

Index of restaurants by name

Diwana Bel-Poori House 62
Indian/vegetarian
121 Drummond Street, NW1
tel 020 7387 5556

The Don 179
Modern European
20 St Swithin's Lane, EC4
tel 020 7626 2606

The Drapers Arms 267
Modern British/ gastropub
44 Barnsbury Street, N1
tel 020 7619 0348

Al Duca 112
Italian
4–5 Duke of York Street, SW1
tel 020 7839 3090

The Duke of Cambridge 268
Modern British/ gastropub
30 St Peter's Street, N1
tel 020 7359 3066

E

E&O 98
Asian eclectic
14 Blenheim Crescent, W11
tel 020 7229 5454

Eagle Bar Diner 5
North American
3 Rathbone Place, W1
tel 020 7637 1418

The Eagle 190
Mediterranean/ gastropub
159 Farringdon Road, EC1
tel 020 7837 1353

The Ealing Park Tavern 377
Modern British/ gastropub
222 South Ealing Road, W5
tel 020 8758 1879

The Earl Spencer 335
Modern British/ gastropub
260 Merton Road, SW18
tel 020 8870 9244

ECapital 26
Chinese
8 Gerrard Street, W1
tel 020 7434 3838

Eco Brixton 321
Pizza
4 Market Row, Brixton Market, Electric Lane, SW9
tel 020 7738 3021

Eight over Eight 364
Asian eclectic
392 King's Road, SW3
tel 020 7349 9934

The Engineer 229
Modern British/ gastropub
65 Gloucester Avenue, NW1
tel 020 7722 0950

Enoteca Turi 330
Italian
28 Putney High Street, SW15
tel 020 8785 4449

Eriki 286
Indian
4–6 Northways Parade, Finchley Road, NW3
tel 020 7722 0606

Escale 351
Turkish
94 Kew Road, Richmond, Surrey
tel 020 8940 0033

Eyre Brothers 212
Mediterranean
70 Leonard Street, EC2
tel 020 7613 5346